Second Edition

CHILDREN with
SPINA BIFIDA

Second Edition

CHILDREN with SPINA BIFIDA

A Parents' Guide

Edited by Marlene Lutkenhoff, R.N., M.S.N.

Woodbine House ▪▪ 2008

© 2008 Woodbine House
Second edition

All rights reserved under International and Pan American Copyright Conventions. Published in the United States of America by Woodbine House, Inc., 6510 Bells Mill Rd., Bethesda, MD 20817. 800-843-7323. www.woodbinehouse.com

Cover illustration: Elizabeth Wolfe

Library of Congress Cataloging-in-Publication Data

Children with spina bifida: a parents' guide / edited by Marlene Lutkenhoff. – 2nd ed.
   p. cm.
 Includes bibliographical references and index.
 ISBN 978-1-890627-77-5
1.Spina bifida. 2. Spine—Abnormalities. I. Lutkenhoff, Marlene.
RJ496.S74C476 2008
618.92'83—dc22

2007039480

Manufactured in the United States of America

10   9   8   7   6   5   4   3   2   1

TABLE

OF

CONTENTS

▪▪ PREFACE

This is a revised edition of *Children with Spina Bifida: A Parents' Guide,* originally published in 1999. That book was written in an effort to provide parents with clear and compassionate information they could use during the first few confusing years of their children's lives. Both professionals and parents contributed to the first edition, and numerous words of wisdom from other parents were shared within the pages of that book. We kept to that same format for this second edition, because most new parents need information and support from both professionals and parents as they make their way through the thicket of medical, education, and legal issues that surround the field of spina bifida.

I wish to thank all the individual authors who contributed to this book—including those who graciously gave their time and expertise both to the first edition and to this edition, and those who are contributing for the first time. And I would like to thank once again the parents who provided the parent statements at the end of each chapter. You will see new pictures of smiling, happy children with spina bifida throughout the pages of this book, for without them, there would be no reason for this book. Thank you to the families who agreed to share their children's photos with us, and to Debbie Frederick for taking many of them. I am also grateful to Barbara Johnson, Director of the Rubinstein Libraries at Children's Hospital Medical Center in the Division of Developmental and Behavioral Pediatrics, for her help in updating the Reading List and Resource Guide.

Thank you to the parents who teach professionals every day what it is like to raise a child with a disability. Thank you for sharing your children with us and for demonstrating to us in countless ways that every life is precious and deserving of the same benefits offered to all. I hope you find this new edition of *Children with Spina Bifida* helpful wherever you are in your journey with your children.

Marlene Lutkenhoff, RN, MSN

FOREWORD

Drake Crittenden Ash

When I think back to my daughter's birth seven years ago, my vision is one of chaos viewed through a thick fog. Nurses run from my hospital room calling for sterile gauze. From a distance I hear the pediatrician, who has been called in because of the baby's mild distress, turn to my obstetrician to announce, "We have a problem. A myelomeningocele." I see the look on my doctor's face as she recoils in disbelief.

Today, as I survey my thriving seven-year-old daughter, I realize that the chaotic early fog has long since lifted. Emily is sitting at the kitchen table creating a work of art in vivid color. She draws on her tremendous imagination to illustrate a world of happy, make-believe characters. She is an active and exuberant little person with many friends and interests and extraordinary inner resources. She attends our neighborhood elementary school, where she is an eager and competent student. Although she has brought changes to our lives, she has also brought richness and a depth of appreciation for the things that we enjoy about our daily existence.

Exactly how and when we reached our present appreciation of Emily's gifts is impossible to pinpoint. In the early days of coming to grips with Emily's disability, I remember feeling extremely overwhelmed by the complexity of this birth defect, and the number of surgeons involved in Emily's care. There were dozens of medical professionals, each one working to impart knowledge of one piece of the puzzle that is myelomeningocele—commonly called spina bifida.

We struggled to understand what the implications of this disability would be for our daughter as we learned that there could be a broad range of orthopedic, neurological, urological, and learning deficits.

Emily's severely clubbed feet and twisted lower limbs were the most obvious sign of orthopedic impairment. The wound on her back, an indication that the spine had not formed properly, was surgically closed on her first day of life.

While Emily was healing from her initial surgery in the newborn intensive care unit, the neurosurgeons educated us about hydrocephalus, a pooling of cerebral spinal fluid in the brain that affects most children with spina bifida. Fortunately, hydrocephalus can be treated by inserting a small device called a shunt. Although we continued to hope that Emily would beat the odds, within a week our tiny daughter was back to the operating room. She emerged from surgery with an enormous bandage covering much of her scalp. Kind nurses reassured us that the shunt would be well hidden once Emily's hair grew in. Today she sports a variety of hair styles with little evidence of this life-saving device.

During the first few weeks of adjustment to our new circumstances, I gained tremendous strength and a sense of normalcy from the presence of our two other children, Danny and Sarah, then aged five and three. The immediacy of their needs kept me moving forward while I grappled with informing relatives, making numerous doctors' appointments, and coming to grips with changed expectations for our future as a family. I wondered if I would be able to return to my job as a musician in a symphony orchestra, and whether we would be able to enjoy a hike in the forest together when Emily grew older.

Much support flooded in from friends and neighbors who wanted to help but didn't always know what to say. One card from a friend who has a child with a disability stands out in my mind today. She wrote that although our new daughter might reach milestones in a different way or at a different time than "typical" children, each one of her accomplishments would seem like a victorious celebration of life. How true those words turned out to be! From the first smile to the first unaided sit, crawl, and step, Emily's achievements were uplifting! They sprang from much hard work and will to embrace life. These moments were sometimes clouded by illness or hospitalization for surgery, but as Emily grew and learned, we began to understand that she was simply our child and that we would equip ourselves to care for her.

Through our Spina Bifida Clinic, we were introduced to several mothers of older children with spina bifida. It was a great relief to share experiences and information with parents who had already faced some of the challenges and decisions we were dealing with. I was grateful to have some of these mothers' phone numbers on hand when I didn't understand something a physician had said, or when I was trying to solve a problem about Emily's day-to-day care. It was also encouraging to meet children with my daughter's disability. This took me one step closer to acceptance of my own role as parent of a child with a serious medical disability.

Today the parents that were such a lifeline in the early weeks of Emily's remain very important to our family. Though we come from diverse backgrounds, our friendships are cemented by many common threads. We share the daily challenge of keeping our children healthy and of balancing our own needs and those of our other children with the tremendous time and energy consumed by spina bifida.

In seeking out medical care for your baby, you may have the opportunity to receive treatment from a team of surgeons, therapists, and other specialists in a multidisciplinary setting. We go to the clinic at Cincinnati Center for Developmental Disorders, under the direction of Sonya Oppenheimer, which is where many of this book's chapter authors work. This clinic has given us continuity of care and a feeling of support that I hope each one of you will have access to in your communities. I have been touched many times by the kindness and compassion others have shown toward Emily. I hope that you, too, will share this feeling and draw strength from it as you set out to raise your child.

Although many things have changed since Emily's birth, many things also remain the same. The frequent medical appointments and surgeries of her early years have given way to occasional check-ups and clinic visits. Now Emily can handle most of her care independently, giving her freedom to participate in the many social and extracurricular activities she loves. I have long since returned to my career as a violinist. But most importantly, I can't think of a single family activity that we haven't been able to enjoy together despite Emily's spina bifida—including many hikes in the woods! Sometimes Emily's participation depends on careful planning or a slower pace, but life definitely goes on with many of the same joys and challenges experienced by families everywhere.

:: Update

In preparation for the second edition of *Children with Spina Bifida* that you hold in your hands, I was asked to update, and perhaps add to, my original foreword for the book. Where can I begin? The cherubic, bubbly seven-year-old who looks out from the pages of the first edition of the book is now chic and stylish at sixteen—a junior at our local high school.

Emily carries on the social life of today's typical teen, from conversations on the telephone and computer, to attendance at all of her favorite band's nearby performances. Learning to drive and sing jazz has replaced the swimming lessons and kitchen table art sessions that occupied her when she was younger.

At home, Emily is extremely independent. She has a good grasp of her medical issues, and meets them with admirable cheerfulness and wry wit most of the time. Some high points of these years have included going to a sleep-away camp for six summers, touring Europe with the orchestra I play in, and discovering some musical talent of her own. Friends are at the top of Em's list. She will choose to spend time with her pals over just about anything.

Of course, there have been appointments, tests, therapy sessions, illnesses, and a major surgery or two along the way. Emily has endured some emotionally trying moments along with the joyous ones. Thus, we have learned to savor stretches of stable health and roll with the punches during medical crises. Supportive friends, family members, and caring medical professionals continue to make a huge difference to our family.

I hope that this book will provide you with answers to many of the questions you may have about your child's health and development. As parents, deepening our own understanding of spina bifida is the best way to insure that we will be able to act as loving caregivers and capable advocates for our children.

1

WHAT IS
SPINA BIFIDA?

Sonya Oppenheimer, M.D.

When you first find
out that your baby has (or will be born with) spina bifida, you will
naturally be scared and confused. There are so many possible medical problems, unfamiliar terms to learn, and uncertainties about
the future. In the beginning, it can be difficult not to focus on your
worries and concerns, especially if you have never known anyone
with spina bifida.

But there are actually many reasons to be optimistic. First and
foremost, you will find that children with spina bifida are really more
like other children than unlike them. As your child grows, you will see
that he has a personality, talents, and interests all his own, and that
spina bifida is far from being his defining characteristic. Second, many
useful medical treatments, educational approaches, and therapies are
available to help reduce the impact of spina bifida on your child's development. And finally, societal attitudes, opportunities, and legal rights
and benefits are constantly improving, making it more and more easy
for people with spina bifida to become independent, welcome members
of their communities.

As a parent, you will work closely with a variety of professionals to help ensure that your child has the opportunities and abilities to lead a successful and fulfilling life. Learning about spina bifida is the first step to helping your child achieve his potential.

■■ What Is Spina Bifida?

As the director of the Spina Bifida Clinic at the Division of Developmental and Behavioral Pediatrics at Children's Hospital Medical Cen-

ter in Cincinnati, Ohio, I have often been asked to explain spina bifida to new parents. Many of these parents have never heard of this disability that has been diagnosed in their unborn baby or newborn. I usually begin by comparing the condition to a spinal cord injury, since parents can relate to that. They may know someone who has had this type of injury as a result of a swimming or car accident. Although spina bifida is not technically a spinal cord injury, it affects mobility in a similar way.

In the simplest terms, spina bifida is a type of neural tube defect that occurs very early in the pregnancy. The neural tube is the embryonic tissue that becomes the spinal cord and brain (central nervous system). In the most common form of spina bifida—myelomeningocele—there is an opening in both the backbone (vertebrae) and skin around it, so that the spinal cord protrudes through the back. The damage to the spinal cord that occurs as the result of myelomeningocele results in the individual losing some sensation and movement in parts of his body. Which parts of the body are affected and to what degree depends on the location of the lesion—the area on the spinal cord that is affected. Usually, however, spina bifida results in problems with mobility and with bowel and bladder control. (See Chapter 5 for more information about how the location of the lesion affects function, as well as for information about other forms of spina bifida besides myelomeningocele.)

Spina bifida is not a progressive disorder—that is, the damage to a child's spinal cord does not get worse over time. It is, however, a lifelong disability that cannot be outgrown. A variety of medical complications are often associated with spina bifida, including hydrocephalus, bladder and bowel incontinence, and scoliosis. Fortunately, as explained in later chapters, there are effective treatments for all of these complications.

About 7 out of 10,000 (1 in 1428) babies born in the United States have spina bifida. The Spina Bifida Association of America estimates that more that 70,000 people in United States live with spina bifida. The incidence is higher in individuals of English/Irish or Hispanic descent, and lower in African-Americans. As more women of childbearing age take folic acid (400 micrograms) prior to conception, the number of children born with spina bifida is expected to decrease. However, at least 30 percent of spina bifida births are not preventable and many women do not plan pregnancies and are unaware of the need for folic acid.

▪▪ A Word about Terminology

You will probably encounter a variety of terms used to describe your child's disability. Here are some definitions to help you sort out the meanings:

- A **neural tube defect** is an opening or problem anywhere along the neural tube that is present at birth. Spina bifida and anencephaly (an open neural tube defect with no brain development) are examples of neural tube defects.
- **Spina bifida** literally means split (bifida) bony spine (spina). The term is used to describe a neural tube defect that occurs anywhere along the spine.
- **Myelomeningocele** is one type of spina bifida in which the spinal cord (myelo) and meninges, or membranes covering the spinal cord (meningo), protrude through an opening on the back into a sac (cele). (Say "my-low-muh-NING-go-seel") This type of spina bifida may also be referred to as meningomyelocele.
- **Myelodysplasia** means abnormal development of the spinal cord. The term is sometimes used interchangeably with spina bifida or myelomeningocele.
- **Hydrocephalus** refers to an excessive accumulation of cerebrospinal fluid in the ventricles (cavities) of the brain.

- **Lipomeningocele** means a skin covered lesion with abnormality of spinal cord but is not associated with hydrocephalus or Chiari malformation.
- **Chiari malformation** is a very common condition in children with spina bifida in which the brainstem and cerebellum are lower down in the brain and possibly compressed due to lack of space.

The primary focus of this book is on the myelomeningocele type of spina bifida, which is the most serious and most common type. As Chapter 5 discusses, there are other types of spina bifida, but the term spina bifida is often used interchangeably with myelomeningocele. In this book, the term spina bifida will be used to refer to the myelomenigocele type of spina bifida, unless otherwise indicated.

■■ Will My Child Live?

Given proper treatment at birth, a baby with spina bifida will most likely survive, if there are no unexpected complications. In fact, the newborns with spina bifida in the intensive care unit are often the healthiest looking babies in the unit. The average length of hospitalization is seven to ten days, unless there are complications such as infection or failure of the wound to heal or close properly. Throughout the hospital stay, your baby's head will be monitored closely for any signs of a buildup of fluid due to hydrocephalus. As Chapter 5 explains, this condition can be treated by surgically inserting a shunt to drain the fluid. With good medical care, people with spina bifida can usually expect to live a normal or near normal lifespan.

■■ Will My Child Walk?

This is an important question that parents ask. How much movement your child has in his lower extremities is determined largely by where the lesion occurs on his back. The higher the lesion, the less chance your child will be able to walk independently. This is because the nerves at the higher level of the spinal cord control lower leg movement. Most children with spina bifida can learn to walk, often with the aid of braces, crutches, and walkers. As they get older, many children, especially those who expend a great deal of energy walking, decide to use wheelchairs. This can enable them to better get around and to keep up with their classmates.

A variety of professionals will help your child develop as much mobility as possible. The orthopedist is the medical specialist who will monitor your child's legs and try to keep them in the best possible position for bracing and movement. Physical therapists can show you how to help your baby begin moving and gain motor skills such as rolling, sitting, standing, and, eventually, walking. Occupational therapists can work with your child to strengthen the upper extremities and develop fine motor skills such as cutting and drawing. They can also show you ways to help your child do self-help skills such as buttoning, dressing, and putting braces on and off.

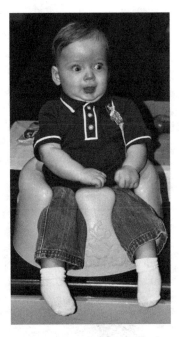

I often tell parents and grandparents that it is important to allow their child to "do his own thing." Teach your child how and then give him opportunities to do whatever he is capable of doing. Sometimes this is hard, but it is so necessary if your child is to grow up to be an independent adult. Chapters 8, 9, and 13 provide more information about how professionals and family members can help your child develop mobility and other needed skills.

■■ Will My Child Have "Normal" Intelligence?

The majority of youngsters born with spina bifida have average or above average intellectual abilities, but their IQ may be somewhat lower (10 IQ points lower) than their siblings'. This discrepancy is probably a result of hydrocephalus. Many have learning problems such as difficulty with math, reading comprehension, and handwriting. They also tend to have significant problems with organization and attention. On the positive side, verbal skills are usually a strength for people with spina bifida, perhaps because their mobility is limited. They are more attuned to sounds at a very early age. They may not be able to physically reach what they want, so they develop the ability to ask for what they want at an early age. Most children with spina bifida attend regular schools, and many qualify to receive special services there, including physical and occupational therapy, and special education services such as tutoring.

▪▪ How Will I Care for My New Baby?

Babies with spina bifida have the same needs as other babies: to be loved, fed, and kept clean. There will be a scar on your baby's back, but by the time he is discharged from the hospital, it will probably be healed sufficiently so that no special care is required. Babies with spina bifida aren't usually any more fragile than other babies.

Diaper changes may be a bit different for you if your baby has difficulty with kidney and bladder functioning. Some babies have difficulty urinating and need to have a catheter (a piece of hollow plastic tubing)

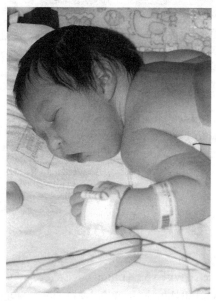 inserted into their bladders to drain the urine. A nurse will teach you how to do this before you leave the hospital. This is a frightening thing for most parents, but once they have done it a few times they become pros and say they could probably do it in their sleep. (See Chapter 6 for more information on urinary concerns.)

Parents often wonder whether they can return to work after having a baby with spina bifida. Usually, you should keep whatever plans you had for child care prior to your baby's birth. Your baby's caregivers can learn how to catheterize, if necessary. Yes, your baby will have frequent doctors' appointments and tests, particularly in the first year. The neurosurgeon will need to check the back area and make certain the shunt is working, if there is one, or make certain that your baby does not need a shunt, if he left the hospital without one. (As discussed in Chapter 5, shunts are used in the treatment of hydrocephalus.) A urologist will monitor kidney and bladder functioning, and an orthopedist will keep an eye on lower extremity functioning. Other professionals your child might see include a developmental pediatrician, social worker, nurse, occupational and physical therapists, and a nutritionist.

Time off from work can be minimized if your child is referred to a spina bifida clinic, as most children with spina bifida are. At such a clinic, your child can see many specialists during one visit. Infants and young children visit the clinic every three or four months. As your child gets older, time between visits will stretch out so he will visit the clinic only once or twice a year. See Chapter 10 for a detailed explanation of a multidisciplinary clinic and a description of the roles of the various specialists.

: Will My Child Grow Up to Be an Independent Adult?

Many adults with spina bifida are able to go to college, find fulfilling jobs, get married, and live on their own with no assistance. Some may need a little assistance in managing self-care (catheterization, bowel program, bathing), but are otherwise quite independent. A few need more assistance in adulthood.

Independence should be the ultimate goal for the majority of children with spina bifida. You can help your child work towards independence from the start by encouraging him to try new skills. If your child cannot do something a certain way no matter how hard he tries, it is time to problem solve and find new or alternative ways. From birth, there will be all kinds of assistance available to help your child make steps in all areas of development needed for independence. In fact, as explained in Chapters 13 and 15, federal law requires that your child be given therapies and educational assistance to help with skill development, if needed. The therapists and educators who work with your family will help you and your child set goals aimed at helping your child achieve the maximum independence.

As with any child, your child needs to grow up feeling that he is a competent person and loved for what he can do. But he also needs to grow up with a healthy sense of self-esteem, so that he can still feel good about himself when he realizes that some things are harder for him, and that he can't be just like his peers in all ways. As Chapter 14 explains, there are many steps you can take to help nurture an emotionally healthy child.

■■ Will There Ever Be a Cure for Spina Bifida?

At present there are a variety of medical treatments, therapies, and educational approaches that can help children with spina bifida grow up to have healthy, fulfilling lives. But there is no cure for the physical and neurological problems present at birth.

In the late 1980s, some surgeons began performing surgery on fetuses prenatally diagnosed with spina bifida. The theory is that early closure of the opening on the back may lead to improved neurological functioning for these babies. This surgery involves making an incision in the mother's abdomen and then, through an incision into the uterus, repairing the fetus's lesion. The surgery is done when the fetus is around 25 weeks gestation. The fetus is still quite small, and delicate tools are needed to operate on such a small area. Once the repair is completed, the mother's uterus is sewn shut and the fetus recuperates in the womb. One of the biggest risks with this surgery is the possibility of premature labor, which carries its own set of complications for both the mother and her baby.

Several centers have reported that the fetal surgery does result in a decrease in the number of children requiring shunts and in the number who show changes in the Chiari malformation. The National Institute of Health has developed a matched control study to determine the effectiveness of fetal surgery. Parents seeking prenatal surgery will either be put into the study group that does receive the surgery or the study group that does not receive the prenatal repair. There is an agreement among centers that only three designated centers will perform fetal surgery on fetuses with spina bifida until the study is complete and sufficient data have been obtained. This trial study is known as the MOMS (Management of Myelomeningocele) study. At the completion of the study, we hope we will know whether fetal repair is indeed beneficial for children with spina bifida.

For parents interested in keeping abreast of this technique and other new developments in the treatment of spina bifida, the best course is probably to join the Spina Bifida Association of America (SBAA), which is listed in the Resource Guide at the back of this book.

■■ Conclusion

Every family expects their lives to change with the birth of a new child. Your family's lives will change too—just in a more dramatic way. You will probably need to learn more and be more involved in helping your child learn than you ever expected. You will also need more support from your extended family, as well as from professionals you probably never expected to deal with. But you will likely also find that parenting your child with spina bifida is more rewarding than you could ever have dreamed. With time, you will also discover that your child is much more like other children than unlike them. Children with spina bifida are first and foremost just children. Their spina bifida should always be secondary to that fact. Enjoy your child!

■■ Parent Statements

I was scared when Brian was born. The medical treatments and all the things I had to watch out for, in addition to the newborn care, were a lot for a first-time parent. When he smiled at me for the first time when he was six weeks old, I felt like I had earned the title "Mom."

❦

The early weeks were extremely difficult because I had had a C-section and I couldn't drive to the hospital to visit our son whenever I wanted. I had to rely on others to take me there and I just couldn't stay as long as I wanted.

❦

When I was told about Vicky and her condition, I was very upset and confused, I didn't really understand what spina bifida was. I also thought "Why me?" "Why us?"

❦

We were very confused—no one said Mark had spina bifida. It was always referred to as the myelomeningocele. We had heard of spina bifida, but who has ever heard of myelomeningocele?

❦

I think raising Tyler will be very fulfilling and rewarding. Helping someone reach their full potential is exciting and suspenseful. Life will never be dull or boring with Tyler around to watch and stimulate. The very term life has a whole new meaning.

❦

Having the opportunity to get to know my daughter and love her as a person has transcended all the low points. I enjoy watching her develop as a person and helping her to challenge herself.

❦

Hearing all the new terminology and learning about all the complications that can go along with spina bifida was so overwhelming at first. I was definitely on information overload in the beginning.

❦

It is hard to adequately describe life with a child with spina bifida. It is wonderful and frustrating, challenging and rewarding, much like any worthwhile undertaking. Joshua, our first child, made us parents, but Lisa, our child with spina bifida, has made us better parents. When adversity hits, you can either be destroyed or be victorious. We are striving for the latter. Keeping a notebook of all events helps tremendously and we still have so far to go, but we'll get there together.

❦

Everyone envisions their child as a super athlete, or really good looking, or extremely smart. Some of our expectations will not be met, but so many have been that we never thought would be. I think an underdog win is so much sweeter and special that I wouldn't trade those wins for anything.

Exploring the Causes of Spina Bifida

Alina L. Flores, M.P.H., C.H.E.S.
Katherine Lyon Daniel, Ph.D.
Joseph Mulinare M.D., M.S.P.H.

❚❚ Why Does My Child Have Spina Bifida?

Nobody knows exactly what causes all cases of spina bifida or other conditions known as neural tube defects. Scientific research, however, provides some information about what happens during development very early in pregnancy that leads to the opening in the spine known as spina bifida. Research has also uncovered some of the factors thought to be related to spina bifida.

Before we get into possible causes, however, it is important for you to understand that the birth of a child with spina bifida is no one's "fault." About 95 percent of babies with spina bifida are born to parents who have no family history of spina bifida or related birth defects. However, some protective actions, such as making folic acid part of your daily diet, can lower the chances of having a baby with spina bifida or other neural tube defect. Although many people have heard about folic acid, many still don't know that women need to take

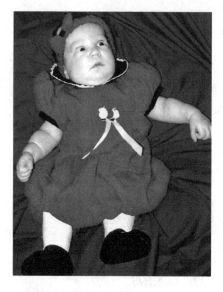

it before pregnancy, and during very early pregnancy, for it to be effective. But even parents who know about every precaution and do everything possible to have a healthy baby can still have a baby with spina bifida.

You have probably been told, or have learned from your own experiences, that children and adults with spina bifida have as much potential for achievement and happiness as people without spina bifida. But you probably still have many questions such as, "Why did this happen?" or "What can we do to reduce the chances of spina bifida in any future children we may have?" This chapter will help you answer these questions.

▪▪ Causes of Spina Bifida

Babies have been born with neural tube defects such as spina bifida for thousands of years. Many scientific studies have tried to determine what occurs during a pregnancy that leads to spina bifida. Because birth defects like spina bifida happen so early in pregnancy, scientists have tried to understand what causes them by focusing on mechanisms of normal development that may be interrupted or changed.

One mechanism being studied is the process of creating DNA, the substance that directs the function of all living cells. DNA is packaged within the body's cells in structures called *chromosomes*. Small sections of DNA that direct the building of body proteins are called *genes*. Thus, DNA acts like the body's blueprints or construction plans. Abnormal or missing genes or segments of DNA might make the blueprint incomplete, and this could interfere with the body's construction or development. Another mechanism being studied is the process of how the cells join together to form tissues, organs, and structures in the developing fetus, as well as how exposure to chemicals or medications may interfere with this process.

Errors in Development

During the very early days of a pregnancy (18–28 days after conception or about 32–42 days after the mother's last menstrual period began), the tissue that later becomes the baby's spinal cord and the brain begins to curve around and fold to form what is called the neural tube. In normal development, this tissue fuses together and then triggers the development of the spinal column and skull bones, which surround and protect the spinal cord and the brain. The spinal cord is a pathway of nerve tissue that controls body and limb movements, sensation, bowel and bladder function, and other functions.

Spina bifida occurs when the fold in the neural tube fails to come together correctly and the protective spinal column does not develop completely. This causes the covering of the spinal cord (the meninges) and often part of the spinal cord itself to push outside of the backbone and into a sac that protrudes from the back. Surgery is usually performed soon after birth to close the opening in the spine and to remove the sac, but some damage to the spinal cord tissue will probably have occurred already.

What prevents the spinal column from developing correctly in babies with spina bifida? There are three broad types of factors that are known to cause or are associated with spina bifida. An association means that scientists don't know whether a factor actually causes an outcome, but do know that the two tend to occur together, so they theorize that the factor and outcome may be related to each other. One category of known causes or associations is *genetic,* another is *environmental,* and still another is *multifactorial*—a combination of environmental and genetic causes.

Genetic Factors

Almost every one of the trillions of cells in the human body contains a nucleus. Within that nucleus are 46 *chromosomes* (containing DNA). Twenty-three chromosomes are inherited from the mother and 23 are inherited from the father. Each chromosome contains genes that carry the instructions for making a cell copy itself and grow properly. There are an estimated total of 20,000 to 30,000 genes on the 46 chromosomes. If even one part of a gene is missing or somehow changed (or mutated) within a chromosome, the overall function of the gene (which tells the cells how to reproduce and grow) can be affected. When these functions lead to a condition that can be traced back to a problem with the genes, it is called a *genetic condition*.

Recently, scientists have found that women with a mutation of a particular enzyme (protein) are more likely to have a pregnancy affected by a neural tube defect. This enzyme, MTHFR (methylenetetrahydrofolate reductase), is found in the body's cells and helps the body use the B-vitamin, folic acid. Women who have the MTHFR mutation do not process folic acid as well as women with normal MTHFR. However, women who take 400 micrograms of folic acid daily are able to overcome this problem. Folic acid will be discussed later on in this chapter as a prevention tool.

Another reason that scientists believe that there may be genetic factors associated with spina bifida is that certain genetic *syndromes* (combinations of birth defects) have spina bifida as a recognized component. Genetic conditions associated with spina bifida include various chromosomal abnormalities or "defects" such as trisomy 13, trisomy 18, and other chromosome imbalances. If your child has been diagnosed with one of these genetic conditions, spina bifida may be part of her condition. Your doctor or a genetic counselor can help explain the specifics of your baby's condition.

Some scientists believe that spina bifida has a genetic cause because members of certain races or ethnic groups have different rates of spina bifida. The reasons are unclear but may be related to genes shared within these groups. For example, in the United States, Hispanics have a higher number of spina bifida pregnancies and blacks have a lower number when compared with whites.

Sometimes specific couples are genetically more likely to have a baby with spina bifida. This can be the case even if no one else in their families has the condition. Just because there is a genetic influence in your family or racial or ethnic group, however, doesn't mean that these genes will definitely be passed on from you to a baby—only that the risk of having a baby with spina bifida may be higher. Unfortunately, we have no easy way to identify most of the genes that may be associated with spina bifida.

Environmental Factors

When studying the causes of birth defects, scientists use the term "environmental" to include factors that affect the internal "environment" of the womb during pregnancy. Environmental factors that may be associated with spina bifida include 1) the use of certain medications during pregnancy such as valproic acid, used to treat seizures; 2) maternal conditions such as insulin-dependent diabetes and obesity; 3) poor maternal nutrition; and possibly 4) hyperthermia (prolonged raising of body temperature such as with a high fever or an extended hot bath).

Other environmental associations, which may be related to nutrition, include lower socioeconomic status and living in certain geographic areas of the United States and the world. For example, pregnancies affected by spina bifida appear to occur more frequently in the eastern United States than in the western states. In certain countries, including India and China, spina bifida appears to be more common. Deficiency of the vitamin folic acid is an environmental association with a definite link to spina bifida; it is discussed in detail in the section about prevention.

Multifactorial Causes

It is very likely that most occurrences of spina bifida and other neural tube defects have "multifactorial" causes, in which both environmental and genetic factors are involved. This means there is some underlying genetic factor that causes a fetus to be more vulnerable to a particular environmental influence—and when the fetus is exposed to that influence, it is at higher risk for developing a neural tube defect.

You may never be able to determine whether your child's spina bifida was related to genetic, environmental, or multifactorial causes. Since it is difficult to know what role genetics might have played in your child's spina bifida, genetic counseling is usually advised for couples considering future pregnancies. See "When to Seek Genetic Counseling" later in this chapter for more information.

▪▪ Prevention Recommendations: Folic Acid

In the early 1990s, research studies showed that women who had a baby with a neural tube defect such as spina bifida could significantly reduce their chances of having a second pregnancy affected by spina bifida by consuming the B vitamin, folic acid, before conception and during the early weeks of pregnancy. As a result, in 1991 the Centers for Disease Control and Prevention recommended that women who have previously had a pregnancy affected by a neural tube defect take 4000

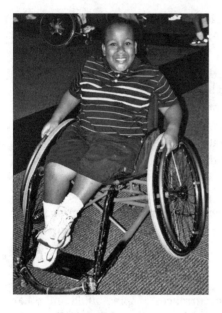

micrograms (4 milligrams) of folic acid daily for at least 1 month before conception and for the first 3 months of pregnancy to prevent neural tube defects.

Since most babies with spina bifida are born to women who have never had an affected pregnancy before, research focused on whether folic acid could reduce the risk for these women as well. In 1992, a research study was done in Hungary among women who wanted to become pregnant. Some of the women were given vitamin pills containing folic acid, while others were given pills that did not contain folic acid. During the study, researchers noticed a significant difference between the two groups. The women who were taking the vitamins containing folic acid had significantly fewer pregnancies affected by neural tube defects than did women who were taking pills not containing folic acid. The researchers soon determined that it would not be ethical to continue the study, so they stopped it and offered all of the participants vitamins containing folic acid.

Following this study, the U.S. Public Health Service issued the second set of recommendations: that *all* women of childbearing age who could become pregnant consume 400 micrograms (0.4 milligrams) of folic acid daily. The reason the recommendation was for all women and not just those who were planning a pregnancy is that more than half of the pregnancies in the United States are unplanned. Because the neural tube forms so early in fetal development (often before a woman realizes she has missed her period), it is important for the mother to have enough folic acid in her body before conception.

What Is Folic Acid?

Folic acid is one of the three B vitamins that the human body needs to make DNA. The natural form of folic acid is called folate, and it is most commonly found in green leafy vegetables, beans, liver, and orange juice made from concentrate. Natural folate in foods is less easily absorbed by the body than folic acid, so even women who eat a diet that is very nutritious may not get enough folate to protect against neural tube defects. In 1998, the Institute of Medicine (IOM) noted that food folate is only about half as easy for the body to absorb as synthetic folic acid found in vitamin pills or in fortified foods. The IOM recommended that all women who can become pregnant consume 400 micrograms (0.4 milligrams) of synthetic folic acid *in addition* to consuming natural food folate.

Since January 1998, the U.S. Food and Drug Administration (FDA) has required that folic acid be added to enriched flour products. This process is called fortification. All products that are made from flour and that are labeled "enriched," such as many breads and pastas, have some added amounts of folic acid, as well as other vitamins and minerals. Since the fortification requirements went into effect, there has been a 26 percent decrease in the number of births affected by either spina bifida or anencephaly (another neural tube defect). But, on average, the amount of folic acid added to fortified foods may still not be enough for all women to meet the recommended daily requirement of 400 micrograms.

It is important for women of reproductive age to understand that they cannot easily get enough folic acid to reduce the risk of spina bifida through diet alone. A simple and convenient way to ensure that folic acid intake is sufficient, however, is to take a daily multivitamin that contains 400 micrograms of folic acid. Women who don't want to take a daily multivitamin supplement can eat fortified breakfast cereals, more enriched breads and pastas, and other foods high in folic acid. Many breakfast cereals contain the full U.S. recommended daily amount of folic acid in each serving, but it is best to always check the label to find the cereal with the amount you are looking for. A list of breakfast cereals that have 100 percent of the daily value is available at: http://www.cdc.gov/ncbddd/folicacid/cereals.htm (Because some cereal companies have increased their folic acid content in their cereals, this list may not include all of the possible breakfast cereals.)

If you've already had a child with a neural tube defect, you are considered at increased risk for another affected pregnancy and may need even more folic acid just before and during any future pregnancy. As stated earlier, the U.S. Public Health Service recommends that women who have had an affected pregnancy should speak with their doctor and consume 4,000 micrograms (4 milligrams) of folic acid daily for at least one month before conception and for the first three months of pregnancy. This is 10 times the 400 micrograms recommended for women who have not had a prior affected pregnancy, and this higher amount of folic acid is impossible to get through diet alone. You should not try to get the 4,000 micrograms of folic acid through multivitamins or breakfast cereals, because very high levels of other vitamins may be harmful to a fetus and perhaps to you. Ask your health care provider about a prescription for folic acid supplements at the higher dosage level before considering any future pregnancy.

Researchers are studying the effects of folic acid on the prevention of other birth defects such as cleft lip and palate and some heart defects, as well. This research has shown that taking folic acid can also reduce the risk of these serious birth defects. Other research suggests that consuming folic acid may also reduce the risk for strokes, heart attacks, and even some cancers, but more research is needed to know for sure.

❚❚ Other Preventative Steps

Besides ensuring that folic acid intake is adequate, couples can take other precautions to help reduce the chances that future children will be born with spina bifida. First, it is important that a mother's medical conditions are diagnosed and treated with the appropriate medications before and after conception. These conditions include in-sulin-dependent diabetes and seizure disorders (epilepsy). If a woman has insulin-dependent diabetes, she is at an increased risk for having a pregnancy affected by spina bifida and other birth defects. Her diet and blood sugar levels should be well controlled and maintained before conception and during pregnancy. A diabetic woman who controls her blood sugar levels before and during pregnancy reduces her risk of having a pregnancy affected by a neural tube defect to about the same level as a nondiabetic woman.

In addition, some prescription medications such as valproic acid used to treat seizures can sometimes cause spina bifida if taken during pregnancy. Your gynecologist, family physician, or nurse midwife can give you more information about making sure your health is at its best before conception.

❚❚ When to Seek Genetic Counseling

If you have already had a pregnancy affected by a neural tube defect such as spina bifida and you are planning another pregnancy, ask your health care provider about genetic counseling before conception. This service should be covered under your health insurance plan, or you can get a referral from your local public health clinic. If you have already had a pregnancy affected by spina bifida, you are considered at higher risk of having a future pregnancy affected by spina bifida or another neural tube defect. In the United States, parents with one pregnancy affected by a neural tube defect have about a 2 to 3 percent chance of having a neural tube

defect in future pregnancies. This is about 20 to 30 times higher than for parents who have not had a previous affected pregnancy. However, when women who had previously conceived a child with a neural tube defect took 4,000 micrograms (4 milligrams) of folic acid before their next pregnancy, that increased risk was reduced by about 70 percent. (The risk of having a second child with a neural tube defect may vary if your child has spina bifida as part of a genetic syndrome.)

Genetic counselors or physicians trained in genetics and birth defects can help you and your partner understand your chances of conceiving another child with a neural tube defect. They can talk to you about how to minimize your risk. They can also tell you about the different types of prenatal tests that are available to detect a neural tube defect after you become pregnant again. See Chapter 3 for more information on prenatal tests and their uses.

Immediate family members (brothers, sisters, sons, and daughters) of a person with spina bifida or other neural tube defect might want to consider genetic counseling before attempting a pregnancy. They have a smaller risk than the parents of a child with spina bifida of having a baby with a neural tube defect, but they still have a greater risk than the rest of the population. The farther away one is from the immediate family—for example, a cousin, aunt, or uncle—the more similar his or her risk is to that of the general population.

It is important to keep in mind that all prenatal tests have limitations; you should discuss these with your health care provider. Most importantly, you should remember that genetic counseling, and the decisions made after counseling, are personal decisions. Although the genetic counselor can provide you with information and guidance, it is up to you to make the decisions that are best for you and your family.

▪▪ Ongoing Research into Causes and Prevention of Spina Bifida

We now know that taking folic acid reduces a woman's chance of having a baby with a neural tube defect, but even women who take the recommended amount of folic acid sometimes have children with spina bifida. While taking 400 micrograms of folic acid daily may prevent up to 70 percent of neural tube defects, researchers are continuing to study what might prevent the remaining 30 percent. We also know some things about the causes of spina bifida and other neural tube defects, but there is still a lot more to learn, and all the causes of spina bifida may never be fully understood.

To people with spina bifida and their families, the slow pace of scientific research can be frustrating. Yet in spite of the challenges of having spina bifida, with good medical care, proper assistance, and encouragement, children with spina bifida can lead full and rewarding lives.

▪▪ Parent Statements

With the exception of the immediate family, most of our relatives and friends found out about Gregory through our birth announcement. In addition to the usual information, we included the following: "Gregory was born with myelomeningocele, often referred to as spina bifida. There is no known cause. We are optimistic and ask that you keep our family in your prayers."

❧

I was embarrassed to tell my mother at first because I thought she would blame me and say I hadn't taken care of myself or eaten properly. She never did, though. She just told me to treat Leslie like I would any other child.

❧

I just cried. I cried and cried, and that's all I could do. I didn't understand what they were telling me or what this would mean for the baby, my family, for me. I didn't even know what spina bifida was.

❧

When I heard that folic acid is recommended for women planning a pregnancy in order to reduce the chance of spina bifida, I thought back to my own pregnancy. When Tim was born, I didn't know a lot about folic acid and I was not a big fan of green vegetables. Was my diet to blame for my son's spina bifida?

❧

Folic acid and its relationship to spina bifida was not common knowledge when my child was born. If I were to plan another pregnancy, I would be sure that I was on the recommended dose of folic acid so that I would have the best chance of having a healthy child.

❧

I was taking folic acid for a whole year before Chelsea was born with spina bifida.

❧

I did everything "right" before and after I got pregnant, and still Henry was born with spina bifida. I second guessed myself and asked "why?" a lot in the beginning, but after awhile I had to push those thoughts to the back of my mind so I could get on with my life.

❧

I am different since Sarah. I feel like I've become a better person. Though I have always been spiritual, my relationship with God has become so much stronger. Having Sarah has strengthened my faith because I can really see and feel His blessings. I also appreciate my other children so much more, and appreciate life in general. I know that Sarah will struggle, but she has life and so much love.

❧

We didn't have any kind of genetic testing or counseling before our first child (who has spina bifida) was born. But my husband and I both decided we should consult with a genetic counselor before I got pregnant again. It was a little scary to hear about every possible thing we could be at risk for with future children, but talking to the counselor was ultimately reassuring.

❦

My child has spina bifida and Down syndrome. I guess when I first heard the diagnoses, I expected Ethan to be very "un" normal. However, as I gazed upon him shortly after he was born I thought, "He's just a baby, a cute baby, and that's all."

3

PRENATAL DIAGNOSIS

Martha E. Walker, M.S., C.G.C.

Many babies born with spina bifida in the twenty-first century are diagnosed prenatally, due to the advances in prenatal screening, ultrasound, and testing that have occurred over the last three decades. Just a generation ago, most parents did not learn of their baby's spina bifida until after the birth. The surprise of the baby's condition contributed substantially to the parents' anxiety. Many people think that prenatal knowledge of a birth defect or serious medical problem allows for better outcomes for the child and the family.

Despite the wide availability of prenatal diagnosis, deciding what to do about such testing is still a very personal decision. If you are reading this chapter, it may be because you have received a prenatal diagnosis of spina bifida and are unsure how to proceed. Or you may already have a child with spina bifida and be wondering whether to undergo prenatal testing during your next pregnancy. You could be an adult with spina bifida, or the close relative of someone with spina bifida, and have questions about the types and timing of prenatal tests appropriate in your situation. This chapter is designed to give women and couples in any of these situations accurate, objective information about their options so they can make the choices that are best for them.

∷ Prenatal Testing

The purpose of prenatal testing is to provide information about a baby's health before delivery. Usually, parents are reassured with normal results. However, if the results indicate that the baby is expected

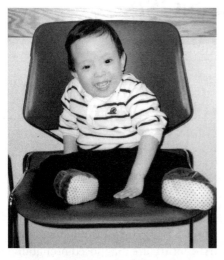

to have a serious medical or developmental problem, then the parents can explore their options and learn more about what to expect after their baby is born.

Any couple has at least a 3 percent chance that their newborn infant may have a birth defect. In 2007, the American College of Obstetricians and Gynecologists recommended that prenatal screening for certain conditions (such as Down syn-

drome) be offered to all pregnant women. More specialized diagnostic testing is typically offered to couples in certain "high risk" categories. For example, couples who have had a previous child with cystic fibrosis (an inherited condition that occurs in 1 in 3000 children) have a risk of 1 in 4 (25 percent) in their offspring. Prenatal testing might also be considered if a close relative of the unborn baby has sickle cell anemia, Tay Sachs disease, muscular dystrophy, or some other single gene disorder which follows a known pattern of inheritance. Other reasons for prenatal testing might be maternal exposure to certain medications or environmental agents, a family history of a chromosome abnormality or balanced chromosome translocation (rearrangement), or a positive "quad/triple screen" maternal blood screening test result (see below). Prenatal diagnostic testing is available for many but not all disorders.

There are also higher risk categories specifically for neural tube defects. As explained in Chapter 2, neural tube defects are usually a result of multiple environmental and genetic factors. If one parent has spina bifida or if a couple has had a previous child, fetus, or close relative with a neural tube defect, the estimated chance of having a baby with spina bifida would be somewhat greater than average. In addition, a woman who has insulin dependent diabetes or needs to use certain medications (such as some anti-seizure drugs) during pregnancy may be more likely to have a baby with a neural tube defect. The pregnancy of a woman with no family history of neural tube defects could be at increased risk if a high level of alpha fetoprotein (AFP) were detected in her blood test. In fact, the majority of women with elevated AFP levels do not have any family history of spina bifida. Your individualized pregnancy risk may be learned by consulting a genetic counselor or genetics physician.

Even if you are considered to be at greater risk of having a baby with spina bifida or another disability, bear in mind that genetic testing is optional and voluntary. On the other hand, even if your risk is not considered to be especially high, you may still request prenatal testing. The next section looks at some of the advantages and disadvantages that parents may weigh as they decide whether or not to pursue prenatal testing.

▪▪ Advantages and Disadvantages of Prenatal Diagnosis

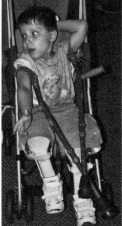

Prenatal diagnosis has been used by thousands of women throughout the world for over three decades. Most women and couples are satisfied with their decision to seek prenatal diagnosis. Since test results are usually normal, the majority of people who have prenatal testing are reassured. It is important to realize, however, that prenatal diagnostic testing cannot check for every possible birth defect or condition. But through appropriate testing, parents can find out whether their fetus has the specific problems for which it has an increased risk.

Advantages

If a serious problem is diagnosed prenatally, parents may feel unprepared to handle the news or proceed with decision-making.

Usually, however, parents have time to either prepare for their baby's delivery or to consider the option of ending the pregnancy. If you are in the situation of having received abnormal prenatal test results, it is important to ask all of your questions and try to get answers from a variety of medical professionals. Genetic counseling is recommended. Genetic counselors provide information, rather than direction, in a way that lets parents make their own decisions. Your beliefs, values, and choices are acknowledged, supported, and respected. Honest discussion with your spouse or partner is also extremely important. Sharing the decision-making process with trusted family members, friends, and your pastor, rabbi, or hospital chaplain is often helpful. Although some individuals may give you pointed advice, remember it is your decision and it must be what is right for *you*.

When parents decide to continue the pregnancy, they can take a number of steps to plan for delivery. For example, parents can educate themselves about the disorder, contact other parents to learn about their experiences raising a child with spina bifida, and consult a nearby multidisciplinary clinic that sees and treats children with spina bifida. Staff members at these clinics are very knowledgeable about caring for children with spina bifida. It is also important to discuss pregnancy management with the obstetrician and/or consult a specialist in maternal fetal medicine (perinatologist).

When spina bifida is diagnosed prenatally, plans are often made for the woman to have a Cesarean section delivery (C-section), which many physicians think is the safest form of delivery for an infant with spina bifida. This form of delivery is scheduled so the neonatal, pediatric, and neurosurgery specialists will be prepared and available to care for the infant immediately after he or she is born. Some major medical centers have a Fetal Care Center whose staff coordinate all of these special arrangements.

Any parents would understandably be very upset upon being told that their baby has a serious birth defect. The process of grief and acceptance requires time. When a prenatal diagnosis is made, the timing of receiving news of the diagnosis is changed, and the parents gain a chance to start preparing emotionally for the birth of their child weeks prior to delivery. As a result, they might be more able to enjoy and care for their newborn after arrival.

Another advantage of prenatal diagnosis is that fetal surgery on a research/investigational basis may be an option when a neural tube defect has been diagnosed prenatally. Spina bifida is one of the relatively few conditions for which *in utero* treatment or therapy is available. See Chapter 1 for information on fetal surgery.

Disadvantages

Prenatal diagnosis has some disadvantages. Unfortunately, prenatal test results do not allow prediction of how severely a child will be affected. Another disadvantage is that some procedures (amniocentesis and CVS, described below) involve a small risk for miscarriage (pregnancy loss). Also, these tests and level II ultrasound are costly and not always covered by health insurance or Medicaid.

A major disadvantage of prenatal diagnosis decision-making comes from a psychological standpoint: Some people simply do not wish to learn of their baby's disability prior to delivery. Many parents would not consider pregnancy termination, and others do not want to be in the situation of making an agonizing decision of whether to continue or end their pregnancy. Pregnancy termination can be carried out as late as 27 to 28 weeks gestation in some parts of the U.S. The medical procedures for pregnancy termination are considered safe for women's reproductive system and physical health. However, if termination is chosen, the parents' grief is often substantial and may be experienced in isolation.

Deciding whether or not to have prenatal testing may require you to intensely examine your family needs, personal values, ethics, and religious beliefs. If you have any doubts as to what to do, it is important to talk with many different specialists in order to obtain all the facts and make an informed decision.

▐▌ Common Prenatal Tests

This section describes the most commonly used prenatal tests. Other, more specialized testing through DNA or biochemical analyses is also available to families with different inherited conditions. For information on these tests, you should consult a genetics specialist.

Maternal Serum Alpha Fetoprotein

The maternal serum alpha fetoprotein (MSAFP) screen has been widely used in the United States since the mid-1980s. People who undergo this test should understand that it is designed to *screen* for open neural tube defects in pregnancies. Results of the blood test tell you what the *chance* for a fetal neural tube defect is. The results do not tell whether or not the fetus actually *has* a neural tube defect. Thus, the MSAFP screen is not a diagnostic test. With appropriate follow-up, the screen can detect 80 to 90 percent of fetuses with open neural tube

defects. This means that, if a woman is actually carrying a fetus with an open neural tube defect, there is an 80 to 90 percent chance she would have a positive (abnormal) MSAFP screen. Use of this blood screening test poses no significant medical risk for the pregnancy or the fetus.

Alpha fetoprotein (AFP) is a protein that is produced in the fetal liver and yolk sac. It is released into the amniotic fluid during fetal urination. From the amniotic fluid and through the placenta, some AFP enters the mother's blood, which may be sampled between 15 to 22 weeks gestation. The expected amount of AFP (normal range) in the mother's blood serum varies according to how far along the pregnancy is. The mother's race and diabetic status are other factors. The median (average) level of AFP in maternal blood serum is 1.0 multiples of the median (MoM). The MoM level is interpreted in the laboratory to produce an individualized risk for an open neural tube defect in the fetus. The individualized risk is usually reported as a fraction, such as 1 in 850, 1 in 52, etc.

When an amount of maternal serum AFP greater than the laboratory cutoff is found, it is called a positive screen. Most laboratories use the AFP cutoff levels of 2.0 MoM (two times the median level) or 2.5 MoM for Caucasian women and 3.0 MoM for African American women. A positive screening test result does not mean that the fetus has been diagnosed with spina bifida or any other birth defect. It means that the pregnancy should be looked at more closely and that further testing should be offered to the pregnant woman.

A common reason for a positive screen is incorrect dating of the pregnancy. That is, the blood serum AFP level may appear elevated because the pregnancy is actually further advanced than originally thought. It is also possible that an elevated AFP is due to normal variation: perhaps the fetus is simply making more than the average amount of AFP. AFP levels tend to run higher in African-American women and in pregnancies with twins or multiple births. The woman's body weight is another factor influencing MSAFP concentration, and serum AFP levels are also affected if a woman has insulin-dependent diabetes. In addition, elevated serum AFP levels are occasionally caused by fetal disorders other than neural tube defects. These include malformations of the abdominal wall, some rare hereditary disorders, placental anomalies, and an increased risk for stillbirth.

Approximately 4 percent of women who undergo the AFP blood test will have a positive screen, and about 2 to 5 percent of women within *that* group are estimated to actually have a fetus with an open neural tube defect.

Positive screening test results are an indication that further testing by amniocentesis and/or ultrasound is necessary in order to get diagnostic information. Genetic counseling is recommended for women who have had a positive screening test result. The genetic counselor will explain the accuracy, limitations, benefits, and risks of other available testing options and will support whatever decisions are made by the woman.

Ultrasound

Ultrasound is a safe and noninvasive method for making an image (picture) of the fetus. A hand-held device called a transducer is moved across the mother's abdomen, and it transmits sound waves to the fetus. When the fetal tissue or bones reflect the sound waves, an image is produced on a monitor similar to a television screen. Ultrasound measurements of femur (thigh bone), head diameter, and abdominal circumference are used for estimating gestational age. "Routine" ultrasound is typically performed by an ultrasound technician.

Level II ultrasound uses the same procedure as routine ultrasound, but it is performed by a perinatologist, a physician who specializes in maternal fetal medicine. The specialist will do a thorough examination of the fetus and check for malformations of any type, including possible changes in the spine anatomy. When level II ultrasound is performed after 18 weeks gestation by well-trained and experienced physicians, approximately 90 percent of fetal open neural tube defects are detected.

Amniocentesis

Amniocentesis is a procedure for obtaining a sample of amniotic fluid from the fetal sac after 14 weeks gestation. Usually, ultrasound is performed simultaneously. The physician inserts a needle through the mother's abdomen (not through the navel) to remove about 15 ml (one tablespoon) of amniotic fluid. The fluid is composed mostly of fetal urine, but it also contains some cells shed from fetal tissues. In the laboratory, the fluid and cells can be tested for certain fetal disorders, including neural tube defects and Down syndrome.

The amniocentesis procedure does carry a risk for pregnancy loss (miscarriage). A recent study estimated that this risk is about 1 in 1600 (less than 0.1 percent), but other studies estimated a risk of 1 in 400 to 1 in 200. Potential effects of amniocentesis which could be harmful to the fetus include infection, vaginal leakage of amniotic fluid, and Rh disease. Although the needle used for collecting amniotic fluid is somewhat long, most women describe the amniocentesis procedure as "not very painful."

To check for the presence of a fetal neural tube defect, AFP levels in the amniotic fluid are measured. This measurement can be performed from 14 to 21 weeks gestation, and the laboratory turn-around time for this analysis is 1 to 4 days. An amniotic fluid AFP level of greater than 2.5 MoM (i.e., 2.5 times the median) indicates there is a significantly high chance the fetus has a neural tube defect.

A second laboratory test checks for the presence of a chemical called acetyl cholinesterase. Acetyl cholinesterase is an enzyme found in nerve and muscle tissue and in red blood cells; with normal fetal development it is *not* found in amniotic fluid. The presence of elevated amniotic fluid AFP and positive acetyl cholinesterase would indicate a high chance, approximately 99 percent, that the fetus would have an open neural tube defect. About 1 to 2 percent of the time, abnormal AFP and acetyl cholinesterase results like these are associated with problems other than neural tube defects, such as malformation of the fetal abdominal wall with involvement of the fetal digestive system. Level II ultrasound examination is recommended in cases where amniocentesis results are abnormal.

Chromosome studies are another test usually performed when a sample of amniotic fluid has been obtained. The chromosome analysis, also known as karyotyping, can rule out conditions such as Down syndrome (which is caused by an extra copy of chromosome 21) and Edwards syndrome (which is caused by an extra copy of chromosome 18). Typically, there are 46 chromosomes in human cells. Most children with neural tube defects do have this expected number of 46 chromosomes and do not have any extra or missing chromosomes. Rarely, however, neural tube defects are caused by a chromosome abnormality such as trisomy 13 or trisomy 18.

Chorionic Villus Sampling (CVS)

Another prenatal diagnostic test is chorionic villus sampling (CVS), a procedure in which a small sample of the chorion (early placenta) is studied for chromosome make-up. The specimen is obtained by inserting a flexible catheter through the mother's cervix or a needle through her abdomen. AFP levels cannot be measured through CVS, so this test is often not chosen by women who want to check the fetus for neural tube defects. CVS is mainly used by women who want to rule out chromosome abnormalities such as Down syndrome, trisomy 13 or 18, or specific single gene disorders.

CVS has the advantage of being performed early in pregnancy, usually between 10 and 12 weeks gestation. The diagnostic information becomes available sooner than with amniocentesis. In general, CVS carries slightly higher risks for the pregnancy than does amniocentesis, and the CVS genetic studies are a little less accurate than with amniocentesis.

The Serum Quad Marker Screen

The serum quad marker screen is mentioned here because it is a blood test offered to *all* pregnant women. Similar to the MSAFP screen, it is performed at 15 to 22 weeks gestation. In addition to AFP, three other chemical compounds in the maternal blood serum are analyzed. Using this test, pregnancies at increased risk for a fetus with Down syndrome can be identified by taking the woman's age into consideration along with levels of human chorionic gonadotropin (HCG), unconjugated estriol (UE3), inhibin, and AFP. Most women will screen negative, meaning there is a relatively low chance that the fetus has Down syndrome. A positive screen means there is a chance of at least 1 in 270 that the fetus has Down syndrome.

In the case of a positive screen, amniocentesis is generally offered to determine whether the fetus does, indeed, have Down syndrome or another chromosomal abnormality. An estimated 67 percent or more of fetuses with Down syndrome may be identified through use of the maternal serum quad screen, combined with appropriate follow-up. Because AFP is a component of this test, the quad screen is just as useful in identifying pregnancies at increased risk for neural tube defects as the MSAFP screen described earlier.

First Trimester Screening

Many women have found first trimester screening to be beneficial. In 2007, the American College of Obstetrics & Gynecology recommended that this option should be offered to all pregnant women, regardless of their age. First trimester screening does not check for fetal neural tube defects, but for certain chromosomal disorders.

First trimester screening is typically performed at a certified ultrasound center at 11 to 13.6 weeks gestation. Ultrasound measurement of the fetal neck area (nuchal translucency) is combined with measurements of the blood compounds free beta and PAPP-A in the mother's blood. Individualized patient risks for Down syndrome and Edwards syndrome (trisomy 18) are then estimated. Detection rates of 91 percent for Down syndrome and 97 percent for Edwards syndrome have been reported. Women who are over age 35 years at delivery have a significant chance of receiving a "positive" screening result with first trimester screening. (Again, this simply indicates the need for more testing; not that the fetus actually has a disorder). Regardless of the first trimester screening results, couples should consider the option of the second trimester AFP screen for fetal neural tube defects.

▪▪ Making a Decision...

If you are in the process of deciding whether to pursue prenatal testing, or if prenatal tests have indicated a possible or probable diagnosis of spina bifida, please be assured that there are many qualified medical professionals who want to support and assist you. To locate someone who can help guide you through the decision-making process, ask your physician for a referral or contact the National Society of Genetic Counselors (www.nsgc.org). If you have Internet access, you will also be able to locate a great deal of information on spina bifida and correspond online with parents who have gone through the same decision-making process.

Remember: Prenatal testing has both advantages and disadvantages. The decisions related to the results of such testing are highly individual. Prenatal testing is most beneficial when parents have a clear understanding of the medical information and the choices available to them.

■■ Parent Statements

We did not choose to have AFP screening for our first child because we believed that whatever the results, we would accept and love our child. Although we did not have the AFP screening, we discovered at the 21-week "well baby" ultrasound that our child had spina bifida. This news was completely unexpected and devastating to us. However, the diagnosis gave us the opportunity to explore fetal surgery to repair his lesion and to hopefully prevent any further damage to his nervous system and also reduce the likelihood of hydrocephalus. While the surgery presented significant risks, we believed that this was the best option for us to give Sean the best possible outcome. The fetal surgery was successful, as Sean is not shunted, has bowel and bladder function, and is able to walk and run without orthotics. He is our pride and joy!

In the pregnancies which brought Sean's two younger brothers, we elected to have AFP screening for neural tube defects only. They are happy, healthy kids without spina bifida.

❧

Our first child was born with myelomeningocele. His diagnosis was a shock! I was terribly upset, especially with having to stay in the OB postpartum ward while they whisked him away to the special care nursery at another hospital. When I became pregnant with our second child, I was glad prenatal testing was available because I really wanted to avoid having any surprises at delivery. My AFP blood test was normal and the level II ultrasound looked fine. I decided not to have amniocentesis. Overall, I was reassured, but I still worried some during pregnancy. Our daughter Kathryn was born on her due date and is very healthy.

❧

Spina bifida was first suspected in our unborn daughter at the routine 20-week ultrasound. When the condition was confirmed by a special-

ist, I remember feeling like the walls of my life were caving in. When my husband and I were finally in our car in the parking lot after that appointment, we both sat there and sobbed. It was good for me to find out before birth that there were problems—it gave me time to accept the situation and strengthen myself mentally. It gave us the opportunity to talk and meet with doctors and plan out our daughter's post-birth care (including needed surgeries).

❧

After several ultrasounds and an amniocentesis, we were told that Tricia had hydrocephalus, an encephalocele, and no cerebellum. The amnio told us her chromosomes were okay and she was a girl! We did not know Tricia had spina bifida until she was born—they looked for it but could find nothing wrong with her spine on the ultrasound. I did not have an AFP blood test.

❧

We had a routine AFP at 18 weeks gestation and received a high number of 6. An ultrasound was done in my regular OB/GYN office, but no defect was noticed so we were sent to a specialist, who did a level II ultrasound. The defect still was not found, so I had an amniocentesis. The results from that test were positive. I had another amnio the day before my baby was born, to confirm that his lungs were strong enough.

❧

Finding out that Kelly had spina bifida ahead of time helped me "be there" for her. One nurse wrote in a report (that I later read), that my husband and I were so calm and positive about the situation that she felt we were in denial—but it was just the opposite. We had worked through our anger and depression and were ready to do whatever we had to do for our baby.

4

WORKING
THROUGH
YOUR GRIEF

Melody Campbell Goettemoeller

It's a very hard thing to do, to look at our blonde, blue-eyed six-year-old and think of grief at the same time. Because almost every moment of the day, she is smiling or singing, or reaching to hold my hand. Our lives are much richer because of her. But our lives have also been much more of a challenge, or series of challenges, as we have worked through various difficulties or different stages of her growing up.

I remember the morning that she was born. We had come to the hospital for a scheduled C-section, filled with hope that everything would go right with the surgery, and with anticipation of finally seeing our child. Our family doctor, Bill, was there with the video camera, taping every precious moment.

The mood in the surgical OB delivery room that morning was very light, almost joyful. I knew each person there because I work in the hospital where I delivered. The anesthesiologist was late and we teased him about that. I can remember the exclamation of "Out she comes" and then the room fell silent. . . . I could feel the tenseness in the air, and I said, "What's wrong? Is the baby O.K.?" It was a long time until I got an answer, and I just lay there quietly while our family doctor worked with the OB nurse to stabilize and examine my baby. He came over and said to me very quietly and gently, "She has a problem with her back and we are going to have to send her to Children's."

I don't remember a lot after that. I'm sure that the medicine that I was given made me forget a lot of things. I can remember the team from Children's coming, and Sandy, the wonderful nurse who ended up caring for Megan and being one of our first teachers about spina bifida.

My grandmother was at the hospital that morning, and even six years later, cannot forget some of the events of that day. She will say, "I can just see her Daddy walking up and down the hall in that surgical mask, the tears running down his face." My husband, too, talks about being alone at Children's during the surgery on Megan's back and placement of her shunt. He was torn between wanting to be with me, and desperately wanting to make sure that everything went all right with his little girl.

I can look back now and see those initial signs of grief as we struggled to understand what we were told and what it would mean to our child's life and to us as a family. As a nurse, I had studied about spina bifida in nursing school, but I really didn't remember much about it. My nurse colleagues brought textbooks to the hospital so that I could read and somehow comprehend what it really meant. Through it all, in those first few days, we had great support. Our families were always there, beside us, or praying for us. Our friends also were very close and constant. Our faith kept us focused and helped us walk one step at a time.

Dr. Ken Moses, in his talks on the fundamentals of grieving, describes the grief related to having a child with a disability as arising from "the loss of a dream." But I really cannot remember dreaming or fantasizing about what my child would be like before her birth. I already had one child, a son, and knew the busy life that went along with having a new baby. I knew that I had to get everything ready before that new baby came, so I scurried about my house busily making preparations. My husband and I went out to eat the weekend before Megan was born and I can remember commenting, "What if something is wrong with the baby?" To which my husband replied, "Whatever it is, we will deal with it together." We didn't realize at the time that we would have to put that promise to a test.

■■ Emotions

I'm sure that as you read my memories of my daughter's birth, it brought back some of the emotions that you felt when your child was born or was prenatally diagnosed with spina bifida. No one can prepare for the feelings that you might experience when you learn that your new baby will have a congenital defect, illness, or some problem.

In the first few days after Megan was born, I still did not believe what I was told. I remember continually asking the nurse, "Are you sure that's what the doctor said? Couldn't it be something else?" The nurse continued to affirm the diagnosis of spina bifida, while I continued to try to deny it. It is said that **denial** in these initial stages is actually a healthy response. It gives you time to draw on your internal and external resources and gather the energy you need to begin to cope with the situation, while the actual meaning of the diagnosis sets in.

I can also remember feeling **guilty.** Had I done something during my pregnancy to cause this? Had I truly done everything I was supposed to? I did find some comfort in hearing others tell me that I had indeed taken care of myself and my unborn baby, and in learning that the causes of spina bifida are still far from being fully understood. I also knew in my heart that I would never have knowingly done anything that might have harmed my child before birth.

Two weeks after Megan's birth, and very shortly before her discharge from Children's, we attended Mass at a church near the hospital. During the service, the tears streamed down my face, as I dealt with very mixed emotions. I was still very sad that she had not been born perfect, and very **angry** that this had happened to her, to me, and to my husband and me as a couple. I looked ahead to her discharge from the hospital and was extremely **anxious** about what the future would hold for us.

The loss of a dream. . . . I realize now that we all have dreams about what our life will be like. These dreams begin when we are toddlers playing with dolls or baseballs and continue to be woven as we grow up. We dream of white houses with picket fences, beautiful sunsets, a loving, happy family with smiling, beautiful children. We don't dream of teal wheelchairs, small walkers, or purple braces, even though that becomes some families' realities. Until we deal with the fact that we have indeed lost our dreams, it is difficult to go on. The emotions that we feel during this time are normal. Recognizing these emotions is a critical part of helping us to deal with the reality of parenting a child with spina bifida.

▪▪ Peaks and Valleys

Our life with Megan has had its ups and downs, its peaks and valleys. We have very much celebrated the good times, and have waded through the dark times hoping that they would be short-lived. And sometimes in the middle of a low point in our lives there is a glimmer of hope, a moment of joy that gives us the strength to keep on going.

Some of our numerous valleys have been related to medical problems. Children with spina bifida usually have many medical difficulties, including urinary tract infections, shunt malfunctions, and problems that may require many surgeries. Our family's valleys revolved around repeated fractures, but the cause and the depth of each family's valleys will differ enormously because each child with spina bifida is unique.

Megan had surgery on her left hip when she was two. After the surgery, she was in a body cast for ten weeks. Everything went well, and the cast came off. However, one month later, she tried to stand up without her braces, fell, and broke her left femur (upper part of her leg).This was the first of thirteen fractures and numerous body casts she was to endure over the next three years. With each new fracture, I remember I had several days or weeks of depression. I literally walked around in a daze at work, often crying at the slightest thought of this continuous, never-ending nightmare. My friends at work were compassionate and allowed me to pour out the sadness and frustration I felt at not being able to get out of this cycle of fractures and casts. Each time it seemed that only after I had cried, and talked out the emotions with my friends and family, was I ready to work with Megan and the doctor on a plan of what we were going to do to heal . . . not only the fracture, but also our wounded spirits.

Even when we were in those continual valleys of broken bones, there were still glimmers of hope or moments of joy. We tried as much as possible to continue on with normal lives and preserve for our daughter some sense of normalcy. We went to the beach last summer with her in a beautiful red body cast. We chose a bathing suit to match the cast, and altered it so that it would go on over the cast. However, we had to get creative when it came to figuring out what a small child does at the beach in a body cast. One of her loves was playing in the sand table at preschool, and that was something that she thought of immediately when she saw all that sand on the beach. My husband, always much more adventurous than I, quickly dug a deep hole in the sand, lined it with plastic, and placed her into it. From this spot, she could easily reach lots and lots of sand and feel the ocean breeze on her face. She has wonderful memories of that vacation, which surprisingly don't include being in a body cast, but instead include visions of waves, sunshine, and sand.

:: Life Goes On: Critical Time Periods

At different times as your child grows up, things happen to bring all those initial feelings of grief and anger back to the surface. Often they are just under the surface brewing, because you continually have to deal with the permanence of the disability. I can remember very recently attending a family reunion. It was held at a park on a beautiful summer day, sunlight beaming down. My husband's family is quite large, and children of various ages, most of them blonde, were running and playing on the nearby playground. My daughter, in her teal wheelchair, was moving quickly down the path toward the playground to meet the other children. The playground was typical, with teeter-totter, jungle

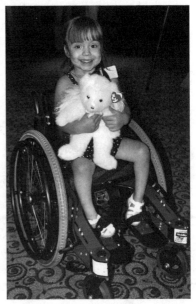

gym, swings . . . the usual equipment. Her pace slowed as she eyed the various pieces of equipment. The other children continued to run and jump, yelling with excitement.

I cried as I watched Megan, knowing that she would never be able to run and jump, or to ride on the teeter-totter the way the other children could. I looked at the strong legs of the other children as they ran, and then looked at the braces that kept my daughter's legs straight. She turned slowly, then returned to me and said, "Mommy, this playground is not built for me." I quickly wiped my tears away, not wanting her to see the sadness in my eyes. Meanwhile, my sister-in-law, Joanna, who had been watching from a distance, came over and pointed out a large, really neat sandbox that was near the back of the playground. My daughter raced towards the sandbox with a huge smile on her face. Joanna lifted her from the wheelchair and placed her in the sandbox. Soon many of the other children were playing next to her, and the tears on my face slowly dried.

In talking to other parents of children with spina bifida, I have found that everyone has had similar experiences. It is impossible to predict exactly what experiences will cause sadness or some other emotion to suddenly blindside us. Often, however, it seems that transitions from one part of life to another—getting the first set of braces, buying the first wheelchair, or getting on the bus on the first day of school—bring those emotions back to the surface. For my family, it helps to always try to celebrate transitions. We turn them into memorable, positive occasions for our child, which helps us move past our sadness or frustration. Experiment and see what works best for your family in these situations.

❚❚ Chronic Grieving

The author Elisabeth Kubler-Ross has written extensively about the stages of grieving that one goes through to reach an acceptance of death and dying. Sometimes the process of coming to terms with a child's disability ia likened to Kubler-Ross's stages of grieving. To me, however, Dr. Ken Moses's concepts of how parents typically cope with a disability seem to ring truer. Dr. Moses describes the grief related to having a child with a disability as occurring in states, rather than in stages. The states of grief relate to the emotions of denial, anger, anxiety, fear, and depression. He describes grief as a process that parents have to work

through in order to accept and to deal effectively with the disability. However, the grief is never finally put away; it is never completely over. Your child will have spina bifida all of her life.

I have found that I have to deal with this grief on an almost daily basis. For example, recently as I was helping my daughter get into the car, she asked, "Mom, is my spina bifida almost better?" I looked at her face, swallowed the lump in my throat, and said, "No, it's just always going to be the same. You will always have it." And she replied very quietly, "Oh." We finished our preparations for travel and went on our way.

Many people have found ways to channel their feelings of chronic grief so that they can affect the lives of their children or others in a positive way. Sandy, the special nurse I mentioned who was with the team from Children's that came and got Megan the day she was born, has a daughter with spina bifida. Whenever an infant is born with spina bifida, she helps care for the baby initially and then later helps the parents learn to care for their baby. Sandy is also active in the local spina bifida support group. Donna Albrecht, who has two children with disabilities, has designed accessible playgrounds. She has also improved handicapped accessibility in her city and has written a book, *Raising a Child Who Has a Physical Disability,* in an effort to help other parents. One of the newspaper journalists in our town, the mother of a young girl with spina bifida, frequently writes in our local newspaper about the trials, tribulations, and joys of parenting a child with disabilities.

Perhaps you don't feel as if you have the special talents of the individuals I mentioned above. You should still be able to find a number of methods of channeling your grief to help your child. For example, you can work for ways to make your child's environment more accessible to her, especially in your own home. This will create some big successes for her once she is able to get wherever she wants to go within her home. You can also look for ways to bring your child together with other children who have spina bifida. This will help her to realize that she is not alone, and give her additional sources of information and support.

Every family is different, but I have found it helpful to discuss my feelings about spina bifida with my child. My daughter has asked me whether I am sad that she has spina bifida. I have honestly told her that it does sometimes make me sad. I have explained to her my belief that God made her exactly the way she is and that she indeed has some big things to accomplish in her life. Grief is something that we recognize, and we try to use it to make our situation better and our resolve stronger.

■■ Finding Support

I mentioned earlier that in the process of dealing with denial, one has to draw on both external and internal supports or resources to help face the situation. In fact, most parents need differing levels and types of support throughout their child's life, not just in the beginning. Internal

supports are the sources of strength within you, such as your religious beliefs or personal convictions. External supports often come from relationships with family, friends, and others that you can draw on for energy and assistance in helping you deal with the ups and downs of everyday life.

Support from Your Family and Friends

My partner in life—my husband, Duane—has been a major support to me, as I hope I have been for him. Since the birth of our first child, we have kiddingly said to each other that it is "Us against the world," implying that our marriage, our bond, always comes first, even when we're engaged in the rat race of working and raising children. It is a struggle to maintain that priority as events happen in our lives, and especially now with the addition of our third child.

My husband and I have always had very different approaches to life and different ways of coping with the reality of our daughter's disability. Because of my training as a registered nurse, I tend to concentrate on the medical aspects of her problems. I am much more protective and fearful because I know what can happen. He is always pushing to allow her to be a child, to experiment, to try things, to be free. We balance each other in a very good way.

When we are in the valleys, we both deal with grief in very different ways. I cry a lot, sometimes loudly and often, until it is all out. I talk on the phone to my friends, and they, in turn, reach out to me, to comfort me. I'm not sure what my husband does. He is always very quiet about his grief, except initially when he too will cry or cover his

face with his hand. He likes to spend his free time outdoors, helping his brothers with the milking or working on building a pond near our new home site.

I think everyone has their own way of dealing with emotions. If you are married or in a significant relationship with someone who is a support for you and your child, learn to recognize how they deal with stress, or how they handle the different emotions. Realize that it is OK for the two of you to have different coping mechanisms. My husband has learned to deal with my long phone calls with my friends, and I have learned to respect his need to spend time outdoors. We try to listen to each other, and allow each other to express emotions when the time is right.

Our families have also been a major source of strength and support. My sister Suzanne has always been there with a sharp wit and sense of humor in every situation, no matter how dark the moment seemed. My sister Jane and my mother have accompanied me on many visits to the spina bifida clinic, busily writing down details and instructions, so that later, when I have questions, everything is written down clearly for me to refer to. My mother-in-law keeps the home fires burning, and cares for my other children during crisis times. My mom has also spent countless hours on the phone, listening to my tales about what my daughter accomplished today, as well as what my current worries are.

Our faith and church life have always been very important to my husband and me. Since Megan's birth, people from our church, as well as from other churches—some very far away—have reached out to us. We have received cards, flowers, gifts, and numerous prayers. Our church community has openly welcomed Megan, and continues to show her prayerful support, as well as always considering accessibility so that she can remain actively involved in church activities.

Use whatever sources of support are available to you, whether that be your family, neighbors, or friends. They can help you through the rough times as well as celebrate the triumphs with you.

Support from Organizations and Professionals

In addition to seeking support informally from family, friends, and other important people in your life, you can also get help from more formal sources of support. For example, The Spina Bifida Association of America is a national organization with a network of local support groups that can provide you with up-to-date information about specific aspects of raising a child with spina bifida, put you in touch with other families in your area, and help you understand your child's educational and legal rights. There are also a variety of national organizations dedicated to supporting and providing information to parents of children with hydrocephalus, learning disabilities, seizures, or any of the other complications that may go along with spina bifida. In addition, if you have a computer and access to the Internet, you can correspond with parents and professionals from around the world through online newsgroups, chat rooms, or bulletin boards devoted to disability issues. See the Resource Guide at the back of this book to get an idea of the national organizations that offer support.

In your community, there may be local groups you can tap for support and information—for example, wheelchair groups such as Winners on Wheels in Cincinnati, Ohio, or special wheelchair ballet groups. The teachers and therapists who work at your child's early intervention center, preschool, or school will also have experience and expertise that can be an invaluable source of information and support. So too do the professionals who work at the spina bifida clinic. You may need to explore your local community to locate all the different sources that might meet your child's, as well as your own, needs for support. Once you find one good source of support, however, you will often find that it will lead you to another.

▪▪ Conclusion

Being a new parent of a child with spina bifida can be overwhelming. As a new parent, your struggles to understand what spina bifida is and how to deal with the medical complications may leave you feeling as if you might never be hopeful again. But believe me, there will come a day when things will look brighter and your hopes for your child and your family will no longer seem unrealistic.

As for my family, we have **big hopes.** Hope that our daughter will be able to achieve everything that she desires. Hope that wherever she goes, her big, bright smile will win people over and allow them to see past the braces and the wheelchair.

This morning as Megan goes out the door for her first day of first grade, her blonde hair is flying out behind her as she races the wheelchair down the driveway. She is yelling, "Mom, it's my first day of first grade! I am soooooo . . . excited!" I have a big smile on my face, and a few tears that I wipe away—but I am so happy to be her mother.

▪▪ Addendum: Ten years later...

It is hard to believe that ten years have passed since I wrote this chapter. My daughter Megan is now sixteen years old, and today is her first day of tenth grade. Her new wheelchair is purple and she wears a brace from her chest down to her toes that has beautiful purple butterflies on it. We have had a rough year. She has been in and out of the hospital fighting a virulent bone infection. She had lost a great deal of weight, and we were beginning to wonder whether things would turn around. Through this particular dark valley, she has emerged as the most persistent, yet patient person I have ever met. She spent many days in the hospital, and, despite the numerous needle sticks for blood, unpleasant diagnostic

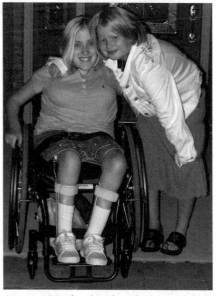

Megan, 16, on her first day of tenth grade

procedures, and pain, she managed to take each day and turn it into a pleasurable and memorable experience. She made friends with the hospital staff, and that became her world until the illness improved and she could go home.

I'm not sure when we learned that each day is new, and to treasure it . . . to not look too far into the future, but be happy in the moment. Megan's disability and the need for frequent medical care and hospitalizations as well as extensive home health care needs have made us take each day as it comes.

Megan has grown. Today she is worrying about whether she can get her driver's license. I am worrying about whether there is enough hair dye in the world to weather this milestone of her life. My husband thinks it is great and is earnestly looking for a car that can be adapted to make her life more independent. Our daughter is also beginning to think about college and is planning to be a social worker.

My husband and I continue to have **high** hopes. More importantly, Megan sees a bright future ahead of her and what does it include? Boys! Yikes! She looks at herself in the bathroom mirror, checking the earrings, making sure her hair is just right, puts on a little lipstick and rolls out the door. Our friend, Judy, helps her get on the lift and into the bus.

The yellow school bus has turned out of our driveway and is on its way to the high school. For some reason, tears are again running down my cheeks. I always cry on the first day of school as I realize how fast the time passes, and that my children are growing up. I know that I have an awesome daughter. It really is my privilege to be Megan's mom!

▦ Parent Statements

I was at the ultrasound by myself and tried to just understand what my OB was telling me, that my baby had a neural tube defect. I cried all the way home, kind of in a panic.

❧

Many of our family members were more upset than I was. I spent a lot of time reassuring them that we would be able to handle these problems.

❧

My mother said God was punishing me for the bad things I had done. The church told me God would not do such a thing, which made me feel better. My siblings were and are very supportive.

❧

My family is overwhelmingly supportive with love and encouragement. We are lucky. I have a sister who had a son with Down syndrome who died at 13 months, so she's been through so much more than we have and she's a wonderful encouragement. Also, several members of our family have learned how to catheterize Jennie so we can take a break. They give support in words and actions.

❧

When I found out my baby had spina bifida, I felt like a black cloud had descended on me. I thought of ramps and wheelchairs.

❧

Our family and friends were very supportive and helpful. I don't know how we would have done it without them.

❧

My best coping technique was my family and their continued positive attitude. My oldest brother is blind and my parents' example over the years continues to be a great source of strength.

❧

My spouse is not the great communicator. He quietly takes all the information in and accepts the information as the will of God. I tend to also quietly process information, but I frequently talk about my frustrations and concerns with a few good friends.

❧

I read everything I could find on the subject (which is not a lot) and talked to other parents who had already been through this experience so we could get a glimmer of what to expect. I told my husband everything I learned. He listened and then he was my ROCK!

❧

I always thought I would never be able to have children because of a medical diagnosis. I was so happy to have a child that I devoted myself to him for the first two years of his life. My husband tried to distance himself from Andrew and would often cry when he looked at him. He blamed himself for the spina bifida.

❧

In the beginning, when Nicholas first came home, all I wanted to do was be with him and learn everything I possibly could, and do everything for him. My life was Nicholas and that's it. My husband dealt with it differently—he kept himself busy with other things, mostly work, and left Nicholas's needs up to me. He helped a lot but didn't feel comfortable with it all and felt better if I just took care of everything.

❧

My husband kept all his emotions inside, while I would cry at the drop of a hat and was always willing to talk with anybody who would listen.

❧

There have been many times when I have felt blessed by having a child with special needs. The time that comes to mind is when I realized that God must have thought a lot of me to give me a child with spina bifida. He must have thought I would be a good parent for Casey. We talk about people having faith in God but I think sometimes God shows he has faith in us.

❧❀❧

There aren't a lot of other kids with spina bifida in our community, but over the years I have found a tremendous amount of support online. I have never met most of these people in person, but we pour out our hearts to one another on a regular basis.

5
Why Is
Neurosurgery
Necessary?

Marion Walker, M.D.
Paula Peterson, R.N., M.S., P.N.P

With proper medical care, most babies with spina bifida can grow to have healthy, fulfilling lives as adults. En route to that healthy adulthood, however, most children with spina bifida will usually need to undergo more surgical procedures and medical treatments than other children. The first surgery usually occurs just hours or days after the baby is born, with others scheduled as needed over the following years.

The most urgent medical concerns facing a child with spina bifida generally involve the nervous system—the brain and spinal cord. This means that a neurosurgeon—a physician who specializes in surgery and surgical aspects of the brain and spinal cord—will be a vital part of your child's healthcare team.

The neurosurgeon is often the first doctor that parents of an infant with spina bifida meet. In fact, it is becoming increasingly common for parents to meet with the neurosurgeon before their baby's birth if spina bifida is diagnosed prenatally. The neurosurgeon performs the first surgery, the closure of the open neural tube. This chapter describes that initial surgery, as well as the other major medical problems related to the nervous system that may occur throughout your child's life, and explains how the neurosurgeon will be involved with the care.

❖❖ Closure of the Open Spina Bifida

To understand what happens during the initial surgery on your baby's back, it is important to know how the spinal cord develops and how the neural tube defect occurs.

The spinal cord begins to develop in the fetus as a long, flat layer of cells and gradually folds to form a tube-like structure called the neural tube. This process is usually completed by the twenty-eighth day of pregnancy.

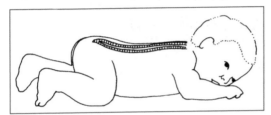

Figure 1. *Baby with a normal spine*

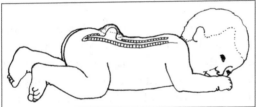

Figure 2. *Baby with spina bifida*

When the neural tube closes normally, the bones, muscles, and skin overlying the spinal cord close properly. When the neural tube fails to fold and close properly, the overlying bone and muscle, and often the skin, fail to close also, leaving the neural tissue in the spine (the neural placode) exposed. See Figures 1 and 2.

The failure of the neural tube to close properly leads to two different forms of spina bifida:

1. In **myelomeningocele,** the skin, muscle, and bone over the opening in the spinal column fail to close properly. Part of the spinal cord and its protective covering, the meninges, protrude through this opening. (See Figure 3.) This is the most serious and most common type of spina bifida. Most infants born with myelomeningocele have significant spinal cord dysfunction. There is rarely any neurological function below the anatomical level of the opening. In other words, if the spina bifida is located at

Figure 3. (left)
Myelomeningocele

Figure 4. (right)
Meningocele

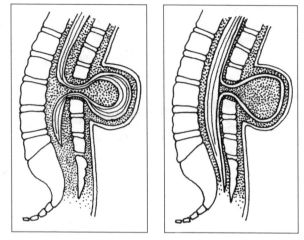

the L3 (third lumbar) level, there would not likely be any normal function in the nerves and spinal cord below L3.

2. In **meningocele,** a very rare condition, the baby's back is covered by normal skin, but part of the protective covering (meninges) of the spinal cord comes through an opening in the spinal column. There is usually a bulge or lump on the back in the midline indicating where the abnormality occurs. (See Figure 4.) There is less likely to be nerve damage, but problems may develop later in life due to tethering of the spinal cord. (See below.)

Occasionally, **spinal bifida oculta** (SBO) is confused with the two forms of spina bifida noted above. SBO results from a very different process and is unrelated to the two types of spina bifida above. In spina bifida occulta, some of the bones of the spine fail to close appropriately, but there is no opening on the back. There may be abnormal skin discoloration or a tuft of hair in one spot on the midline of the back, but there is usually minimal or no nerve damage. (See Figure 5 on the next page.) Most people with spina bifida occulta do not even know that they have the condition. The mildest form, a simple bony abnormality, may be present in up to 25 percent of the "normal" population. Some forms of SBO are associated with tethered spinal cord. This problem is discussed below.

A common form of SBO is a condition known as a **lipoma** or lipomyelomeningocele. A lipoma is a collection of fatty tissue that is attached to the end of the spinal cord. There is often a bulge or dimple

Figure 5. *(left)*
Spina Bifida Occulta

Figure 6. *(right)*
Lipoma

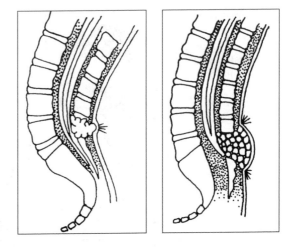

on the back, rather than an open sac. (See Figure 6.) This condition may cause problems similar to myelomeningocele, so a baby born with a lipoma will need much of the same care as a baby born with spina bifida. The initial surgery needed for a baby with myelomeningocele, however, may not be necessary during the first few days of life. This is because the abnormality is covered by normal skin.

Preparing for Surgery

When a baby has myelomeningocele, a neurosurgeon will generally close the open back 24 to 72 hours after birth. The infant is evaluated for other possible associated conditions before surgery is done. Before the surgery, much care will be taken to prevent further damage to the open area by keeping it covered with moist, sterile dressings.

Prior to the initial surgery, the neurosurgeon will determine how much movement and feeling your baby has. (Nerves ordinarily relay information about movement and sensation between the central nervous system and other body parts. Thus, damage to nerves results in impairment of movement and/or feeling.) Movement and sensation is usually easily checked at the bedside by performing a neurological examination. The level of motor function can be assessed by observing your baby's muscle movements, whereas the sensory function can be determined by responses to various painful stimuli, such as a pin prick or a pinch. Examining your baby prior to surgery helps document whether or not there is any loss of function associated with closure of the opening of the myelomeningocele.

The point at which function is affected is referred to as the "level" of spina bifida. The level would be defined as:

- **Cervical,** meaning nerves from the neck region are affected. It is rare for a lesion to be this high.
- **Thoracic,** meaning nerves from the upper part of the body down are affected. Only rarely is a thoracic lesion high enough to affect how the arms function.
- **Lumbar,** meaning nerves from the lower part of the body down are affected. These nerves control the feet, ankles, calf, knee, thigh, and hip. This is a common area for the opening to occur.
- **Sacral,** meaning only nerves at the very end of the spinal cord are affected. These nerves control the bladder and bowel and are affected in almost 100 percent of people with spina bifida.

Determining the exact level of a child's spina bifida is sometimes very difficult. In addition, the degree of muscle paralysis and imbalance is not the same in every child with the same level of lesion. This can make it hard for doctors to predict how spina bifida may affect your baby's movement and sensation. In general, however, the lower the defect is on the back, the less loss of function there will be. The higher the defect is on the back, the greater the loss of function. For example, a child with a thoracic level lesion would usually not have function in the nerves affecting the thoracic, lumbar, and sacral regions. A child with a lumbar level lesion would usually not have function in the nerves affecting the lumbar and sacral regions. As noted above, bladder and bowel function is almost always affected, regardless of the level of the lesion.

What Happens During and After Surgery?

The purpose of this initial surgery is to return the spinal cord to its normal position in the spinal canal and to prevent further damage or infection. It cannot, however, make the spinal cord function normally. The neurological defect present at birth will be present throughout life. The neurological function, however, should not deteriorate unless there is a known, and usually treatable, cause.

Surgery is performed under general anesthesia. The surgical procedure typically takes one and a half to two hours. There is rarely any significant blood loss. The surgeon closes the open neural placode to

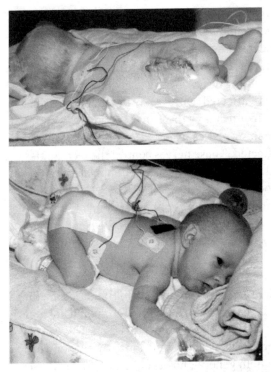

make the spinal cord a normal tubular shape, potentially lessening the amount of tethering that may occur (see below). The normal covering of the spinal cord (the dura) is then closed over the spinal cord. Finally, the muscle, fascia (connective tissues), and skin are closed. Usually, the baby has enough skin surrounding the opening to close over the opening. Less commonly, a skin graft is needed. Care and handling will be individualized according to the hospital's philosophy of treatment and your baby's specific needs. The surgical site will heal in approximately one week.

■■ All about Hydrocephalus

Another neurosurgical concern that arises in about 80 percent of babies with spina bifida is hydrocephalus. Hydrocephalus literally means water (hydro) on the brain (cephalus). The term refers to an excessive amount of cerebrospinal fluid collecting in the cavities or ventricles of the brain.

Cerebrospinal fluid (CSF) is normally produced and absorbed at a constant rate in the brain. It bathes the brain and acts as a cushion during movement. Hydrocephalus results from either a blockage to the normal flow of CSF or a deficient absorption of cerebral spinal fluid because of abnormal circulation. In children with spina bifida, hydrocephalus occurs because the pathway of fluid flow in the brain is obstructed.

The signs of hydrocephalus in infants may include some or all of the following:

- Head growth above "normal" or showing abnormal increased rate of growth;
- Soft spot is bulging and tense (check with your child in a sitting position when he is not crying);
- Change of behavior—usually extremely irritable, may become very tired;
- Vomiting or lack of desire to take food;
- Prominent scalp veins;
- Eyes may have a "sunset" appearance (whites of the eye are prominent)

The signs of increased fluid in older children (after the soft spot has closed) are:

- Irritability and/or tiredness ("whiny");
- Headache;
- Loss of appetite;
- Vomiting;
- Visual disturbances (double vision, crossed eyes, blurred vision);
- Behavioral changes.

Treatment

A surgical procedure known as a shunt is ordinarily performed when progressive hydrocephalus is confirmed. During this procedure, a shunt is surgically inserted in the fluid cavities of the brain (ventricles) and connected to a length of tubing that runs under the skin and usually all the way into the abdominal cavity but sometimes into the atrium of the heart or other organ. The shunt allows the excess CSF to drain from the brain, reducing pressure and the risk of possible brain damage. (See Figure 7.)

Some neurosurgeons feel that if a baby is going to develop hydrocephalus requiring a shunting proce-

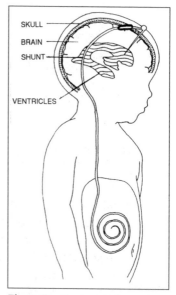

Figure 7. *Treatment of hydrocephalus with a shunt*

dure, this will occur when the infant is less than two weeks old and that the likelihood of needing a shunt decreases after two weeks of age. You should discuss this issue with your neurosurgeon if your baby has not developed hydrocephalus by the time he is discharged from the hospital.

After the operation, the tube under the skin and the valve which regulates fluid flow from the brain to the abdominal cavity can be felt under the skin. If the shunt is not working, the signs and symptoms that occurred before the insertion of the shunt will reappear. If this happens, contact your physician or clinic.

If your child's shunt malfunctions, he will need a revision—an operation to repair or replace the malfunctioning shunt. A shunt series—an x-ray that shows the pathway of the shunt—can help determine whether the malfunction is due to the placement or disconnection of the tube. Frontal and side views of the head as well as the abdomen are taken to determine whether the sections are together and the shunt is in place. A CT scan can document the size of the ventricles and further help in diagnosing shunt malformation.

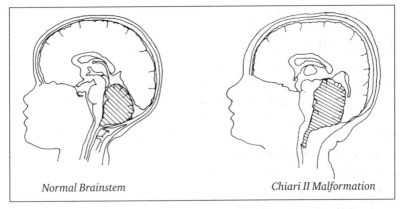

Normal Brainstem   *Chiari II Malformation*

Figure 8.

A small number of children with hydrocephalus may benefit from a relatively new surgical procedure called endoscopic third ventriculostomy. This procedure allows the neurosurgeon to open up a new pathway for cerebral spinal fluid flow as an alternative to placing a shunt or removing an existing shunt. This procedure appears to be more successful in older patients with myelomenigocele. Parents should talk to their child's neurosurgeon regarding the advisability of this procedure.

Other Neurosurgical Concerns

:: The Chiari II Malformation

The Chiari II malformation is a difference in the structure of the brain involving the lower brainstem, upper spinal cord, and the lowermost portion of the cerebellum. About 85 to 90 percent of children born with spina bifida have this malformation. Only a small percent of children, however, show symptoms and problems that eventually require surgical management.

What Does All This Mean?

To understand how the Chiari ll malformation may cause problems for a child with spina bifida, you need to know some basics about brain anatomy and function.

The **brainstem** houses centers which control the heart, breathing, and blood pressure, plus those centers which affect swallowing, vomiting, sneezing, and coughing. In addition, many of the cranial nerves that supply fibers to the head, eyes, and neck originate in the brainstem.

The **cerebellum** is the portion of the brain that controls balance and coordinates muscle movements. It assists in helping infants and children develop good control of their head, neck, and trunk.

When the Chiari II malformation is present, the brainstem and cerebellum are pushed down, and compression may occur due to lack of space (see Figure 8).

In addition, the fourth ventricle is elongated and enters the cervical area of the spinal cord. This may block the normal flow of cerebrospinal fluid and increase the compression on the brainstem. It also results in increased intracranial (within the skull) pressure or displacement of cerebrospinal fluid into cysts in the spinal cord. When this occurs, an infant or child may show the signs of shunt malfunction listed above, as well as the signs of brainstem dysfunction identified below.

What Are the Signs and Symptoms of Problems with the Chiari II Malformation?

1. Respiratory distress (difficulty breathing);
2. Apnea (cessation of breathing) any time;
3. Stridor (high pitched, noisy breathing);

4. Inability to swallow, as well as a weak suck response, resulting in feeding difficulties and inability to handle fluids;

5. Upper extremity weakness and numbness (funny feeling).

When Do Signs and Symptoms Usually Occur?

The most common sign of a problem caused by the Chiari ll malformation is stridor. It occurs most often in infancy up through the
first decade of life. In addition, infants most commonly have feeding
difficulties, apnea, or upper extremity weakness. When older children
are experiencing difficulties due to the malformation, signs usually
include upper extremity weakness, respiratory distress, and, less commonly, stridor.

How Are the Problems with the Chiari Malformation Diagnosed?

If your child has the Chiari malformation, its presence will be
noted on the CT scan completed during the newborn period. Suspicion
of problems with the malformation will be raised if your child begins
to have any of the above signs and symptoms.

Magnetic resonance imaging (MRI) is by far the best way to diagnose and define the malformation. A baseline MRI is often completed
between 9 and 12 months of age. The lower part of the brainstem including the cerebellum is clearly viewed at that age. If problems occur prior
to that time, the neurosurgeon may request an MRI. Other diagnostic
tests may also be requested. See the section on "Testing" at the end of
the chapter for more information on CT scans and MRIs.

What Is the Treatment?

Shunt malfunction is the most common cause of Chiari II symptoms. If your child's shunt is not functioning properly, the neurosurgeon
will revise the shunt and make sure that it is functioning. If your child has
not previously had a shunt and is now experiencing Chiari ll symptoms,
a shunt will most likely be placed. Often these procedures can alleviate
the pressure on the brainstem and therefore reverse the symptoms.

Some children, even after shunting procedures, continue to
exhibit signs and symptoms of the Chiari ll malformation. Treatment
then may include:

▪ the continued use of oxygen, through a plastic tube with
small prongs placed in the nose;

- a tracheostomy—an opening made through the neck and into the trachea to assist with breathing;
- a gastrostomy tube—a tube that is passed surgically directly into the stomach and allows formula to be given. This may be frightening at first, but is actually easily managed at home.

If these treatments are being considered for your child, the neurosurgeon will discuss your child's options with you.

∷ Tethered Cord Syndrome

By definition, to tether means to "restrict" or "bind with." Therefore, "tethered cord" may be defined as a spinal cord that is bound down or restricted by scar tissue. The tethered cord cannot move freely as the child bends and moves about, and the small blood vessels nourishing the cord are stretched, resulting in decreased blood flow to the spinal cord and nerves.

The potential for developing the tethered cord syndrome begins when a newborn's myelomeningocele defect is closed. Magnetic Resonance Imaging (MRI) of the spinal cord performed at nine to twelve months of age has shown that 100 percent of all infants with spina bifida have a tethered cord. But treatment is not usually recommended until the infant or child begins to show the clinical symptoms of tethered cord syndrome described below. These symptoms typically appear as the spine grows in length, stretching the spinal cord.

Symptoms of Tethered Cord

Symptoms of tethered cord syndrome can appear at any time, but are most likely to become evident during periods of rapid growth. These periods are individual, which makes it important to always be aware of signs of tethering.

Loss of Neurologic Function

Progressive weakness in the lower extremities (legs and feet) represents a significant change and usually indicates a tethered cord. This change most often shows up as increased difficulties with walking or decreased use of the lower extremities. The change or difficulty in walking occurs due to weakness or increased muscle tone (spasticity). Spasticity or increased tone requires a child to use more energy to move his extremities. As a result, he makes slower and fewer movements. Increased tone can also cause joints to become deformed and less responsive to orthopedic procedures such as heel cord lengthenings and simple ankle and foot surgeries.

It is also important to consider other possible causes for changes in your child's walking patterns or use of extremities. These may include improperly fitted shoes or braces, a dislocated hip, or weight gain. Each of these problems is readily identified, and, when corrected, your child should regain his usual functioning. However, if progressive loss of function does occur, it is often associated with tethered cord. For early recognition of these problems, your child should have regular follow-up evaluations of muscle function performed by a physical therapist and reviewed by a neurosurgeon.

Back Pain

Back pain caused by a tethered spinal cord typically occurs with activity and improves with rest. The pain tends to progressively worsen with time until your child undergoes surgical intervention. It is important to remember, however, that some children with clinical signs of the tethered cord syndrome do not experience pain.

Changes in Bladder Function

Deterioration in bladder function is one of the most common signs of tethered cord syndrome. This is difficult to recognize in a young child who has not yet learned to stay dry. An older child who has previously been able to stay dry using a bladder management program may begin to have more difficulties staying dry.

Sometimes changes in bladder function may be directly related to problems with the urinary tract (e.g., a urinary tract infection). The cause may also be deterioration of spinal cord function due to tethered cord syndrome. For this reason, it is important to have your child assessed by the urologist as well as the neurosurgeon. This is often done simultaneously to assure that the evaluation is completed as quickly as possible.

Scoliosis

Scoliosis (curvature of the spine) is common in children with spina bifida and can have a variety of causes. (See Chapter 8.) If other causes are not found, then progressive scoliosis may be a symptom of tethered cord syndrome.

Surgery to untether the cord should be done before the curve becomes so severe that it limits function and mobility. If the scoliosis does not improve following release of the cord, then a spinal fusion may be necessary. A spinal fusion is a surgical procedure in which bones of the spine are fused (joined) together to reduce the degree of curvature, and is discussed in more detail in Chapter 8.

Monitoring for Tethered Cord Syndrome

Baseline studies are generally completed early in a child's life. The following tests are most commonly done and serve as a basis for future comparison.

1. Manual Muscles Test (MMT) may be done after your baby's lesion is closed and before he is discharged from the hospital. This test may be repeated as indicated every three to six months. The MMT is a very important and reproducible test performed by the physical therapist. During the test, an instrument called a dynamometer is used to measure lower extremity strength. Objective criteria are used to describe results and to document function, making it easy to compare the results of subsequent tests with earlier tests.
2. Magnetic Resonance Imaging (MRI) of the head and spine may be recommended on baseline and then compared with future scans. See below for a description of MRI testing.
3. Spine x-rays can show early signs of curving.

When concerns about tethered cord arise, the following studies may be done and compared with the baseline information:

1. Magnetic Resonance Imaging (MRI) of the complete spine and lower part of the brain.
2. Manual Muscle Test (MMT) and dynamometer readings.
3. Urological assessment, including a urodynamic study known as a CMG (cystometrogram). This study documents how well the bladder empties and filling capacity pressures, as well as functioning of the sphincters.
4. Close monitoring of the child by a neurosurgeon.

What Happens During and After Surgery?

Surgery to release a tethered cord is straightforward. Using the operating microscope for increased vision and light, the surgeon cuts away dense scar tissue from the spinal cord. Fatty or cystic tissue, if present, may also be removed.

Your child will probably remain in a flat (horizontal) position for 24 hours or longer, and will be rolled from side to side frequently. To prevent leakage of cerebrospinal fluid through the new incision site, activity needs to be resumed slowly.

Pain control will be an important part of the postoperative care. Your child may receive pain medication through a small tube placed near the spinal cord during surgery. This is known as an epidural catheter. Children with epidural catheters must be carefully monitored to make sure that the pain medication does not mask signs of neurological deterioration. After the first day or two, pain medication can usually be given by mouth.

Once your child is allowed to resume activity, he may receive physical therapy for passive and active exercises. Most children are out of bed walking or in a wheelchair by the end of the first week.

Bladder management is an important concern following surgery. A catheter is usually placed in the bladder during surgery to ensure continual emptying. It is removed after three to four days. Clean intermittent catheterization (CIC) is then resumed unless your child was not on that type of bladder program before surgery. (See Chapter 6.)

Bowel management is also important to prevent constipation. Some type of "clean out" (suppository or enema) is usually given one or two days after surgery. Once the bowel is cleaned, the program used before surgery is re-started.

Your child will be discharged from the hospital approximately one week after surgery. Full activity, including school attendance, can usually be resumed within four weeks. Follow-up will include visits with the neurosurgeon, a manual muscle test (MMT), and a urodynamic test (CMG).

What Are Possible Complications after Surgery?

How much a child's functioning improves after surgery for tethered cord syndrome varies. However, your child's problems should not worsen unless the cord begins to tether again. Re-tethering is not uncommon, making it extremely important to continue monitoring your child for the signs and symptoms of tethered cord syndrome.

Approximately 10 to 15 percent of children show signs of shunt malfunction after tethered cord surgery. This can occur up to six months after surgery, but the greatest risk is within the first month. Your child should be followed closely by your neurosurgeon for signs and symptoms of shunt malfunction during this period.

Temporary worsening of muscle or bladder function is not uncommon after surgery. However, almost all children eventually regain their baseline level of function, and many improve.

Children who need repeated procedures for re-tethering are more likely to lose some neurological function. This is a result of scarring due to repeated procedures. Rest assured, however, that your neurosurgeon will follow your child very closely and recommend surgeries only when absolutely necessary.

▮▮ Syringomyelia

One final problem that can affect the nervous system of children with spina bifida is syringomyelia. Syringomyelia is a disorder in which a fluid-filled cavity, called a syrinx, forms in the spinal cord. (In other words, it can be compared to hydrocephalus of the spinal cord.) It is caused by high pressure of cerebrospinal fluid that can't exit from the fourth ventricle and is therefore forced into the central canal of the spine. Syringomyelia can lead to problems with neurologic function, resulting in symptoms similar to those caused by tethered cord (scoliosis, increased muscle tone in the extremities).

The most common cause of syringomyelia in children with spina bifida is shunt malfunction. Consequently, shunt revision is often the best treatment for this disorder. Treatment may depend on other neurological concerns, and occasionally involves a surgical procedure in which fluid is shunted from the syrinx into the chest or abdomen. Follow-up examinations and scans are important to monitor the success of the surgery. After treatment, children usually regain the neurologic function they had prior to syringomyelia.

▮▮ Tests Used to Monitor Brain and Spinal Cord Function

To monitor and treat the neurosurgical concerns described in this chapter, your child's doctor will rely on a variety of sophisticated testing procedures. These tests enable the doctor to distinguish between two or more problems that produce similar symptoms, and also to pinpoint the extent of a problem. As a parent, it is important for you to understand in advance what these tests involve. That way you can help prepare your child for the procedure and reduce any anxiety he might be feeling. Although the tests are all painless, the equipment used can seem intimidating to a small child who does not know what to expect.

CT Scan (Computerized Axial Tomography)

CT scan is an x-ray exam that enables tissues inside the body to be viewed. A computerized scanner is used to produce a series of cross-sectional images of the body area that needs to be examined. Images from many angles taken in sequence can then be used to build a three-dimensional picture. In children with spina bifida, most scans are performed on the head to monitor hydrocephalus. The ventricular system can be viewed and the size of the ventricles can be documented.

Your child will be positioned on a padded table with his head supported. A strap across his forehead will hold his head still during the exam so that clear images can be produced. The table slides into the open area of a large doughnut-shaped device, which is open in the front and back. This is a scanner ring and contains the x-ray tube. The table will move slightly for each scan, and buzzing and clicking sounds can be heard. This is controlled by a computer. A scan of the entire head takes approximately 30 minutes. The technician performing your child's scan may or may not be able to give you an idea of the results, but it is vital that you review the scan with the neurosurgeon afterwards. The neurosurgeon is the one who will make recommendations based on the results of the scan.

MRI (Magnetic Resonance Imaging)

MRI is a diagnostic tool that uses magnet energy to produce a clear, two-dimensional picture of the brain, cervical canal, and/or spine. Images can be obtained in any direction or plane. MRI is not an x-ray. No radiation is used; instead a large magnet, radio waves, and a computer are employed. CT scans are preferred to check the size of the ventricles; otherwise, MRI scans are usually recommended.

Infants and young children require sedation in order to remain motionless. Your child will be comfortably positioned on a padded table with his arms at his sides and his head in a head rest. Soft Velcro straps will be placed on his arms to ensure a snug and safe fit. Your child will also wear soft ear plugs, since the MRI machinery makes a variety of noises.

To begin the test, the table is moved into a tunnel-like tube in which the magnetic field is generated. The test can last up to an hour, depending on which area of the brain or spine is being examined. Extensive evaluations of the entire spine and head may have to be performed on two separate visits. When the MRI is completed, your child will be sleepy because of the sedation and will need to be monitored until he is awake and aware of his surroundings. While technicians or others may give you an idea of the results, again it is vital that you review the MRI with the neurosurgeon for the "official" results.

Ultrasound

Ultrasound is a diagnostic tool that uses high frequency sound waves beyond the range of hearing to make an image of the organ or structure that is being studied. The sound waves are then projected onto a screen and a photograph is made. (This is the same test that most pregnant women have to visualize their fetus.)

Before your child's ultrasound begins, gel will be placed on the skin over the area to be studied. This is to prevent air from entering between the skin and transducer (the ultrasound source). Your child will need to lie still while the transducer, a wand-like device, is being passed over the area. The ultrasound is a simple, safe method to monitor the size of the ventricles when determining the need for a shunting procedure. Its use is limited to infants, as it cannot be used once the soft spot on the head is closed.

▪▪ Conclusion

Many of the neurosurgical issues associated with spina bifida can be frightening to families. However, the good news is that medical professionals have made major progress in learning how to treat these problems through close observation and surgical intervention. As a parent, you can do a great deal to ensure that your child's neurosurgical problems are dealt with in a timely manner. First, you can make sure you understand how to monitor your child for problems that might develop. And second, you can promptly communicate any concerns you might have to your child's medical team. When parents, the pediatrician, and specialists work closely as a team, your child's health can only benefit.

■■ Parent Statements

My initial reaction to Scott's diagnosis was shock, and then almost denial. Of course, my baby's defect couldn't be that severe. Things would be okay. The doctors would fix it. I wanted to believe they would "close up the back" and the other problems would go away too.

❧

In the beginning, it was so hard to go to the doctor's office or clinic. I really felt we were only looking at what was wrong or what he couldn't do. I would come home from visits and wonder if anyone saw what a beautiful baby he was or did they only see the spina bifida, hydrocephalus, club foot, tibial torsion, hearing impairment, etc.

❧

Ignorance is the number one public problem. Once educated, people are generally understanding. One incident I clearly recall is being in the grocery store after our son had just had craniotomy surgery. He had staples around his whole head. A tackily-dressed lady came up and asked, "What's wrong with his head?" I am not proud of this, but I popped my eyes out at her, rubbed my hands together, and vampire-like said, "He had BRAIN surgery!"

❧

We were hoping our son would not have to have a shunt, but it became apparent after a week that he needed one. He had surgery at the age of twelve days. It was necessary and we thank God that it was available.

❧

It is always in the back of our minds that our son's shunt could malfunction. Our son took a bad tumble down a full flight of stairs and within a few days developed severe headaches. We just knew his shunt was mal-

functioning. He had had it for almost four years without any problems, but now it seemed it was blocked. We took him in for a CT scan and were told his shunt was working fine, but he was experiencing headaches from the fall. We were extremely relieved.

❧

Every time James had to have a shunt revision, it was very discouraging, because just when we thought they finally got it right and he was okay, something would go wrong with it again. He has had four shunt revisions, all before the age of one. The first year was very hard. He was in the hospital every month the entire first year.

❧

I know a lot of parents of children with spina bifida and some of them have never had shunt problems.

❧

The hand weakness my daughter developed due to a syrinx/cyst on the spine was unexpected and increased the severity of her disability. As her parents, we needed to come to a new acceptance of her disability. This new acceptance seems to have to come at each stage in my daughter's life. We now do not know if she will be able to drive or not—a new challenge in acceptance for us.

❧

I know I sometimes panic. Every time he gets a headache, every time he cries loudly, every time he becomes nauseous, I worry that something is wrong, but most of the time I think we treat him pretty normally.

6

Urologic Concerns

Nan Tobias, M.S.N., R.N., C.N.P.

Most parents of young children only have to concern themselves with the end result of the urologic process—with changing wet diapers. But when you have a child with spina bifida, there are many more urologic concerns, including potential problems with the functioning of the kidneys, ureters, bladder, and urethra. At a minimum, your child will probably need special assistance emptying her bladder. At worst, she could develop a condition that could potentially damage her kidneys. Fortunately, many urologic problems can be prevented with vigilance, and also can be effectively treated with medications, surgery, or other means. This chapter discusses the most common urologic concerns, along with their prevention, diagnosis, and treatment.

■■ Normal Urinary Tract Functioning

To understand why children with spina bifida have urologic problems, it helps to understand how the urinary tract normally functions. The urinary tract consists of the kidneys, ureters, bladder, and

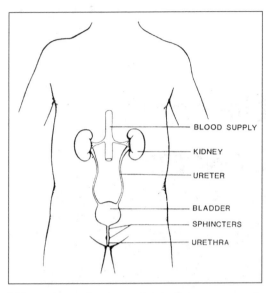

BLOOD SUPPLY

KIDNEY

URETER

BLADDER

SPHINCTERS

URETHRA

urethra. (See Figure 1.) Blood continuously circulates through the kidneys, which filter out the body's liquid waste products. These waste products include excess water, salts, and toxins. The urine, made in the kidneys, travels down the hollow ureter tubes, and is stored in the urinary bladder.

The bladder normally functions under very low pressure. This is a result of the bladder's muscular wall being in a relaxed state. The bladder fills to a certain volume. When this volume is reached, stretch receptors in the bladder wall send a message to the brain via nerves inside the spinal cord that it is time to empty the bladder. Urine then exits through the urethra as the bladder wall contracts (tightens) and the sphincter muscle relaxes.

:: How Spina Bifida Affects the Urinary Tract

Children with spina bifida are usually born with a normal urinary tract and with the capacity to produce urine. Maintaining that normal urinary tract can be a challenge, however.

As discussed above, the bladder usually sends a message that it is full to the brain along nerves inside the spinal cord. When spina bifida occurs, however, the nerves are damaged and messages from the bladder cannot get to the brain. Changes occur within the muscular wall of the bladder due to the lack of proper nerve connections. These changes make the bladder wall stiff and unyielding. This type of bladder is referred to as a *neurogenic bladder*. When there is urine in the bladder, one of two things can happen: 1) urine may leak out uncontrollably; or 2) it may be stored at very high pressures inside the bladder.

Urinary Incontinence. Urine leakage (*urinary incontinence*) can occur for two reasons: 1) the sphincter muscle at the bottom of the bladder doesn't work well; 2) the bladder muscle is rigid and stiff. This rigid bladder wall may become so stiff that urine is forced out through the sphincter muscle. If you have a baby with spina bifida, it is a good idea to observe how often you need to change her diaper. Does your baby seem to hold urine for long periods (3-4 hours or more) or are the diapers wet in small amounts very frequently? These observations will help the urologist evaluate the bladder's functioning.

Note: Many babies with spina bifida begin a catheterization program soon after birth. If your baby is already being catheterized, it is important to periodically measure the amount of urine drained from the bladder and to observe whether your baby urinates between catheterizations.

Vesicoureteral Reflux. Sometimes, the bladder muscle wall can become so stiff that it cannot stretch well. The bladder may hold only a small percentage of the urine that it should be able to hold. It is much like trying to blow up a balloon that will not let the air in. The bladder wall may be so rigid that urine is actually pushed backwards up the ureters to the kidneys again. This condition is called *vesicoureteral reflux*. Vesico-ureteral reflux does not have visible symptoms. Testing for this condition is described under "Diagnostic Evaluation of the Urinary Tract," below. If not treated, reflux can lead to kidney infection and kidney damage.

Hydronephrosis. If vesicoureteral reflux becomes severe, it can cause the kidneys and ureters to be swollen. This condition is called *hydronephrosis*. Hydronephrosis can occur for a number of reasons. In children with spina bifida who are receiving appropriate care, the most common reasons are: 1) vesicoureteral reflex; and 2) kidney or bladder stones.

Kidney and Bladder Stones. Stones may form in the kidneys or bladder of a person with spina bifida due to standing of urine or due to repeated infection. When urine does not flow normally, the chemical compounds in the urine can cause sediment to build up and stones to form. Likewise, certain bacteria that cause infection in the urinary system can cause stone formation.

If stones occur in the kidney, they can cause a blockage of urine, and are therefore likely to cause an obstruction in the urinary tract. They can lodge where the kidney joins the ureter or where the ureter connects to the bladder. This obstruction will cause the kidney to swell and lose function. A person with a normal, intact spinal cord experiences severe pain if this happens. A person with spina bifida may experience little or no pain at all.

Preventing Infection and Stone Formation

An infection caused by bacteria inside the bladder is called *cystitis*. An infection that involves the kidneys is called *pyelonephritis*. A child with spina bifida who has cystitis may not experience many

symptoms, due to the interruption of spinal cord function. She may, however, experience discomfort with catheterization (see below) or have increased urinary leakage. Pyelonephritis can make a child very ill. Generally, when the kidneys are infected, symptoms can include fever, chills, nausea, and vomiting, as well as an overall feeling of being unwell. Treatment with IV fluids and IV antibiotics may be necessary.

The following guidelines will help prevent urinary tract infection and promote healthy habits:

- Keep the skin clean and free from urine and bowel movements. There are bacteria (germs) in bowel movements, and bacteria grow in urine if it is left on skin and clothes for long periods. The bacteria can then travel to the bladder and cause infection. Particularly if reflux is present, or even if it is not, the bacteria can also travel to the kidneys and cause a kidney infection.
- Encourage your child to drink plenty of water and juices daily. Doing this will help flush out bacteria that do get into the bladder. The following table will help you calculate your child's daily fluid needs.

Weight	20 lb.	30 lb.	40 lb.	50 lb.	60 lb.	70 lb.	80 lb.
Mini. Fluids Needed	32 oz.	40 oz.	48 oz.	54 oz.	56 oz.	60 oz.	64 oz.

■ Help your child stay away from foods and liquids that can harm the bladder and cause it to work less effectively. These substances include:
1. caffeine, found in soft drinks, tea, and coffee;
2. carbonation, found in soft drinks and some bottled water;
3. chocolate; and
4. citrus products, including grapefruit, oranges, lemons, limes, and tomatoes and their juices.

This does not mean that your child can never again have these foods and drinks. It does mean that it is much healthier for the body to have other foods and fluids and to consider these four substances as treats to be consumed only on special occasions.

Medications may also be placed into the bladder in order to prevent stone formation. Some people are more prone to developing stones than others. Those prone to stone formation generally carry many infections in the bladder, do not empty their bladders well or frequently enough, and/or have a great deal of bladder mucus. Generally, people who have a great deal of bladder mucus have undergone bladder augmentation surgery. (See the section on "Surgical Treatments" below.) Your child's urologist may recommend using a catheter and a syringe full of normal saline (salt water) or other types of medication in order to "wash out" the bladder and get rid of the mucus.

■■ Diagnostic Evaluation of the Urinary Tract

Everyone with spina bifida needs to have a *urologist*—a doctor who specializes in keeping the urinary tract healthy. Generally, your child's spina bifida team will include a urologist. If it does not, it is important that your child visit a pediatric urologist within the first month of life. Periodically, the urologist will perform certain tests to monitor the kidneys and bladder, described below.

Renal Ultrasound

During a renal ultrasound, pictures are taken of the kidneys, ureters, and bladder with sound waves. It is a very simple test that gives information about the structure of the urinary tract. A technician will place a warm, soothing liquid on your child's back and abdomen, then rub the skin with a wand that looks similar to a microphone. An image will be shown on a screen and special pictures will be developed. The pictures will show whether there is swelling in the kidneys (*hydronephrosis*) or ureter (*hydroureter*); whether the bladder wall looks normal; and whether the bladder empties completely with catheterization, or, in some instances, with voiding. How often this test is ordered will depend upon your child's age and the findings on past ultrasounds.

Voiding Cystourethrogram (VCUG)

This test is an x-ray of the urinary tract that is taken after a special fluid is placed into the bladder with a *catheter*—a thin plastic tube. The x-rays show a close-up picture of the bladder wall and any changes that may have occurred as a result of high pressures due to the spina bifida. This test will also reveal the presence of any vesicoureteral reflux (backwards flow of urine towards the kidneys). If your child has reflux, this test will need to be done every year or so. If your child does not have reflux, it will be done less often.

Renal Scan

A renal scan is a test that may be done if the kidneys have not shown evidence of growth over a period of time or if the kidneys appear scarred on an ultrasound. This test shows how well and how fast the kidneys filter the blood. In addition, it shows how much of the overall kidney function is done by each kidney. It can also show in greater detail how much scarring or damage the kidneys have.

Urodynamics

Urodynamics is a test to measure the stiffness of the bladder wall. It is done by passing a catheter, with a pressure monitor, into the bladder. As the bladder is filled with water through the catheter, pressure readings are measured. If this test indicates a stiff bladder wall with high pressure readings, it may mean that your child's current bladder program is not as effective as it needs to be. The frequency of catheterization may need to be increased. Additionally, if your child is not currently taking medication to relax the bladder wall, she will probably need to start. If your child already takes medication, she will need either a higher dose or an additional medication. Catheterization and medication to relax the bladder wall will help keep the kidneys functioning well, promote kidney growth, prevent kidney damage, and promote continence. See "Medications for the Urinary Tract" for information on medications that might be used.

Not only does this test measure the stiffness of the bladder wall, but it also measures the strength of the urethra. If the urethra is too weak, it will not be able to prevent urine leakage. Certain medications and sometimes surgery can make a weak urethra stronger.

Cystoscopy

Cystoscopy is a procedure that is often done using a general anesthetic, but may be done without. If your child has little or no sensation below the waist, a general anesthetic may not be needed. This procedure involves passing an instrument much like a telescope up into the bladder through the urethra. The urologist will look into the "scope" and be able to directly visualize the urethra, bladder, and the lower portion of the ureters. This procedure may be necessary prior to major urinary tract surgery, to evaluate the appearance of the urinary tract when a child has vesicoureteral reflux, or for other reasons.

■■ When Intermittent Catheterization Is Needed

Intermittent catheterization involves inserting a hollow plastic tube called a catheter into the bladder in order to empty urine. More specifically, the catheter is inserted through the urethra and into the bladder. Generally, the procedure is done four or five times each day in order to promote bladder emptying, prevent infection and stone formation, and reduce bladder pressures. The catheter is inserted, the urine is drained, and the catheter removed each time.

A variety of factors is involved in determining when to begin a child with spina bifida on an intermittent catheterization program. There are two different philosophies. First, some urologists think that all newborns who have spina bifida should be started on such a program soon after birth. By using catheterization from the start, infections and incomplete bladder emptying should not become problems. In addition, it may be possible to prevent hydronephrosis and vesicoureteral reflux from occurring. Furthermore, it is the rare person with spina bifida who does not eventually need to catheterize her bladder, and the thought is that prevention is the best form of treatment.

On the other hand, some urologists think that it may not be necessary for some children with spina bifida to catheterize their bladders for a certain portion of their lives. Most often, this time period occurs in infancy and the preschool years. If a newborn's bladder shows evidence of good emptying, no reflux on a VCUG, and normal kidneys on an ultrasound, it may be safe to allow the child to void on her own for a period of time. Some think that taking this approach may make it more difficult on the child and family when catheterizations are begun at a later age. If a child and family become accustomed to the catheterizations at an early age, then the procedure is accepted early on. If, however, at age three or four, the family is told they must begin catheterizations (due to infection, poor kidney growth, or damage, for instance), it will be much more difficult for the child and family to adjust. In addition, by not catheterizing the child from birth, the risk for damage to the urinary tract is greater.

Certain conditions are indications that a catheterization program may be required. These are:

- Kidney or bladder infections;
- Incomplete bladder emptying with urination;
- The presence of vesicoureteral reflux;
- Poor kidney growth;
- Kidney damage;
- A poorly functioning bladder as indicated by urodynamic results;
- Urinary incontinence in an older child.

Most children with spina bifida do require catheterization due to one or more of these reasons, or because their urologist believes in the "prevention" method of caring for the urinary tract. Before catheterization became an accepted method of caring for the urinary tract in people with spina bifida, many went on to develop kidney failure and required dialysis. Since the 1970s, the use of intermittent catheterization (along with medication, discussed below) has promoted healthy kidneys and prevented many serious consequences to the urinary tract. It has also helped many people with spina bifida stay dry during the day and/or night.

Learning to Catheterize Your Child

Many parents are frightened when they first learn that they will need to catheterize their child's bladder. They may be very concerned that they are not capable of performing such a procedure and that they will somehow harm their child. While these fears are natural, they are almost always unfounded. The procedure does take time, effort, and practice to learn. Nearly every parent who has ever attempted the procedure has been successful, however. Rarely, a parent may be physically incapable of catheterization due to a neuromuscular disease that reduces strength or coordination, visual difficulties, or the amputation of an arm or hand.

Generally, a nurse on the hospital unit or in an outpatient setting will teach you how to catheterize your child. Many nurses will provide written information or video materials as well. Remember: the advantages of performing the catheterizations and preventing damage to your child's urinary tract far outweigh the risks.

Probably the biggest fear parents have about performing the catheterizations is that they will harm their child. Two potential ways that a child could be harmed are by: 1) introducing infection into the bladder, and 2) causing trauma to or damage to the urinary tract.

Infection can be introduced into the bladder if you are not careful about washing your hands, if you do not cleanse your child's genitals, or if you do not clean your child's catheters properly. Bacteria live virtually everywhere in the world—on your skin, on your hair, on furniture, carpets, etc. You will be taught to wash your hands and how to prepare and store your supplies. Infection due to poor technique happens occasionally, but again, the risks due to not catheterizing are generally much greater.

The second fear, hurting your child, happens only in the rarest of circumstances. You will be taught to catheterize your child by inserting the catheter very gently. Sometimes, particularly in boys, it may be necessary to hold firm, steady pressure against a tight sphincter (the muscle at the bottom of the bladder), but you should never FORCE or use excessive pressure when inserting a catheter. If you do force a catheter and push very hard, it is possible to harm the urethra or bladder. It is, however, quite impossible to poke a hole through the bladder. When the catheter enters the bladder, it will just curl up inside the bladder if you insert it too far.

When you are first learning to catheterize your child, it is a good idea to place her on a bed or a blanket on the floor. The area should be well lit so you can see well. When catheterizing a taller or preschool-aged child, it is often helpful to have another adult assist you, until you and your child become accustomed to catheterizations. If you do not have a family member or friend who can help, it may be possible for a nurse from a home care agency to help you during this time of learning and adjustment. If you think you would benefit from a nurse visiting in your home, discuss this with your urologist or nurse.

Parents often ask how much urine their child should be putting out. How much fluid your child drinks will, of course, affect urinary output, but here are some guidelines:

Age	Amount
1-2 days	30-60 cc
4-5 days	70-250 cc
6-10 days	200-300 cc
10 days—2 months	250-450 cc
2 mos.—1 yr	400-500 cc
1-2 yrs	500-700 cc
3-5 yrs	600-1200 cc
6-8 yrs	700-1300 cc
8-14 yrs	800-1500 cc

❚❚ Medications for the Urinary Tract

Medications to Promote Continence

Children with spina bifida often have a stiff, tense bladder wall because the nerve impulses are interrupted in the spinal cord. Medications are commonly used to calm this stiff, tense bladder wall. These medications include Ditropan, Ditropan XL, Probanthine, Levsin, Detrol, Detrol LA, and Oxytrol patch. These medicines work to relax the bladder muscle, reduce the pressures inside the bladder, and as a result, in the kidney as well. When the overall pressures within the urinary tract are reduced, the kidneys can function more effectively and grow as expected. These medicines also help promote urinary continence by allowing the bladder to store more urine under lower pressures.

Although Ditropan is a very effective medication for the bladder problems associated with spina bifida, it sometimes causes significant side effects when taken orally. These side effects may include heat intolerance, constipation, and blurred vision. The XL tablet causes fewer side effects but it must be swallowed whole. If your child has side effects, the urologist may suggest that the Ditropan be given directly into the bladder through a catheter. This method of administration is not effective for everyone, but may be an option to try to eliminate the side effects. Another option is to administer this same medication through the skin with a transdermal patch. The patch is worn continuously and medication is slowly released and absorbed into the blood stream.

Some other medications that calm a tense bladder wall are also commonly used. Probanthine and Levsin are medicines that have been around for many years and have proved to be effective for many people. Detrol and Detrol LA are newer medicines being used with children. Information is still being gathered about their effectiveness.

Another medication that can be used to promote urinary continence is one that helps tighten the bladder neck and sphincter muscle. Pseudoephedrine may reduce the leakage of urine by helping muscles at the bottom of the bladder to tighten. This medication has been shown to be safe over the long term.

Antibiotics

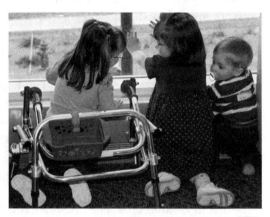

Most people who catheterize will have bacteria in the bladder at least some of the time. When bacteria are present in the urine, but do not cause any problems or symptoms of infection, the condition is called *asymptomatic bacteriuria.* Generally, there is no need to treat this condition. Certain bacteria that are present in the urine, but do not cause any illness, have been shown to be protective to the bladder. These bacteria protect against other more virulent (disease producing) bacteria from taking over and causing an infection. Studies have shown that sometimes when the protective bacteria are destroyed by a treatment course of an antibiotic, a new bacteria invades the bladder, causing symptoms and infection.

In general, it is best not to treat bacteria in the bladder if they are not causing problems. An exception to this rule is often made, however, if bacteria such as *Pseudomonas* or *Proteus* are present. These bacteria can be related to the formation of stones in the bladder and should generally be eradicated from the bladder by using an antibiotic.

An antibiotic should also be given when symptoms of infection accompany the bacteria in the urine. Symptoms that indicate an infection is present and should be treated include:

- Fever;
- Pain in the lower abdomen or flank area;
- Pain during catheterization or voiding;
- Nausea and/or vomiting;
- Loss of appetite;
- Generally not feeling well;
- Urinary leakage or incontinence.

Other illnesses that could cause similar symptoms must, of course, be ruled out (e.g., influenza, throat infection, ear infections).

Urinary tract infections are more common in girls, primarily due to the nature of the female anatomy. The urethra in a female is short and so it is quite easy for bacteria to climb from the skin into the bladder. If the bladder is not emptied on a frequent, regular basis, these bacteria multiply and can start an infection in the urine. Boys can get infections in the urinary tract as well, most commonly because of a poorly functioning bladder.

Both girls and boys with spina bifida are more likely than other children to get urinary tract infections. This is due to the changes in the bladder from lack of appropriate nerve connection in the spinal cord. Because of the high bladder pressures, there is less blood flow to the urinary tract, which can affect the body's ability to fight off infection. When the pressures inside the urinary tract are reduced with medication and catheterizations, the body has a much better chance of keeping away infections.

If your child has had one or more kidney or bladder infections, the urologist may prescribe a low, "suppressive" dose of an antibiotic to help "suppress" infection. A suppressive dose may also be prescribed if your child has vesicoureteral reflux. Even if your child takes a suppressive antibiotic, the protective bacteria that were discussed earlier often remain in the bladder. Although you may have heard or read about the overuse of antibiotics today, many times they are necessary to preserve the health of your child's urinary tract. If you have concerns about the use of antibiotics, discuss them with your child's health care provider. In most instances, the risks to the urinary tract are greater without the use of preventive antibiotics.

If antibiotics are necessary, they may sometimes be given directly into the bladder instead of by mouth. Medications given in this manner are pushed through a catheter and into the bladder with a syringe, after the bladder has been emptied. It is a simple procedure that can be done at home.

▪▪ Surgical Treatments

Sometimes children with spina bifida need surgery to protect kidney function, prevent kidney and bladder damage, or promote continence. Surgery will only be considered after a thorough urologic evaluation, and your child's overall needs will be considered prior to any surgery. Below are descriptions of surgical procedures that are common in children with spina bifida.

Ureteral Reimplantation

When reflux of urine into the kidneys is likely to result in kidney damage or when kidney damage has already taken place, this procedure may be performed. In order to prevent the backflow of urine, the ureter tube is surgically re-positioned. The ureter is tunneled through the bladder wall so that urine cannot easily flow backwards towards the kidneys. This surgery is highly successful in stopping reflux from occurring.

Urethral Slings and Bladder Neck Suspension

A urethral sling or bladder neck suspension may be necessary when the bladder neck is *incompetent,* meaning it allows urine to leak even with the use of medication. During a sling procedure, a connecting portion of the child's own tissues (shaped much like a sling) is created and passed underneath the urethra in order to elevate it. Elevating the urethra and bladder neck places them inside the abdomen rather than in the pelvis. Here the pressure changes are less likely to cause urinary leakage.

A bladder neck suspension is a similar procedure in which sutures (stitches) are passed through the area near the urethra and upwards through connecting tissues. This procedure also elevates the bladder neck. When there are increases in abdominal pressure, the urethra closes down so that leakage does not occur.

The decision as to which of these two procedures to use is made by the surgeon. The surgeon will consider your child's individual anatomy, perhaps other diagnostic results, and his or her own experience in making a choice. Both techniques have good success rates.

Artificial Sphincters

These devices are not commonly used, but may be beneficial for some children with spina bifida. They too are used when urinary incontinence cannot be controlled with medication alone. The device consists of a cuff surgically placed around the bladder neck or urethra. Constant pressure is maintained in the cuff in order to prevent urinary leakage. When it is time to empty the bladder, a pump implanted in the scrotum or labia is squeezed. This process transfers fluid from the cuff into a reservoir balloon. With the pressure removed from the bladder neck, a catheter can then be passed into the bladder to drain the urine. After the bladder is emptied, the pump reactivates and transfers the fluid from the reservoir balloon back to the cuff.

Many complications are associated with artificial sphincters, including leakage of urine and sphincter fluid, tissue erosion (wearing away of the tissue around the urethra), tube kinking, sphincter malfunction (where the artificial sphincter does not function well), infection, and kidney damage if the artificial sphincter is not cared for properly. Certain urologists have had better experiences with these devices than others. Some urologists prefer not to use them at all. It would be prudent to discuss with your child's urologist his or her own opinion about the artificial sphincter.

Bladder Augmentations

For many children with spina bifida, an intermittent catheterization program and medication to reduce bladder pressures is enough to protect kidneys from damage and promote urinary continence. Sometimes, however, bladder pressures cannot be sufficiently controlled with these methods. Your urologist may recommend that your child's bladder be "augmented" with some other tissue from within your child's own body. Common tissues used for this procedure include stomach, small bowel, large bowel, or ureter. The other selected tissue is sewn onto your child's bladder. This creates a bladder with a larger capacity and lower pressures. After the surgery, your child may continue to need medication to lower pressures within the bladder. Bladder augmentation surgery is generally very successful in promoting a healthy urinary tract and continence.

Mitrofanoff Creation

As children grow and begin to seek more independence, it becomes more and more appropriate for them to be able to catheterize themselves independently. Some children, however, may have difficulty catheterizing themselves due to poor manual dexterity or logistics. For example, if your child needs to transfer out of her wheelchair onto the toilet in order to catheterize, she may not have the time or muscular strength and coordination to do this on her own. Due to the nature of the female anatomy, it is virtually impossible for girls to catheterize while sitting in a wheelchair. Overweight men or boys with spina bifida are likely to have similar difficulties if their large abdomen prevents them from seeing the genitals while seated in a wheelchair. A procedure called a Mitrofanoff is quite helpful in such instances.

A Mitrofanoff involves surgically creating a tube from some other tissue in the child's body, such as the appendix, ureter, or small bowel. The tube is then placed so that it runs from the bladder through the abdominal wall and out through the skin. The opening is generally located to one side or the other and below the level of the belly button. Some surgeons will create the opening within the belly button. The location of the opening will depend upon your child's anatomy and your surgeon's surgical technique. Your child can then catheterize her bladder relatively quickly through the tube while sitting in her wheelchair. Urine does not leak through this opening.

▪▪ Conclusion

Keeping your child's urinary tract healthy through preventative measures is of highest priority. Ideally, the healthy habits your child develops at a young age will last a lifetime. Diagnostic testing will monitor your child's urinary tract health and pick up problems quickly when performed on a routine basis. Sometimes your child may need medical treatments and surgery for specific problems. If so, use this chapter as a guideline to understand your child's diagnoses and health care needs. It will give you a basic understanding of urinary tract problems and help you formulate questions to ask your urologist and other health care providers. Whatever management regime your child will need to follow, remember to encourage her to be as actively involved as possible. With time and practice, she will most likely learn how to take care of herself and to be completely independent in this area.

❚❚ Parent Statements

When our son was a year old, we found out that his kidneys were swollen from retaining urine in his bladder. We had to learn to cath him four times a day. Once we did this, his kidneys returned to normal and there was no remaining damage.

❧

We have people ask us all the time, "How can you stand to cath him?" The alternative (not cathing) is not an option. We now have a child with healthy kidneys.

❧

Our long-range goals are that our son try everything to see what his limitations are, if any. Our short-term goal is that he learn to cath himself by age seven or eight so he will be more independent in his self-care.

❧

Accepting the fact that we had to begin catheterizing our daughter was hard for us. We knew it was for her own good, but it was still difficult for us. Now we are old pros!!

❧

A difficult treatment decision for us revolved around catheterization. For me it was one of the most terrifying tasks in the world.

❧

I wasn't sure about whether to have Doug undergo surgery for a Mitrofanoff. Now I'm glad we went ahead with the surgery because it has made it easier for Doug to catheterize himself.

❧

I regret that we delayed encouraging Jamie to cath. We didn't understand that the advantages outweigh any of the problems that can occur.

❧

I was happy when Josh was able to tell us his bladder was full. It made it possible to cath him right away rather than wait until he was perhaps in pain. Some people take the ability to know when to urinate when their bladders are full for granted—not us, not anymore.

BOWEL

MANAGEMENT

Deborah B. Mason, R.N., M.S.N., C.P.N.P.
Kathy Santoro, M.Ed., R.D., L.D.
Ajay Kaul, M.D.

Most parents of young children look forward to the day when their children will be able to stay clean and dry on their own. For children with spina bifida, this goal usually takes a considerable amount of work to achieve, but it can be reached.

As Chapter 6 discussed, there are a number of factors that make it physically difficult for children with spina bifida to achieve urinary continence. For most children with spina bifida, there are just as many, if not more, factors that contribute to problems with bowel continence. As with many problems, the degree of bowel involvement in children with spina bifida depends upon the site and extent of the spinal defect. However, few children with spina bifida have complete bowel control, and constipation is quite common. Fortunately, a good, consistent bowel management program can minimize these problems. The goal of this type of bowel program is to achieve timed elimination of stool through the use of oral laxatives, suppositories, and/or enemas.

Although bowel problems are not as serious a medical problem as bladder dysfunction, they can be a source of considerable discomfort and social disability. This chapter will therefore explain why bowel problems occur and what you and your child can do to manage them.

■■ Normal Bowel Function

To understand why children with spina bifida have bowel problems, it is important to know how the digestive system typically works. The gastrointestinal system is a hollow tube divided into segments called the esophagus, stomach, small intestines, colon (large intestine), rectum, and anal canal. This tube has muscular walls which are supplied by nerves that exit off of the spinal cord. When stimulated, these nerves cause the muscular wall of the gastrointestinal system to contract or relax, thereby mixing and moving the food or feces down to the anus. This occurs without conscious effort.

When we eat, food causes the stomach to swell, which in turn stimulates contraction in the colon (gastrocolic reflex). These contractions help move the feces toward the rectum. As the feces move, water is absorbed, giving form to the stool. (See Figure 1.) As feces fill and distend the rectum, it causes relaxation of the internal anal sphincter (rectoanal reflex) and the feces move down into the anal canal. The sensitive skin lining the anal opening is able to discriminate between solid and liquid feces and gas (anal sampling). This information is then sent up to the brain via the spinal nerves. The brain makes the final decision to have or not have a bowel movement. This decision

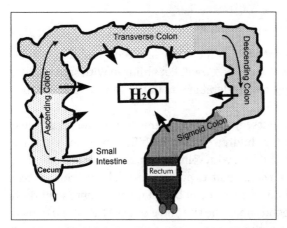

Figure 1. The colon absorbs water from the stool, so that it hardens as it passes from cecum to the rectum, depicted by the increasing density.

is then passed down through the spinal cord to the external anal sphincter, which is under voluntary control. To defecate, the external anal sphincter is relaxed, thereby allowing the feces or gas to be evacuated.

Clearly, for digestion and elimination to proceed smoothly, many body parts must function properly and work together. Lesions in the brain, spinal cord, gastrointestinal system nerves, or the muscular walls of the gastrointestinal system can all impair movement of food through the intestines.

❚❚ Bowel Problems in Children with Spina Bifida

Children with spina bifida usually do not have normal rectal sensation or function of the last part of the colon above the rectum ("hindgut") and anal sphincters. This is because the rectum and anal sphincters are both supplied by the lower spinal nerves, which are usually abnormal in children with spina bifida. Typically, this results in bowel incontinence, which means difficulty controlling when feces are released as a result of an inability to squeeze the external anal sphincter effectively. Factors such as a decrease in activity, limited ability to push, medications, difficulty in removing clothes, and diet may further contribute to difficulties in achieving continence in a child with spina bifida.

Constipation. Another bowel problem that children with spina bifida commonly have is constipation—hard, infrequent stools which are difficult to pass. This problem is usually due to feces moving too slowly through the lower bowel. The slow movement allows nearly all of the water content of the feces to be absorbed in the colon, resulting in hard stool. The hard stool can form a large mass that blocks or obstructs the bowel, resulting in discomfort and pain. Children with spina bifida may also have difficulty pushing out hard stool because their abdominal muscles are weak. This, in turn, makes it even more likely that a stool mass will develop. Additionally, their hindgut may not contract effectively to push the stool down.

Fecal Impaction. Fecal impaction refers to the formation of a large amount of stool within the colon that cannot be passed. Fecal impaction may occur in children with spina bifida because: 1) they are physically inactive due to their spinal cord lesion, and 2) because they have weak muscles in their abdomen and diaphragm. Fecal impaction leads to incontinence by blocking movement of solids through the anal canal. Soft or liquid stool leaks out around the stool mass, making it look like the child has diarrhea. If your child has increasing constipation with constant leakage of liquid feces from a full rectum, hospitalization may be necessary to clean out the impacted stool.

Rectal Prolapse. Rectal prolapse refers to the rectum protruding through the anus. (This looks like a floppy piece of tissue coming out of the anus.) It often occurs while a child is straining to have a bowel movement. Although this may appear frightening to parents, usually the rectum returns to its normal position afterwards. Infrequently, the rectum will continue to protrude, most often in children with an inactive bowel and a weak anal sphincter. It this happens to your child, you should see your physician. Usually this condition can be reversed with laxatives and a good bowel management program. Surgery is seldom necessary.

▪▪ Bowel Management Programs

Various methods can be used, either in combination or alone, to treat bowel problems in children with spina bifida. These methods, which are discussed individually below, include:

1. Bowel habit training;
2. Dietary modifications (usually high fiber) to optimize the consistency of the stool;
3. Biofeedback training;
4. Medications—laxatives, stool softeners, suppositories, enemas;
5. Surgery.

When these methods are used to train a child to have a self-initiated bowel movement at the same time every day to prevent constipation and fecal impaction, they are known as a "bowel management program."

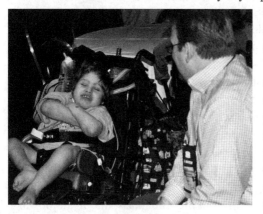

It will take time and patience to find out what works best for your child, but the physicians and nurses on your spina bifida team will help you. Because the nerves that supply the bowel are very low in the spinal cord, virtually all children with spina bifida have to follow a bowel program. However, bowel function differs from child to child, and a program that works for one will not necessarily work for another.

Regardless of the specific elements included in your child's bowel management program, his bowel program should allow him to:

- Empty his rectum of feces one or two times per day to prevent incontinence or leakage of stool;
- Avoid stool impaction or obstruction;
- Actively participate in his bowel program;
- Eat a high fiber diet.

The development of a bowel management program that will lead to fecal continence in most children with spina bifida begins in infancy. When your child is younger than three, it is important for him to have a bowel management program focused on preventing constipation and fecal impaction. Regular evacuation (cleaning out) of the rectum prevents recurrent impaction, pain, and rectal prolapse. Preventing these problems also simplifies later efforts at bowel training. At age three, a more aggressive approach is used.

Before your child begins a formal bowel program, it is important for him to have an initial assessment. This may include a physical exam in which the doctor checks to see whether the lower left area of your child's abdomen feels hard, and feels inside the rectum for hard stool. This exam is usually done around age three.

Initial evaluations may also include an anal manometry evaluation. This test determines the strength of the external anal sphincter muscles and measures your child's ability to sense stool in the rectum. During this exam, a silicone balloon is inserted in the rectum and inflated at intervals. The procedure doesn't hurt.

The most successful programs start with reserving time each day to empty your child's colon completely. The best time to try is 15 to 20 minutes after a meal to take advantage of the gastrocolic reflex (normal contractions in the colon occurring when you eat or drink). The child sits on the toilet and uses a variety of techniques to empty the lower colon. This may include digital (finger) stimulation and manual removal of the stool and/or the use of enemas or suppositories. (See below.) Many children with spina bifida can begin learning to do this at around age three, when they are able to sit on a toilet.

There are a variety of steps that you can take to help ensure that your child's bowel management program will succeed:

1. Make sure that he is not afraid of the toilet, bathroom, or the process of defecation. These fears may be caused by leaving your child alone, placing him on the toilet be-

fore he has developed good sitting balance, or showing obvious signs of impatience or anger when your child fails to "perform."

2. Try to make your child's bowel management program as pleasant as possible, by keeping your child warm, comfortable, and entertained.

3. Do not expect success overnight.

4. Be sure to give your child positive reinforcement when he produces results, rather than criticizing or punishing him for failing to perform.

5. Finally, encourage your child's independence as much as possible, even at three years of age. For example, encourage him to strain his abdominal muscles while sitting on the toilet, if he can.

Your child should wear disposable diapers or incontinence pads until he is having few accidents and soiling episodes. For some children, it may be unreasonable to expect daytime and nighttime continence. Instead, it may make more sense to focus on achieving "social" continence so that the child does not have accidents at school or in other social settings where soiling may be embarrassing.

An important part of any bowel management program is to have the family keep a daily symptom diary. You should record what time self-initiated bowel movements occur, what time accidents occur, and what time enemas or medications are given. It is also helpful to record toileting times. Bring this diary to clinic visits to help your child's team assess his progress and to determine what changes need to be made in treatment. You may also want to post this information in chart form on the bathroom door at home and use the charts to reward your child. He may find it reinforcing to receive stickers on his chart when he has bowel movements on the toilet or accident-free days.

Components of a Bowel Management Program

Initial Disimpaction

Before beginning a bowel program, it is often necessary to completely clean out your child's bowel (disimpaction). You will be instructed to give your child a stimulant or osmotive laxative or an enema the night before starting the program. A variety of enema types may be recommended by your physician, including saline enemas, phosphate enemas (Fleets™), or tap water enemas. Milk and molasses enemas are no longer recommended due to serious side effects, some of which have been life threatening.

Be sure to follow your physician's instructions carefully about the amount and frequency of the enemas. Enemas are preferable to suppositories for initial disimpaction because they produce a bowel movement more quickly and completely. An abdominal x-ray may be ordered to see if the bowel has been completely cleaned out. Once the bowel clean-out is accomplished, your child will be placed on his regular daily program.

Potty Training

Because children with spina bifida may not be able to feel when their rectum is full, potty training is different than it is for most other children. However, sitting on the toilet is as appropriate for your child as it is for any other child. Not only will your child feel more "normal" when he is sitting, but gravity will also assist in emptying the bowel.

Early Stages. The "potty training" part of bowel training is called *scheduled toileting*. Here the first step is for your child to become accustomed to sitting on a potty for five to ten minutes, three or four times a day. The goal is to increase your child's tolerance to sitting on the potty for a few minutes. Your child may not understand why he is sitting there, so it is important that you remain matter-of-fact and patient.

Have your child sit on the toilet when a bowel movement might occur. This is usually after meals. In the early stages of toileting, it is important to:

1. Introduce your child to sitting on the potty for a few minutes and gradually increase the time to five to ten minutes. Sometimes a kitchen timer with a bell and books to read may help.
2. Schedule the times on the potty so that toileting occurs after each meal and at any other time when a stool is likely.
3. Use a regular potty chair rather than an adult-size toilet since your child may not be able to balance well. The sturdy, wooden potty chairs with arms are best.

Regular Toileting. Your child should attempt to have a bowel movement within 20 minutes after a specified meal each day. Placing him on the toilet after a meal takes advantage of the fact that food tends to stimulate bowel activity. Your child should sit for no more than ten minutes. Breakfast is usually the best time because the gastrocolic reflex is likely to be the strongest. If your child is in school, you may need to wake him an hour earlier to allow for an unhurried routine. If this is difficult to fit into your family's morning schedule, your child's toileting time may be set for after dinner.

Your child should always attempt to have a bowel movement following the same meal every day. Try not to skip a single day (even when on vacations) and do not switch back and forth between breakfast time and dinner time. If your child has multiple daily bowel accidents, it may help to have him try to have a bowel movement after two or more meals. Over time, the frequency of bowel movements on the toilet will increase despite the absence of an urge. Bowel programs take time, so you need to be patient and persistent.

Pushing. Children with spina bifida with higher lesions may not have the strength in their diaphragm and abdominal muscles to push out stool. Sometimes having your child blow on a small party horn during attempts to have a bowel movement may be helpful. Grunting while pushing (Valsalva Maneuver), tickling, or laughing may also help.

Response to Accidents. Whoever is caring for your child should check for bowel accidents several times a day so that accidents can be detected soon after they occur. This checking also provides more opportunities for positive reinforcement when your child is accident-free. When your child has an accident, the response should be matter-of-fact rather than punishing. As he gets older, it is important to teach him to check for accidents and to recognize the odor that signifies gas or stool has escaped.

Digital stimulation. Digital stimulation is often used in addition to regular toileting. It involves inserting a finger into the rectum as far as possible and moving it around inside. This movement is often enough to cause a contraction that will push stool out. When your child is an infant, the little finger should be used instead of the index finger. A vinyl latex free glove can be worn and the finger that is inserted should be well lubricated with K-Y Jelly or Lubrifax. In addition, fingernails should be kept short. When your child is older, he can be taught to use digital stimulation himself.

Enemas. Enemas work by stretching the bowel, loosening stool masses, and causing a reflex emptying (evacuation) of stool. Sometimes enemas are routinely given every day or every other day. There are a variety of different types of enemas and enema solutions. Tap water enemas have been found to be just as effective as normal saline enemas. The normal saline enema is a solution consisting of tap water with a little added salt. The amount of salt depends on the child's weight and how much fluid is used. Other types of enemas have a stimulant (such as bisacodyl or senna) in it. Small volume enemas (Enemez mini enemas) are also commonly used as it acts as a stimulant to evacuate the bowel. Your doctor will tell you what is best for your child.

Because children with spina bifida have poor muscle tone in their rectum, retaining fluid is a problem. Special enema kits have been developed to help your child retain the fluid. Ask your doctor or nurse for advice as to the type of enema solution to use and where to purchase enema kits.

Nutritional Considerations

Diet plays a major role in bowel management. Specific foods such as caffeinated beverages, certain fruits, or those containing artificial sweeteners (sorbitol) may cause loose stools or may stimulate stools at appropriate or inappropriate times. Therefore, recognizing your child's response to particular foods is important. A response may be desirable at some times but unacceptable at others. For example, some adults with spina bifida drink coffee in the morning to stimulate bowel movements, but must avoid coffee the rest of the day since caffeine is not generally recommended for people with spina bifida.

Of all the dietary recommendations, eating a high fiber diet is most important. Dietary fiber is the component of plant foods that is not digested or absorbed in the intestines. Foods high in fiber can soften the stool by acting as a sponge to absorb water and provide bulk, making the stool easier to push out and keeping it formed so it won't leak out easily. There is, however, no conclusive evidence that taking extra fiber significantly improves constipation.

Good sources of fiber are fruits, vegetables, grains, and cereals. These foods should be routinely included in your child's diet, but not to the exclusion of other nutrient-dense foods. Since high fiber foods may quickly fill a child's smaller stomach capacity, it is important to make sure he also eats other foods that supply essential protein, fat, calories, vitamins, and minerals.

To help your child accept a nutritious diet containing higher fiber foods, involve the whole family. Children are more likely to accept new foods when parents and siblings eat them too. Offer your child choices of snacks or mealtime items, but try to make sure all options are nutritious. For example, "Would you like a bran muffin or an apple?" Try new fiber foods gradually and be willing to reintroduce the food several times before expecting your child to readily accept it. Let your child help purchase and prepare the foods for meals and snacks.

The following are good sources of fiber:

FRUITS

- Prunes, figs, pears, apples, strawberries, grapes, peaches, raisins, melons, oranges, cherries, plums, pineapples, and berries. Also juices with pulp and prune juice.
- Be sure to cut pieces into small bites, and encourage your child to chew carefully and slowly to avoid choking. Grapes and cherries should be cut into quarters.
- *Caution:* some tropical fruits have been known to cause problems in children allergic to latex.

VEGETABLES

- Broccoli, cauliflower, cabbage, peas, green beans, corn, squash, carrots, spinach.
- Try them cooked or raw with a dip.

GRAINS

- Whole grain breads, crackers, rolls, rice, pastas, cornbread, bran muffins, granola, oatmeal, or other cereals containing 3 to 4 grams of fiber per serving or more.
- Try mixing one-half of a high fiber cereal with one-half of your child's favorite cereal.
- Bake fruit breads or zucchini breads and oatmeal cookies with raisins.

NUTS AND SEEDS

- Sunflower seeds, peanuts, Brazil nuts, and cashews.
- *Warning:* Infants, toddlers, and young children should *never* be given nuts or seeds on which they could choke.

SNACK IDEAS

- Cookies (oatmeal, bran, raisin, granola)
- Bars (zucchini, banana, carrot, or cereal bars)
- Sandwiches on wheat bread
- Oatmeal or cereal
- Whole wheat crackers or graham crackers
- Yogurt with fruit
- Jello with fruit
- Fruits with yogurt, caramel, or whipped cream for dipping
- Raw vegetables with ranch or cheese dip
- Milkshakes blended with fruit

How much fiber is necessary? This varies from age to age and from child to child. However, the "rule of thumb" is your child's age plus 5 equals the suggested grams of daily fiber. Children may need more or less to have a success-ful bowel program, especially older children. Teens and adolescents likely require close to the adult recommendation of 25 to 30 grams per day.

Adequate fluid intake is important in preventing constipation when a high fiber diet is eaten. Most children ages 1 to 4 need between 32 and 56 ounces of fluid per day. Older children usually need 64 ounces or more per day. To encourage your child to accept fluids, offer sips throughout the day or try frozen fruit ices and popsicles, puddings with sliced fruits, yogurt, milkshakes, or Jello with fruit.

Medications

During the first year of life, a child's stools are usually soft, so impaction is less likely. Often infants have a bowel movement with urination. However, by the second year, most children with spina bifida require some medication to keep the stool soft and ensure daily

■■ TABLE 1   Medications Used In Bowel Management

Use only with doctor's advice.

Type of Medication	Examples	How It Works
Bulk-forming laxatives	Malt Supex Methylcellulose (Citrucel) Psyllium (Metamucil)	These medications absorb liquids in the intestine and cell to form a soft, bulky stool. This bulky mass then stimulates the bowel.
Hyperosmotics	Magnesium Citrate Milk of Magnesia Magnesium Sulfate Sodium phosphate (Fleets, oral or enema)	These medications encourage bowel movements by drawing water into the bowel from surrounding tissue. This then results in a soft stool mass and increased bowel action.
Osmotics	Miralax Lactulose Sorbitol	These medications encourage bowel movements by drawing water into the bowel from surrounding tissue. This then results in a soft stool mass and increased bowel action.
Stimulants	Senna (Senekot) Bisacodyl (Dulcolax)	These medications encourage bowel movements by acting on the intestinal wall. They increase the muscle contractions that move along the stool mass.
Stool softeners (emollients)	Docusate (Colace)	This medication encourages bowel movements by helping liquids mix into the stool and prevent dry, hard stool masses.
Miscellaneous	Glycerin suppository	This medication draws water into the bowel from surrounding tissue. This produces a soft stool mass and increases bowel action.

emptying of the bowel. Continence is more easily achieved if the stools are formed and reasonably firm, rather than the consistency of soft paste or hard marbles.

Important factors to consider in choosing a medication for your child include: how safe the dose is for children, whether it has a minimum of side effects, how easily it is given, its effectiveness, and its safety in long-term use. To help determine which medication at which dose is best for your child, the medical staff caring for your child will also want to know about your child's elimination patterns. Table 1 lists medications typically used for bowel control.

Laxatives. Laxatives are medications that encourage bowel movements to relieve constipation. There are different types of laxatives, each working in different ways. Types of laxatives include: bulk formers, hyperosmotics, lubricants, stimulants, and stool softeners (emollients). Some products contain more than one type of laxative. For example, a product may contain both a stool softener and a stimulant. In general, these combination products may be more likely to cause side effects because of multiple ingredients. In addition, they may not offer any advantage over products containing one type of laxative. Most laxatives are available without a prescription, but be sure to check with your doctor for any special instructions for proper use.

Information
To allow bulk-forming laxatives to work properly, it is important to drink plenty of fluids. Results are usually seen in 1 to 3 days.
Each dose should be taken with a full glass or more of cold water or fruit juice. Usually produces results within ½ to 3 hours following a dose.
Each dose should be taken with a full glass or more of cold water or fruit juice. Miralax is mixed in 4-8 oz of water. Usually produces results in 1-2 days.
Stimulant laxatives are usually taken on an empty stomach. Result are slow if taken with food. Usually results are seen 6-10 hours after dose is given. Results from a Dulcolax suppository are usually within 15 min. – 1 hr.
Docusate should be given with milk, fruit juice, or formula to mask the bitter taste. Results are usually seen in 24 – 72 hrs.
Do not lubricate the suppository with mineral oil or petroleum jelly before inserting into the rectum. This may affect how the suppository works. Moisten only with water. Results are usually seen in 15 min. – 1 hr.

Suppositories. Sometimes children with spina bifida need a suppository to help clean out the stool. A suppository is a solid, cone-shaped medication that is inserted into the rectum. It will melt at body temperature and soften the stool immediately around it. The suppository stimulates the stool and frequently results in immediate emptying of the stool accumulated in the lower colon. For children with spina bifida, suppositories are often used in combination with other stool softeners and regular toileting.

The two suppositories most often used are: glycerin and Dulcolax. These are both available in drugstores without a prescription. If a glycerin suppository does not produce a bowel movement, a bisacodyl (Dulcolax) 5 mg suppository usually will. Some children may require a suppository two or three times a week, in addition to oral medication. Some bowel programs involve the use of bisacodyl every day to trigger rectal evacuation and establish a regular pattern of evacuation. Once a pattern is established, usually after 10 to 14 days, this medication is given every other day. Glycerin suppositories may help soften the stool but are usually ineffective in completely emptying the rectum.

Here are some helpful hints for suppository use in children:

1. Take the suppository out of the refrigerator and allow it to reach room temperature before inserting. (Suppositories must be stored in a cool place because they soften at room temperature.)
2. Place your child on his side with knees bent or in a face-down position.
3. Use latex-free gloves. Lubricate your finger and the suppository with a water-soluble lubricant such as KY Jelly. A tube of KY Jelly lasts a long time and makes clean-up easy.
4. Place the suppository well inside the rectum against the bowel wall. Hold in place for 3 to 4 seconds.
5. Your child should remain quiet (preferably lying down) for 20 to 30 minutes after insertion. Stay by him and be firm about the need to lie still. A book or other diversions may help.
6. If your child has a very weak external sphincter, it may be necessary to hold his buttocks together so that the suppository remains inside long enough.
7. After 20 minutes, place your child on the toilet for 10 minutes.

8. Your child should be seated on the toilet or potty chair with his feet supported. Teaching your child to grunt will help him have a bowel movement. Remember, reassurance is important.

If more than one or two days pass without results, the amount of stool softener needs to be immediately increased. Finding the best time of the day to give a suppository for your child takes experimentation and patience.

Biofeedback Training

Some children with spina bifida have tried biofeedback training as part of their bowel management program. As part of a bowel program, the goal of biofeedback is to teach the child how to contract the external anal sphincter to prevent a bowel movement. This is done through anal manometry, which was described above. A child involved in biofeedback has regularly scheduled appointments over a period of time to help him gain a clear understanding of his sphincter function. Biofeedback is combined with daily sphincter exercises to increase the strength of the muscles around the anus. Biofeedback may increase the chances of a more successful bowel program, although some experts feel it is unclear whether this method is effective for children with spina bifida.

The children most likely to benefit from biofeedback training are those with low, incomplete spinal cord lesions who have frequent bowel movements. Children older than five years with some degree of rectal sensation can be trained to contract their external anal sphincter appropriately. Children with high spinal cord lesions are unlikely to benefit from biofeedback training because they do not have enough innervation of the external anal sphincter to learn the response and they have difficulty sensing when their rectum is full. Children with high spinal cord lesions can usually avoid bowel accidents by having a bowel movement at a regular time each day. Ask your doctor if he feels biofeedback is a reasonable treatment for your child.

Surgical Options

If medical management fails, a highly successful surgical technique called a cecostomy has been developed for administering enemas. This involves creating a small port or opening in the right lower abdomen which opens internally into the cecum (beginning of the large intestine). The child's appendix is sometimes used as a connector between the cecum and the skin port. If the appendix is not available, the cecum is used to create a stoma (an opening into the intestine from the skin/abdomen). A catheter is used to inject enema solution into this port, which then flushes out the entire length of the colon through the rectum. Once the colon is cleared of feces in this manner, the child remains continent until more stool is formed. The port can be designed so that there is no leakage around it. An enema is given once every day to every other day and your child can be taught to give it to himself. The usual recommendation is to flush out the colon first thing in the morning, if time permits, or after school.

This procedure is most often done around school age, and can considerably enhance some children's quality of life. However, no surgical procedure is simple and free of complications, so be sure to ask the surgeon about possible drawbacks if a cecostomy is recommended for your child. About 85 percent of children with spina bifida are able to achieve fecal continence with this technique.

■■ The Psychological Impact of Incontinence

Children with bowel incontinence worry about soiling their pants or worse—having an accident so serious that people around them will notice the odor or stain. The fear of having such an accident can cause children to miss out on school, work, and social events. They may also avoid developing close relationships and have trouble socializing due to fear of social isolation and ridicule. In addition, incontinence can affect a child's self-esteem and sense of well-being. Generally speaking, bowel incontinence tends to have more of a social impact than urinary incontinence does.

Some children with spina bifida may have emotional difficulties due to incontinence. Reactions of shame, denial, loss of self-esteem, and despair are common when incontinence is severe or chronic. These reactions may lead to significant depression and social disability. A child may feel isolated and rejected by peers despite his family's efforts. He may feel insecure and regress in other areas of development.

Accidents can be particularly devastating for children with bowel incontinence and can lead to increased dependency on parents. You should therefore make every effort to help your child work towards having a bowel movement at a predictable time within the privacy of the home.

However, occasional accidents may be unavoidable. You and your family need to understand how helpless your child may feel in this situation and provide sensitive support. You should also be aware that repeated episodes of incontinence may reflect other emotional problems.

Bowel incontinence threatens the quality of life just as much as an acute medical problem does. It impairs a child's ability to feel like a part of his community. Children who are incontinent need to get past the dread of being incontinent in public and understand that nothing is as bad as the dread they place on themselves. To achieve this, they need to understand that having bowel movements is a biological fact, and not something to be embarrassed about. They also need to understand their own bowel management program and to always be prepared. At a minimum, preparations should include: 1) bringing along a change of clothes and some wipes for emergencies; and 2) doing a bowel program before going out, or at least checking the lower rectum for stool and manually removing any stool present. Some people wear disposable undergarments for extra security.

As a parent, you can help by encouraging your child to seek information and find understanding. It is also crucial to communicate openly and positively with your child about his bowel management to help defuse any negative emotions and stress he feels about this activity. Some children might benefit from counseling or opportunities to talk to others about these issues.

∷ Helping Your Child Help Himself

Individualized bowel programs are not do-it-yourself projects. The professionals working with your child will play an important role in developing a program that will work for you and your whole family. These professionals will rely on accurate reports and responses from you. In a multidisciplinary type of setting, the nurse will likely be the person who will help you and your child problem solve until a good bowel program is in progress. It is important that both you and your child are comfortable with him and are able to ask him questions about a very private subject. You should feel free to get in touch with him whenever you have concerns.

Bowel programs are such an integral part of the lives of children with spina bifida that caregivers are usually able to talk openly with others about these issues. This is important, as child care workers

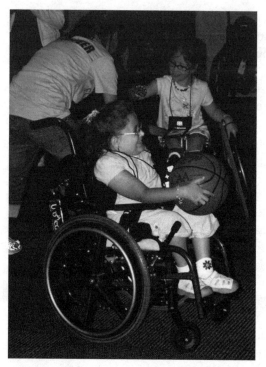

and teachers may need to have detailed information about your child's toileting needs and abilities. As your child takes over responsibility for his bowel program, he will also need to learn to feel comfortable talking about these issues.

As your child gets older, the professionals working with him will help you adapt the program so that he can ultimately learn to manage his own toileting needs. You can help by having expectations that your child will learn to be independent, and by allowing him to do as much as possible for himself. Many kids with spina bifida can handle their own bowel program by early adolescence.

▪▪ Conclusion

Bowel management is a complex process for children with spina bifida. The management techniques used are not the same for every child and it may take several months for your child's bowel program to become a routine or for you to achieve success. There will be days when you and your child will be discouraged, so it is important to remember to stay calm and be patient. You should also be prepared for the process to be interrupted when your child is ill. Despite setbacks, however, the goal of continence is well worth the effort. With the support of their families and others, many children with spina bifida can achieve at least social continence.

◼◼ Parent Statements

One of the things I hope Melissa will achieve in the future is bowel and bladder continence.

◈

One of the challenges of being out in public with a child who has a physical disability is having to wait for a handicapped stall. This is especially infuriating when the person coming out is able-bodied.

◈

The words, "He'll never have bowel or bladder control" were probably the most crushing.

◈

My husband is a planner and he keeps most of his emotions to himself. I'm the opposite way; I deal with things one day at a time, one problem at a time. I couldn't even think about Pablo's bowel program for preschool or kindergarten when he was only two years old. Right now, I worry about Pablo's bowel program for the day. I worry about NOW; my husband worries about what we are going to do WHEN xyz happens.

◈

Working on bowel and bladder control is discouraging. There are no perfect solutions, and trial and error seems to be the norm. Sometimes we think we will never get this under control.

◈

Finally feeling like I had my daughter's bowel management routine under control made me feel good.

8

ORTHOPEDIC CONCERNS

Luciano Dias, M.D.
Joy Ito, R.N.
Marlene Lutkenhopp, R.N., M.S.N.

Most parents dream of the day their baby will take her first steps. Fortunately, most children with spina bifida have the potential to walk. They may, however, need a variety of types of special equipment to help them walk. In addition, they may find that walking is not the most efficient way of getting around for them. Your child's *mobility*—or ability to move around on her own—will depend on a variety of factors, including the level of her spina bifida and medical complications that might be present at birth or arise later. This chapter explores these factors in detail, and also introduces some of the types of equipment and treatment that can be used to improve mobility. Chapter 9 offers more in-depth information on therapies and equipment that can increase your child's mobility.

▪▪ How Well Will Your Child Walk?

One of the hardest things for parents of a newborn with spina bifida to hear is, "We will just have to wait and see what your child's potential will be." Most parents want definitive answers that profession-

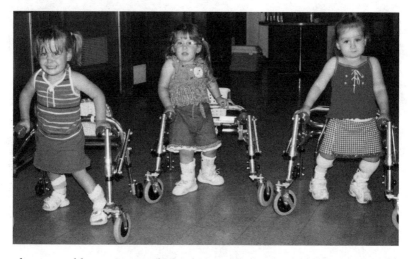

als are unable to give. Each newborn will develop at her own pace. In general, however, children with higher level lesions need more bracing and other adaptive equipment to help them walk than children with low level lesions. Your child's innate motivation and cognitive abilities will also affect when she will begin crawling or walking. The range at which children with spina bifida begin walking is quite variable. A child with a very low level lesion may begin walking around 12 to 18 months. However, most children need some type of external support to begin walking due to their weaker lower extremities. Some children first work on learning to stand with a standing frame. Then, once they are ready for bracing at around three years, they may begin walking with bracing and a walker. Some children with a very high level may not be able to walk at all, especially if their sitting balance is poor.

How well your child walks, and whether she continues to walk throughout her lifetime, is highly related to the level of her lesion. Children who have sacral level lesions will walk with no support. However, since the gluteus muscles in the buttocks are weak, they often walk with a lurching gait. Children with low lumbar level lesions will walk with crutches and short braces known as AFOs (see Chapter 9). And children with high level lesions require high braces known as RGOs or HKAFOs (see Chapter 9). They usually stop walking around 11 to 13 years of age because the energy requirements are very high. Your child's walking ability will also depend on facts such as obesity, orthopedic deformities (see below), balance, and her ability to use her arms and hands.

Professionals sometimes use the labels below to describe a child's walking abilities:

- A **community ambulator** is someone who is able to walk most of the time, perhaps with the use of braces, a walker, and/or crutches.
- A **household ambulator** primarily walks within the house and uses a wheelchair when out and about.
- A **therapeutic ambulator** walks very little, primarily for exercise.
- A **wheelchair user** uses a wheelchair as her primary method of mobility.

Recently, a new classification has been used for children with spina bifida, the Functional Mobility Scale (FMS). It takes into consideration how the child walks in 3 set distances: 5 yards, 50 yards, and 500 yards. For each distance, the child is given a rating from 1 to 6, with 1 meaning the child can't walk, but must use a wheelchair for that distance, and 6 meaning the child is able to walk without support. As an example, an FMS of 3-3-3 means that a child can walk with AFOs and crutches for 5, 50, and 500 yards. A FMS 3-3-1 means that she can walk with AFOs and crutches for 5 and 50 yards but uses a wheelchair for 500 yards.

Whenever possible, it is beneficial for a child to walk, even if only as a therapeutic ambulator. Standing helps strengthen bones and prevent contractures. Standing can also improve breathing and the function of the kidneys and bowels. In the end, it's not as important how your child walks as it is to help her become independently mobile.

■■ Roadblocks to Developing Mobility Skills

Gross motor skills—movement skills involving the large muscles of the body—normally develop in a set pattern. First a baby achieves head control, then rolls, sits, crawls, and walks. Almost all children with spina bifida follow this same pattern of development. Their development is slower, however, and they usually need assistance from physical therapists or early intervention specialists to achieve these skills. Don't be too concerned about *how fast* your child develops a new skill, but rather *how well* she develops that skill. See Chapter 11 for in-depth information about the differences in development common to children with spina bifida.

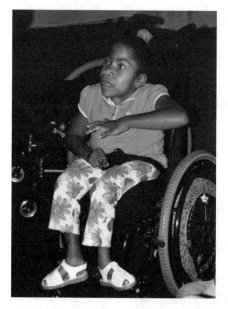

Much of your child's delay in motor development will be related to reduced sensation and movement in her lower limbs. In addition, delays may be caused by certain *orthopedic* problems—problems with bones, muscles, tendons, or other structures of the body that result in motor delays or deficits.

Because of the high risk of orthopedic problems, an orthopedic physician (also known as an orthopedist or orthopedic surgeon) will be an important member of your child's spina bifida team. An orthopedic physician specializes in diagnosing and treating orthopedic problems. With your child, his ultimate goals will be: 1) to get her moving, with or without an assistive device such as braces, and 2) to help your child maintain optimal function. In monitoring your child, the orthopedist will look at sensory and motor function, limb alignment, sitting balance, and how well your child walks. The doctor will also look for signs of specific orthopedic problems and recommend braces or other treatments. Frequency of visits will vary depending on your child's needs.

When a child who is walking has gait problems, the orthopedic surgeon can do a comprehensive orthopedic evaluation and use computerized gait analysis to help identify the underlying problem and more accurately decide the best treatment approach.

The following sections describe orthopedic problems that commonly occur in children with spina bifida at certain stages of development.

Early Infancy

About 30 percent of infants born with spina bifida have clubfoot. Clubfoot needs to be corrected so that your child will eventually be able to fit into braces that will help her walk. A first step in treatment might be for you to learn to do stretching exercises with your child. *Serial castings* or splints may also be used. During serial casting, your child wears a series of casts over a period of several weeks. The casts can be applied at the doctor's office and are used to gradually bring your child's foot or feet into the desired position.

Often exercises and serial casting cannot correct the problem and surgery is necessary. Surgery for clubfoot is frequently done around the age of ten months. Your child's foot will then be casted until healing occurs. After surgery, bracing will be necessary to keep your child's foot in its correct position.

Infants with spina bifida can develop deformities secondary to lack of muscle action. For instance, a child with a high level lesion can develop contractures at the hip and knee because when she lies down, her hips and knees are naturally flexed. Using a splint at night such as the total body splint that maintains the hip, knee, ankle, and foot in proper alignment may be indicated.

The Toddler and Preschool Years

During this stage of development, children are usually actively engaged in moving and exploring. Your child with spina bifida will also want to explore her environment, but may just need a little help. The orthopedic physician, in collaboration with the spina bifida team, will decide when it is time to begin using braces (orthotics) to provide the

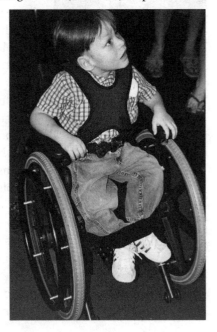

support necessary for walking. As Chapter 9 explains, there are a variety of bracing devices. The orthopedic physician and/or the pediatric rehabilitation physician and the physical therapist will work together with you to decide what type of brace your child needs. The orthotist will then measure and make a customized brace for your child.

The goal is to get your child in an upright position, even if she may not be a functional walker. If she has a high level lesion, she may be placed in a standing frame, a device that will support her in an upright position. Putting a child in a standing frame gives her a sense of accomplishment, frees her hands to play with toys, and strengthens her muscles and bones. If your child has a lower level lesion, she will need less bracing. Still, finding the perfect fit between child and brace can sometimes be difficult, costly, and frustrating. Many hours of physical therapy, encouragement, and practice may be necessary before your child takes her first step.

Besides bracing, other types of equipment such as scooters, belly-boards, hand-operated tricycles, and wheelchairs are often introduced at this age to increase a child's ability to move around. See the following chapter for more information.

From School Age to Adulthood

As your child grows, it will be important to maintain the mobility that was so carefully achieved during the preschool period. The orthopedist will monitor your child's walking ability and the fit of her braces. He will take periodic x-rays of your child's back and legs to look

for problems that may develop. When necessary, he will use surgery to prevent or treat problems.

It is vital for your child to continue to see her orthopedist on a regular basis, whether she walks well or is strictly a wheelchair user. If problems are left unattended, your child may develop contractures or progressive leg deformities, and no longer fit into her braces. She could also develop hip or spine problems that prevent her from sitting correctly in her wheelchair. See the next section for information on these and other potential complications.

Your child's growth and increasing weight will affect how she walks. It may seem that just when everything is working together nicely, your child has a growth spurt and her braces no longer fit. Sometimes it may feel like you are playing a catch-up game with endless visits to the orthotist. Weight has a tremendous influence on walking. A child who weighs too much will tire easily because of the extra effort she expends getting up and walking. As walking gets more and more difficult for her, she will tend to do it less and less and may gain more weight. This makes it vital to encourage your child to eat healthy foods and to remain active.

If your child requires surgery during this age range, she will most likely need casts for a period of time while the muscles and bones mend. How much casting will depend on the surgery. Your child might be in anything from a short leg cast to a *hip spica cast*—a cast that goes all the way up to the chest area and may include one leg or both. If a hip spica is used, an area will be cut out for bathroom purposes. Casts can be fairly heavy and awkward, and your child may or may not be able to walk with them on. For details about casts and cast care see Chapter 9.

One of the most extensive orthopedic surgeries your child may have at this age is scoliosis surgery, which is discussed in the next section.

▪▪ Common Orthopedic Problems in Children with Spina Bifida

The preceding overview of orthopedic problems that children with spina bifida often have at particular ages is, unfortunately, not exhaustive. There are also a number of orthopedic problems that can occur at any age. Although reading about all the potential problems can be worrisome at first, remember that not all children will have all, or even most of these problems. Also, knowing about potential problems in advance can help you be alert to early signs that a problem is developing. Then effective treatment can be started as soon as possible.

Many orthopedic problems are best treated with surgery. In fact, you should know that your child will most likely need some type of orthopedic surgery during her lifetime. Your child may even have to have the same operation done more than once, since bones and joints that are carefully put into alignment sometimes revert back to their original position over time.

It is often difficult for parents to know when or if they should agree to a certain procedure. Orthopedic surgeries are seldom a matter of life or death, which makes decision-making all the more confusing. You can, of course, ask for a second opinion, but surgeons often have different ideas about what operations should be performed and when.

This makes it very important that you have a good relationship with your child's orthopedist and value his opinion. Do not be afraid to ask him to carefully explain the proposed surgery, including all the possible risks and benefits, so that you can make an informed decision.

As mentioned before, the use of gait analysis will help the orthopedic surgeon select the best procedure(s) for improving your child's function. For a walking child who is older than four, gait analysis should be part of the preoperative evaluation. Gait analysis is done at a special center with a team who has experience in studying the gait of children with neuromuscular problems. Using special cameras and computer technology, the team obtains an in-depth evaluation of the child's gait. A complete study usually takes about three hours to complete.

Fractures

Children with spina bifida are more likely than other children to have fractures. Their increased risk is probably due to their reduced activity. Bones that aren't used tend to get weak and osteoporosis often develops.

The good news is that fractures in children with spina bifida tend to heal quickly. The bad news is that re-fractures are common. Because of reduced feeling and a subsequent lack of pain, your child may not even be aware that she has a fracture. Sometimes swelling and warmth are the only signs. An x-ray is done to confirm a fracture.

Fractures are especially common after orthopedic surgeries and after a limb has been immobilized in a cast for a long time, especially if the child was immobilized in a spica cast. For this reason, the surgeon should keep immobilization to a minimum and give your child a standing cast if possible. Sometimes surgery is necessary to correct the fracture. A minor fracture may only require a soft cast or brace.

Because of decreased sensation to the lower extremities, care must be taken to reduce the risk of pressure sores from casts. It is important that casts be well padded, especially around joints. Odor and drainage may be a sign that a pressure sore is developing under the cast and needs to be checked out. See Chapter 10 for more information on pressure sores.

Contractures

A contracture occurs when there is an unbalance of the underlying muscles and tendons at a joint. As a result, the joint does not have full movement. The most common contractures in children with spina bifida are in the hip, knee, and ankle. Contractures can be present at birth or develop over time. A contracture is referred to as "fixed" when a joint cannot be moved to its fullest extent. A contracture that can be "reduced" refers to tight muscles that can still be moved through the full range of motion.

To prevent contractures, the physical therapist may recommend that your child routinely do exercises to keep the muscles stretched out and flexible. He or she can also show your child exercises to maintain her *range of motion*—or ability to move her joints in all directions. The orthopedist may also prescribe splints and braces to try to keep muscles and bones in proper alignment. See Chapter 9 to read about different types of braces.

Hip flexion contractures are fairly common in children with spina bifida. With a hip flexion contracture, the child's knees are bent and the child walks with a crouched gait. Children who sit for extended periods in a wheelchair are at risk for developing hip flexion contractures simply because their hips are in one position for a long time.

The heel cord is another muscle that sometimes becomes tight in children with spina bifida. A very tight heel cord causes the heel to be pulled upward. Tight heel cord muscles make it difficult to put on shoes and walk. The surgical procedure to correct this problem is called heel cord lengthening.

If a contracture becomes fixed, surgery may be necessary. In the case of a hip flexion contracture, surgery is performed when the contracture interferes with a child's gait or makes wearing braces difficult. The tendons around the joint are released (cut) to lengthen them. The child then usually wears a cast covering the hips and legs for two weeks afterwards. In the case of tight heel cords, the heel cord or Achilles tendon is surgically cut so that the foot can be returned to a more neutral position.

Hip Dislocation and Subluxation

Hip subluxation means the leg bone is partially out of the hip joint, while hip dislocation means the leg bone is completely out of the hip joint. Either condition may be present at birth or develop over time. Hip subluxation and hip dislocation occur when some muscle groups in the area are working and others are not. Often, there are no visible signs that a child has a subluxed or dislocated hip. Often these hip problems are not discovered until your child is having a physical exam and x-rays.

Treatment of hip problems varies depending on the level of the lesion and the child's ability to walk. Research has shown that when a child has a low lumbar lesion (walking with support and AFO braces), hip dislocation is not the main factor influencing the child's gait. Instead, it is contractures (usually flexion and adduction) that cause an asymmetrical gait. In this situation, treating the contractures will improve the child's gait. On the other hand, when a child has a sacral level lesion (walking with no support), surgical treatment of the hip subluxation or dislocation is necessary to improve the child's gait.

Spinal Curvatures

Children with spina bifida may have three types of spinal curvatures:

1. **Kyphosis**—an exaggerated curving out of the spine. This occurs in a small percentage of newborns. Surgery may be necessary at some point in the child's life if the kyphosis is of such a degree that breathing or sitting balance is affected.
2. **Lordosis**—an exaggerated inward curving of the lower spine sometimes referred to as "sway back." This type of curvature usually occurs as the result of hip flexion contracture. Often, lordosis is not treated unless sitting balance is affected. The first step in treatment would be to treat the hip flexion contracture. (See above.) Sometimes spinal fusion, discussed below, is also necessary.
3. **Scoliosis**—a sideways (lateral) curvature of the spine. This is the most common spinal curvature, and affects over 50 percent of children with spina bifida.

The orthopedic doctor will periodically look at your child's back and take x-rays to monitor development of scoliosis. As Chapter 5 explains, the development of scoliosis could be a sign of tethering, especially in children with low lumbar and sacral level lesions. Scoliosis can also occur as a result of a shunt malfunction or hydromyelia. In most cases, it occurs because the connection from the spinal cord to the spinal muscles and soft tissue is altered.

The degree of scoliosis is measured by taking spine x-ray films and using a ruler to measure angles. The orthopedist monitors the degree of scoliosis and how fast it changes to help him determine when and if surgery is needed.

Untreated scoliosis can cause a child to sit with more weight on one buttock. This can lead to the development of a pressure sore. Children with severe scoliosis may develop respiratory problems if the curve puts pressure on the lungs and restricts breathing.

If your child has a mild case of scoliosis, a plastic body jacket brace might be recommended as a treatment. This brace is worn during the day and covers the entire trunk area.

If your child's scoliosis is severe, she will need spinal fusion surgery. This is a complex procedure, and will be delayed until your child is around 10 or 12, if possible, in order to give her time to grow. The purpose of surgery is to fuse (join) the bones of the spine to halt the progression of the curve. The part of the spine that is fused will no longer grow and will be stiff. After surgery, it takes 6 to 12 months for the spine to fuse completely. Scoliosis surgery is major surgery and recovery from surgery takes 6 to 8 weeks. A brace is usually worn for the first few months after surgery.

∷ Conclusion

The orthopedic care of children with spina bifida has changed a great deal in recent years, especially with the use of gait analysis. Today, children do not usually have as many orthopedic surgeries as in the past, and the surgeries that are performed are often more successful. In addition, there have been improvements in preventive care and in the ability to diagnose problems earlier. Still, the risk of orthopedic concerns cannot be ignored, due to the very nature of spina bifida. This  risk can best be minimized when you and your child are knowledgeable about possible complications and work with the orthopedic physician to keep on top of any concerns.

▪▪ Parent Statements

We told his brothers and sisters that their little brother was born with a hole in his back and that one day he may walk, but differently.

❦

Someone in the family knew the mother of a son with spina bifida and she became my source of information when my baby was prenatally diagnosed with spina bifida. It was extremely helpful to have her to talk to. When they finally found the lesion on the ultrasound, the doctor said the lesion was around the L4-L5 region. I asked what that meant and he really didn't answer me. I called my support friend and she was all excited. She let us know that that area was pretty much a zone in which the kids can learn to walk.

❦

My son is aware that he doesn't walk as fast as his friends, but that doesn't stop him. He knows no obstacles.

❦

We thought that Marcus would not be able to walk when we first found out about spina bifida. But our son walks, rides a bike, and is a social butterfly. He has surpassed every expectation we had for him before birth.

❦

Tricia had to wear a body cast after her back surgery to correct her kyphosis. She looked so uncomfortable and I felt bad that I couldn't do anything about it. I sat by her bed night and day and felt kind of alone. I thought Tricia was the only baby who had ever been born like this and nobody knew what I was going through.

❦

Some of the more difficult treatment decisions for us revolve around hip surgeries and other surgeries where results are less certain and the doctors say things like: "It may help or it may not" or "Some patients see better results, some see no change, some actually do worse after surgery." Those surgeries are hard because you never know if you are doing the right thing. You just have to make the decision you are comfortable with, hope for the best, and not second guess yourself.

❧❀❧

It's hard to resist the temptation to just pick Ben and his walker up when he gets tired. I want him to be independent, though, and I realize he needs to learn.

❧❀❧

Every one of Chris's accomplishments has special meaning for me. Most parents are excited about their child's first steps, but Chris has been walking for 11½ years now, and sometimes I still get emotional just watching him walk. I will never take it for granted.

9

PHYSICAL THERAPY

Jill Harris, M.A., P.T.

By now, it is probably clear to you that children with spina bifida have a variety of medical needs. Among the most obvious needs are those that affect your child's development of motor (movement) skills. The previous chapter discussed medical treatment for problems that can impair motor skills. This chapter looks at the role of physical therapy in improving and maintaining motor skills. In addition, it explores the various types of specialized equipment that can be used to help position a child with spina bifida or to enhance his independence and mobility.

■ What Is Physical Therapy?

Physical therapy is a profession that teaches the client and the family techniques and exercises to reduce pain, maintain skin integrity, and to improve function, movement, and activities of daily living. These can be practiced at home as well as in the community. The goal is to enable someone with motor problems to move efficiently and to do the activities that are necessary and enjoyable to function in the home, school, and community. Physical therapy can involve: 1) increasing strength, balance, and flexibility through exercises; 2) preventing orthopedic problems with exercises and positioning devices; 3) making adaptations to household layout and equipment; 4) recommending specialized equipment; 5) analyzing posture, bracing, and movement problems.

Many parents wonder how physical therapy differs from occupational therapy. Although both types of therapy are concerned with improving developmental motor skills and activities of daily living, physical therapy emphasizes gross (large) movements of the body, such as those made by the arms, legs, and trunk. In contrast, occupational

therapy emphasizes fine movements, such as those made by the fingers, hands, and face. Also, occupational therapy places more emphasis on splinting, feeding, dressing, arm and hand movements, and writing and perceptual skills.

The professional who is qualified to evaluate and treat a child's limitations in the area of gross motor skills and sensation is the physical therapist (PT). A physical therapist is a health care professional who has at least a certificate or bachelor's degree in physical therapy and has licensure in the state in which he or she practices. As part of their degree program, physical therapists are required to have clinical practice, but how much varies with each university program. Your therapist may or may not have additional degrees (master's or doctorate) or certificates in specialized areas of treatment.

Your physical therapist may have a physical therapy assistant work with you and your child during the therapy session. Physical therapy assistants have associate degrees (two years of college) and have passed a state licensure examination. They are also required to have clinical experience as part of their degree program. The physical therapy assistant follows the goals and therapy program that the physical therapist has written and discussed with the family. Both therapist and assistant are required to take continuing education courses each year to maintain their license.

As a parent, you will probably find yourself incorporating physical therapy into daily activities with your child. The physical therapist will teach you exercises to do with your child at home, as well as techniques for advancing his developmental and functional skills (walking, handling stairs and curbs, etc.) and skills needed for school (getting in and out of a chair, getting on and off the bus, getting on and off the toilet). Your involvement in your child's physical therapy program will be crucial. This is because the PT can only spend a limited amount of time with your child, but to make progress, your child needs to "practice" these functional and motor skills daily in the environment where he will use the skill.

██ Why Do Children with Spina Bifida Need Physical Therapy?

Your child's need for physical therapy will depend on a number of factors, including:

- the degree of paralysis;
- sensory deficits (difficulties discriminating light touch from deep pressure, heat from cold, position of body parts, and pain);
- joint deformities;
- developmental reflexes (voluntary movement responses that help a child survive);
- cognitive abilities;
- strength; and
- ability to perform activities of daily living

In general, however, children with spina bifida benefit from early physical therapy instruction, teaching of their families, and direct "hands on" intervention. The frequency and the content of physical therapy sessions will vary. Depending on your child's needs, your family might be given occasional suggestions from a physical therapist in a spina bifida clinic, or might receive weekly therapy over a period of years, either in your home, in an outpatient setting, or in school.

One key reason that most children need physical therapy is that spina bifida limits the way nerves receive messages about hot and cold, pain, and movement or position sensations in the legs and trunk. Spina bifida also impairs the nerves' ability to send messages to the muscles to move the legs and lower body, causing weakness or paralysis. When children have weakness or paralysis in their trunk and/or limbs, they may not achieve motor skills such as rolling, sitting, and standing within the typical timeframes. With the help of a physical therapist, they may be able to find ways to move using other muscle groups that are not affected by the spina bifida. If their other muscles are unable to take over, then the physical therapist can help by suggesting equipment or bracing.

Another reason physical therapy may be necessary is that children with spina bifida undergo surgery to close their skin and spinal defect as newborns. During these operations, muscles are surgically cut to make repairs to the underlying nerves and spinal column. Any time a muscle is cut, weakness will result. These weak muscles need exercise so they can become strong and functional.

Physical therapy often plays an important role if later surgical procedures are recommended. For example, a physical therapist can help with positioning in the bed and relearning skills such as rolling, getting to a sitting position, and transferring out of bed to a chair, commode, wheelchair, or assistive device. A physical therapist will also teach your child exercises to help maintain position or function of his joints or muscles after surgical correction. In addition, the PT might need to teach your child how to care for a brace.

Older children with spina bifida may need physical therapy to prevent muscle contracture (tightness) from developing or worsening as they grow. They also need to practice functional skills and improve the speed of doing these skills.

Strengthening is an ongoing part of physical therapy programs and can help children keep up with the increased demands placed on their bodies by their increasing weight and height. As their bodies get fuller and heavier, some children with spina bifida find it is too difficult to continue to walk and must be taught how to use a wheelchair and to transfer in and out of it. Eating a nutritious diet, exercising, and keeping active are important things for your child to learn from the beginning.

▪▪ When and Where Should Physical Therapy Begin?

A physician may refer your child to a physical therapist for evaluation during the newborn period. If not, ask your doctor if and when your child would benefit from a referral to physical therapy. Physical therapy may be offered by a local spina bifida clinic in a pediatric hospital or outpatient facility or by an early intervention program in your community. There may be pediatric physical therapists listed under "physical therapy" in the yellow pages of your phonebook. You could inquire if they have experience with spina bifida or at least with children. Chapters 13 and 15 discuss how to seek therapy through the local early intervention program or school system. If you decide to seek services in a hospital or outpatient clinic, you will need to check with your HMO or health insurance plan to see if and where physical therapy is covered.

It is best if physical therapy is started at an early age. At this point, parents are taught ways to position and move their baby's extremities, as well as how to encourage developmental skills. Learning these skills early in your child's life can help prevent or slow down deformity. Your baby may need splints or braces, depending on the extent of involvement to nerves and muscles. Splints and braces can help stretch muscles and position bones in good alignment for future weight bearing. Last but not least, working with a physical therapist early in the developmental process can provide your family with much-needed support and information, and help you feel more comfortable with your new baby.

Physical therapy can be provided in a variety of settings: hospital, clinic, rehabilitation facility, school, private office, early intervention center, or your own home. The setting may depend on your child's medical status (the ability to travel to a facility where he would be exposed to other people), family transportation, travel distance, and family schedule. There are advantages to both home therapy and facility-based therapy. In your home, the therapist has an opportunity to see you and your child interact in a familiar environment. This enables the therapist to make recommendations using the toys and equipment at hand and provide suggestions knowing the family home. The clinic, rehab facility, early intervention center, or hospital provides greater access to other professionals on the premises, if additional information is needed, and greater access to a variety of equipment to try with your child for fit and function. If your child receives physical therapy at a facility, videotapes may be made so you can show them to any absent family members or to the orthopedist. In some hospitals, Day Treatment is an option. It allows a child to receive multiple therapies during the day but go home to be with his family for the evening and night. Therapy can be given intensely for several hours for two or more therapies. Sometimes it is a good idea for a child to receive physical therapy both at home and at a facility, providing him with the best of each setting.

:: How Will the Physical Therapist Work with My Child?

Before beginning work with your child, the physical therapist must first evaluate him. The therapist will ask you questions about your observations of your child's movement, interactions, and strengths. The therapist will also evaluate joint motion, flexibility, developmental reflexes, developmental skills, sensation level, muscle strength, leg length, and deformities. He or she may ask what pieces of equipment you already have and/or what equipment would make caring for your child easier.

This evaluation will be summarized in a written document and should include the therapist's recommendations. Once your child's evaluation is complete, the PT will discuss the findings with you and determine goals for your child. A letter will also be sent to the referring physician with the evaluation results and recommendations.

If your child is a newborn, it will be difficult to accurately evaluate his strength and sensation. However, as communication and developmental skills mature and body awareness increases, the therapist will be able to provide more accurate information about his abilities. This information will be used in making both short- and long-term predictions about your child's needs (equipment, braces, and home and school adaptations).

The therapist will want to know your family's concerns before designing a program with specific goals. The physical therapy program will be individualized for your child, depending on the level of his functioning muscles and their strength, his developmental skills, head and body control, and other factors. Some of the specific goals the PT may work on with your child over his childhood are listed in Table 1.

Positioning

One of the physical therapist's earliest concerns will be to ensure that your baby is positioned so that he can best achieve developmental milestones.

Your child may initially be positioned in a side lying or adapted stomach lying position (propped half way between side and stomach lying). The therapist can show you how to prop your child in these positions with rolled towels, baby blankets, or with the use of adaptive equipment. (See the Resource Guide for some sources of adaptive equipment.) These positions allow the spinal stitches and wound to heal without irritation or pressure. These are also good positions for the child to begin early head lifting and turning, following a toy with both eyes, and using the arms to bear some body weight or move both hands together.

After the wound has healed, your baby may be placed in a back lying position for sleep, and for activities that encourage reaching. The PT can show you how to prop your child in a reclined position by using pillows and infant seats. This position allows for feeding and encourages head control, object tracking, and eye contact.

Splints

Some babies with spina bifida have changes in the alignment of their joints that may cause problems later on when they use their joints in weight bearing or to move in daily activities. If problems with your child's joint alignment are observed, a physician may order splints. A splint is a positioning device that holds the joint or body part in a normal position to prevent or correct the deformity. It is worn periodically throughout the day, but taken off for several two- or three-hour periods so that the skin can be kept clean and free of pressure. Splints may be worn during naps and sleep if no red marks (pressure sores) or blisters appear during the day. Splints can be made from a variety of materials depending on what the therapist prefers for the size, weight, age, and body part. They may be made by a physical therapist, occupational therapist, or an orthotist (brace specialist).

Swaddling

Your physician may recommend swaddling if your child holds his legs in a frog-legged posture with knees bowed out and heels together. Swaddling is done by placing a pillow or rolled towel between the knees, wrapping both legs lightly together with a soft baby blanket, and securing it with a pin. This reduces muscle tightness at the hips and knees.

Swaddling should only be done at times that you can observe your child and see how he is reacting to this positioning. This way, you can change your baby's position or adjust the snugness of the wrap if necessary. Swaddling at night and naptime is not recommended because there are additional blankets restricting your child's movements and you cannot monitor how your child is positioned.

∷ TABLE 1   Physical Therapy Goals

Developmental Skills
- Prop on arms (lying on stomach)
- Roll over
- Rotate to sit
- Sit
- Creep (commando style on belly)
- Crawl on hands and knees
- Tall kneel
- Half kneel (one knee bent out in front)
- Pull to stand
- Stand
- Walk around furniture
- Walk

Functional Skills—Activities of daily living that are used in the home and community.
- Rolling over in bed
- Getting to sit
- Sitting skills (with or without use of hands to assist)
- Feeding skills
- Transfer skills:
  - in and out of bed
  - on and off the toilet
  - in and out of the bath tub
  - in and out of a chair
  - in and out of a car
  - up and down to the floor
- Brace application and removal
- Skin care
- Carrying an object
- Making a bed
- Setting a table
- Brushing teeth
- Combing hair
- Dressing

Mobility Skills—Skills associated with independent movement in the home or community

- Walking (with or without braces or an assistive device)
- Falling techniques
- Moving around objects (stepping over a toy, going around a table)
- Picking up objects off the floor
- Carrying an object while moving
- Standing and reaching overhead for an object
- Stairs (ascending and descending)
- Ramps and curbs
- Elevators and escalators
- Drinking fountains
- Wheelchair mobility (transfers in and out, forward/backward propulsion, turns, ramp and curbs)

Gross Motor Skills—These are motor skills that are done with the entire body or with an entire limb (arm or leg). When these skills are introduced depend on age readiness, as well as your child's balance, coordination, flexibility, and muscle strength.

- Stand on one foot
- Throw, catch, kick, bounce a ball
- Hop on one foot
- Jump forward, backward, up and down, off a step, over a line
- Hit a ball with a bat, racket, or club

Children who demonstrate sufficient leg strength may be able to:

- Run
- Gallop
- Skip
- Jump rope
- Pedal a tricycle or bicycle

Positioning Devices

There are a wide variety of positioning devices that a physical therapist might recommend for your child. Examples include: adaptive chairs, prone boards, side lyers, crawlers, and standing devices. There are stuffed fabric positioning aids that allow different positions with one device. Some of these devices are stationary, mobile, upright, or reclined with or without power assist so the child can move while in the proper position. All of these devices improve your child's posture so he can have better use of his limbs and can better interact with other people. These devices can be obtained through catalogs and brochures your therapist may have access to, on company websites, or through licensed vendors of durable medical equipment. Your therapist or physician can recommend companies in your area.

In selecting positioning devices, it is wise to use a team approach so that the total needs of your child are considered. Each professional who works with your child will view a piece of equipment and the benefits it provides him from a different perspective. As a parent, you too may want it to accomplish specific goals for positioning, growth, and quality. Let's not forget cost, too, and whether it is a "covered benefit" under your health plan(s). All of these considerations must be taken into account before you purchase an item.

Carrying

Your physical therapist can recommend the best way to carry your child so that neither he nor you is injured. How your child should be carried will depend on whether a specific part of his body needs to be protected and to what degree. A general rule of thumb when carrying a child with spina bifida is to keep him as close to you as possible to avoid possible injury to limbs. Parents should always lift with their knees bent to avoid back injuries.

Exercises

At different stages in your child's life, the physical therapist will teach you a variety of different exercises. These exercises may have some of these overall goals:

1. to help keep your child's muscles stretched out and joints moving through their full range of motion;
2. to help your child achieve gross motor and functional skills;
3. to strengthen weak muscles;

4. to improve endurance in movement, function, and gross motor skills;
5. to improve balance and coordination;
6. to reduce stiffness due to immobility;
7. to relieve pressure on the skin and muscles;
8. to improve fitness level;
9. to reduce obesity;
10. to increase control over muscles that assist in elimination of body waste;
11. to improve joint alignment;
12. to improve posture;
13. to improve breathing and lung expansion

Stretching Exercises

As explained in Chapter 8, if your child's muscles are not moving spontaneously or voluntarily, he may develop contractures—shortened, tight muscles that pull a limb out of position and prevent joints from working properly. As long as your child is still growing, a stretching program will be helpful to prevent tightness from developing in muscles. Your child's muscles may also need to be stretched daily so he is able to perform activities of daily living. Some children may need to keep muscles stretched out so they can easily put on braces, clothes, and shoes. The program, number of repetitions, and frequency should be guided by a physical therapist according to your child's specific needs.

Stretching can be uncomfortable at first, but discomfort subsides as the muscle lengthens. Children tolerate stretching if it is made fun through singing, activities, and play. It is helpful to vary the room or the surroundings where these exercises are done. Depending on your child's age, the muscle to be stretched, and the exercise position, your child may be able to do stretching exercises unsupervised as he grows older.

If your child has had surgery, your doctor may ask that the PT teach you exercises to maintain the surgical correction as your child grows taller and heavier. The type of surgery and the area of the body will determine when and if your physician will request a physical therapy stretching program. Many types of orthopedic surgeries use a stretching and/or strengthening program when the wound has healed. The physical therapist will begin exercising your child and provide you with a list of written exercises to do at home. It is important for you to fit these exercises into your family's daily routine as an extension of the therapy session.

Developmental Activities

It is important for every child to master developmental skills. The child with spina bifida is no exception. Developmental motor skills that the PT will work on with your child include: propping on forearms or hands while lying on the stomach, rolling over, getting into and out of a sitting position, creeping, crawling, kneeling, standing, and walking. To determine when your child is ready to work on each skill, the therapist will look for the presence of certain developmental reflexes. For example, your child needs to have the arm reactions that help him keep his balance or protect himself from a fall before learning to sit and walk.

Strengthening Exercises

The PT will provide written instructions for exercises that will allow your child to improve strength, balance, and coordination as each developmental skill is mastered. For example, the therapist may work on increasing strength in your child's upper back, arms, and chest by weight bearing on arms alone, through wheelbarrow walking, and by using a scooter board—a rectangular board with swivel wheels. The therapist may recommend that the exercises be performed with the use of light weights (both cuff and dumbbells), pulleys, weighted balls, or elastic bands to make the activity more difficult and increase muscle strength and endurance. To make the activity fun, your child's limbs might be weighted while playing with toys, tricycles, scooters, or wheeled carts. Be sure your therapist uses products that are nonlatex. You can download a list of common latex items and substitutes from www.sbaa.org

Maintaining muscle strength at an optimum level will provide maximum support for your child's joints. This is always important, but especially so if bracing (see below) will be needed for your child in the future.

If your child does need braces on his lower limbs, it is important to work on arm as well as leg strength in his physical therapy program. The arms assist the weaker legs in climbing stairs, carrying objects, and holding on while the legs are lifting and carrying the body.

Electrical Stimulation. For children who have weak muscles that have innervation, strengthening exercises can be enhanced by using either:

> 1. low intensity threshold electrical stimulation (TES), which is delivered at night when the child is sleeping; or

2. neuromuscular electrical stimulation (NMES), which can be used any time of the day.

These nonpainful forms of electrical stimulation can be used on young children (three to four years and older) to enhance the strength that they gain from their home exercise program. Electrical stimulation helps to keep the muscle in a state of readiness and maintains or advances the strength—it complements the exercise program. Each by itself is not as effective as both together.

Physical therapists who have received advanced training and certification through a TES course (Continuing Education Course) are able to use the units that deliver the electrical stimulation. These certified therapists are able to acquire the units, set the correct parameters (settings on the machine), and position the electrodes on specific muscle groups that would benefit from strengthening. They change muscle groups periodically, depending on the child's needs. Pediatric physical therapists in a clinic, rehabilitation facility, or hospital generally have access to the NMES units. Your therapist will determine if your child is a good candidate for this treatment. He or she can also assist you with the process of working with your medical health insurer to determine if this would be a "covered benefit" for your child.

Functional Skills

An important goal of physical therapy is to teach your child skills that will allow him to function independently in the home, school, and community. These include feeding, grooming, transfers, housekeeping, and other skills listed in Table 1.

The physical therapist will demonstrate the activity with your child and show you how to assist your child at home. Suggestions may be provided on how to simplify the activity, or to break the skill down into parts that are

easier to do. The therapist will have your child practice the skill over and over, suggesting different ways to do the skill, if necessary. The physical therapist may watch you practice your home program and provide reassurance or suggestions. Suggestions may include when and how often to practice the activity, as well as how to incorporate it into daily use.

Once your child has learned a skill, it is important to let him become independent in practicing and using it. You may need to gently prompt or assist as your child takes on more responsibility. It cannot be stressed enough that your child needs to practice these functional skills every day so he can do them as quickly and efficiently as possible. You are teaching your child today to prepare for the future (and remember, you are not growing any younger).

Other Exercises

There are other reasons for children with spina bifida to exercise in addition to those described above. One key reason is to reduce weight or to prevent your child from gaining too much weight. This type of exercise is especially crucial if your child is in a wheelchair or not very active due to weak muscles. Exercises to burn off calories can be done with or without music. Exercise repetitions should be stressed. Your child may use weights if he is physically able to use them.

Another important reason for wheelchair users to exercise is to relieve the pressure on their skin, bones, and muscles from sitting. The best way to do this is for your child to lift his seat briefly out of the wheelchair by doing a push-up using the arm rests every 20 minutes. If your child cannot do this, he should learn to rock his body side to side to give pressure relief.

A few children do muscle strengthening to improve control of their bladder and rectum, as well as the muscles in their legs. There are very specific exercises for these areas of the body.

Some children need to do exercises to improve their balance and coordination during walking and/or gross motor skills. These exercises are assisted with balls, ladders, ropes, rings, balance beams and boards, uneven surfaces, and even water. Water therapy can assist in developing coordination, strength, and competence in swimming. Therapeutic horseback riding can also help some children improve their balance and coordination and provide an opportunity for animal bonding and animal care.

Depending on your child's needs, he may need physical therapy for months or even years. Toys help in making therapy fun, creative, and functional. Your physical therapist can help you select toys that would help your child explore his environment, build strength and flexibility, and develop or learn a functional or gross motor skill. In some physical therapy facilities, animal assisted therapy is also used to teach and improve skills and attention, as well as to provide a change to keep the child interested in therapy.

∷ Will My Child Walk?

Most children with spina bifida are able to learn to walk. As Chapter 8 explains, however, walking is usually easier for children with low level lesions than for children with high level lesions. In addition, braces and assistive devices (canes, crutches, and walkers) are often needed to achieve the goal of walking.

Your child's physical therapist will look for signs that he is ready to walk, with or without braces. In particular, the therapist will look for protective or parachute reactions (reflexes) when your child is learning to sit. These include the ability to put a hand out to protect his body from tipping over when his weight shifts forward, backward, or to the side. This parachute response is very important when learning to walk, as it protects your child if he falls. The presence of parachute reactions is used to determine walking readiness in a child without adequate muscle strength in the legs.

Another sign that your child is ready to walk is that he is trying to pull himself up on furniture to get to a standing position. In addition, balance awareness of body position in space is crucial for voluntary movement and walking. If your child has adequate strength, he may try to stand without holding onto furniture. One milestone that your child does *not* need to achieve in order to walk is creeping and crawling. These provide excellent weight-bearing practice for improved arm strength and limb coordination, but are not necessary for walking.

Usually, brain maturation allows children to develop protective reactions so they can control their balance. Some children with spina bifida, however, have changes to their brain control centers (cerebellum) that do not allow them to gain control over their balance or their awareness of body positioning. Difficulties in this area may not be apparent until the child begins attempting to sit independently. As the child rises higher off the floor, he may show problems with other developmental skills such as kneeling or standing. Children with these difficulties are helped by working on balance/coordination activities, strengthening, and timing exercises to improve the speed of their protective response. They may need to have walkers and crutches adapted (by weighting the assistive device), to allow additional time to move their limbs and provide sensory awareness, and/or be provided protective gear (helmets or joint padding). Some children may benefit from using a wheelchair for long distances if attempting to walk is too frustrating.

Whether or not your child is expected to walk, the physical therapist will undoubtedly work with you to provide opportunities for standing. Adaptive equipment such as prone boards, supine standers, wheeled mobile standers, and standing tables will be selected for your child considering his age, size, medical status, and orthopedic problems. There are wheelchairs that also allow standing, but they are heavier to move and may be used as a second wheelchair but not for primary mobility.

Standing provides many benefits that your child can not get any other way:

- Standing challenges the lungs and heart, allowing them to work more efficiently.
- Standing makes the circulatory system pump the blood upward through the limbs, back to the heart.
- Bones maintain their strength as they are forced to hold up the weight of your child's body.
- The bladder and bowels operate more efficiently when the body is standing, as gravity aids in eliminating waste products.
- Standing provides pressure relief to the skin and underlying tissues so pressure sores (ulcerations) are not as likely to occur.
- Standing provides a different perspective to viewing the person's surroundings.

Your child may find standing to be fun and enjoyable if favorite toys, activities, reading, games, and interactions with others are used to pass the time. Your child may begin by standing for a brief ten-minute period. Ideally, you will gradually be able to increase the time standing to 30 to 60 minutes, twice a day.

If your child has adequate strength to support his weight, you should encourage him to walk as you would any other child. Encourage him to attempt to pull to stand, side step (cruise) around furniture, and walk too. As discussed below, bracing may or may not be necessary for your child to learn to walk.

Will My Child Need Braces?

Ordinarily, certain nerves in our bodies tell specific muscles whether to hold joints tight to support a standing position, or to release joints to allow movement. When nerves or muscles aren't working because of spina bifida, braces (orthotics) can help to support and protect the joints. This allows the limb to be used to its maximum potential for functional skills. Braces are also used to maintain normal joint alignment, to correct deformity (e.g., toeing in), and to stretch tight muscles.

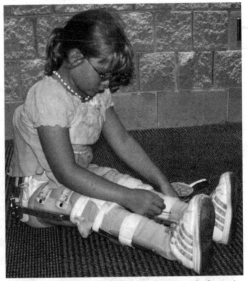

Hip knee ankle foot orthosis (HKAFO) with thoracic lumbosacral orthosis (TLSO)

There are a variety of styles and types of braces. In general, however, they are lightweight devices made of plastic or metal that are secured to the limb with cotton, leather, or synthetic straps. Braces for children with spina bifida are designed to give different levels of support and movement, depending on the level of the spinal lesion. The four basic levels of bracing are:

1. Braces consisting of a spinal jacket (Thoracic lumbosacral orthosis—TLSO) covering rib cage, low back, and buttocks, or a pelvic band attached to braces that extend from the hip to the foot (called "hip knee ankle foot orthosis"— HKAFO); A variation of this is the reciprocating gait orthosis (RGO), which allows a reciprocal movement of the legs instead of legs moving together in a "swing" motion.

2. Braces that extend from hip to foot only (called "long leg braces" or "knee ankle foot orthosis"—KAFO);

3. Braces that extend from below the knee to the foot; ("short leg braces" or "ankle foot orthosis"—AFO);

4. Braces that support the foot only (either a dynamic ankle foot orthosis—DAFO—or a shoe insert called the University of California Brace—UCB).

In addition, some children need a lift in their shoe or on their brace. This might be necessary if one leg is shorter than the other leg. In children with spina bifida, this may occur because one hip bone is poorly positioned in the socket or even out of the socket. The pelvis may be tilted so that one side is raised higher than the other side or the child may have had a fracture that overlapped slightly in the healing process. Using a lift on the shorter side allows the child to have better posture and places equal weight on each foot. It also decreases the chance that deformities of the spine and hip will worsen.

Reciprocating gait orthosis (RGO)

There are many variations of the basic types of braces. For instance, cables or straps may be added to long or short leg braces to rotate the leg inward or outward while walking. Joints may be added to allow the brace to move the same as joints of the body (to flex, extend, and rotate), or the brace may be constructed in one solid piece for standing. A solid circular base may be attached to the braces to allow independent standing. A reciprocal gait orthotic makes hip movement easier with cables (on the spinal jacket) that assist the muscles as the child shifts his weight side to side (like a walking doll).

The decision as to whether to use braces and when to begin is important to your child's development and function. Your child's age, medical health, developmental skills, and reflexes will help to determine when he is first fitted for braces. A rough rule of thumb is that braces can begin to be used for standing at around the age your child would be able to stand if he did not have spina bifida (11 to 15 months). He should also demonstrate the balance skills and protective reflexes that are needed to stand or walk (see above). In addition, your physician (usually the orthopedic physician) will need to evaluate your child's joint range of motion, presence or absence of deformity, and muscles. Restricted joint motion or muscle contracture can affect the efficiency, fit, and wearing time of braces until the muscle gradually becomes more flexible. If the joint or muscle is rigid or unable to be stretched, surgery may be needed (see Chapter 8). If your physician feels your child would benefit from bracing, he or she will give you a prescription, stating the type and style of brace your child needs. It is important for you and the physical therapist to communicate your child's abilities, therapy program, and goals to the physician.

The orthotist is the professional who will make the braces. Some physical therapists have special training to make orthotics that fit in the shoe. You will have to schedule an appointment and bring the prescription. The orthotist will evaluate the area to be braced prior to making a cast, noting any bony prominences and points where pressure may need to be relieved. The price of bracing varies depending on the style and type of brace. Prices may also vary between orthotists in the same community, as well as between different parts of the country. You will need to check with your insurance or managed care organization to find out if they have a contract agreement with a specific vendor or not, in order for payment to be covered.

Making Sure Braces Fit Well and Are Comfortable

The braces should always fit your child comfortably and be applied easily. The braces should allow freedom of movement at all joints. A rule of thumb: you should be able to pass a finger between the brace and the skin to prevent tightness or excess pressure. The center of each orthotic joint should line up with the center of the body's joint that it is to control. Any pressure marks under straps or from brace contact should disappear 10 to 15 minutes after removing the brace. There should not be blisters or red marks on your child's skin. Wearing time of braces may be started at a half-hour three times a day and increased over several months to five to ten hours a day. How easily your child is able to tolerate his braces will depend on his age, use, and needs.

You or your child should check the skin under his brace(s) at least twice daily. Teach him to use a mirror to check areas that are difficult to see—buttocks, back of thighs, calves, heels, and balls of feet. Be sure your child always wears socks, tights, leotards, or hose under his brace to protect the skin. (These also provide warmth.)

Braces are usually designed to be worn under clothing (pants, dresses, and underwear). However, they can be made wider so that they can be worn over clothing. Your child's age, the amount and type of bracing, toileting status, and personal preference need to be considered in this decision. Infants and toddlers are not aware or concerned about appearance and most are in diapers. As children grow older, they become aware that not everyone has braces and that some braces worn over clothing make using the toilet more difficult. In the teenage years, looking like everyone else becomes important for socialization.

A short leg brace can be easily disguised with a sock. Long leg braces become more obvious when worn over pants and may not be as acceptable to some children. If your child wears clothing over his braces, you need to buy clothes in larger sizes so the brace(s) does not wear holes in the garment. When in doubt, choose clothes based on their fit rather than their looks.

What about Assistive Devices?

An assistive device is a piece of equipment that supports and/or balances someone so that they may walk independently and expend the least amount of energy. Many children with spina bifida find an assistive device helpful when they first begin to walk.

The choice of assistive device (walker, crutches, or canes) depends on the amount of support and balance needed, and may change over the years as a child grows. Some children start with a walker and progress to canes or crutches as their strength, balance, and coordination increases. Other children may start with crutches/canes and choose to go to a walker as they get taller and heavier, if they find it too difficult to walk long distances or are afraid of falling or being pushed in school. Some children with spina bifida may use canes or crutches when they are very young, but later develop enough balance, coordination, and strength to walk without an assistive device. Some only use the device when they need to enhance their strength for long distances or to climb flights of stairs.

Some commonly used styles of assistive devices include:

Walkers. These are light metal frames used for support in walking. Frames may provide support either in front of the child or behind him. The **anterior (orthopedic) walker** provides support in front, and allows the body to lean slightly forward onto the arms. With wheels on the front, it allows a faster speed. When used without wheels, it is a very stable, slow device. The disadvantage is that it does not encourage spinal extension as does the **posterior walker,** which provides support in back of the person. This walker, if provided with wheels, allows good posture and speed efficiency.

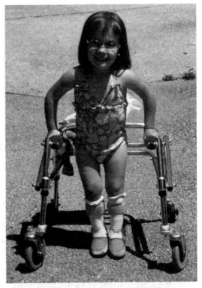

Posterior rolling walker; ankle foot orthosis (AFO)

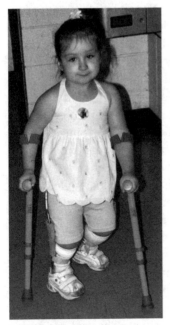

Lofstrand crutches

Lofstrand Crutches. These crutches have cuffs that go around the forearm and handles for the child's hand. The child can hop, swing between them, or alternate his legs, allowing quick and efficient movement. They also allow the user to climb stairs, which is difficult to do with a walker. These crutches are used when the child has developed good upper body strength and coordination so that he can control both arms together (without the stabilization of the center bar on a walker). These crutches should not be used by children with hip flexion contractures, as the child needs to lean slightly forward to use them, which can maintain or increase a contracture.

Canes. There are **quad canes** (four-legged canes) that allow children to use a variety of gaits: 1) fast reciprocating (alternating legs), 2) hopping, and 3) swinging. The quad cane assists both balance and strength when walking short or long distances. With this type of cane, the child can choose which style of gait to use, depending on the circumstances and the surroundings. The **straight cane** helps balance a child so he can walk long distances. Children who use straight canes usually use a reciprocal gait. Both styles of canes allow the child to climb stairs.

Would My Child Benefit from a Wheelchair?

The answer to this question is not a simple one, nor is the answer of *when* to decide. Your physician, therapist, and child will be your guides as to the form of mobility that is most useful at different ages. Whether your child would benefit from a wheelchair does not need to be decided immediately. However, as your child approaches school age, you will

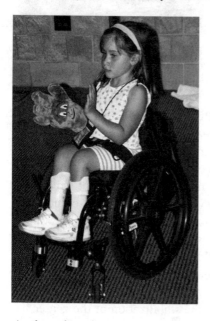

have to consider how he will get around the playground during recess, to classes, the cafeteria, and bathrooms, as well as participate *efficiently* in fire drills.

Not all children with spina bifida need a wheelchair. Some need a wheelchair only to travel very long distances, such as at the mall or zoo. Others use a combination of walking and wheeling to get around their home, school, and community. Young children may use a combination of wheeled mobility stander to get around their home and a stroller for the community. Some children may use a wheelchair when they are tired or when the terrain is rough. If and when a child uses a wheelchair is primarily determined by the degree of paralysis.

It is beneficial for children with spina bifida to wheel their chair to keep their arms strong. However, this strength gain must be weighed against how long it takes to get to the destination (efficiency) and how much energy the child has left when he gets there. The goal is independent mobility, but not at the expense of all of a child's strength and energy. Children who have very high muscle tone (spasticity) in their arms and weak hand muscles may need to consider the benefits of a (motorized) electric wheelchair or scooter. There are many other ways to maintain strength and endurance (see the section on "Exercise," above).

Despite the many advantages of wheelchairs, deciding on and purchasing one for the first time can be a traumatic experience for many parents. Some feel that buying a wheelchair means they have given up on their goal of walking for their child. A wheelchair can also be seen as an outward sign that their child has a disability. In reality, a wheelchair may be the primary means of mobility for some, but it will be just another way of moving about for others, and will be used in conjunction with walking. For children whose walking is very limited, the wheelchair becomes their ticket to independence. It is amazing how rapidly many children adjust to their wheelchair.

Choosing a Wheelchair

Today there are many different types of wheelchairs, including sports wheelchairs used for racing and other active physical activities. The type and style of mobility device (wheelchair, stroller, motorized scooter) you select will be influenced by your answers to these questions:

- How capable is my child physically?
- Would my child's age affect the selection of type of device and when?
- How good is my child's hand control and hand strength?
- Does my child have head control? Trunk control?
- Does my child tire easily so that a recline feature or "tilt in space" is needed?
- Does my child need to have his legs elevated?
- Would a stroller or a wheelchair address my child's needs?
- Is there a piece of equipment that allows both my child or another person to propel it?
- Where do I wish to use the mobility device? Inside? Outside? Both?
- How long of a time (months? years?) would my child need to use a mobility device?
- How often would my child need to use a mobility device?
- For how long at a time would my child sit in the mobility device?

- Would my child be able to maneuver the device?
- Would a (motorized) electric device be needed?
- Would "power wheels" help my child propel the wheelchair?
- What make(s) and model(s) of mobility devices are available?
- Which vendors (stores) carry these products?
- Could my child "test drive" the chair/scooter/stander?
- Are there wheeled devices that would allow my child to build strength in his arms and/or legs before we make a final decision?

Wheelchairs come in a variety of sizes, models, and styles. They can be **manual** (propelled by the user), **push** (propelled by someone other than the user), **recliner** (chair can be positioned in varied positions of tilt back), **standing,** or **(motorized) electric. The chair can have power (motorized) components, such as wheels, seat, and tilt.** The chair may have a collapsible frame or a rigid frame. A collapsible frame allows the chair to grow with the child and fits easily into the trunk or back seat of a car. A rigid (nonfolding) frame is used in sports and racing chairs. These chairs are great as a second chair for the person who enjoys sports.

The backs of wheelchairs can be firm, soft, or custom molded, come in a variety of heights, and can have extra padding placed in them to provide support where needed. They can also be removable.

The seat of the wheelchair should be firm. Custom molded seats and cushions (e.g., gel, Roho™, Jay™) may help those children who have orthopedic problems that lend themselves to pressure points and sores (tailbone, buttocks, and hip joints). Some wheelchair vendors do "pressure mapping" to determine where pressure needs to be relieved for the wheelchair user. A general rule of thumb is that the seat and wheelchair frame should be parallel to the floor and not tipped downward so pressure sores don't develop on the tail bone or pelvic muscles.

The type of tire you select will depend on your family's lifestyle, as well as your child's hand strength. Pneumatic (air-filled) tires work best on uneven terrain, while hard rubber tires work well on smooth surfaces, such as floors and sidewalks. Some wheels have "no flat tires" to prevent breakdown in inconvenient places. Most wheelchair wheels are removable to make lifting and storing the wheelchair easier. Power wheels can be substituted on some wheelchair styles.

Wheelchair arm rests are adjustable and removable or swing away. Leg rests that swing away allow for easier transfers. The foot rests may divide and flip up, may be a single plate that flips up on one side or be fixed for rigid frame wheelchairs. Transfers in and out of the chair should always be considered when selecting or designing a custom wheelchair. Most wheelchairs allow for such additional custom features as trays, pouches for supplies, and holders for crutches, oxygen, or other equipment needed by the individual.

Your physical therapist can provide suggestions about wheelchairs based on your child's specific needs. It is helpful to have the wheelchair vendor send a representative to a therapy session to discuss the pros and cons of wheelchairs with you and the therapist in one session. Wheelchairs vary greatly in price depending on the company, wheelchair type, accessories, country of manufacture, and where you live.

Many factors must be considered when deciding whether a very young child (two or three years old) should be in a stroller or a wheelchair. First, you should consider your child's desire to be independent in mobility. Second, you should get expert medical advice from your child's therapists and physicians. And finally, you should check with your medical health payor (insurance, managed care, Medicaid) to see what kind of coverage they provide. In addition, you may wish to rent or borrow an appropriately sized wheelchair for a short period before deciding.

Before reaching any final decisions as to the type of wheelchair to purchase, it is unfortunately necessary to ask the payor of your medical care (insurance, HMO, PPO, Medicaid) whether they have any stipulations on mobility devices. There may be limitations on *where* you can purchase a device and how *often* a mobility device will be paid for by them, as well as on what *type* will be funded. This may have some impact on your decision of what type of mobility device to buy and when.

:: My Child Is Having Surgery! Oh No, a Cast!

The statement every parent hates to hear: "Your child needs surgery!" If your child needs orthopedic (bone and/or muscle) surgery, a cast may be a necessary part of correcting the problem. (Some orthopedic surgeries do not immobilize with a cast but use an external fixator, wires, rods, plates, nails, and screws, depending on the area of the body and the procedure the physician chooses.) Casts hold the bones, joints, and muscles in a desired position until healing occurs. Casts, like braces, come in a variety of types, shapes, and colors. They are made from plaster or fiberglass. Sometimes they are needed for days, and sometimes weeks.

Types of Casts

Casts are applied to protect and immobilize the surgical area. They extend a level above and below the healing area to keep it in the best position for healing to occur. After hip surgery, for example, a hip **spica cast** may be applied. This is a cast that extends from the bottom of the rib cage to the calf with an open area for hygiene. Frequently the ankles and feet are included as well. Sometimes the surgeon has some leeway in deciding how long the cast will be, depending on whether one side or two sides are corrected. This extensive cast is needed to hold the hip and prevent twisting, bending, or slipping of the healing bones and tissues.

A **long leg cast** is a cylindrical cast that encloses the leg from thigh to foot. It may be straight or bent at the knee. A **short leg cast** extends from the calf to the toes. It may or may not enclose the toes. The cast may even point the foot downward, outward, or inward, depending on the surgical procedure and the corrected limb position. There may be a cast shoe or boot applied over the cast when your doctor wants your child to begin weight bearing or walking. An assistive device (walker, crutches, or canes) may be needed to assist with providing support and balance. The doctor and the physical therapist should discuss with you the best type to use with your child, and arrange for you to get it, if you don't have one.

Daily Life with a Cast

As a rule, casts should not be immersed in water. A single cast may be kept dry with a plastic cover while showering. Casts need to be kept *out of the water* when taking a bath. Water tends to break down the plaster or cement, allowing the cast to become brittle and loose. Synthetic casts made out of fiberglass or plastic are more resistant to water than plaster ones but still should be cared for in the same way.

Toileting needs are usually not a problem with a short or long leg cast. Toilets can be adapted with grab bars and a higher raised seat or a commode chair that can be placed over the toilet or be free standing at bedside. The height of the commode chair can be adjusted, and, if needed, a commode chair with armrests that drop to allow transfers from a bed can be used. Initially, your child may need assistance or supervision to get up and down from the toilet, to prevent falls. Always be careful in a bathroom around sinks, tubs, and showers due to water and rugs on the floor. If possible, rugs should be removed or put to the side to prevent assistive devices from sliding.

If your child has a hip spica, however, toileting requires more adaptations. Usually a diaper, urinal, or bedpan can be positioned within the cut-out area of the cast for your child's toileting needs. After a bowel movement, your child will need to be turned onto his stomach for hygienic cleansing.

Positioning becomes very important if your child has a hip spica cast or long leg cast. The weight of the cast(s) may make it impossible for your child to roll over, until he gets used to it. Your child should be turned every three to four hours, either side to side or onto his stomach and back. This lessens the chance of developing pressure sores on the skin. Pillows are useful when varying your child's position and can help make him more comfortable. An egg crate mattress pad (wavy like an egg carton) can be obtained thru most hospitals or medical vendors to reduce skin irritation and prevent pressure sores.

Occasionally, the skin under a cast will itch. Pouring cornstarch into the cast should help. You may want to seek medical advice from your orthopedist if this does not solve the problem.

While your child is recuperating, consider taking him for a ride in a wagon or cart in which he can be comfortably positioned. The change of scenery and activity can make the time your child is in the cast more pleasant. Your physical therapist and physician can help you plan for your child's mobility needs, as well as for his transportation home from the hospital.

When traveling in a car or van, a child in a cast should only be transported in the back seat or on a rear seat that has been folded down.

There are straps that go through the seatbelts and shoulder harnesses that secure a child over 40 pounds to the seat. Some hospitals provide these as part of their orthopedic service. You may want to ask your doctor if the hospital provides cast seatbelts or restraints before your child's hospital stay. You may need to obtain a car seat from the hospital that accommodates your child's new body position. Your physical therapist may be able to assist you in obtaining an appropriate car seat.

As your child heals, your doctor will determine when the cast should be removed and if your child would benefit from physical therapy. It may be necessary to have a physical therapist evaluate your child as the surgery will have made changes to the muscles, joints, or both. The therapist may provide exercises and positioning ideas, help with selecting adaptive equipment (shower/bath chairs, shower massage, hair washing trays, etc.) for the home, or suggestions on home adaptations (grab bars, railings, ramps, room design) for safety and efficiency. Your doctor may recommend that therapy be given in your home through a home health physical therapist or suggest seeing a therapist in the community.

▪▪ Hi Ho! Hi Ho! It's Off to School We Go!

Preparation for preschool or kindergarten should be a carefully planned progression for your child—and so should the physical therapy program that may accompany his schooling! Physical therapy is provided to many preschoolers three to five years of age, provided that the therapy **complement educational goals.** The therapy has to help the child accomplish tasks that he will need to do **in school.** Examples of such tasks include getting on and off the bus or in and out of a chair, climbing stairs, and long distance walking. Physical therapy in the schools may not teach skills needed outside of school, such as making a bed or transferring in and out of a bathtub.

Chapters 13 and 15 discuss the evaluation process the school will use to determine whether your child qualifies for physical therapy or other special services at school. If your child qualifies for services, a meeting will be scheduled with you, your child's teacher, therapists, and, if needed, other school personnel to identify goals; how they will be met, and in what time frame. The frequency and length of therapy sessions should also be discussed. All of these details and more will be written down in a document called an Individualized Education Program (IEP). (See Chapter 15.)

After your child enters kindergarten, physical therapy will continue to be provided as long as your child has not reached the goal of being able to function independently in the educational setting. Once this is accomplished, then therapy is discontinued. It may or may not continue through high school. One role of the school-based therapist is to teach functional skills that will be used in the classroom, cafeteria, hallways, and bathrooms. Skills related to drinking fountains, stairs, curbs, and busses need to be included too. These skills can also be used in the community, home, and workplace, but are a necessity at school. Consequently, achieving these skills should be considered appropriate goals in your child's IEP. To achieve these skills, your child may do exercises to strengthen and stretch muscles during therapy sessions. Balance and coordination exercises may also be a part of your child's program if they will help your child master functional skills. Most schools have a variety of children's toys that can make the therapy fun and the time go quickly.

Another role of the school PT is to adapt equipment—for example, by padding prone and supine standers for trunk control and preventing pressure points; by positioning wedges on chairs to improve posture and make it easier to get up; and by padding crutch grips. Your therapist will also make suggestions about purchasing equipment that would be helpful to your child's mobility, positioning, transfers, and functional skills. If a mobility device is being considered, the therapist may give you ideas and suggestions and help you make choices from the many styles and types.

Many school therapists make suggestions on braces and brace adaptation and on establishing good working relationships with the physicians and local brace companies. They may set up a meeting that allows the child, parent, orthotist, and therapist to discuss bracing concerns and suggestions. They will teach your child how to get the braces on and off until he is able to do it easily.

The physical therapist should establish a good working relationship with the teacher, teacher's aide, principal, and other school personnel who are working together to help your child accomplish his school goals. The therapist will want to establish good communication with you as well. This may be done through telephone conversations or messages, traveling notebooks, notes pinned to your child's back, email, and invitations for you to observe the therapy session. If you have a concern that needs to be addressed immediately, a phone call is usually the quickest way to contact the physical therapist. If the therapist is difficult to reach by phone, try calling the teacher or principal; they may have the therapist's work schedule and be able to contact him or her.

If your child will be home schooled, your community, home health, or clinic physical therapist may design a program of exercises, mobility, or activities for you to do with your child that would be progressed as therapy goals are reached. Families may need to look into local availability of swimming classes, YMCA teams or classes, hippotherapy (adapted therapy on horseback), and community programs that offer a variety of individual or team sports or classes (chess, cards, Tae Kwon Do, etc.) to keep your child active socially and physically with other children. Your physical therapist will need to evaluate and discuss with you which programs, community skills, equipment, exercises, transfers, and mobility training would benefit your child, as well as how frequently to do them.

■■ Finding the Right Physical Therapist for Your Child

Parents sometimes feel the need to find a private physical therapist for their child. Perhaps they think that their child might benefit from working on nonschool-related skills, want ideas for strengthening their child at home, or wish additional therapy to complement the program at school.

One way to find a qualified therapist is to call the National Spina Bifida Association and ask whether your state has a spina bifida clinic and where it is located. Most states have at least one pediatric hospital in which a spina bifida clinic may be located. A clinical PT associated with a spina bifida center or spina bifida team should have a comprehensive grasp of the issues related to working with your child. He or she will have seen many children with spina bifida, and should be familiar with the wide range of abilities and problems that can occur. Contact the clinic coordinator or call the physical therapy department and ask to speak to the therapist assigned to the clinic or to someone who has experience working with children with spina bifida. If this hospital is far from where you live, ask the therapist to recommend a pediatric physical therapist near you who has worked with children with spina bifida.

Many physical therapists have had experience working with children, but may never have worked with a child with spina bifida. If you are unable to find a therapist with experience working with spina bifida, a therapist who has advanced clinical degrees in pediatrics or neurodevelopmental treatment (N.D.T.) would be helpful. You may wish to call the American Physical Therapy Association and ask for the Pediatric Section to get a referral near your community (see the Resource Guide). You can find the names of physical therapists in the yellow pages, and your county board of MRDD (Mental Retardation/ Developmental Disabilities) or a local chapter of Easter Seals or United Cerebral Palsy may also assist you.

◼◼ Conclusion

Your child may learn to move or perform self-help skills differently than children who do not have nerve and muscle changes. However, the goal of learning to do things independently is the same for your child as it is for all growing children. Your physical therapist can help you and your child learn skills and use strategies to reach specific goals.

◼◼ Parent Statements

Abby receives OT and PT in school. Whenever we face a challenge, the therapists help me and Abby work out a way that allows Abby the opportunity to do things for herself.

◈

Our daughter has been in a body brace and a hip spica cast (a cast that goes from the ankle up the hip in one leg and around the entire waist) at different points in her life. I never imagined that she would have any mobility in these restrictive devices, but she surprised me and was able to crawl and sit up in them.

◈

I think it's good not to have extremely high and unrealistic expectations for your child, but you should also maximize the opportunity to help them achieve what they can (don't restrict them).

◈

I am discouraged by the horrific price mark-up on the assistive equipment my child needs. There should be a law!

❧

Brian started using a wheelchair due to surgery on his legs and skin breakdown. There are advantages to using a wheelchair like speed and freeing his hands so he can pick up or carry things. Brian prefers a wheelchair at school. At other times it is more convenient for him to use crutches because it's easier for him to get in and out of cars and up and down steps. We're fortunate that Brian has the option of using either a wheelchair or crutches.

❧

Kari was about 10 years old when I began to notice that most of her energy was going into ambulation so that she was too tired to carry books and do other activities. By the time she was 13, she had transitioned full-time to the use of a wheelchair. Kari seemed thankful to have the use of her arms back.

❧

*The therapist thought Will was heavy enough and could sit up enough to propel himself in a wheelchair. I was glad for him but it was hard at first for me to see Will in the wheelchair because it meant he wasn't going to walk. I hadn't had false hopes that he **would** walk, but this made it so final.*

❧

Although my son can walk, I've been considering a wheelchair for when we're at the mall, the zoo, or an amusement park, etc. We would keep it in the car so he wouldn't become dependent on it. It would strictly be for those times when walking would be too tiring for him.

10

OTHER MEDICAL CONCERNS

Roberta E. Bauer, M.D.
Geri S. Pallija, R.N., M.S.N., C.S.
Renee S. Rodrigues, M.D.

Many of the preceding chapters have discussed medical concerns unique to children with spina bifida or other spinal cord injuries. However, children with spina bifida also have medical issues common to all children, and some children with spina bifida have medical complications not directly related to spinal cord dysfunction. This chapter covers these concerns, as well as factors to consider in selecting and working with medical professionals.

▪▪ Routine Medical Care

Despite the number of chapters in this book devoted to possible medical complications of spina bifida, there is some good news. Children with spina bifida have normal immune systems. That is, with proper immunizations, they are no more likely than any other child to come down with childhood illnesses or community acquired infections, and they can recover just as quickly.

Like other children, children with spina bifida can receive their routine medical care from a physician in their community. Choosing your child's physician, however, is an important decision. The physician does not have to be an expert on spina bifida, as your child's general pediatric care will be the same as that needed by any child. He or she does, however, need to be comfortable with evaluating your child for problems related to spina bifida. The doctor should also be comfortable working with the spina bifida team professionals to help with those evaluations (see below). This is because the physical changes that come with spina bifida are lifelong and will present different challenges as your child ages. For example, there are no cures for lack of sensation or for bowel and bladder incontinence, and there will always be a need to check for medical complications of these problems.

Ideally, you should choose a physician who is willing to work as part of a team to give your child the best care. You may want to consider issues such as wheelchair accessibility of the office or restrooms. Other considerations might be whether or not the physician is a provider for your insurance company or for the special insurance or assistance programs available to children with disabilities. In addition, it is important to find a doctor who will be able to direct you to other specialists to answer questions he or she can not address. Above all, you should look for someone you can trust who treats you and your child with respect and who welcomes your questions.

The members of your spina bifida team may be able to suggest primary care physicians near you who are experienced in the care of children with spina bifida or who are recommended by other families. Local medical associations, public health nurses, and local hospitals often can provide a list of physicians who are accepting new patients. You may also wish to talk with other families in your local spina bifida association or support group for recommendations.

Immunizations

Immunizations are important for preserving health and preventing diseases caused by infections. Having spina bifida does not interfere with the immunization series or schedule in any way. Prior to leaving the hospital, your baby can have her first immunization against hepatitis, as recommended, and then continue the series.

At 2, 4, and 6 months, the basic immunizations against diphtheria, whooping cough (pertussis), tetanus, polio, pneumococcus, and hemophilus influenza can be given. The measles, mumps, and rubella (MMR) and chicken pox (varicella) vaccines can be given after one year of age. If your child has airway problems that would make influenza a more serious illness for her, your doctor may suggest influenza immunizations every year during flu season.

Initially, immunization injections are given in the thigh. Your child might not feel the shots if the nerves that carry sensation to the thigh are affected by her spina bifida. If the lack of sensation begins lower on the leg, she will probably protest as most children do when they receive injections.

Your Child's Growth

Your physician will monitor your child's growth by measuring her weight, height, and head circumference at each visit.

Height

Your doctor will measure your baby's length to help track the appropriateness of growth. When children grow in length, what is actually producing most of the change is the growth of bones in the back or spine and in the long bones of the legs. Children with spina bifida have differences in the formation of the vertebra, or back bones, that change how they grow. They have a much higher risk of having curving (kyphosis) or twisting (scoliosis) of the back bones, which changes the rate at which length or height increases (see Chapter 8). Because the bones themselves formed differently where the birth defect occurred, those vertebrae may grow differently too. The growth rate of the legs is also affected when the nervous system control is abnormal. For complicated reasons, paralyzed legs grow more slowly and reach shorter lengths in adulthood. The net effect of these differences is that children with spina bifida are often shorter than would be expected based on nutrition, growth hormones, and genetics.

Your physician may choose to plot your child's arm span (comparable to height but not affected by spina bifida bony changes) on the growth curves to help track normal growth rates. Sometimes a bone age is determined by taking an x-ray of the bones in the hand and wrist. If shorter stature is being caused by hormonal or nutritional problems, your child's bone age will be younger than her actual age. Further evaluations would then be necessary to address this type of growth problem.

Children with spina bifida are at higher risk for some hormonal changes that can also affect height. First, changes produced by hydrocephalus may be responsible for resetting the timing of the onset of puberty. If your child begins developing breasts, acne, or pubic hair earlier than expected in your family's history, the doctor may suggest evaluations for *precocious puberty*, and medications may be prescribed to delay the completion of puberty. The hormones of puberty are actually the messengers to the growth plates in bones which tell them to stop growing. So, if children with spina bifida do enter puberty earlier than other children, they may have fewer growing years. This can also result in shortening their adult heights.

The second hormonal change that can affect height involves human growth hormone. This is a chemical produced in the brain. The control of its production is complicated and can be affected by the changes that come with spina bifida. If your child's length, arm span, or bone age is coming along at a slower rate than expected, your doctor may evaluate whether human growth hormone is being produced appropriately. If there is a deficiency of human growth hormone, it can be replaced by regular injections under careful physician monitoring until puberty occurs.

Weight

Watching your baby's weight gain helps assure that she is getting enough calories to have the energy to grow and develop. Breast milk

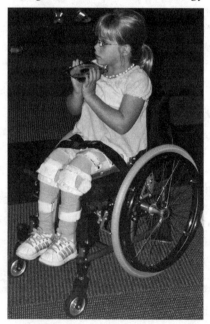

and infant formula that contains iron, vitamins, and calories provide your child with absorbable iron to build blood cells and prevent low blood counts, or anemia. Waiting until four months to start solids will help your baby get a good start nursing or taking formula before she develops the ability to move solids around in her mouth to swallow.

As your child grows older, promoting growth but preventing obesity becomes especially important. Obesity has unwanted effects on the cardiovascular system and on metabolism for all of us. In a child who needs to use her upper extremities to weight-bear on crutches, the elbows and shoulders need to support more force than nature and evolution ever prepared them for. Unnecessary weight can add even further stress to those joints.

If your child uses a wheelchair for mobility, she uses fewer calories than she would in standing and walking. This makes monitoring calorie intake very important. Likewise, if your child is making the transition from walking with braces and crutches to using a wheelchair for more of her mobility, calorie intake will need to be decreased to prevent excess weight gain. In addition, it is wise to monitor weight gain if your child's activity level drops after surgical procedures or while bracing adjustments are necessary.

A nutritionist or dietitian can help determine what your child needs to eat to maintain nutrition without gaining excess weight. To determine a healthy diet and activity level for your child, the nutritionist may recommend special measurements of skin fold thickness and fat accumulation, as well as blood tests that help determine rates of metabolism. Finally, it will be vital to help your child develop the lifelong habit of finding enjoyable activities to maintain fitness and to help burn calories.

Head Circumference

Your physician will measure your baby's head circumference on a regular basis. Under normal circumstances, head growth is caused by cell division and growth of the brain expanding in volume inside the skull. The head circumference grows most quickly during the first three months after birth, slows a bit over the next three months, and then slows a bit more over the next six months. Then, once the soft spots or fontanelles have closed, head circumference changes at a much slower rate. These predictable rates of change are reflected on the growth curves for head circumference that were determined for children who did not have hydrocephalus.

If your baby has hydrocephalus, the fluid accumulation may have expanded her head circumference before birth. Once the shunt is in place, your baby will have some room inside her skull to allow the developing brain to grow; therefore, for a time after hydrocephalus surgery, head circumference may not change. If it continues to grow at a faster rate than expected for her age, your physicians may be concerned that the shunt is not functioning properly. To determine whether normal brain growth and healing are occurring, the doctors may order CT scans or MRIs which show the developmental changes that typically occur as a child gains more control over posture and voluntary use of her body. (See Chapter 5 for more information on CT scans and MRIs.)

If your baby does not have hydrocephalus that requires a shunt, your doctors will still pay very close attention to changes in head circumference. They will also examine fontanelle tension and your baby's eye movements and appearance to assure that pressures inside the skull remain normal.

Other variables affecting head size include genetic influences and factors that affect when the bones in the skull fuse together and stop growing. Sometimes the pressure inside the skull spreads the bones farther apart from each other than usual. The fontanelles may also remain open longer than in children who never had increased pressure caused by hydrocephalus.

Because of all of these issues, your physicians will carefully monitor your child's head circumference. They may also show you how to measure head circumferences to help them monitor possible changes that may suggest problems with the shunt.

Fevers

All babies get especially close attention if they develop fevers. Like any baby, your child should be seen by a physician if she is younger than two months old and has a rectal temperature of 100.4 degrees Fahrenheit (38 degrees Celsius) or higher. Your doctor may also ask to see your child beyond this age if she develops a fever. You should definitely call your doctor if your child has a fever and:

- is difficult to arouse;
- does not seem fully conscious of her surroundings;
- is unable to eat or drink; or
- seems to be suffering from headache, stiff neck, or severe abdominal pain.

Children with spina bifida may develop infections from shunts and/or bladders that do not empty completely. Your doctor will want to make certain that infections involving your child's shunt, urine, or skin do not exist. If your child's fever is persistent or if your child seems especially ill, the physician might order blood work, urine catheterization for culture, and even take fluid from the shunt.

Fever is one way the body protects itself against germs, and it is a sign that the body's defenses are in action. Fever can make babies uncomfortable and fussy, though. It is safe to give your child medication to relieve fever symptoms even while you are calling the doctor to find out the cause of the temperature. However, first record the temperature, then give your child the appropriate dose of acetaminophen or ibuprofen recommended for her weight. Aspirin is not recommended for children with fevers because of an illness called Reye's syndrome that gets worse when aspirin is given.

Always measure your child's temperature with a thermometer. Merely feeling the skin is not an accurate way to determine whether there is a problem with the entire body's heat regulation. Your child's body sends heat to the skin to get rid of it, and sometimes the skin will feel warm to the touch even though no fever or infection is present. Measuring the temperature inside the body (by ear, mouth, or rectum) is the best way to detect a temperature elevation that needs investigation.

∷ Childhood Illnesses

As discussed in Chapter 6, the only childhood illnesses that children with spina bifida are more likely to have are bladder and kidney infections. Otherwise, children with spina bifida are not any more likely than other children to *get* typical childhood illnesses such as ear infections or the flu. *Recovering* from colds or the flu, however, may take longer for some children with very high lesions. This is because the muscles controlling breathing can be affected in a way that makes it more difficult to clear secretions and cough. Most children with spina bifida, however, do not have any respiratory changes that interfere with recovering from colds or the flu.

Skin Injuries

Your child can be at risk for certain kinds of injuries to the areas of her skin that are *insensate*—that have minimal or no feeling. First, your child can develop skin infections that she may not notice because they do not hurt or itch in the areas where her nerves do not sense pain. If skin is scratched or cut over areas that lack sensation, be sure to wash and clean the area well. Using a triple antibiotic ointment may help to avoid infection.

Burns

Insensate areas of the skin are more easily burned, even by temperatures that would not cause injury to skin with normal sensation and circulation. You may wish to lower the temperature on your water heater in your home to avoid the scalding temperatures that could produce burns in bath water. Certainly, you should always check the water temperature with your own hand before placing your baby's feet or body in the water. You should also teach your child to check temperatures with her own hand before placing her feet on hot surfaces. Checking visually for skin injuries over insensate areas should become a part of your child's daily hygiene routine just like washing behind her ears.

All children should wear sunscreen to protect against ultraviolet rays that cause sunburn now and skin cancers in the future. Wearing protective clothing such as kneepads or water shoes over skin that may be injured during crawling or swimming is also advisable.

Frostbite

Frostbite can occur more easily in the winter because your child will not feel the discomfort of cold feet that are becoming injured by frigid temperatures. Blood circulation increases when movement occurs, and if the nerves do not allow movement, your child does not have that defense against frostbite either. To help your child avoid frostbite:

1. avoid long outdoor exposures to winter temperatures;
2. have her wear layers of warm clothing to help insulate her body from cold and keep the warmth inside;
3. help her carefully warm up when back inside.

If your child's skin appears white and cold and is not returning to normal color with return of warmth inside, elevate her feet to body level. Add warm swaddling clothes around the feet to encourage blood supply to the area. If color does not improve in fifteen minutes, even with warm clothes, exposure to normal inside temperatures, and elevation, your child may need further evaluation and treatment by medical personnel. Skin care is covered in more detail in the section on "Pressure Sores," on page 167.

Fractures

As children grow taller and heavier, the force of weight being carried by the bones is the body's signal to send more calcium to add thickness to bones. Your child may therefore break bones in her lower extremities more easily if they are not strengthened by normal weight bearing. Even if your child will likely use a wheelchair for most of her mobility, your doctors and therapists may suggest a bracing and standing program during her growing years to help the bones develop appropriately. This is discussed more fully in Chapter 9.

If your child fractures a bone in an area where she does not have feeling, she may not have any complaints. The only sign that something is wrong might be warmth or swelling over the area. Even if your child is not experiencing any pain, your doctor will want to check for broken bones so that they can be splinted or casted to help them heal. See Chapters 8 and 9 for more information on the treatment of fractures.

:: Specialized Medical Care

Although a pediatrician will be able to handle much of your child's routine medical care, your child will have some medical needs that are outside of the expertise of a pediatrician. Most children with spina bifida see a *multidisciplinary team* to look after these specialized needs. A multidisciplinary team is a group of physicians and health care professionals with different areas of expertise who assess the needs of children with spina bifida on a regular basis. This team provides care that looks at the whole child and prevents any duplication of services, thereby also providing cost-effective and preventative care. A visit to each physician individually would be very time-consuming as well as costly in terms of loss of work for parents.

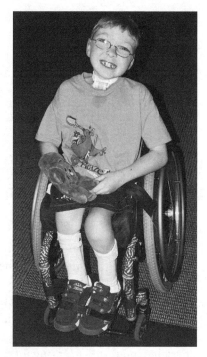

Most major medical centers that have pediatric units have spina bifida clinics (sometimes called myelodysplasia or myelomeningocele clinics) where your child can be seen by a multidisciplinary team. To locate a team in your state, contact the national Spina Bifida Association listed in the Resource Guide at the end of this book.

The Multidisciplinary Team

Teams may be made up of slightly different specialists according to people's availability and interest, but they usually consist of the following team members:

- Developmental Pediatrician
- Nurse
- Urologist
- Social Worker
- Neurosurgeon/Neurologist
- Physical Therapist
- Orthopedist
- Occupational Therapist
- Speech Therapist
- Gastroenterologist
- Physiatrist
- Dietitian
- Vocational Rehabilitation Counselor

Consultation should also be available with:

- Ophthalmologist
- Psychologist
- Allergist
- Pulmonologist
- Geneticist
- Orthotics
- Enterostomal Therapist
- Equipment Providers

A *Developmental Pediatrician* is a pediatric doctor who has additional training in child development and pays particular attention to how the child grows and attains skills through physical, intellectual, emotional, and social development. This doctor is often the director of the team and coordinates care with the other specialists. The role of clinic director can also be filled by a physiatrist (see below) or another physician interested in caring for people who have spina bifida.

A *Urologist* is a surgeon with specialized training in the function of the kidneys, ureters, and bladder, as well as the parts of the reproductive system. Preventing and treating urinary tract infections, preserving kidney function, and helping your child achieve urinary continence are all areas the urologist specializes in.

A *Neurosurgeon* is a surgeon with specialized training in the structure of the brain and surgical procedures necessary to maintain the health of the brain and spinal cord. The neurosurgeon closes the skin over the back to protect the spinal cord from further damage or from infection in the initial hours after birth and evaluates whether shunting for hydrocephalus is necessary. He or she helps to assess the way the shunt is working as your child grows and replaces or repairs shunts that are not relieving hydrocephalus. If your child needs any surgeries related to the skull bones or the spinal cord, the neurosurgeon will be in charge or involved. This doctor diagnoses and treats problems related to Arnold-Chiari malformation and tethered spinal cord. For more information on neurosurgeons, see Chapter 5.

A *Neurologist* is a doctor with specialized training in how the brain functions and in the treatment of any disorders of the brain from a medical perspective. He or she diagnoses and treats seizure disorders, headaches, or other brain dysfunctions. This doctor may also provide medications and interventions for children with increased muscle tone, or spasticity.

An *Orthopedist* is a surgeon with specialized training in bone, muscle, and tendon structure and function. This doctor assesses your child's hips, legs, ankles, and feet function in order to make recommendations for bracing and subsequent standing and walking. He or she keeps a careful eye on the spine for signs of curvature and on the hips to assure that the bones are in appropriate positions to support weight. Your orthopedist can help to explain when walking is expected and how much bracing or assistance with equipment will be needed. He or she will work closely with the therapists and the orthotists, especially while your child is growing and her needs are changing rapidly. Chapter 8 provides more information on orthopedists.

A *Gastroenterologist* is a doctor who has additional training in how the digestive system works and has expertise in bowel management issues, feeding concerns, and treatment of digestive tract problems. He or she can prescribe medications to help with heartburn or constipation and can diagnose and treat stones in the gallbladder and problems with malabsorption or diarrhea. On some teams, these issues are addressed instead by the pediatrician or other specialists.

A *Physiatrist* is a doctor who has specialized training in physical medicine and rehabilitation techniques. He or she shares expertise in bracing and equipment adaptations with the orthopedic surgeons and orthotists. This doctor has a good understanding of what therapists can do with exercise, electrical stimulation, and ultrasound to help with pain or muscle imbalances. A physiatrist works with therapists as part of a team to help children learn skills that will enable them to function in their environments.

The team *Nurse* is familiar with each of the medical issues related to spina bifida and provides families with additional information and coordination of care to meet their needs. The nurse can be an important link to various resources both within the hospital and out in the community.

The *Social Worker* can help families learn to cope with issues that arise related to raising a child with a chronic condition. He or she also helps families locate resources to assist in caring for their child. Like the nurse and the team director, the social worker helps to ensure that the whole child is not forgotten in our efforts to attend to the health of each body system.

The *Physical Therapist* (PT) specializes in helping children improve their gross motor skills—the skills such as sitting and walking that involve large muscles of the body. The PT will teach the parents exercises to stretch their child's muscles and keep them working together equally. He or she will evaluate timing and necessity of bracing and will consult with your physicians about the need for prescriptions for devices such as wheelchairs, crutches, walkers, standing devices, etc. The PT will then teach you and your child how to use this equipment. Sometimes a PT evaluates the child and then a physical therapy assistant carries out the recommendations of the PT. This most often occurs in the school setting, where PTs may just see your child intermittently when changes in educational or therapy goals are needed. See Chapter 9 for more information on physical therapists and physical therapy.

The *Occupational Therapist* (OT) specializes in helping children improve their fine motor skills—skills such as writing or using a spoon that involve small muscles of the body. The OT will evaluate how your child uses her upper extremities, head, and neck. He or she will teach the parent and the child exercises to help improve function and coordination of eye/hand movements. The OT can be especially helpful in adapting tools or clothing to allow your child to become increasingly independent in self-care tasks such as dressing, feeding, toileting, recreation, and activities of daily living.

The *Speech-Language Pathologist* (SLP) evaluates and treats problems with speech (producing and combining sounds to make words) as well as language (how the child takes in information and expresses herself). Sometimes children with spina bifida and/or hydrocephalus experience learning difficulties, and the SLP can help in assessing memory, language processing, and attention.

The *Dietitian* or *Nutritionist* evaluates nutrition and makes recommendations for changes to promote optimal health, prevent obesity, and manage constipation.

A *Vocational Rehabilitation Counselor* evaluates adolescents to see what their interests and skills are. He or she works with the adolescent to determine career goals and identify additional training or available educational opportunities.

An *Ophthalmologist* is a surgeon with specialized training in how the eye functions. He or she evaluates vision and diagnoses and treats eye disease and vision problems. The ophthalmologist can prescribe glasses and perform operations to assist with aligning and maintaining the health of the eyes.

A *Psychologist* is a nonmedical professional who is trained to evaluate mental processes and provide therapy or counseling to help with these processes. He or she can perform formal psychological testing to help determine the best classroom setting for your child. Psychologists can also advise parents on how to deal with problems in behavior, as well as help family members understand their feelings and how those feelings and beliefs affect behavior.

An *Allergist* is a doctor with additional training in evaluating and managing allergies. Some of these physicians are pulmonary (lung) specialists; others study immunology and how the body's defenses work. Children with spina bifida who develop serious reactions when exposed to latex (see below) often benefit from the expertise of allergists.

A *Pulmonologist* is a doctor with additional training in the evaluation and treatment of disorders related to breathing. If symptoms of Chiari II malformation are interfering with the regularity of your child's breathing when she is awake or asleep, a pulmonologist can provide helpful recommendations to minimize the effects of irregular breathing. A pulmonologist can also help determine the best timing of scoliosis surgery if curvature of the spine interferes with the space available to take deep breaths.

A *Geneticist* is a doctor with additional training in conditions that are determined by our genes. He or she helps identify genetic conditions and also counsels families about the risk of recurrence of neural tube defects or spina bifida in subsequent pregnancies. Chapter 2 describes genetic counseling in more detail.

An *Orthotist* is a professional who specializes in creating, building, and fixing orthotic or bracing devices. He or she may also supply other helpful adaptive equipment. See Chapter 9 for more information.

An *Enterostomal Therapist* is usually a registered nurse with additional training related to ostomies, or openings (stomas), made into the body to assist with functions such as urination, bowel movements, etc. These therapists can help with skin care and can suggest products to help keep skin and stomas healthy.

Equipment Providers sell durable medical equipment, such as wheelchairs, crutches, adaptive equipment, home/vehicle modification devices, and medical care supplies.

Together the multidisciplinary team will be able to provide the best care for your child, since professionals with expertise in all of the disciplines that could help your child and family are available in one setting. If your child has a health problem, more than one of her body systems may be affected. It is therefore important that your child be seen in the team setting to assist with sorting out complex health care issues. Most spina bifida clinics try to make the clinic/team visit a "one stop" trip with x-rays, ultrasounds, diagnostic/laboratory tests, and patient education all scheduled in one day. For school-aged children, this makes for a long day at least once a year. For infants or toddlers, visits are usually more frequent to assess growth and development.

The multidisciplinary team usually has a coordinator who can assist you in planning for your child's assessment and make sure all necessary team members are available the day you visit the clinic. If there are particular professionals you feel your child needs to see, or you are not sure who to see, contact the coordinator to discuss this. The coordinator might also help make sure that your health insurance plan is followed if referrals are needed to see particular team members or if permission is needed to see those outside of a preferred provider list.

Often the team will provide your family with a copy of the clinic report. You may request a copy of this report for your own records. It may be helpful to keep a file of these reports to keep track of the names of your team members and also in case you need to share medical information about your child in another setting, such as an emergency room, at the school, or on vacation. If written goals for your child are not provided, it is a good idea to keep your own record of the visit and make a note of any tests, x-rays, or teaching that needs to occur on future visits. You may also write your questions down ahead of time and ask the clinic coordinator which professional could best address your concerns if you are not sure.

The section below discusses some of the medical concerns that may be addressed by your child's team. Other concerns typically managed by spina bifida teams are covered in Chapters 5, 6, 7, and 8.

▪▪ Special Medical Concerns

Latex and Other Allergies

Since World War II, products containing latex or rubber have improved the quality and performance of many items that we use daily. The medical field has benefited from the use of latex to advance standards of health care for us all. Sterile latex gloves have provided protection against bacterial and viral infections, saving millions of lives and improving our quality of life. Bladder infections and potentially life-threatening kidney infections have been reduced through the use of first metal, then latex catheters for intermittent catheterization. As with many medical advances, however, new problems have also been created.

As children with spina bifida were exposed to latex over time, some developed allergic reactions to the protein contained in the latex. These reactions included hives (large, red, swollen areas on the skin); a severe drop in blood pressure, resulting in "light-headedness" or even fainting; and swelling of the breathing passages. In the mid-1980s, medical professionals became aware of the connection between latex and some life-threatening, severe allergic reactions that occurred during surgery.

Prevention of Latex Allergies

Allergic reactions to latex can now be avoided by providing a latex-free environment in the hospital, the operating room, the child's home, and in the community. Many hospitals, especially those that specifically care for children, have changed to latex-free products and procedures to protect those who are sensitive to latex. If your child has experienced symptoms related to latex exposure, check with your hospital to find out what its specific latex protocols are and be sure all health professionals who care for your child are aware of this sensitivity.

Any child with spina bifida is at risk of developing an allergy to latex and should avoid it both in the hospital and where possible in the community. It is especially important to avoid latex products that are placed in the mouth, bladder, or rectum, where contact with mucous membranes (the lining of the body) occurs. The latex protein is easily absorbed into the blood stream from mucous membrane, and this greatly increases the likelihood of developing an allergy to latex.

If your child is not allergic to latex, preventing exposure can help ensure that she does not become allergic. Latex gloves and party balloons are the most common items that cause allergic reactions. Rubber urinary catheters and enema catheters can also cause problems, as can pacifiers or nipples on baby bottles. Toys made of rubber, including basketballs or Koosh balls (toys with spider-like rubber projections), can produce skin reactions. You can obtain lists of items containing latex, as well as latex-free alternatives, by contacting the Spina Bifida Association of America.

Precautions for Children with Latex Allergies

If you think that your child has had a reaction to latex, make an appointment to see an allergist. He or she can determine whether an allergy exists and prescribe any treatment or preventative measures your child may need. Also make sure that your child has a medical alert bracelet or tag identifying her latex allergy in case she is not able to give that history and you are not with her at the time of medical care. Carrying an emergency kit with non-latex gloves and antihistamines, such as diphenhydramine, is very useful. Some children need to carry a syringe of epinephrine (Epi-Pen™) with them at all times to be given if they come in contact with latex and have a severe reaction. Your family and child (if appropriate) should be taught how to give the epinephrine and to recognize when it is needed.

Ask if there is a policy regarding latex precautions wherever your child receives care, be it a hospital, dentist's office, emergency room, orthotist shop, school, camp, or through your local paramedic or ambulance service. If there is not, assume that the staff is unaware of this issue. Be ready to provide education and also protection for your child by carrying latex-free gloves and closely monitor products used in the care of your child. You may want to phone ahead and ask to have the first appointment of the day. Also ask whether the room has been wet-dusted in the cleaning process.

Food Allergies

The proteins in rubber that cause an allergic reaction are similar in structure to the proteins found in some tropical fruits. Bananas seem to cause the most common *cross-reaction* (an allergic-like reaction to a substance similar to one that the body is sensitive to). Kiwi fruit, papaya, passion fruit, avocados, and chestnuts may also cause a reaction in people with latex allergies, just to name a few.

Swelling of the lips and mouth, along with itching of the roof of the mouth, are symptoms of a reaction. The over-the-counter medication Benadryl™ or diphenhydramine may be given to alleviate mild symptoms. Follow the instructions on the label for your child's age and weight. This medication may make your child sleepy. Call 911 immediately if your child has difficulty breathing. Alert your physician to any prolonged reactions after eating one of these fruits.

If true latex allergic symptoms occur after eating any of these fruits, your child should avoid them. Also check the content label on fruit juice mixtures, as many include tropical fruits that may not be listed on the front label. If your child has had a reaction to any fruits on the list, it probably is best to avoid the others until you have had allergy testing.

Taking Allergies Seriously

Remember, if your child swells severely, wheezes, or has trouble breathing after touching or being near latex products, she needs immediate medical attention and access to epinephrine. Call 911 or go immediately to the nearest emergency room. Latex allergy is lifelong and can be a life-threatening problem once developed. Preventing an allergy from developing by avoiding exposures during surgery or medical or dental procedures is in your child's best interest.

Pressure Sores

Pressure sores occur when skin breaks down on an area of the body. Usually pressure sores occur due to friction or prolonged pressure on an area where a child has impaired sensation to the skin. Often they occur over a bony prominence, such as the ankle, heel, or buttocks. Your child's first pressure sore may occur with new braces that rub and wear a hole in the skin over the ankle or heel, or with shoes that become too small and rub the toes. These sores usually are not severe and generally do not require antibiotic therapy. Discontinuing the braces until healing occurs and then altering the bracing so that the rubbing does not occur usually solves the problem.

Prevention of Pressure Sores

The take-home message here is that daily inspection of your child's skin is critical to ensure that nothing she wears is too tight or pinches her in areas of the body that she cannot feel. This also applies to the waist line, especially over the bony spine area, and the groin area where a diaper may become too tight. Teaching your child to check those places with you is an important part of self-care, just like taking a bath or brushing her teeth. Have your child use her sense of touch for the areas of her body that she cannot see. As she becomes older, also teach her to use mirrors to inspect parts of her body that are harder to see to check for any areas where the skin is broken, reddened, or bruised.

If your child spends much time in a wheelchair, proper seating to distribute her weight and prevent pressure on the buttocks or lower spine area is very important. The company that provides your child's wheelchair may have *pressure mapping* available to help ensure proper weight distribution in the seat. Pressure mapping is done with a pressure-sensitive seat/back pad that will diagram the areas of the body where the pressure is most intense (such as the *ischium* or lower part of the hip bone). Once those areas are identified, supports can be added to the chair to reduce pressure to those vulnerable areas. Specially molded seating tailored to your child's anatomy can be made to lessen the likelihood of developing pressure sore areas.

Equally important, you need to teach your child to frequently change position while sitting. Your child should shift her weight at least every half-hour. Wheelchair push-ups are a good way to keep the blood flow to the buttocks adequate and to prevent pressure sores. Your child should learn to support herself with hands on the wheelchair armrests, extending her arms with her body up and off of her chair for a slow count to ten. Wheelchair push-ups should be done at least every hour. This means that the armrests need to be on the wheelchair at all times. If the armrests are in the way when your child is propelling the chair herself, then the seat position is inappropriate and needs adjustment. The armrests are really important in assisting your child to change position.

Some families use a wristwatch and set the alarm to go off about every 20 minutes to remind their child to change position. Other ways to remember are with each television commercial or with every change of class in school. Your child will probably remember best if she is involved in deciding what the cue will be to remind her to change her position in the chair. Any area that remains red after 20 minutes of pressure relief is a problem area, and your child should stay off of that area as much as possible.

Treatment of Pressure Sores

Pressure sores on the buttocks are more serious than elsewhere on the body. One reason is that the child needs to stay off the area completely by lying on her stomach or her side until the wound is healed. This is very difficult to do in a busy family setting, in which both parents work and school attendance is necessary. The other reason is that pressure sores on the buttocks are more easily infected. Bowel and bladder incontinence can lead to bacteria getting into the open area, and the underlying tissues, muscle, and bone may become infected over time if healing does not occur.

Treating pressure sores on the buttocks may require extensive surgery. The surgeon may need to rotate a flap of skin from the area beside the pressure sore to cover it with healthy skin and also bring along the underlying muscle and connective tissue layers to provide some muscle padding to protect the bony prominence area. It is an extensive surgery and cannot be done repeatedly. In severe cases, the deep infections may get into the bloodstream or underlying bones, requiring long-term IV antibiotics.

Preventing pressure sores on the buttock area is extremely important to your child's health. Remember: changing position frequently is the main way to prevent pressure sores. Your child should also eat a healthy diet and maintain a weight that is appropriate for her age and height in order to keep her skin healthy and assist with healing. Your therapists and equipment providers can help to assure that braces and equipment fit well and are well maintained. This can help to stop pressure area problems before they become serious.

Common Eye Problems

As infants, our vision develops as both eyes aim at the same spot at the same time. These two images are than fused by the brain into a single three-dimensional image, which gives a perception of depth to what we see. To get this clear, three-dimensional image, our eye muscles must work together to focus on the same image.

During the first two or three months of life, it is common for one or both of a baby's eyes to turn in or out once in a while, giving the impression of crossed or wandering eyes. This is believed to be caused by the immaturity of the infant's central nervous system and usually stops occurring by six months of age.

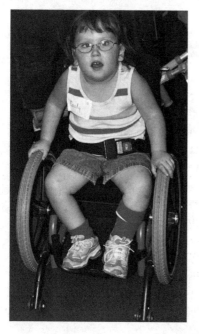

If eyes continue to be misaligned (point in different directions) after the age of three months, a condition called *strabismus* may be present. In *esotropia*, the most common form of misalignment, one eye turns inward. In *exotropia*, one eye turns outward. When one eye turns inward or outward, two different pictures are sent to the brain—one from the straight eye, and one from the misaligned eye. After a time, the brain starts ignoring one of the images and then sees only the image from the dominant eye. This helps the child to see clearly again, but it also causes her to lose depth perception. This condition is called *amblyopia*.

Strabismus occurs in 3 to 4 percent of the general population and is most commonly seen in children under the age of 6 years. About 50 percent of these children have a family history of strabismus. In children with spina bifida who have hydrocephalus, strabismus is much more common than usual. Some studies have shown that the number may be as high as 30 to 60 percent. Six muscles control our eye movements, and anything that interferes with that muscle coordination can interfere with how our eye muscles work together. Children with hydrocephalus are more prone to eye muscle disorders since the cranial nerves that control the muscles may be affected by the increased pressure within the brain and skull.

Treatment for strabismus usually involves placing a patch over the dominant eye, forcing the child's brain to pick up the image from the misaligned eye. If patching is begun early enough, strabismus may not progress to amblyopia. If patching does not improve the condition, surgery may be required to help align the eye muscles.

During surgery, the tension of the eye muscles in one or both eyes may be adjusted, so that the muscles can work in a coordinated fashion. Under general anesthesia, the surgeon makes a small incision in the covering of the eye to reach the muscles that attach to the sides, top, or bottom of the eye. The eye is not removed from the socket. Recovery time is rapid in children, and they are able to resume normal activities within several days. When surgery is done early on, it is usually successful in aligning the eyes. Sometimes, however, further surgery may be needed later in order to keep the eye muscles in alignment.

If your child is suspected of having strabismus, she should be seen by an ophthalmologist. Your ophthalmologist will discuss the appropriate treatment for your child's condition and any complications that may occur. Your spina bifida team can make a recommendation to you for a referral.

Premature Puberty

Some children with hydrocephalus begin to go through puberty earlier than usual. If your daughter develops breast buds before the age of eight or your son begins to get acne or chest or groin hair before age nine, discuss this with your physician. Hormones can be given to delay the maturation process and allow puberty to occur at a time closer to that of your child's peers. Lupron or leuprolide acetate can be given by injection every four weeks to block the naturally occurring gonadotropin releasing hormone in your child's system that is causing the early maturation. A pediatric endocrinologist can order blood tests to evaluate your child's hormone levels. He or she can also help you and your child decide whether to use hormones to help manage premature puberty.

Body Temperature Regulation

If your child's spina bifida causes a loss of body sensation in the abdomen or up into the chest area, a large proportion of her body surface area lacks sensation. If the skin lacks sensation, the body's ability to regulate its own temperature is also affected. One reason is because there is less control over the blood vessels that ordinarily get wider or smaller to help get rid of excess heat that the body produces. Children with spina bifida may also lose their ability to perspire in the same areas where feeling is lost. If a large proportion of your child's body is unable to perspire, she may have difficulty controlling her body temperature during heat waves. She just does not have as much functional skin to perspire and to dilate blood vessels to cool herself down effectively. She may have problems keeping her mind focused as her temperature rises or feel nauseated or weak. These symptoms can progress to the confusion or loss of consciousness of heat stroke if not properly treated.

If your child shows heat-related symptoms, move her to a cooler area, offer her a cool beverage, and sponge her skin with cool or room-temperature water to restore her normal temperature. If the symptoms persist or worsen, seek medical care.

If your child has problems with heat regulation, you will need to work with her school to make sure she is in an air conditioned class-room during hot weather. Also, you will need to make sure she is not sent outdoors to play when the temperature is too hot or too cold for her. You may need a note from your doctor to get the school to take you seriously about these issues.

Deep Vein Thrombosis

Another effect of lack of sensation is that there is decreased control over blood vessels that are controlled by the nerves. Less movement and less change in the blood vessels can lead to poorer circulation in the legs. When the blood pools in the legs and takes longer to return up to the circulation in the abdomen and on to the heart, there is a risk of some of the blood clotting in the slowest blood vessels. These vessels can actually become clogged in a way that does not let the blood flow through at all, resulting in a condition called *deep vein thrombosis*.

When veins become clogged, it is harder for blood to circulate through the tissues. That, in turn, makes it harder for wounds on the legs to heal and easier for pressure sores or infections to start. Sometimes tissues surrounding the clots may become inflamed, resulting in *phlebitis*.

Attention to positioning, range of motion, and proper fitting of seating and braces can all help to prevent these types of problems before they start. In addition, you should notify your physician if you notice poor color or swelling in your child's feet.

Phlebitis is typically treated with compression via surgical stock-ings, ambulation, anti-inflammatory medication, and possibly surgery to remove the clot. Thrombosis is identified with ultrasound imaging and is treated with anti-coagulation (blood-thinning) medications under the direction of a hematologist (physician who specializes in blood disorders).

Antibiotic Use

Antibiotics are medications used to treat bacterial infections. They can cause a variety of side effects. Some antibiotics give children looser bowel movements. They may also make it easier for yeast to grow in the mouth or diaper area, so an added medicine to combat yeast may need to be prescribed. In addition, antibiotics, like any medicine, can cause allergic reactions, such as hives, breathing difficulties, or rashes.

Side effects of antibiotics are no different in children with spina bifida than in other children. However, children with spina bifida may be treated more often with antibiotics than other children if they have frequent urinary tract infections or have had shunt or surgical infections (see Chapter 6 for more information on using antibiotics to prevent or treat urinary tract infections).

To minimize side effects from antibiotics, your physicians should take care to determine whether your child has an illness that is caused by bacteria by checking cultures or blood work. Your child should not be on antibiotics for a viral illness, since antibiotics treat bacterial infections only. When antibiotics *are* needed, you should ensure that your child takes them every day as prescribed until the course of medication is completed. This helps to lessen the likelihood that your child will become intolerant of the medicines and that the germs will become resistant to the effects of the medicine.

Seizures

Seizures are involuntary bodily movements, changes in consciousness, or both that are triggered by changes in electrical activity in the brain. Seizures occur in about 20 to 30 percent of children with spina bifida. If your child has a shunt that has repeatedly been modified, has had shunt infections, or has other structural changes in the brain in addition to hydrocephalus, she is more likely to fall into the group that experiences seizures. Children with spina bifida who do not have hydrocephalus and shunts have a 2 to 8 percent chance of having seizures.

Types of Seizures

There are many different types of seizures. The entire body can be involved, with rhythmic stiffening and flexing of the arms and legs followed by a period of unconsciousness or tiredness and weakness. These generalized or *tonic-clonic* (formerly called "grand mal") seizures are rarely mistaken for anything else. However, other types of seizures can be much more subtle. In focal or *myoclonic* seizures, just one extremity may twitch repeatedly and uncontrollably. A head bob followed by a loss of muscle tone may be a sign of *atonic* seizures if it is something that recurs. Eyes rolling to one side or upward when your child does not seem to be aware of what is happening around her can be a form of *akinetic* seizure. Staring spells that are associated with lapses in awareness can be an especially subtle form of seizure activity known as *absence* (or "petit mal") seizures.

No particular type of seizure is characteristic of hydrocephalus. There is also no set time that seizure disorders begin, although peaks of onset have been found around infancy and adolescence.

Diagnosis of Seizures

If your child is having unusual behaviors and does not seem to be making consistent progress in learning or awareness, your physician may consider seizures as a possibility. An *EEG* (electroencephalogram), or brain wave test, may be scheduled to look for seizure activity. Typically, sleep-deprived EEGs are ordered. This means your child will be asked to stay up late the night before the brainwave test and then to come to the EEG lab sleepy but awake. Sensor leads will be positioned over the scalp to detect changes in electrical activity in your child's brain below. No needles are used, but the leads will be applied with a sticky substance that will need to be washed out of your child's hair afterward. Your child will then be asked to lie still, and readings will be taken while she thinks and falls asleep. Your child may be asked to watch lights blinking rapidly at a regular rhythm or to breathe in and out rapidly in an attempt to induce hyperventilation. Both of these maneuvers can make some forms of seizures more likely to occur.

Although catching a seizure on the EEG is helpful for diagnosis, this actually happens infrequently. What is more typical is to find areas of the brain that give off irregular electrical activity that is out of sequence with the typical rhythms of activity found in the state of consciousness. If the patterns are noticeably different on the EEG, they may be helpful in diagnosing a possible seizure disorder. If the patterns are subtly different, your physician may ask to do a longer EEG while your child's behavior is videotaped. This requires hospital admission but allows for correlation of behavior with the electrical recording. Ambulatory EEGs can be conducted in the home. For this procedure, your child would have the leads placed on the scalp in the hospital and then be sent home with a backpack containing equipment to record electrical activity, usually for 24 hours. You could be asked to keep a diary of any unusual behavior. Both of these studies increase the chances of catching a seizure on EEG.

Treatment of Seizures

Sometimes seizures can be an early sign of shunt malfunction or infection. They can also be set off by an imbalance in the salts and minerals dissolved in the blood, or by bleeding or pressure inside the head. The new onset of seizures will therefore always prompt your physician to make sure that your child is otherwise healthy. If shunt problems and other problems are ruled out, your child will likely be evaluated by a neurologist. Often the neurologist will prescribe anticonvulsant medications to help reduce the frequency of seizures.

In many children, a single anticonvulsant medication will provide excellent control of seizures, reducing the frequency or eliminating seizures completely. Other children need higher doses of anticonvulsants or the addition of a second or third anticonvulsant. How well seizures can be controlled with medication is highly variable, depending on the kind of seizure and the underlying brain changes.

Anticonvulsants need to be taken regularly to keep the level of medication in your child's body consistent. Your physician may ask for blood levels (blood tests) to ensure that the amount of medicine is right for your child's weight and type of seizure. Other types of blood tests, such as liver function tests, blood cell counts, and salt levels, may also help ensure that your child is not experiencing side effects of the medications.

Side effects vary but may include liver injury, decreases in infection-fighting cells, low blood sodium, or changes in the way other medications are used up in the body. Most anticonvulsants make children a little sleepy, moody, or unsteady on their feet when they are not used to the medication in their systems. Your doctor will tell you which effects to expect for your child's anticonvulsant. Often, however, side effects are more noticeable in the first two weeks after medications are started and then become less bothersome. Long-term use of some anticonvulsants has been linked to learning changes in children with seizure disorders, so the goal is to control seizure frequency without sedating the child.

If your child's seizure disorder is very difficult or impossible to control with medication, your doctor may evaluate her to see whether a neurosurgical procedure might eliminate the seizure focus. The need for this type of operation is extremely rare and is certainly not a concern for most children with spina bifida who have seizures. Your neurologist will share information with you about the risks and benefits of surgery. An implanted device known as a vagus nerve stimulator (VNS) may also be an option. Your neurologist will discuss this device with you if it may be helpful for your child.

What to Do If Your Child Has a Seizure

You should ask your doctor for a prescription for rectal diazepam (Diastat™). This is a suppository that can be given on an emergency basis at home if a child has been seizing for more than 4 or 5 minutes. If the seizure continues, call 911 or go to the nearest emergency room. In addition, you should alert your physician if your child is experiencing a change in seizure frequency or type.

Otherwise, move your child to a safe place where she cannot fall or hurt herself. Turning her on her side helps to keep her tongue out of the airway and prevents choking if she happens to vomit. If she is having difficulty breathing, keep her airway open by tilting her head back and thrusting her lower jaw forward. Ask your child's physician to demonstrate this maneuver for you. Do not place anything in your child's mouth to hold her tongue down or keep her mouth open. Most seizures are self-limited (under 5 minutes), and the best course of action is to wait these out.

▉▉ Making Hospitalizations Easier for You and Your Child

Children with spina bifida must often make trips to the hospital, so it is important to help your child view these visits in a positive way. Because your child will follow your lead, what you say and do before and during her hospital stay are of utmost importance.

Preparing for a Hospital Stay

How soon you let your child know that she will be admitted depends upon her age. Toddlers do well with only a couple hours notice to prepare. Preschoolers should be told the day before with very brief explanations of what will occur. Elementary-school-aged children usually enjoy being included in the preparation a few days ahead of time and benefit from simplistic, honest information.

Remember, you know your child best, and you know how she handles change. If she acts anxious about going to the hospital, it may be because she wants to control her own life, not necessarily because she wants more information. Do not give her too much information that she may not understand. Your answers should be brief and honest.

If the operation will hurt, tell her so, with reassurance that she will be given medicine to help make the pain go away. Spend more time allowing her to ask questions and helping to pack.

Make sure your child picks out several of her favorite toys to take along. She will also need to take along her special security object if she has one. Taking their own pillow or pillow case often makes children feel more comfortable, especially if a parent cannot be with them at all times.

If your child is going to the hospital for a planned surgery, ask whether the hospital has tours for young children. These are often fun, hands-on experiences. Call well in advance to be sure you are able to participate. Often if parents and family members know what to expect, then their child is much more calm during the real thing.

While waiting for surgery in the preoperative area, your child may encounter a Child Life specialist. He or she can keep your child busy with reading, arts and crafts, and other activities and can also review with her what the sights, sounds, and sensations will be when she goes into the operating room. Often parents are able to accompany their child into the operating room and through the initial anesthesia. Your surgeon should be aware of the hospital's policy on parents in the operating room or refer you to the department of anesthesia to discuss this ahead of time.

Ask about visiting your child in the post-anesthesia room or recovery room. You may be the best person to calm your child if she is frightened when she awakes. If you yourself are very fearful of this type of situation, by all means, send in another family member who is more calm and comfortable. Your child will usually be given medication for pain and sometimes may sleep through the entire recovery period. When you are with your child, let her know you are there, and then sit with her quietly, or hold her if possible. Try not to stimulate her too much by talking or touching, since this may make her more fretful as she recovers from anesthesia.

In an Emergency

If your child is admitted to the hospital unexpectedly, there is little time for preparation. Try your best to stay calm and explain what is happening at your child's level of understanding. It is a good idea to keep your own record of your child's history, illnesses, surgeries, x-rays, tests, and hospitalizations in a notebook so that you can grab it as you leave for the hospital. Also include the names and phone numbers of each of your child's physicians. This is very helpful if you are going to a hospital where your child has not been seen before or if your child's medical record is not readily available for some reason. The notebook will also help you give an accurate history when things get busy. You can even give it to staff to copy so that you do not have to give each detail and can spend more time comforting your child.

Keeping Your Child Comfortable in the Hospital

When your child is spending several days in the hospital, you need to decide whether to stay with her at night. Whether you spend the night depends on your child's age and whether or not she is able to express her needs to staff. Where you stay, either in the child's room or a parent dorm, depends on your child's age and the reason for hospitalization. Sometimes, there is a small fee for a parent dorm and/or the requirement that you wash the linens and straighten the room prior to leaving. If you must return to work during the day, try to arrange for a relative to spend time with your child.

If you choose to remain with your child, you may participate in her care as you are able to. If you have spent the last several days and nights sleepless with a sick child and really do not feel like providing your child's bath, cathing, or bowel regimen, let the staff know that you would really prefer a break from this for a time. Some families prefer to give as much care as possible, and others view a hospital stay as a temporary rest from that part of care. Time can then be spent playing new games, reading stories, or catching up on homework. Talk this over with your child's nurse at the beginning of each shift to be sure there is no confusion as to who is responsible for your child's routine care.

If you must leave your child for a while and she can tell time, leave her a watch so she can keep track of when you will return. Encourage her to make friends with a nurse you trust who can keep an eye on your child in your absence. Make sure the staff knows where you can be reached at all times and when you will return. You can keep a tablet at the bedside to jot down this information for all to see. It also helps if you make a note of the names of each nurse caring for your child so that you can address them personally or ask for their assistance when necessary.

If your child is being admitted to a hospital associated with an academic institution (known as a "teaching hospital"), your child may also be cared for by medical residents. Residents are medical doctors who are undergoing training for their chosen career paths. Their supervising doctor is known as the attending physician. All of these doctors are committed to providing the best coordinated medical care possible for your child. They are there to answer your questions and assist you and your child throughout the hospital visit. They also remain in contact with your child's regular pediatrician. If any medical personnel do not introduce themselves, ask them what their names and roles are. This is common courtesy, and you should know who is caring for your child. Also, be sure that everyone who is caring for your child has proper identification.

Keeping Up with School Work

If your child is missing school, ask her teacher to send home the books and assignments. You can then bring the assignments to the hospital if your child is up to doing the work. There often is a teacher assigned to the hospital who can assist your child with school work. The hospital tutor will communicate with the school about your child's progress so that plans for additional educational needs can be developed. Your doctor needs to write an order for the teacher to see your child.

While your child is doing schoolwork, take the opportunity to have a break for yourself, visit friends, make phone calls, or visit the parent library, if there is one, to seek out information related to your child's condition. If your child is unable to attend school for more than a week or two, ask your doctor for a prescription for tutoring and to include an approximate date when your child will return to school.

Coping Emotionally

When your child's diagnosis is complex or when many physicians, each with a different opinion, come to see your child, things can become pretty tense and confusing as treatment options are being determined. If you find it overwhelming to try to absorb information from so many sources, you can ask that all information be relayed to you and your family by one physician with whom you have a good working relationship. If your primary care physician is the one who admitted your child, this usually works well. If a specialist on the team admitted your child and consulted the other physicians, each may be giving you information about your child that may be difficult for you to sort out by yourself. Ask for help before it becomes too overwhelming! Remember, you're probably tired, hungry, and not at your best when your child is ill; no one is!

If problems arise in care that cannot be worked out with your child's nurse, feel free to ask to speak to the nurse who is in charge of the unit, or contact your child's physician with your concerns. Remember, you are the consumer and you should be comfortable with the care your child is being given. If you have questions, ask them, and if answers are not forthcoming, ask for another opinion.

Most families try to focus on the positive aspects of their child and her recovery while in the hospital. Staying positive assists your child in the recovery process and keeps you focused as well. If you find this difficult to do, there are many professionals available to help you. You may ask for the assistance of your pastor, the hospital chaplain, another parent, a social worker, or a clinical nurse specialist in psychology or psychiatry. Remember: You are not alone.

For some families, any visit to the hospital produces great anxiety. Others may plan the hospital visit to include other sites and activities to make it seem more of an excursion. If it is possible to plan ahead for an admission, it generally helps to encourage your child to participate in getting ready. As mentioned above, let her select some favorite toys to bring along. You may also wish to buy an autograph toy for her to take to the hospital. These types of toys (such as teddy bears or stuffed dogs designed to be doodled on) not only serve as a souvenir of the stay but also give your child a ready-made social interaction even on days she would rather hide under the covers. Encourage friends and visitors to send cards and books or other small gifts for entertainment but to keep visits brief and attuned to your child's comfort level. Most importantly, remember that your child will follow your lead with regard to a trip to the hospital. If you keep your attitude positive, she is much more likely to feel positive about the whole experience, too.

■■ Parent Statements

My family is very supportive, but they ask lots of questions. Sometimes it seems like I answer the same questions 50 times. I sometimes think they don't grasp the severity and the wide range of defects associated with spina bifida.

❧

Our family doctor was not only ignorant about Jeremy's needs, he was unwilling to learn and accept suggestions from the specialty doctors at the myelo clinic. Sooooooo, we got a new family doctor.

❧

The hardest treatment decisions we have had to make involved whether or not to do elective eye surgeries. The outcome of any surgery is never guaranteed, so you have to weigh the potential benefits against possible risks. For us, it took two eye surgeries to correct our daughter's major problems and we have been reluctant to do any others.

❧

The most discouraging thing about spina bifida is that it doesn't go away. It's not something you recover from like chicken pox or a broken leg. Most of the time I don't think about Katie's limitations. However, hospital check-ups at the clinic force me to face reality—that Katie has problems and always will. When you think you've dealt with one problem and are used to it, there's a new problem to face. There's a new problem waiting for you around the corner.

❧

I worry about precocious puberty. I want my daughter to have time to learn to respect her body and to know how to assert herself so that others respect her body also.

✺

It was hard to be separated from my baby for the first two weeks that he stayed at Children's Hospital (an hour and a half from home). He had pneumonia and two operations in that time and I worried about him. I was afraid to leave him in the nurses' care because they had other babies to care for and some nurses weren't as knowledgeable as others. I was really glad when we got to bring him home.

✺

We have seen lots of pediatricians. Their initial reaction to our son is typically "What is spina bifida?" But I am happy to say that once we explain, they have all taken the time to educate themselves and help us with our needs.

11

YOUR CHILD'S DEVELOPMENT

Patricia Manning-Courtney, M.D.
Harriet Hadley Valentin, M.D.

All children, with and without disabilities, go through a process of changing and acquiring new skills known as development. Development is a very individual process for each and every child. Rarely do two children develop exactly like each other, even if they have very similar abilities or disabilities. There are many factors that affect development in children, particularly genetic and environmental factors. These and other related factors directly affect the rate at which a child develops. Development can and should be monitored, just like height and weight. If problems with development are detected, then parents and professionals alike can employ appropriate interventions and strategies to stimulate development.

Like any child, your child with spina bifida will follow a unique path of development. Although having a spinal cord lesion usually affects development in at least some manner, spina bifida per se does not place any set limitations on a child's development. The rate of your child's development and his or her respective pattern of strengths and needs will ultimately be determined by a wide range of factors, not just the spina bifida.

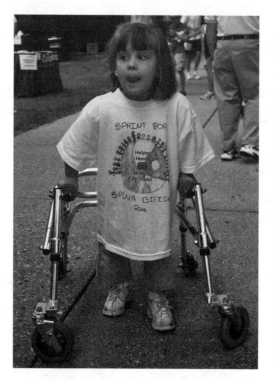

This chapter provides an overview of the information you need to help monitor and stimulate your child's development. To help you understand and recognize how your child is progressing, it begins with an overview of typical development. It then identifies specific ways in which spina bifida may affect a child's development and offers suggestions to help you assist your child in overcoming possible roadblocks to their development.

▪▪ What Is "Normal" Development?

"Normal" development actually encompasses a wide spectrum. Each new skill or "milestone" a child achieves may occur within a broad range of ages that is considered "normal." For example, while many children begin to walk at around one year of age, the age range that is considered normal for walking is from around eight months to eighteen months. In addition, children may achieve some skills early or right on schedule and other skills somewhat late, and still be considered to be developing "normally."

While an early rate of development is encouraging in any child, it is not necessarily predictive of later abilities. Just because one child acquires a skill such as walking before another child does not mean that the earlier walking child will be "smarter." Making steady progress in all areas of development is more important than the rate of development in any one area.

Many factors affect the rate at which a child develops. Some of these factors are due to "nature" and others to "nurture"—that is, due to genetic or environmental factors. Genetic factors that influence development include the traits that children inherit from their parents. For instance, children whose parents walked at an early age might be more likely to walk at an early age also. Environmental factors are the things we expose our children to as they are developing, such as books, music, and other stimulating activities that may influence development. For most children, both nature and nurture interact to influence the overall rate of development.

Other factors influencing development include a child's unique personality traits, such as motivation and temperament. Some children are naturally more outgoing, energetic, and strong-willed, while others may be more passive, quiet, or even-tempered. These differences may not only affect the rate of development, but also the appearance of overall development. For instance, it may seem as if an outgoing child is developing language skills at a faster rate than a quieter child, even though both children are actually developing in a similar fashion. Prematurity is another factor that can influence development, as premature infants often take a little longer to acquire specific skills, especially early on.

In "normal" development, skills usually develop in a particular sequence. This sequence probably reflects the way that the brain and nervous system develop and mature. For example, cooing, babbling, and then using single words is a typical sequence in language development, and sitting up, creeping or crawling, and then walking is a typical sequence in gross motor development.

Keeping track of the developmental milestones a child acquires is a useful way to monitor development. The section on "Major Developmental Milestones" which follows offers a starting point for monitoring your child's progress. Observing and identifying your child's individual temperament, motivation, and pattern of strengths and weaknesses is also a helpful way to monitor development, as well as to determine ways to stimulate and maximize that development.

** The Major Areas of Development

Development is typically broken down into four to six major areas. These are: gross motor, fine motor, language, cognitive, social, and self-help skills. Development within each area may follow its own path, yet all the areas of development are interrelated. For this reason, delays in one area, such as in acquiring language, can affect development in another area, such as social skills. A brief description of each area of development follows.

Gross Motor: This area includes motor (movement) skills involving the large muscles of the body, such as crawling, climbing, and walking. These are the skills that allow a child to move around and explore his environment. Muscle tone, strength, and control are important factors in determining how and when these skills develop.

Fine Motor: These are the movement skills that involve smaller muscles, such as the muscles in the hands. Grasping objects and using writing utensils are major skills in this area. Control of facial muscles and eye muscles may also be included in this area, as well as eye-hand coordination.

Language: Language skills give us the ability to communicate with others in the world. There are two broad types of language skills. Receptive language is the ability to remember and understand spoken words, gestures, or symbols used to communicate. Expressive language is the ability to use spoken words, gestures, or symbols to communicate with others. It is not unusual for a child to develop receptive language skills before expressive language skills.

Cognitive: Cognitive skills are somewhat harder to define, but they generally describe the abilities to reason and solve problems. Early cognitive concepts that young children typically master include:

- Object permanence—the understanding that something continues to exist when it is out of sight. For example, Mom's face is still there even when she hides it behind a blanket to play peek-a-boo
- Cause-and-effect—the understanding that an action causes a specific result. For example, if you remove the bottom block from a tower, the whole tower will fall down.
- Means-to-end—the idea that you can use an object or strategy to achieve a desired result. For example, if you climb onto a kitchen chair, you can reach the cookie jar.

Cognitive skills can be hard to measure and evaluate in younger children, and may reflect development in the other developmental areas described above. As children get older, there are standardized tests, usually administered by a psychologist, to measure cognitive skills. Measuring cognitive abilities is sometimes a useful tool when a child is having learning or school difficulties.

Social: Social skills are the skills we use to interact with other people. Babies begin to develop these skills as they recognize and relate to their parents and other family members. In older children, play skills, the ability to share, waiting their turn, and reading other children's cues all reflect social skills. Like cognitive skills, social skills may not be easy to measure in children, yet they play an important role in determining how a child will relate to the world around him.

Self-Help: These are the skills such as dressing, brushing teeth, and bathing that a child develops as he learns to take care of himself and his daily needs. As they learn self-help skills, most children grow from being totally dependent on adults to becoming more independent. Many self-help skills are taught, and the ability to perform some skills will depend on progress in the other areas of development. For example, dressing is an important self-help skill, which is dependent on the development of fine motor skills that allow children to pull on socks, pants, and fasten buttons or snaps.

■■ Major Developmental Milestones

It is beyond the scope of this chapter to list every developmental milestone during childhood. This section will therefore highlight only the most commonly discussed milestones in each developmental area that occur during the first five years. There are many charts and books you can refer to for more detailed information on specific milestones. A few of these are listed in the Reading List at the back of the book.

As you read through this section, remember that there is usually a wide range of ages for what is considered "normal" for acquiring a particular milestone. Also remember that a child's rate of development in any one area is less important than consistent, steady progress in all areas.

Gross Motor Milestones

One of the first obvious gross motor milestones is head control. This usually occurs within the first two months of life. Head control allows for development of subsequent motor milestones, including rolling back and forth (which occurs between four and ten months), and sitting without support (which occurs between five and nine months).

Crawling is a major motor milestone that usually precedes walking. However, children can exhibit a wide range of crawling patterns, which usually begin to emerge between seven and twelve months. The type or pattern of crawling is probably not as important as the fact that the child is making an attempt to get somewhere. Some children crawl on their bellies, others creep on their hands and knees, while still oth-

ers may prefer to roll to get where they want to go or scoot on their bottoms. Some children may crawl for a very short time before walking, and a few may not crawl at all prior to walking.

Walking is a much-anticipated milestone, and marks the transition from infancy to toddlerhood. As mentioned above, the most-often quoted average age of walking is twelve months. However, as for all milestones, there is a range of ages which is considered normal for walking. Some children who are developing "normally" walk as early as eight months and others not until eighteen months. Many factors influence the age at which a child will walk, outside of the obvious physical factors. In some families, most members walk later, while in other families, walking early is the rule. For the large majority of children, the age at which they begin walking is not as important as the fact that they have acquired walking. In fact, in many children, the age that walking is mastered does not predict what a child's later skills will be like in other areas. That is, just because one child starts walking sooner than another does not mean that he will be ahead of the pack in all areas of development.

After walking, the major motor skills that are developed revolve around improving walking, developing running and climbing skills, and being able to go up and down stairs. Other commonly described gross motor milestones are tricycle riding by about three years of age, and skipping by about five years of age.

Fine Motor Milestones

Fine motor milestones are usually less obvious than gross motor milestones, yet are equally important in allowing a child to interact with the world. In early infancy, a baby holds his hands primarily in a fisted position. During the first two to four months of life, the baby will begin to keep his hands open for longer periods of time, allowing them to do a wider variety of activities, such as holding objects and bringing them to his mouth. By four to five months, a child can begin to reach more purposely for objects, and between five and seven months, he may be able to transfer objects from hand to hand. Initially, a child uses his whole hand to pick up something, in what is described as a raking grasp. Eventually, the grasp becomes more refined, involving just the thumb and pointer finger, between nine and twelve months. This finer grasping pattern, or pincer grasp, allows a child to manipulate smaller objects, such as finger foods. Interestingly, a child's ability to willingly release an object develops concurrently with the ability to grasp an object.

After development of the pincer grasp, fine motor skills are further developed through the use of various tools, such as eating and writing utensils. These important skills are developed in the second year of life, and set the stage for later important fine motor skills, particularly writing and using scissors.

Language Milestones

The earliest language milestones occur long before a child is actually saying words. Language understanding begins in the first few months of life, when babies show a response to sounds, such as startling or opening their eyes. The first language expression milestones occur at the same time, when babies begin to vary their crying patterns to indicate different needs. Between four and nine months, as the baby begins to recognize more familiar sounds, he also makes more specific noises. He coos, then babbles, and also imitates other noises. As language understanding increases, more appropriate responses to familiar sounds develop, such as responding to "no" and his name, and taking part in verbal routines such as "bye-bye."

True words begin to appear sometime between nine and twelve months, and are usually preceded by "mama" and "dada." Some typically developing children may not say their first words until sometime after twelve months. It is, however, very important to rule out hearing loss when there is a concern about late talking.

Between the first and second year of life, the number of words in a child's vocabulary steadily increases. At 18 months, some children may know up to 50 words. At the same time, the understanding of language steadily increases, including the ability to identify body parts, follow simple commands, and point to specific items in pictures. Many children can combine two words by two years of age. However, only their parents or other familiar people may be able to understand them.

By three years of age, a child is usually using pronouns, plurals, and complete sentences. Three-year-olds may also be able to identify some colors and state their name and age, and are mostly understandable to most people.

After three, language understanding and usage becomes increasingly more complex. Telling stories, understanding and answering "what," "where," and "how" questions, and asking many of their own questions are all skills that children develop between three and five years of age.

Cognitive Milestones

Milestones in cognitive development may be the least obvious of all the milestones, yet this does not diminish their importance. On the contrary, these are the skills that may best predict a child's ultimate abilities to learn and succeed in school and function as independently as possible. In the first one to two years of life, measuring these skills may be fairly dependent on the development of all the above-described

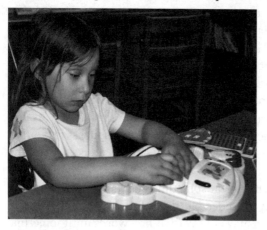

skills. For example, certain measures of early cognitive development require that children manipulate blocks or foam board pieces, which involve fine motor skills.

Children first begin to explore their environment through their senses—by tasting, touching, seeing, smelling, and hearing things. This stage of cognitive development is often referred to as the sensorimotor stage. During this stage, usually between four and eight months, a baby gains interest in where objects are, their appearance, and any changes that occur. The baby may be able to follow the path of a fallen object with his eyes. Object permanence, or the ability to recognize that something is present even if it is hidden or temporarily removed, develops between nine and twelve months. It is during this same age that many babies show fear or anxiety with unfamiliar people or settings, otherwise known as stranger anxiety. Many babies in this age range can begin to understand that certain objects, such as a comb or a cup, have a specific purpose, and can demonstrate this by imitating combing their hair or drinking from a cup.

Between one and two years of life, children increasingly understand the purpose of objects and no longer simply focus on what they look or feel like, or what noise they make if you bang them. This phase may be described as a symbolic stage. When a child pretends to brush his hair with a toy brush, he is demonstrating his understanding that the brush has a purpose. Later in preschool and school-age years, more elaborate problem solving and logical thinking develop. Learning the ABC's, how to count, and other early academic skills are not necessarily cognitive skills, but they reflect certain areas of cognitive development such as memory. These types of skills are again not as obvious as walking and talking, but can be measured using specific tests involving puzzles, blocks, and other similar items.

Social Milestones

The earliest social milestone may be the social smile, which develops around six weeks, although sometimes this milestone is classified under language. Later, around ten months, children begin to exhibit stranger anxiety, preferring to stay with familiar individuals. An important social skill that children work on as toddlers and preschoolers is learning how to play with other children. Younger children initially prefer to play alone even if other children are present. As they age, children will typically begin to play alongside, but not necessarily with other children. This type of side-by-side play is also known as parallel play. By around the age of three, most children have usually started playing interactively with peers.

Self-Help Milestones

Between one and two years of age, children learn a few selected self-help skills such as feeding themselves and undressing. Many more self-help skills begin to develop when a child is between ages two and three. It is during this time that children become adept at removing shoes and socks, often to their parents' dismay. They also learn to unzip large zippers and manipulate large buttons. They can use a spoon and even pick out and get their own cereal for breakfast. Between ages three and four, children are usually able to use the toilet independently and wash their hands unassisted. Between four and five, children can cut their food with a knife, and by the age of six, children can usually dress themselves completely, including tying their shoes.

■■ Development in Children with Spina Bifida

Like all children, children with spina bifida show a tremendous amount of variability in their development. They do not all develop at the same rate, nor do they all excel or have difficulties in the same areas. Children with spina bifida are at greater risk for developmental difficulties, but not all children with spina bifida have developmental delays.

Many children with spina bifida develop numerous skills in the same sequence as other children do. However, some children may not achieve certain skills—particularly gross motor skills such as crawling—at all. These children may still be able to move about on their own, however, especially with assistive aids.

Because of the wide range of lesion levels in children with spina bifida, it is impossible to specify average ages for reaching particular milestones for children with spina bifida. The following sections, however, describe in a general way how spina bifida may affect development in each area. These may or may not be areas of concern for your child, depending upon the level of the lesion.

Gross Motor Skills

This is the area of development that is usually affected the most by spina bifida. Not surprisingly, it is often the area that parents are most concerned about when they learn that their child has spina bifida. In general, children with higher level spina bifida have the most difficulty mastering gross motor skills.

Gross motor deficits are often noticeable shortly after birth. A child with spina bifida often doesn't exhibit the active leg movement typically seen in newborn infants. Head control, rolling over, and sitting may all take a little longer to master. Similarly, crawling and creeping may develop differently in some children, or not at all in others. Children with spina bifida who do not crawl can be quite creative in finding other ways to scoot and move around. For example, they may use their arms to propel themselves forward "commando style," or scoot along on their bottoms. The important point is not how they are moving, but that they are indeed moving around.

The primary question that most families have about gross motor skills is, "Will my child walk?" This question may be very difficult to answer when your child is born, but there are some factors that can help in predicting later walking abilities. A child with a very high level lesion is less likely to walk than a child with a lower level lesion. This is because more of the nerves that control leg muscles are affected in children with higher level spina bifida. If your child has very low level spina bifida and also shows good leg muscle movement and strength at birth, he can be expected to walk.

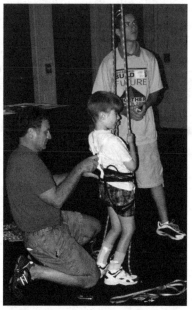

For most children with spina bifida, however, only time will tell. Usually within the first year or two of life, a child's ultimate walking abilities will become clearer. Again, leg muscle movement and strength are usually the key determinants in predicting who will walk.

Children with spina bifida exhibit a wide range of walking abilities. Some children with spina bifida can walk without any assistance at all, and it may even be very difficult to tell that they have spina bifida from the way that they walk. Other children walk somewhat differently, and some walk with assistance, such as with crutches or a walker. See Chapter 9 for information about assistive devices.

Running, jumping, and typical stair climbing are skills that are beyond most children with spina bifida.

Fine Motor Skills

Fine motor skills are less likely to be significantly affected, even in children with higher levels of spina bifida. This is because the nerves that control the arms and hands are located much higher in the spinal cord than is usually affected in children with spina bifida.

Initially, fine motor skills may develop right on track. However, as fine motor skills become more complex, many children develop subtle difficulties in this area. Since many children with spina bifida need their arms for balancing or walking, their hands are not as free to explore their environment. This can contribute to their fine motor skills delays.

Younger children may dislike coloring and cutting because of their fine motor delays. Older children often have problems with handwriting. Tasks that require good hand-eye coordination such as completing puzzles and copying words from the blackboard tend to be particularly difficult. The reasons for these difficulties may be more related to brain differences of children with spina bifida than to problems in the spinal cord. These problems occur more often in children who have associated hydrocephalus.

On occasion, children with spina bifida will have either increased muscle tone or weakness in their arms. For these children, fine motor skills are more significantly affected. Children with significant fine motor difficulties often benefit from occupational therapy (see Chapter 13).

Language Skills

In many children with spina bifida, language skills develop normally or close to normally. This is because these skills are not directly affected by the back and spinal cord abnormalities. Some children even have a specific strength in their language abilities, compared to some of their other abilities.

In some children with spina bifida, slightly excessive talking is noticed, and is sometimes referred to as "cocktail language." Children with this pattern of language are important to identify because their language comprehension may not be as strong as their expressive language. This pattern of language may be difficult to detect in young children, as most preschoolers often seem to talk excessively to their parents. As your child grows older, however, it will become evident if he has word-finding problems. If he does, he will use words inappropriately, making it clear that he does not understand the meaning behind the words.

"Cocktail language" is misleading, because children who talk well are perceived as having good overall language skills, when actually they do not understand everything that is being said to them. Comprehension is therefore a problem and can affect academic skills. The inability to adequately reason and understand tends to be a lifelong problem.

Children with spina bifida do not generally have difficulty with speech production—that is, with correctly forming the sounds needed to speak. Rarely, speech production may be a problem if the lesion level is high enough to involve the trunk muscles that are responsible for lung expansion.

As in children without spina bifida, children with spina bifida who have delayed speech or language should have their hearing evaluated. Hearing problems do not occur any more frequently in children with spina bifida than they do in children without spina bifida.

Cognitive Skills

Children with spina bifida tend to have "normal" intelligence, even if they have significant motor impairment. That is, when tested using standard intelligence tests, their scores or IQs (intelligence quotients) tend to fall in the average range. An average IQ is 100. However, the range of average IQs is often considered to be about 80 to 120. Many children with spina bifida tend to score in the lower average range (80-90) on tests of intelligence.

A few children with spina bifida have mental retardation—IQ lower than 70, resulting in significant delays in the ability to function at home, school, and in the community as independently as peers do. (Other terms for mental retardation you may hear include cognitive disabilities, intellectual disabilities, or, in the United Kingdom, learning disabilities.) While only a small proportion of children with spina bifida have mental retardation, the percentage of children with spina bifida and mental retardation is probably slightly higher than the percentage of children without spina bifida who have mental retardation. Children with severe hydrocephalus may be at greater risk for this type of cognitive disability. Frequent shunt malfunctions, especially those that are not addressed quickly, may also lead to more cognitive delays. One thing that does not usually lead to cognitive delays is delays in other areas of development, such as gross motor skills. If a child with significant gross motor delays has cognitive delays, it is probably not due to the gross motor delay.

Many children with spina bifida also have more trouble learning in some areas than in others. For example, they may be stronger in language skills, and weaker in basic problem solving or math-based skills. The discrepancy, or gap, between the strong areas and weaker areas of intelligence may result in specific learning problems. If these conditions cause problems in learning academics in school, a child may be diagnosed with a specific learning disability (see Chapter 13). A specific learning disability is a measurable discrepancy between a child's overall cognitive abilities and his performance in a specific academic area, such as reading, writing, or math. Early signs of specific learning disabilities may be difficult to detect, and specific learning disabilities usually do not become evident until a child is in first or second grade. If your child is suspected of having a specific learning disability, his cognitive skills will be tested using standardized intelligence tests. The more details we know about a child's cognitive abilities, the better able we are to maximize his learning abilities.

There is increasing evidence that children with spina bifida may be more likely to have difficulties in other areas related to cognition, particularly memory, attention, and organizational skills. Children may be diagnosed with attention deficit disorder (ADD) or attention-deficit/hyperactivity disorder (AD/HD) if they have specific difficulties with paying attention, concentrating, controlling impulses, and distractibility. Many professionals who work with children with spina bifida have observed that these problems occur more frequently than in children without spina bifida. A study involving the Cincinnati Children's Hospital Medical Center Spina Bifida Clinic found that almost half of the clinic patients screened in that setting had some attentional problems. Children with spina bifida seem more likely to exhibit ADD, rather than AD/HD. That is, they are more likely to have problems with focusing their attention than with hyperactivity. As discussed in Chapter 13, some children with ADD or AD/HD respond to medications that help them focus and pay attention.

Problems with attention, memory, and organizational skills may not directly affect overall cognitive abilities. However, they may affect learning, particularly in an intellectually stimulating environment such as a classroom.

Self-Help Skills

The development of self-help skills in children with spina bifida is most significantly affected by the degree of motor impairment. For example, children with higher level lesions who do not walk have more difficulty with basic self-help skills such as dressing, toileting, and bathing. They can, however, learn ways to assist with these tasks, and make it easier for the person actually performing the task. Children with lower level lesions may have only mild delays (if any) in self-help skills, or may have delays related to a specific area, such as fine motor skills. Fine motor problems could affect a child's ability to use eating utensils, fasten buttons or zippers, or tie shoes.

Clearly, the degree of bladder and bowel involvement will affect development of toileting skills (see Chapter 7). Children with spina bifida can, however, develop skills that assist in this process. For instance, they can bear down with a bowel movement or assist with, and eventually perform, catheterization.

Most children with spina bifida also need to learn self-help skills that other children do not. They learn to take braces off and on, learn to transfer from wheelchairs, or, as mentioned above, learn self-catheterization.

To develop self-help skills, your child, like every child, needs to be provided with opportunities and encouragement to learn to do these skills himself.

Social Skills

Early social skill development in children with spina bifida (social smile, awareness of family members) may not differ at all from children without spina bifida. Later skills, such as cooperative play, may also progress typically in children with spina bifida, sometimes in spite of delays in other areas. If children with spina

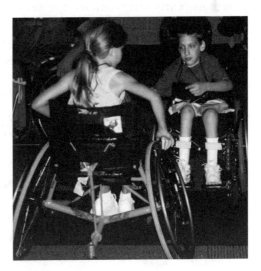

bifida do develop delays in social skills, it may be because they are not given enough opportunities to develop social skills by playing and interacting with peers. Problems can also develop if children with spina bifida are held to different standards than other children. For example, if they are not expected to solve their own problems, make their own decisions, or behave like other children, they may develop difficulties with self-esteem or with getting along with others. For more information about keeping your child's social skills on track, see Chapter 14.

■■ How You Can Help Your Child's Development

With the Help of Therapists and Other Educators

There are specific therapies available for children with delays in certain areas of development. As Chapter 9 discusses, physical therapy can help maximize children's gross motor skills. Physical therapists can help teach your child how to use different types of equipment and aids that make movement easier. Occupational therapists focus on fine motor skills. Speech and language therapists help children with pronunciation problems as well as with more complex problems with understanding or producing language.

These therapies and other special services are available to babies and young children with spina bifida through early intervention programs. Early intervention involves developmental stimulation and therapy designed to help minimize delays due to a disability or developmental problem. Early intervention also includes support and training for the families of children with disabilities, aimed at helping them learn to stimulate and facilitate the development of their child. As Chapter 13 explains, early intervention programs are available in all states, for children aged birth through three years of age, often at no cost to the family. From age three on, children with spina bifida may continue to qualify for therapies or special educational help through the school system if developmental delays persist. Again, see Chapter 13 for information about how these programs can help and how to find out whether your child qualifies.

Some parents of older children seek private therapy in addition to, or instead of, therapy provided through the school. Schools generally provide therapy only when a delay interferes with functioning within the school environment. As a parent, you might be interested in obtaining therapy to help your child with skills such as dressing or grooming needed at home, but not at school. Insurance companies vary tremendously as to how much private therapy they will support. See Chapter 15 for more information about getting the maximum benefit from your insurance.

Stimulation at Home

As with any child, you can do many things to stimulate and encourage development in your child with spina bifida. Providing opportunities for exploration (wide-open spaces), as well as a variety of items for interacting with (both toys and nontoys!) allows your child to use all his senses to learn about the world. Talking, singing, and reading to your child will increase his exposure to language and help him develop language skills. Encouraging independence, rather than automatically doing everything for your child, will help him develop self-help skills. Tolerating messes is important when your child is learning to do a variety of skills independently, from feeding himself, to pouring his own juice, to dispensing his own toothpaste. Providing lots of opportunities for your child to meet other children and adults will help in the development of social skills. Finally, seeking out current information on spina bifida, through local or regional support groups, local clinics, the Internet, or books, assures that you will be up-to-date on current intervention practices and possible new treatment opportunities.

■■ Conclusion

It can be worrisome to hear all the ways that spina bifida could delay your child's development and frustrating to hear that only time will tell how the condition will delay it. However, you do not (and should not) have to just sit idly by and wait for your child's development to unfold. There are many ways that you can work together with therapists, special education professionals, and other health care professionals to help your child learn skills and adaptive meth-

ods for accomplishing goals. The outlook for children born with spina bifida today is very different than it was for children born decades ago, thanks to the vast array of services available today to facilitate development. Most children with spina bifida are able to attend regular school in regular classes, and have many options for leading productive and fulfilling lives in adulthood. Every small step you help your child accomplish today will help to bring him closer to that promising future.

Remember that you are not alone and that numerous other parents in your shoes have learned how to maximize the development of their own children. Some of their personal statements follow.

❚❚ Parent Statements

My expectations for Beth have definitely changed, but not necessarily in ways I expected. I've had to change my expectations of when things will happen (she crawled at 13 months, not at 9 months; she walked at 2 years with braces, not at 12 to 18 months), and I've had to change my expectations about how things get done. Beth uses the potty, but not the way I expected when I pictured potty training a "normal child."

❧

We have Jimmy on a schedule for catheterization and medicine needs, but other than that we purposely do not treat him different than our other two boys. If we are letting him do something that might be a little daring in someone else's eyes, such as going down the slide, our opinion is—if he doesn't try it, how is he going to know if he can do it?

❧

I like to read books and articles about "typical" development, although I know some parents of kids with disabilities do not. I find it gives me a good roadmap of what lies ahead for my child, and it is also very encouraging to me when I see that she's acquiring some skills right on target, if not before.

❧

We are excited over every developmental victory because it is so hard for our daughter to do things with her legs. We feel she will always be an overachiever.

❧

When I watch Katie try so hard to do things that are such a challenge, it brings me a lot of joy. No matter how hard it is, no matter how painful, or how much she really doesn't want to do something, she not only tries but she gives it her best.

✥

Abby is extremely motivated to keep up with other children. She has learned to use her braces and walker much earlier than expected and is always willing to try new things. She goes for what she wants.

✥

Kevin is mostly a "floor kid" at two and a half years. We constantly have to remind ourselves that he is age appropriate in everything but physical (motor) development.

✥

Since Children's Hospital was too far way for us to drive to regularly, we found a center close to us that had a good physical therapy program as well as a day program for children with disabilities. Sarah started attending when she was two and a half years old. She could have started at one year, but I was reluctant to let her go sooner. She learned to play with sand and Play Doh, went on field trips, learned to walk with crutches, rode special bikes, and made friends too. When she turned three, our township provided transportation to the program for free.

✥

The only child with spina bifida we had any knowledge of was my husband's sister who was born in the 1950s before back closures and shunts were routine. We pretty much prepared ourselves for a child who would not be able to walk. Our son walks, rides a bike, and is a social butterfly. He has surpassed every expectation we had for him before his birth.

12

PARENTING A CHILD WITH SPINA BIFIDA

Alysoun Taylor

When you first re-
ceive your child's diagnosis, you may wonder how you will cope. It all
seems so overwhelming at first, but after the dust settles, most parents
do rise to the occasion. The question is not so much whether or not you

will be able to cope, but whether
you will cope well. Will you, your
child, and your family merely survive, or will you thrive?

Chapter 4 looked at some
of the feelings parents often have
initially when a child is diagnosed
with spina bifida, as well as some
early coping techniques. This
chapter takes a more in-depth
look at strategies parents can use
to preserve their emotional health
and also discusses the effects that
spina bifida can have on the emo-

tional life of the entire extended family. In addition, this chapter covers daily care issues, including playing with your child, bathing, discipline, transportation, and promoting independence, with an eye toward helping parents minimize the stress involved in caring for their child.

❖ Adjusting and Coping

Taking Care of Yourself

In order to thrive, each of us has basic needs that must be met. Beyond food, clothing, and shelter, we need love, support, and someone to talk to. We all need time to ourselves and a chance for recreation. Parents need to feel competent, and they need to get enough rest. Adults need to have interests of their own to pursue.

Your child needs a lot from you. She needs you to be there for her for the long term. When you decided to have a child, you didn't sign up for the 100-meter sprint, you signed up for the marathon. Any distance runner will tell you that you can't finish a marathon unless you pace yourself. You need to be careful not to become so wrapped up in your child's needs that you neglect to take care of your own.

Accept Help

The first thing you need, especially in the beginning, is rest. Every problem seems worse when you're tired. Your family and friends may wear you out with their concern for you. You need to be a little selfish and tell them what they can do that is really helpful to you. Accept offers to help with your housework. You may want to send out a birth announcement explaining the basics of your child's condition so that you don't have to answer the same questions over and over again. Make up a mailing list, and then put a couple of your well-wishers to work addressing envelopes for you. Many families keep loved ones up to date through e-mail and personal websites. Again, don't hesitate to ask a friend or family member to help you with your e-mail correspondence if it feels overwhelming.

My daughter was born in December. We had lots of help with food and transportation back and forth to the hospital before I was allowed to drive, but the most meaningful gift we received was a Christmas tree. We hadn't had time to get our own, and one day we came home from the hospital and there it was in our living room.

As your child grows older, it is very important that you do not allow yourself to become the only person who can care for your child. This is especially important if you are a single parent. If you don't have close friends or family members who can help you, consider social service agencies that offer respite care. Your health insurance may cover home health care. If your child just needs intermittent catheterization, they will probably not pay for a nurse to watch your child, but they may pay for someone to come in and do the catheterization. This may be all the help a relative or friend needs to be able to watch your child while you get away for a few days.

Get Information and Support

One of the things you will need most in the beginning is information. Your doctor can help you to obtain books to read, and some helpful publications are listed at the back of this book. What most parents really want in the beginning, however, is someone to talk to. If you contact the Spina Bifida Association of America (listed in the Resource Guide), they can tell you where the nearest local chapter is. The nurses and social workers at the hospital may also assist you in making contact with other parents. It is important to bear in mind, however, that there is no "typical" case of spina bifida. The effects of spina bifida are distributed over a broad range, and another parent's experience may be very different from your own. Also, your personality and attitudes are individual, and you may not become lifelong friends with the first parent you meet whose child has spina bifida. If you keep trying, though, chances are you will find someone you can talk to and share experiences with.

Besides looking for support from other parents of children with disabilities, it is wise to strengthen your relationships outside the disability community. This will help you maintain a balance in your life and increase your opportunities for meaningful relationships. It is difficult to find time to make friends when you are taking care of a baby, but not impossible. If you are a single parent, it is even more important for you to have other adults to talk to.

Streamline Your Life

Many families find that they need to focus on the things that are most important in their lives. They may choose to give up some of their outside activities and responsibilities and focus on family life. It is important to find the right balance: too many activities outside the home can lead to stress and exhaustion, but too few can leave parents feeling trapped and isolated. It may be best to focus on the activities that give you the most enjoyment and fulfillment and drop those activities that bring more stress than they're worth.

Take Time for Yourself

Whatever your interests are, it is important to find time for them. Adults need to have activities that stimulate their minds, lift their spirits, and keep them involved with the adult world. You may decide to join a bowling league, or a community chorus. You may not have time for community theater when your child is a baby, but you can find the time to attend performances. You may even find that you have a talent for dealing with children with disabilities. Many parents discover that they enjoy caring for children with special needs and go on to develop interests in medicine, physical therapy, or special education.

Take Care of Your Emotional and Physical Health

Each person deals with the stress of daily living a little differently. Some people thrive on it, while others can become easily overwhelmed. You will need to find a strategy for dealing with stress that works for you. Some people find physical exercise to be an excellent way to burn off stress. Others enjoy relaxing in a hot tub with a good book. For some, spending time with friends is rejuvenating.

You should seek professional help if you are having difficulty managing stress or if you are experiencing severe anxiety. Many parents, with and without children with disabilities, feel overwhelmed at times. The wise parents seek help before things get to a crisis level. There are mental health professionals in your community who can help. Look under "Mental Health" in the Yellow Pages of your telephone book.

Stress can bring on or exacerbate depression. Depression is not feeling stressed out, and it is not "the blues." Many times depressed individuals do not even realize they are depressed. You should familiarize yourself with the symptoms of depression. They include: a change in appetite or sleep patterns, decreased interest in activities, and feelings of sadness. If you think you or your spouse may be suffering from depression, you can seek help from your family physician. Effective treatment for depression is available, but if left untreated, the effects on your family can be devastating.

Another area of concern is your physical health. You need to make sure you find a way to get the exercise you need. Physical exercise is good for your long-term health, and many people find that it increases their energy levels. In addition, staying in shape can help you avoid injuring your back. You will probably be doing a lot of lifting and bending over, and you need to make sure you do all you can to keep your back healthy.

You may need to make adjustments in your home to allow you to use good body mechanics when caring for your child. For example, when our daughter had hip surgery and was in a spica cast for many weeks, we rented a hospital bed that we could raise and lower to allow us to care for her without bending over as much. If you do begin to have aches and pains in your back, feet, or elsewhere, it is a good idea to seek treatment for them as early as possible. Many problems don't go away, but get worse, and it's difficult to enjoy life when you are in pain.

Enjoy Family Life

Above all, remember to enjoy life and enjoy your child. My daughter's first pediatrician told us that children with spina bifida are more like other children than they are different from them. Children with spina bifida can and do thrive, and you can thrive as well.

Our daughter is the light of our lives. She is intelligent, happy, and good-natured. She is very personable and loves nothing more than playing with her many friends. She enjoys racing in her wheelchair, and at the tender age of seven, she has already won three ribbons. The highlight of first grade was her science fair project about leaf-cutter ants (she thinks they are "so cool"). I cannot imagine our lives without her. We know she faces additional challenges as she grows and matures, but we think she has enough spunk to see her through them all. And we will be there, cheering her on all the way. That's what families do.

Maintaining Your Marriage

Raising a child with a disability can place tremendous strain on a marriage. I remember our doctor telling us, soon after our daughter's prenatal diagnosis, that when something like this happens, strong families become stronger, while weak families are ripped apart. That may be a bit simplistic, but you will need to take special care to preserve a healthy relationship with your spouse.

When you were dating, you may have asked yourself what kind of parent your future spouse might be, but it is unlikely that you se-

lected each other based on how each of you would respond if you found out your baby had spina bifida. You will be charting new waters together as a couple, and it is important to be accepting and supporting of each other's reactions. In the long term, it will be very difficult to function together as a team unless you can develop similar outlooks and attitudes toward your child's disability, but you will need to give each other time to come to that point.

Share Responsibilities

Unless both parents work full-time and take turns taking the child to the doctor and therapists, it is likely that one of you, usually the mother, will learn more about spina bifida than the other. During therapy sessions, one of you may pick up a lot of jargon that the other doesn't understand. To some extent, this sort of division of knowledge takes place in any family. For example, Mom knows where the library cards are and what time story hour is, and Dad doesn't have a clue, or vice versa. It is not necessary for both of you to be on exactly the same level in everything. It *is* a good idea to make sure both parents get a chance to at least meet your child's various doctors and therapists, and it's helpful if both of you can be present for really important doctor visits.

Both parents do need to stay involved, and each parent needs to know how to care for the child when the other is away. Parents need to strive for a division of responsibility that works for their situation, and recognize each other's contributions. The parent who may be more involved needs to be careful not to act superior to the other, while the parent who can't remember the jargon needs to be careful so as to avoid becoming marginalized. It is better to make decisions about your child's needs and who will be responsible for what together. This way one parent will not feel that he or she is carrying the greatest load, which often leads to resentment.

Keep the Lines of Communication Open

Communication is essential. Each of you will experience many strong emotions in response to your child's condition, including sadness, anger, guilt, disappointment, and resentment. The two of you will not necessarily be experiencing the same emotions at the same time, however. To encourage one another to talk about what is really on your mind, it is therefore essential to listen without judging and without telling one another how you *should* be feeling. If these emotions are not properly expressed and dealt with, they will work their way out in ways that can be very destructive to the marriage bond. When couples *can* share such strong feelings together, it truly can strengthen their bonds and deepen their love for each other.

If you and your spouse had trouble communicating before, now may be the time to seek counseling to help you learn how to share with one another. Couples who *were* doing fine at communicating may discover they now need a little help. You may each have different ideas about how to handle a situation. Or one of you may not even want to think about a particular issue yet while the other wants to talk about it all the time. If you cannot reach a compromise, seek outside help in resolving your differences.

Be Prepared for Bad Days

Every married couple faces relationship obstacles when they become parents. The pitfalls you face when you raise a child with a disability are much the same, only some of the pits may be a bit deeper. For example, you may disagree over how protective you need to be, or about how to handle certain aspects of your child's medical care. You will both face drains on your time, energy, and finances.

Managing the care of a child with a disability is like having an extra job, over and above regular parenting and employment. On those occasions when you spend the entire day in hospital waiting rooms, it can feel like a job you do in total isolation. At the end of the day, you need your spouse to recognize and appreciate what you did. These are the times when nerves are frayed and tempers can easily flare. You can find yourself striking out in resentment, or your spouse can allow feelings of inadequacy to come out as anger.

I often say that before our child was born, I had an average amount of patience. After she was born, I had the same amount of patience, and she got all of it. I had none left over for my husband. To some extent, parents simply have to be mature enough to accept that they don't have the time and patience for each other that they had before they became parents. Each must be willing to make allowances for one another.

Take Time to Be a Couple

A marriage relationship that is neglected too long will wither and die. It's OK to put your children's needs before your own most of the time, but you need to set aside time for each other too. Each of us needs different things to feel loved and validated. We need to learn to express those needs to each other, and to give each other the tools to meet those needs.

You need to have some type of respite care that allows you to spend time alone together. Most children with spina bifida can be left with regular babysitters, at least between catheterizations. Just be sure to select sitters who are old enough and mature enough to handle the responsibility, and make sure they know how to handle any situation that might come up. Many parents find that carrying a cell phone brings them great peace of mind, but try not to call home too often. Remember, this is supposed to be a break. If your child has nursing concerns that require extra skills, such as a tracheotomy, you probably still have some options available to you for respite. Your insurance may pay for nursing care while you are away. In addition, there are agencies available in many communities that provide free or low-cost respite care. Ask your spina bifida team about these resources.

It is good for your child to be left with a sitter occasionally. It may help to keep her from becoming overly dependent upon you, and teach her emotional independence. Most kids love knowing more about their home and routine than the sitter does. It makes them feel like the expert.

Appreciate Your Child Together

It's not enough for parents to share their sorrows and trials together. They also need to share their joy. I can't imagine feeling any prouder of a child than I do of my daughter. We live in awe of her strength, determination, and spirit. Every success is sweeter when your child has obstacles to overcome, and I am so thankful to have my husband with me to enjoy all that she has brought us. I am a stronger person for having him in my life. Maintaining a successful marriage is a lot of work, but is well worth the effort.

■■ Grandparents, Relatives, Friends

When your child is first diagnosed with spina bifida, whether it is before or after her birth, you have a lot to deal with. One of your first challenges is telling your family and friends. Each person's reaction is influenced by her own attitudes, experiences, and biases. Just as each parent reacts a little differently, so too will the relatives and friends.

Some people will respond as if you had just told them your child died; others will be relentlessly positive, even to the point of denying the problems you face. Some people will tell you to pray for a miracle. Unfortunately, there are even some people who still see the birth of a child with a disability as a judgment from God for the parents' misdeeds, though most of them blessedly keep their ideas to themselves. People will want to know what caused it, and some people would actually prefer to think it's your fault rather than face the reality that sometimes bad things just happen for no predictable reason.

Breaking the News

Breaking the news to your family and closest friends will be one of the hardest things you will ever have to do, and there is really no way to be prepared for it. No one likes to be the bearer of bad news. You may know in your head that this was not your fault, but in your heart you may feel as though you are letting everyone down. Your loved ones will want to rally around you and help in any way they can, but initially they may not know what to say. This is a very vulnerable time, and if someone says the wrong thing, like "There's never been anything like this in our side of the family," it can be particularly hurtful. It's hard to be tolerant and forgiving when you are going through such a crisis.

At such a difficult time, it is important to conserve your own strength, emotionally as well as physically. If you can't face telling a particular person, find someone else to do it for you. Ask a close friend, a member of the clergy, a doctor, nurse, or social worker at the hospital, or another family member to break the news. If you find out about your child's spina bifida at birth, you can ask the hospital not to put your calls through until you are up to talking.

Although you may wish to withdraw a little in the beginning while you adjust to the news, it is important to keep the lines of communication open. You do not need to deal with your child's disability alone. When people have a chance to see and interact with your child, it will be easier for them to see her as a person rather than as a calamity. People will begin to respond to your lead. If you project a positive attitude about your child's future, you will see that reflected in the people around you. If you are very negative, your loved ones will also tend to be more somber. You can't expect yourself to keep everyone else cheered up, but at the same time you will probably want everyone around you to feel hopeful for your child's future.

One approach is to explain your child's situation briefly in a birth announcement. You can include statements that express both your hopes for your child, and your need for support, such as the following: "We love our daughter very much, and we expect her to live a full, rich life. We know that with the loving support and help of our family and friends, we will get through this difficult period of adjustment. We know that we will face challenges as our daughter grows, but we also know that she will bring us much joy, which we hope to share with all of you."

Your friends may want you to talk to everyone they know who has a child with any kind of disability. You should proceed at a pace that is comfortable for you. Some parents become instant activists, while others would just like to have some privacy. It is important, however, not to cut yourself off completely. Every parent has the need for information and reassurance.

Changing Attitudes

Attitudes toward disabilities have shifted a great deal in a short period of time, and not everyone has kept up with them. Many people simply lack experience with children with disabilities, and are unaware of such basics as the federal law (IDEA) requiring schools to include them in regular classrooms whenever possible. Many people will tell you to "treat her as if she were normal," while other people will tend to be overprotective and indulgent.

You will need to learn to respond to the different attitudes you encounter. If you have a friend whose patronizing comments drive you crazy, you may decide to spend less time with that friend. If the hurtful attitudes come from family members, however, they can create more difficult problems.

Sometimes people just need to be enlightened. For example, people often do things for children with disabilities without even thinking. If you explain that your child needs to learn to do things for herself, they will usually be willing to change their behavior. Another example might be when your child learns a new skill, such as walking with braces, and your family quite naturally responds with excitement and pride. Sometimes you might be concerned that their reaction will put too much pressure on your child to succeed, but simply explaining your concerns may be all that is needed.

Asking for Help

Most families want to help in any way they can. When grandparents, aunts, and uncles are willing to help out, including learning such skills as how to take down a wheelchair, put your child's braces on, or catheterize her, their support is invaluable. Some grandparents may not be physically capable of caring for a child with spina bifida, but their emotional support can still be important. If they treat your child in a positive way, they will increase her sense of security and belonging.

Sometimes it can be very difficult to ask for the kinds of help you really need. How do you ask someone to help with your child's bowel program? If you are blessed with the type of family who volunteers, you are fortunate indeed. Still, even though it is hard to ask, it may be necessary. Not only do you need respite, you also need to plan for your child in case an emergency takes both parents away from her for any length of time.

Handling Tense Situations

As helpful as family members can be, sometimes they behave in ways that are just plain bad for your child, and then you have no choice but to intervene. People sometimes talk about people with disabilities as if they were not even there. You may have to firmly ask them not to say negative things in front of your child. If you can't get your sister to stop being overprotective, or Aunt Lulu to stop referring to your child as "crippled," you may be able to deal with the situation by talking to your child about how it makes her feel. When problems among family members can be worked out, everyone benefits.

Many people simply can't bring themselves to confront family members. It is important, however, not to bottle up negative feelings toward your family. When you hear about family feuds caused by seemingly minor incidents, it is usually because family members have been harboring resentments. The best recourse is usually to be honest and up-front. Talk to the person you are having a problem with either face-to-face, or through a letter or e-mail, if that feels more comfortable. If your relationship with family members is causing you stress, you may just need someone who will listen to you blow off steam, or you may need to consider getting professional counseling.

▪▪ Siblings

If your child with spina bifida has brothers or sisters, her disability will affect them as well. If they are older siblings, one of your first concerns will be breaking the news to them. If you receive the diagnosis before birth, you may think you can wait to tell the children, but children are very sensitive to their parents' moods, and you will need to offer them some explanation of what you are going through. If you don't, they might think they are responsible for whatever is going on.

Talking about Spina Bifida

How, when, and what you tell your children will vary according to their ages. Very young children may only need to know that the baby has a problem and will need to be in the hospital a little longer than you expected. When the baby comes home, she will not seem so very different from other babies, and you can explain the baby's differences gradually as she grows. Older children can be given more specific information, but it will be a lot for them to absorb, just as it was for you, so you should try to make your explanations as simple as possible.

One way to explain paralysis to young children is to compare the nervous system to a telephone or to an electrical appliance. Even very young children understand that when an appliance is not plugged in, it doesn't work. It's not broken, it just doesn't work. You can explain that people's arms and legs are usually "plugged in" to their spinal cords. When parts of the body are not plugged in, they do not work.

If your baby has a lengthy hospital stay, you should consider bringing the children in to see her, if your hospital allows it. You may worry about your children's reaction to the monitors and I.V., but it may be very reassuring to see that the baby looks just like a baby after all. If a visit is not possible, photos or videos are the next best thing.

Talking about Feelings

You will want to shield your children from your own feelings of upheaval. You may try to be reassuring and as if you are in control of the situation, but you will need to be sensitive to your children's perceptions. They will want reassurance, but they will also want honesty. They will want the explanations you offer to correspond with what they are sensing from you. Remember, the birth of a new sibling can be traumatic even under the best of circumstances. You will have precious little emotional energy available at this time, but try to give them whatever you can.

The most important way to help children develop into emotionally healthy adults is to teach them to verbalize their feelings. This is especially important for the siblings of children with disabilities. You can't just explain the situation once and be done with it. Your children will have many questions over the years and experience many different emotions as they grow. You may want to make a conscious effort to have a heart to heart talk with each of your children every so often.

Some common emotions that siblings experience include feeling that they were responsible for what happened; worrying that they, too, may "catch" spina bifida or become disabled; and even feeling embarrassed about their brother or sister. If they feel embarrassed, they may also feel ashamed for feeling embarrassed. They may have difficulty understanding the permanence of the disability, and they may not understand that their sibling will be able to function independently in spite of her limitations.

Your child with spina bifida may have feelings of resentment of her own. If she has younger siblings, it may be very difficult for her to watch them learn to walk. She may feel left out of their sporting activities, and resent the ease with which they seem to make friends. She may see her disability as more of a burden when she compares her abilities to those of her siblings.

It is important to be accepting of all of your children's feelings and concerns. These feelings are all very normal, and you need to make it safe for your children to share their thoughts with you. If you feel that one of your children is having particular difficulty in dealing with her sibling's disability, you may wish to seek counseling for her, preferably with a counselor familiar with these issues.

Balancing Your Children's Needs

It is very common for siblings of children with disabilities to resent the child with a disability. The child with a disability gets more time and attention, and may receive special gifts, privileges, and attention from people outside the family. Brothers and sisters may come to feel unimportant and unappreciated compared to the "special" child. If you ask them to help, they may feel put upon, and they may resent what they see as a double standard when they are expected to do things the child with spina bifida is not.

Much of this is completely unavoidable. Your child with a disability really does require more of your attention than your other children do, and there is no way you can change that. What you can do is to make sure you openly acknowledge the situation, and the unfairness of it, and make sure you find a way to set aside time to be with your other children one on one. You may not be able to give them an entire Saturday, but you can go for a walk, just the two of you. You will not be able to make things equitable, but you can make sure each child feels loved and special.

You will also need to take an honest look at your own behavior from time to time. Are you doing more than you need to for your child with spina bifida? Are you failing to hold her responsible for behavior that contributes to family disharmony? Are you allowing any of your children to manipulate the situation to their advantage and play on any feelings of guilt you may have? Every now and then, when your child says, "It's not fair," ask yourself if you really are being as fair as you can under the circumstances. None of us is a perfect parent all of the time, but if you honestly think you are doing the best you can to balance all of your children's needs, and if you are teaching your children to verbalize their feelings and concerns, they will probably be fine. Remember, no child thinks things are fair all the time.

Sharing Information

It is important to keep your children informed about what is going on. When I was three or four years old, my younger brother had casts put on his feet because he was pigeon-toed. When he was ready to have them taken off, my mother took me along to the doctor's office, but didn't tell me what was going to happen. I will never forget the terror I felt when the doctor took the saw to my brother's feet. I was the kind of child who tended to keep things inside of myself, and I don't even know if my mother or the doctor understood why I started crying.

There are resources available to help you deal with your children's sibling issues. Some useful publications are included in the Reading List at the end of this book. There are also seminars and activities, all centering around siblings of children with disabilities. Many activities give siblings a chance to meet other children in the same situation. For example, the national Spina Bifida Association has had formal sibling programs for many years as a part of their annual conference. Children with disabilities benefit from meeting each other and seeing that they are not alone, and their siblings can benefit from the same kind of contact. Ask your pediatrician and spina bifida team if they are aware of sibling group meetings in your community.

Appreciating One Another's Gifts

Although having a brother or sister with spina bifida may sometimes seem like a burden, there are benefits as well. Most parents report that their children are more compassionate, and they are proud of the way their children stick up for children with all types of disabilities. They will likely grow up to be more sensitive, empathetic adults, and many go into professions that allow them to make use of their experiences.

There is no way you can ensure that your children will grow up to be friends, but each of your children has unique gifts to offer the others. Your child may feel motivated when she sees how much her siblings can do, and the acceptance she feels from her siblings may be just what she needs to find the confidence to make friends with other able-bodied children. And she can teach her siblings to be loving, nurturing, and sensitive adults.

∷ Day to Day Living

Just as you teach your children without disabilities how to dress, bathe, brush their teeth, etc., so too will you need to teach your child with spina bifida how to do these tasks. It is true that it may take your child with spina bifida longer to learn these tasks and there may be more to learn, such as putting on braces and catheterizing. Still, the rewards of seeing your child accomplish something new will be well worth the effort. Your child will want to play, go places, and have a chance to be a productive member of your family just like your other children.

Bathing Your Child

Bathing a child with spina bifida can present some challenges. Sponge bathing is recommended until the stitches in the back are removed or absorbed and the incision looks clean and healed. (This takes about 10 days to 3 weeks.) Depending on her level of function, your child may outgrow her baby bathtub long before she has sufficient balance to maintain herself in the water, even with traditional bath aids. A special bath seat might work or you can simply climb into the tub with your child (wear a swimsuit if it makes you more comfortable). Ask your physical therapist and other parents for additional suggestions.

As with all children, you need to be careful about the temperature of your child's bath water. Since your child may have little or no feeling in her lower extremities, you may want to install a water temperature regulating device on your faucet as extra protection against burns. As your child grows, bath time can provide a good opportunity for you to teach her to be cautious about any lack of sensation in her lower limbs. You can teach her to test the water temperature with her hands and remind her that her legs can become burned even if she can't feel the heat. You can teach her to inspect her feet for injuries, pressure marks, or foot fungus. This is also a good time to help her learn to name her body parts. A child with little function in her lower body will probably be aware of her legs and feet, but you may have to point out her heels, ankles, shins, calves, etc.

After the bath, be sure to dry your child's legs thoroughly. If your child tends to get foot fungus, you can use powder to fight the fungus and keep them dry. It's also helpful to make a point of letting your child's feet get some air at times. For example, you may wish to avoid pajamas with feet. Most children with spina bifida wear shoes and socks almost all the time, because they can't feel their feet and because many of them wear braces on their feet.

Getting into and out of the tub can become a problem as your child grows and gets bigger. There are many ways to adapt bathtubs and showers so that your child can be independent with bathing. For example, you can add bars to grab onto or buy a hoist or lift that helps your child into the tub. Physical therapists have catalogs and can make suggestions, and almost all medium-sized cities have home health care supply stores where you can look at what's available. Many such assistive devices are very expensive, and health insurance usually will not pay for them. However, you may be able to find funding assistance. Some local chapters of the Spina Bifida Association offer assistance, and many state and local agencies offer assistance based on family income. Often they will offer provide assistance even for middle-income families who do not qualify for other types of aid.

Feeding Your Child

Many children with spina bifida have a strong gag reflex. That is, they start to gag or choke if something touches their tongue or palate. You may notice this particularly as your child begins to eat textured foods. Despite this problem, most children with spina bifida are able to eat and gain weight just fine. (In fact, as discussed in Chapter 10, too much weight gain is often a problem as children grow older.) If your child continues to have trouble with gagging, however, a speech-language pathologist or an occupational therapist trained in this area will be able to help you. A dietitian can help you teach your child to gradually tolerate more texture.

Sometimes children with spina bifida have poor sitting balance, making it difficult for them to feed themselves. Your physical or occupational therapist can suggest adaptations or equipment that will help your child sit independently so that her hands are free to hold utensils.

Bedtime

Your child with spina bifida will probably not need any special care during the night. Usually parents do not catheterize the child in the middle of the night unless specifically requested to do so by their urologists. As a rule, no special bed is required and your child should be able to sleep soundly all night long.

If your child is in a wheelchair and is unable to bear weight on her legs, she will learn how to transfer in and out of her wheelchair onto other surfaces. Sometimes a transfer board will be useful when your child is moving from her wheelchair to her bed. The physical or occupational therapist working with your child will help determine the best way for your child to do transfers.

Teaching Self-Care Skills

There are many tasks your child will need to learn in order to care for herself. You need to begin teaching her as early as possible, but you

also need to be patient and realistic. If your child has to use a complex strategy to do something that should be simple, such as putting on her shoes, it may be much easier for her to learn when she has had a chance to develop her cognitive skills a little bit more. And although encouraging independence is important, you can't expect yourself to go through a lengthy ordeal every time your child needs to get dressed.

One strategy my family uses is to emphasize self-care skills during the summer and on weekends when we have more time. During the school year, I help my daughter get dressed on school mornings, but I allow her to do as much as she can for herself on weekends. Another easy thing to do is to buy clothes for your child that facilitate self-dressing: loose, stretchy fabrics, shirts that open in the front or pullover shirts, slip-on shoes. Remember, however, that clothing needs to be stylish as well as functional.

Your child's occupational or physical therapist can help you to develop strategies for most aspects of daily living. She can help you to select from the many assistive devices available to help with dressing and reaching, and to assess which tasks, if any, are simply too difficult for your child to master. Your most important contribution will be a positive attitude and an expectation that your child will succeed if you both persevere.

Play Time

Play is a child's work, as the saying goes. Although your child may have to work harder to play than other children, she can still benefit in many ways from well-thought-out playtimes.

First, your child needs to simply have fun playing with you and her siblings. Perhaps the most important thing a child with spina bifida needs is to feel completely loved by her family. All family members need to feel comfortable with each other. If a child senses that she makes her own parents nervous, she will not have the confidence to mix with other children naturally. One easy way to help your child achieve this sense of belonging is to play with her often, and show her that you enjoy her company.

Second, your child needs to experience movement through play. She may have to struggle to achieve balance in an upright position, and may feel insecure in other positions. She may even resist positions for cuddling that seem very natural to other children. The key is to respect your child's fears and work into it gradually. Some activities to get your child used to movement include swinging, swimming, and playing atop a large therapy ball. Your child's physical therapist can give you additional guidance. Whatever you do, make sure the emphasis is on having fun.

Finally, your child needs to learn to play independently. Not only will this give you a much-needed break from caring for your child, but it will also give her a chance to practice and experiment with concepts and motor skills on her own, as well as exercise her creativity. To encourage your child to play on her own, arrange her playthings so that she is able to select and get them herself. Place toys in plastic bins on the floor or on low shelves. Be creative and find different ways your child can move about during play. Perhaps a scooter  board will work if your child isn't crawling (see Chapter 9). Once your child is able to stand, make sure she has fun standing activities available, such as a workbench, an easel, or a toy kitchen.

Swimming

Swimming is a great activity for children with spina bifida, but it does present a few challenges. For one, you will have to have a bowel management program that prevents accidents in the pool, or you will have to use very secure swimming undergarments. Special swimming undergarments for people with disabilities are available from companies such as Duraline.

Many people assume that a child with paralysis will feel "free" in the water, but it can be scary at first. Just as they have to learn to feel secure in different positions on land, they will need to get oriented in the water. You may be able to find a therapeutic swim program in your area, or your local recreation center may offer adaptive swim classes. It may take extra time for your child to learn to swim, but even children with very little control of their legs can become strong swimmers using only their upper bodies. Once your child learns to swim, she will be able to enjoy swimming as a social activity, and she will have a valuable exercise option that will last a lifetime.

Swimming in shallow water poses a special hazard for children who don't have sensation in their lower limbs. The bottom of the pool may be rough enough to cause serious abrasions on your child's skin. One option is to have your child wear tights under her swimsuit. The skin will be protected unless the bottom of the pool rips through the tights. Other options are to avoid the shallow end altogether, or to teach your child to visually inspect her feet for signs of abrasions. If your child can walk in the water, water socks may be sufficient to protect her.

Dancing

Most children love to dance. If your child is light enough, you can pick her up and dance with her, but as she gets older she will most likely find her own ways to move to music. This is not the time to lament the fact that your child will not grow up to dance for the New York City Ballet. It's important to allow your child to enjoy her body in her own way. In many communities, you can even find dance classes for kids who use wheelchairs. If you've never seen wheelchair dance, you may have difficulty imagining how graceful and beautiful it can be.

Sports

Karate, baseball, tennis, water skiing, kayaking, basketball, rock climbing—you name it, if there's a sport, there's a corresponding wheelchair sport. You may feel your child is too young for wheelchair sports, but she's never too young to start watching others play. Even if you don't expect your child to use a wheelchair, don't rule out wheelchair sports. Traditional sports can be difficult for children who have to work harder to walk, while wheelchair sports can be fun and fast. See the Resource Guide for organizations that sponsor wheelchair sports and/or activities.

Outdoor Play

Most kids also enjoy playing outside. Many parks and nature reserves have trails that are accessible to wheelchairs. No matter how your child gets around, she will probably have more difficulties in grass, but there are some things you can do to enable her to mix with other children. If you build a backyard swing set, you can incorporate a sandbox. When your child isn't swinging, she can play in the sand. Other children will be able to play with your child and still be as active as they want. You can use other things to draw neighborhood children into your yard, such as sidewalk chalk or a fun collection of bubble wands and a big jug of bubble juice.

Some kids with spina bifida can use motorized riding toys. One child's older brothers played Little League ball, and he used a motorized bike to get around the park. There are many styles of hand-operated or hand-assist bikes available. They can be quite costly, but families tend to pass them around as children grow out of them, through formal and informal lending closets. Remember to equip your child with a well-fitting helmet if she is going to be riding on any kind of bike or riding toy.

Transporting Your Child

Unless your child is recovering from surgery, she will most likely use a regular car seat. It may take her longer than usual, however, to progress from an infant seat to a regular seat belt. Young children with spina bifida are sometimes very slight in build. The lower body may have less muscle weight, and some children are just small for their ages. Your pediatrician can help guide you as to when it is safe for your child to make the transition into a forward facing car seat, a booster seat, and eventually a regular seat belt. Because most older children and adults with spina bifida have at least some balance difficulties, it is best to use the shoulder belt in addition to the lap belt. Be sure to adjust the shoulder belt so it doesn't cut across your child's face or neck, and never put the shoulder belt under your child's arm.

Treatment for some conditions, such as hip dislocation, can interfere with car seat usage. Sometimes children have to spend some time in a body cast, called a spica cast. Special safety harnesses have been developed to allow children in casts to be strapped into a back seat. Many children's hospitals now rent these harnesses to parents for a nominal fee. Most hospitals have a discharge planner who can help with these types of issues, but you may have to ask. If your hospital cannot provide a safety harness, you may have to make a few phone calls to other children's hospitals in the region.

Some bracing devices used to position a child for hip development do not cause a problem. Others are simply incompatible with car seat usage. You may have to remove the brace when your child rides in the car. If your child wears leg braces in the car, they can also cause a problem. Besides the spica cast harness, there are other types of harness devices available. Your local school system's transportation department may be able to assist you in locating such a device if you can't use a car seat, or if your child becomes too big for the car seat but still needs extra support.

If your child uses a wheelchair, her school bus will be equipped with a lift. Inside the bus will be various types of tie-down devices to secure the wheelchair in the bus and allow your child to ride in the wheelchair. The school will probably assume that your child will ride to school in her wheelchair. However, many children with spina bifida use lightweight wheelchairs without any support behind the child's head. These children may be safer, especially when they are young and lightweight, if they are transferred to a regular bus seat equipped with a seat belt, or to a car seat or booster seat.

So far there have not been any serious accidents involving buses and tied-down wheelchairs, so many bus companies feel that this type of transportation is safe. Wheelchair tie-downs are also used in public transportation, and they have the obvious advantage that an adult with a wheelchair can travel independently without the need of assistance to transfer in and out of her chair. Additional studies to determine whether this is a safe mode of transport for all types of wheelchairs and to develop ways to enhance the safety of transportation in a tied-down wheelchair need to be completed.

As children with spina bifida grow, many families invest in vans with wheelchair lifts and tie-downs. Other families prefer to stow the wheelchair in the rear of the car while the child rides in a regular seat. The size and weight of the child, the child's ability to transfer in and out of the car, and the strength and health of the parents or care givers are all factors to be considered.

Many public transportation facilities, ranging from commuter train stations to tram rides at amusement parks, are equipped to deal with wheelchairs, but it is still wise to call ahead. Often you will find that only half the buses are equipped with lifts, and you may have to wait. With the passage of the Americans with Disabilities Act, accessibility to many public places has improved greatly, but you can still run into nasty surprises. Churches are often inaccessible or only partly accessible. On the other hand, sometimes facilities are available if you only think to ask. For example, most zoos and amusement parks have first aid stations which they will gladly let you use to catheterize your child. See Chapter 15 for more information about accessibility issues.

Community Activities

Much of your child's time will be taken up with doctor visits, therapy sessions, and bowel and bladder programs. It's easy to neglect all the "normal" child activities, but your child needs to develop her interests and talents just like any other child. As mentioned earlier, if you look around in your community, you will probably find some type of sports activity for children with disabilities, but you can also enroll your child in many

activities right alongside her peers without disabilities. Some examples include library story hours, recreation center activities such as art and music lessons, craft classes, and scouting activities.

If your child can participate without any special assistance, most programs will accept her willingly. If she does need assistance, some civic recreation centers and parks departments have programs to provide "buddies" to facilitate participation. As explained in Chapter 15, however, your child cannot be excluded from any recreation program that is open to the public, thanks to the Americans with Disabilities Act (ADA).

▪▪ Discipline and Responsibilities

Newborn babies are completely egocentric: they are concerned only about themselves and their own needs. Our role as parents is to teach them that they are loved and wanted, and to teach them their place in the family and in the world. We teach them their place in the world through discipline. Children who are not effectively disciplined can become self-centered, demanding, and irresponsible, while children who are abused can grow up to be abusive and unsure of themselves. The child who is given loving, consistent discipline will most often grow up to be a loving, responsible adult.

Children with disabilities need discipline just as much as other children. In fact, if you want your child to be as "normal" as possible, discipline is essential. This means you must set clear expectations, with clear, consistent consequences for misbehavior, and you must give your child responsibilities. Naturally, you will have to make adjustments and there will be special considerations.

Discipline at Home

Saying No. One of the earliest challenges you may face is that your child with spina bifida may not be able to get into as much mischief as she should. During the toddler years, children are constantly getting into things and going where they shouldn't go, and parents are constantly telling them "no." Although this process is exhausting, it is very effective in teaching children what "no" means, and who is in charge. It may take longer for your child to learn these lessons, but if you are clear and consistent, she will get it eventually. Sometimes parents inadvertently make it harder for their child with spina bifida to learn the meaning of "no." They are so happy when their child finally starts walking that they fail to say "no" when they should. This only leads to confusion for the child since she will eventually have to learn that there are some things she cannot have.

Spoiling Your Child. Another pitfall is that there will probably be times when your child is hospitalized or when her mobility is severely limited after surgery or other medical events. Also, she will likely spend quite a bit of time in waiting rooms. During these times, you will do your best to keep her amused and she can easily become "spoiled." For example, you may allow more television time than usual, and then you will have to deal with getting her used to less television again. It helps if you do not rely on television too heavily. Despite your best efforts, however, your child is likely to get used to having extra attention from you, and perhaps even extra gifts and privileges. She will not want to give those things up when things get back to normal. At such times, you will probably be exhausted yourself and not at your best.

Such lapses in discipline are not only inevitable; they are necessary. It would be cruel not to make allowances for a child who is being restricted and perhaps going through emotional trauma as well. Once the physical restrictions have passed, you can gradually but firmly ease back into your normal routine.

Sometimes parents try to "make it up" to their kids through food. All parents do this at times, such as when they take their children out for ice cream after they get a shot. Parents of children with spina bifida need to guard against this tendency. Your child already has many factors in her life that can cause a tendency toward obesity. You must be careful not to teach your child to use food for comfort.

Effective Methods of Discipline for Younger Children. When your child is very young, it may be difficult to find effective methods of discipline. If your child's mobility is already impaired, she may not be terribly impressed by "time out." Also, because your child has a legitimate need for physical assistance to complete many tasks, it can be very challenging to teach her to take responsibility for herself and to have initiative.

Still, there are things you can do. Insist that your child say "please" and "thank you" when she needs assistance, and try to get her to ask for help before you step in. This is difficult and time consuming, but the more headway you can make in this area, the easier things will be when she gets to school. You may find it helpful to read as much as you can about various discipline techniques, and then try to adapt them. The Reading List provides some suggestions of helpful books.

The most effective method of discipline we found when our daughter was a preschooler was to take things away from her. Whenever possible, we would take away something directly involved with the misbehavior. For instance, if she threw a toy, we took the toy away. This type of direct connection between the misbehavior and the consequence is especially important for toddlers. As our daughter matured, we would take away a favorite toy for other types of misbehavior. I don't recommend taking away a toy that a child uses for security unless she is misusing it. Young children have a very limited understanding of time, so it is not necessary to take a toy away from a toddler for long. Depending on the age of the child, a few minutes to a couple of hours is usually sufficient. Longer lengths of time are unlikely to bring additional benefits. When you return the item, be sure to remind your child that she needs to behave in order to keep all of her privileges. As your child gets closer to school age, you can take things away for longer periods of time according to the severity of the disobedience.

But be careful to make sure your child understands what you are doing. Children with spina bifida can feel frustrated at their inability to control their environment, so it's important to avoid making them feel even more powerless. Try to emphasize that proper behavior brings greater freedom and greater control.

Depending upon your child's level of impairment, it may not be possible to bring her up to the same level of personal responsibility that she would normally have had by the time she starts school. Many children with spina bifida are distractible, and their lack of initiative only adds to their difficulty in following classroom instruction and completing their work. Still, if you are firm and consistent with your child when she is little, you lay the foundation of respect for authority.

Effective Methods of Discipline for School-aged Children. The good news is that as your child reaches school age, many more discipline tools become available to you. By now, the toddler who wasn't impressed by time out will probably hate being confined to her room. You can use charts with pictures for very young children, but as they learn to read it becomes easier. In the morning, you can give your child a list of things she needs to do to get ready for school. Then try to leave it up to her to ask for the help she needs. (You may have to get her up very early at first to avoid missing the bus.)

Older children also respond well to incentive charts and contracts. For example, you can make a contract with your child that spells out what each of you is expected to do to contribute to family life. Allow your child to contribute her ideas to the contract, and then have each family member sign it. Then, when your child fusses about cleaning her room, you can remind her that she signed a contract. This can help to deflect her anger away from you and to teach her that responsibilities are part of life. You may wish to include in the contract such things as going to the doctor, therapy sessions, and bowel and bladder programs. Your child will appreciate your acknowledgment that much of her time is out of her control, and it gives you a way to recognize her for cooperating.

Incentive charts are very useful for children who have a hard time remembering their routine. You can have a chart that lists all of your child's chores or each step in getting ready for school or bed. You need to place the chart where your child can see it, whether she is in her wheelchair, walking, or scooting on the floor. She can check each item off as she completes it and then receive a small reward, such as a sticker or a penny, when all the tasks are complete. You may want to offer a larger reward for long-term cooperation, but be sure your child understands that the most important reward is her own feeling of accomplishment and the family harmony that comes when children do their part without fussing.

Discipline in Public

Most parents hate to have to discipline their children in public. People can be so judgmental. If you lose your patience and snap at your child, they judge your worst moment as if it represented all that you are as a parent. Disciplining a child with spina bifida in public presents special challenges.

One of the things you hear over and over again when you have a child with a disability is that if you treat her like any other child she will grow up to be "normal." People really mean it when they say it, but they don't think it through. Your child will pull at their heart strings and they do not want to see you be stern with her. But someday, your child will grow up, and she won't be a cute little kid with spina bifida anymore. The very people who indulged her when she was six will say she is spoiled when she is eleven.

When your child is little, many people will try to make her feel special. People will think she is deserving of everything from free ice cream to free tickets to Disney World. They will tell you to go to the front of the line; at the zoo, they will pull their kids back from the railing so that your child has the best view. If your child uses a wheelchair, she will be able to part crowds like the Red Sea, but you have to keep up with her because the crowd closes up again after the wheelchair passes through, and she can get away from you.

When you discipline your child in public, people will give you dirty looks. Never mind that she was running a little old lady down with her wheelchair; someone will tell you, "Now dear, she's doing the best she can." While you're trying to teach your child to manage her chair safely and considerately, people will be scurrying to get out of her way, saying, "She's OK," "It's all right," "Excuse *me!*" The message your child gets is that it's perfectly all right if she wants to wheel her chair down the middle of the grocery aisle or even zig zag!

These messages can be hard to counteract, but we have a responsibility to prepare our children to fit into the real world. Children with disabilities may get the red-carpet treatment when they are young, but when they are grown they are more likely to be ignored. If you want your child to integrate into society, good social skills are vital and good discipline is absolutely essential to socialization. So brace yourself to endure the dirty looks. Your child's future is worth it.

Chores

It is very important for your child with spina bifida to have responsibilities and to make a contribution to the family. This will also promote family harmony, as your other children won't resent their brother or sister with spina bifida because she doesn't have chores and they do.

Many housekeeping tasks can be adapted to get around your child's limitations. For example, you may have to bring the dishes to the table for her, but she can set the table from there. Or if you want your child to feed her pet, keep the food where she can reach it when she's sitting on the floor.

Children learn more than just responsibility from doing chores. For instance, sorting laundry can help a child learn organizational skills. Folding laundry can be more difficult, but it's a great opportunity to work on motor skills and coordination.

You can't expect any child to learn a complex task all at once. Sorting laundry begins with just pulling out all the white things, and folding can begin with folding washcloths. Do not assume your child knows how to complete a multi-step job until she understands all the steps involved. For example, "Clean up your room" can be an overwhelming demand. Giving more specific instructions such as, "Put all your toy cars in this bin" may be more effective. For the older child who still has difficulty cleaning her room, you can make a list of each step in the process or help her make her own list.

As your child gets older, keep looking for ways to empower her at home. Our daughter could only reach a couple of shelves in our pantry, and she couldn't reach the cabinets where we kept the dishes. So we started keeping everything she wanted to reach on the one shelf she could access by herself—snacks, cereal, whatever she needed. We even got her a separate set of dishes in a fun print. Because her dishes look different from the others, they always get returned to her own shelf. You can also buy milk in half gallon or smaller containers so it's easier for your child to pour her own milk.

■■ Self-Advocacy

Educating your child about her disability is a big part of helping her to become independent. By the time she starts school, she should be able to answer basic questions about herself. You will also want to talk to her about how to handle questions and staring, and how they make her feel. I've tried to teach my daughter to distinguish between legitimate interest, as from classmates, and idle curiosity, as from strangers we see on the street. I've taught her she must not respond to rude questions by being rude, but that she is not obligated to explain herself if she doesn't want to. When I told her she needed to be patient with young children because they have not yet learned that their questions are rude, she started telling them they were being rude. I had to add that it was up to their parents to teach them not to be rude.

When strangers ask me about my daughter, especially children, I now refer their questions to her. I believe that this is part of allowing my daughter ownership over her disability.

Helping your child become an active participant in her own medical care is also important. If you want her to see to her own medical care when she is grown, you need to involve her as much as possible as she is growing up. She may be too young to decide for herself whether she needs a particular orthopedic surgery, but perhaps you can let her help you decide when to schedule it.

Another idea is to help your child keep a calendar of her appointments. My daughter is now seven, and she wants to know the purpose of each medication she takes. This type of interest should be encouraged. Rather than just dragging your child from appointment to appointment, try to take the time to explain the purpose of each visit.

You can also get books from the library that illustrate how the nervous system and muscles work. And don't neglect to teach your child about healthy habits and fitness. Our daughter has hand weights and push-up bars and loves to do her exercise routine and show off her muscles. If you teach your child to take pride in what she *can* do with her body, she is much more likely to want to take care of it.

** A Safe and Accessible Home

Whether or not your child uses a wheelchair, you will probably need to make some adjustments in your home. You may have to install a ramp to your front door or rearrange the furniture. If you have stairs in your home, you will need to be cautious. If you have single steps, perhaps leading into a sunken room, make sure your child knows where they are. These steps can be hazardous to both wheelchairs and children walking with braces. To make your house more wheelchair accessible, you may need to widen doors and make your bathrooms more spacious. In addition, you might want to replace existing carpeting, as thick carpets make wheelchair mobility harder.

Most kids want to be included in everything everyone is doing, and watching Mom and Dad do things is an important way to learn the life skills necessary for independence. You will want to find ways to get your child into as many areas of the home as possible, and to position her safely while she watches or helps you work. If you live in a multi-level home and your child cannot climb stairs, you can investigate chair lifts, residential elevators, or even the possibility of moving to a more accessible home.

There may be funding available in your community to help pay for alterations in your home. Ask your spina bifida team for this type of resource. Also, some residential improvements qualify as medical deductions for tax purposes, so keep careful records of any alterations you make.

You may not think that you need to be careful about placing hazardous substances out of reach, but never underestimate a child's resourcefulness. Our daughter once pulled on the tablecloth until her vitamins came within reach and then swallowed several of them. Just as with any child, it is wise to invest in socket covers and cupboard latches to help keep your child safe.

Some children with disabilities are very fearful of being trapped in a fire. One way to increase fire safety is to call your fire department. They will keep a record of your child's condition, and which room she sleeps in. You should also teach your child how to call for help and consider installing a telephone in her room. Unless she can stand without braces, you will need to put them someplace where she will be able to reach them, whether she is standing, sitting, or on the floor. All families are advised to have and practice a fire emergency plan. In the event of an emergency, all children need to be able to exit the house on their own. For a child with spina bifida, that might mean crawling out.

■■ Update

It's been nearly ten years since I originally wrote this chapter. My daughter is now almost seventeen, she's learning to drive, and this year, she had a date for Homecoming. My daughter has grown into a beautiful young woman. Physically, she is extremely independent. She takes care of all her own personal care, and she has acquired most of the cooking and cleaning skills she will need to live independently.

In revising this chapter, I found that I still agree with nearly everything I wrote originally. The basic concepts I introduced in this chapter do not change as your child grows older: good communication, advocacy, and fostering a can-do attitude are important at every age. I would like to add just two pieces of advice:

1. Never give up.
2. Believe in your child.

Never Give Up

You must never give up. No child is likely to develop "perfectly." For children with disabilities, development and maturity can be very uneven. Your child with spina bifida is likely to try your patience at times. Some people refer to the development of children with serious medical issues as being like "Swiss cheese." Children may look normal overall, but there are likely to be "holes" in their development. For example, some children with spina bifida do not pay attention to, or process, social cues as well as other children, leading to social lapses. As suggested earlier, some struggle with personal initiative. Others may learn to project an image of the well-adjusted poster child, masking serious emotional issues. And some children may try to create greater privacy and independence from their parents by becoming skilled at lying.

As your child interacts with the wider world, some people will make too many allowances for her; others may seem hard and unsympathetic. I've dealt with a succession of teachers who think that all my daughter needs is someone who will be "tough" with her. As if I haven't tried that already.

As my daughter has moved through public school, I have often wished that she didn't have to grow up in the same timeframe as her peers. Children have so much to learn and master in such a short period of time. Children with disabilities are expected to cover all that same ground, plus deal with the complexities and limitations of the disability, all in the same length of time. No wonder there are holes!

Believe in Your Child

More then anything, our children need for us to believe in them. Believing in them means trusting that with time, patience, and the right support, they will grow up to be well-adjusted, whole adults.

You can't change the world's time table, but you can adjust your own expectations to give your child enough time to grow up. For instance, our daughter is highly intelligent and capable, but she struggles

with study skills. After she graduates from high school, we think the best option for her is attending the community college for a year or two before heading off to a four-year university.

Perhaps the hardest thing we parents must do is accept that we cannot control the outcome for any of our children. All we can do is to create the right conditions for success. For your child with spina bifida, that means never giving up on advocacy until she is given the right accommodations and interventions. I'm not suggesting that you go into every situation prepared for a fight. On the contrary, most teachers and other adults want to do what is best for your child. And it pays to listen to the advice of professionals with experience. But as your child gets older, it may become more difficult to figure out what she needs, and everyone involved in her life will have to be willing to try different strategies to find the ones that will meet both her physical and emotional needs. It may take time, effort, and persistence, but you can find the right support for your child.

Remember, after you have done your part, the rest is up to your child. When times get difficult or you encounter one of those "holes," it can be hard to remember what a really good job you are doing overall, but that is something that all parents experience in varying degrees. And all parents must teach their children to take responsibility for their own future.

❚❚ Conclusion

In the early days of learning to cope with the challenges that spina bifida brings, your life may seem unmanageable. As your family learns new skills and develops a routine, however, things will most likely improve. True, there will still be days of frustration and confusion, but there will also be days of happiness and contentment. Over time, you will find that parenting a child with spina bifida is more like than unlike parenting any child.

❚❚ Parent Comments

I remember thinking it was a good thing that Jacob had an older brother who could stick up for him if other children made fun of him. It turned out that no one ever made fun of Jacob, except his older brother.

❦

My other children sometimes do not receive the attention they need because I am busy with Kelly. Sometimes they have difficulty dealing with the stress. But I believe that having Kelly for a sister has made them more compassionate toward others.

❦

Our family members were understandably shocked when they heard the news of our baby's condition. They all needed time to grieve and adjust their expectations. We made sure the lines of communication were open and that they felt comfortable asking questions about their concerns—no matter how "dumb" the question seemed.

☙❈❧

I felt that my husband's parents initially resented the fact that Michael was not healthy. Now they overcompensate to the point of neglecting their other grandchildren— for instance, always asking how Michael is, but not asking about our other kids.

☙❈❧

After the initial shock wore off, both sets of grandparents rallied around and have been very supportive. They have spent a lot of time educating themselves about spina bifida and special education issues. Around holidays and birthdays they are always sure to ask if there is a certain toy or piece of equipment that would be helpful for Katelyn to receive as a gift. This definitely helps with our finances.

☙❈❧

Due to his physical limitations and decreased endurance, we don't expect Paul to do as many physical chores as my other children. But he does carry out other less demanding chores that take equal amounts of time.

☙❈❧

Maria's an only child, but her cousins treat her just like their sister. They are always more than happy to include her in their games and activities.

☙❈❧

At first having Abby around was hard on my other children. I think seeing her get so much attention and having to give up their time with us so we could be with Abby made it really difficult. Now that Abby is almost two years old, they have become very close to her, very protective of her. I also think having Abby has made them more aware of other children with special needs, and it gives them a better understanding of people with disabilities in general. I believe Abby has made our whole family a lot closer. She is definitely very special to all of us.

☙❈❧

Our daughter with spina bifida is the oldest of our three children. The other children are quite young, so how having a sibling with a disability will affect them remains to be seen. I am hopeful, though, that having a sister with special needs will make them more sensitive and compassionate in general. I firmly believe we all have "disabilities"—some people's are just more visible.

❧

We are easier on Brenda as far as discipline and chores are concerned.

❧

Her brothers and sisters absolutely adore her. And seeing and understanding her disability has made them more comfortable with other kids or adults who are different or have disabilities. I think they'll grow up to be better and more compassionate people thanks to her.

❧

Sometimes I have to bite my tongue to keep myself from interceding in my children's arguments. I know my son with spina bifida needs to learn to compromise and settle his own problems, but I do feel an urge to "rescue" him sometimes.

❧

At the very beginning, parents cope and adjust to the fact that their precious new baby may not be able to get around the same way others do. Later they learn about other problems—urinary infections, muscle imbalances, shunting problems. By the time these things are taken care of, your child has started school and learning differences are becoming apparent. Dealing with these differences takes patience and negotiation and lots of repetition.

❧

I have to say that I don't think my husband and I take enough time for ourselves. We really only go out to dinner or a movie a couple of times a year—mostly when we have relatives visiting who offer to baby sit.

❧

My husband wants to understand all the medical issues and spends lots of time on the Internet looking things up. I don't mind knowing this information, but I'd rather get a summary from him and not have to think about every single detail.

❧❀☙

I've kept a journal since my daughter was born. It helps me to sort out my feelings and concerns. I might not be ready to talk about a concern right away, so this gives me a "safe" way to vent my feelings.

EDUCATING YOUR CHILD WITH SPINA BIFIDA:
One Size Does Not Fit All

Vicki Jahns, M.Ed.

No two children learn in exactly the same way. Some children catch on to academic subjects with little or no problem. Others excel in some subjects, but stumble over others. And still others need extra help to learn most subjects. Regardless of your child's potential to learn, however, chances are that he will require at least some help at some time in his life to maximize his learning potential. The help could be as minimal as extra assistance with homework completion, or it could be as extensive as a modified and highly individualized approach to curricular goals.

For your child to receive the special help with learning that he needs, he may need to enter the special education system. Understanding how this system works is important for families. Special education programming is as individual as the type of hat one wears. Comparing developmental stages and special education with hats may make the process seem a little less formidable. So, put on your reading hat and let's walk through the process of *Learning through a Lifetime.*

❚❚ From Sunbonnets to Graduation Caps

We will begin with a sunbonnet. It is the very first hat of all. When our children are at the sunbonnet stage, which begins with birth, we shelter, protect, and nurture them. We support, enrich, and assist with good beginnings for learning. Many of the things you can do to help your baby learn and grow are the same as for any child. They include:

- Read your baby any book. Read even before he can understand the words. Your baby will benefit from the rhythms of speech and you will lay a good foundation for future speaking and reading.
- Take your baby with you outside, to the store, or on visits to friends and relatives to develop a close bond and expose him in a secure way to new environments.
- Talk to your baby about everything; what you are doing, how you are feeling, what you need at the grocery store.
- Play music for your baby. Babies like simple rhythms and complex symphonies.
- Seek community activities, such as swimming, to meet other young families and to provide exercise and recreation.
- Hold your baby, because it's important for you and your baby to feel close.
- Join a parent group to meet other parents, to share the common concerns of other young parents, and to learn the creative solutions they may have.

There is one more important thing you can do specifically if your child is having, or is at risk of, developmental delays:

- Enroll your baby in early intervention.

❚❚ Early Intervention

A federal law known as the Individuals with Disabilities Education Act (IDEA) requires that all states provide early intervention services for children with special health care needs from the ages of birth to three. These services are designed to enhance the development, or minimize delays, in children who have, or are at risk of developing, disabilities.

They are also meant to support the goals and hopes parents have for their growing child. Services might include:

- **Family Support**—assistance in connecting with services and resources that can help the family in raising their child with a disability and in staying together as a family. For example, the family might be assisted in locating and applying for financial programs that would help offset the cost of raising a child with spina bifida.

- **Special Instruction**—instruction designed to give the parents guidance in supporting their child's overall development. For example, an early intervention specialist or teacher might show the parents ways to encourage their infant to reach for and explore toys.

- **Physical Therapy**—therapy designed to help children improve their gross motor skills. For example, a physical therapist might work with a young child who is having difficulty sitting independently or rolling over.

- **Occupational Therapy**—therapy designed to help children improve fine motor skills, oral motor and feeding skills, and difficulties processing sensations (such as under- or oversensitivities to touch). In the early months, an occupational therapist might be involved if a child is having feeding difficulties such as chewing or swallowing or difficulty accepting solid food.

- **Speech-Language Therapy**—therapy intended to help children develop their speaking skills, as well as their abilities to understand and produce language. A speech-language pathologist—the therapist qualified to provide speech-language therapy—might work with a two-year-old who is not combining single words into short phrases. On some early intervention teams, the speech-language pathologist may also help with feeding difficulties.

- **Service Coordination**—ensuring that a child receives all the services he needs, that professionals on a child's team communicate with one another when necessary, that the child's progress is monitored, and that the family's needs are taken into account in planning the child's early intervention program. The service coordinator, who may be an early intervention specialist or other professional on the team, is also responsible for overseeing the development of the document describing the child's early intervention program, the Individualized Family Service Plan (IFSP). See below.

Early intervention's philosophy is family centered. This means that: families have a choice as to when and if they want to use early intervention service, they can prioritize their needs, and they are members of the team. Some, if not all of the services, your child receives through early intervention can be provided right in your home or at an early intervention center site in your community. Another important philosophy of early intervention is to provide coordinated care. Coordination of services means that your child receives what he requires without duplication or repetition. In some communities, all early intervention services are provided at no cost to families. In other communities, parents are charged on a sliding scale for some services.

Your pediatrician or your spina bifida clinic can help you get in touch with the people who provide early intervention in your community. If you do not desire services at birth, that does not mean you cannot access the system at a later time.

A diagnosis of spina bifida automatically qualifies your child for early intervention. He will, however, need to be assessed by a team of therapists and educators before he begins receiving services. Assessments will be done to help identify your child's unique strengths and needs in all developmental areas: gross motor, fine motor, communication, cognitive.

An Individualized Family Service Plan (IFSP) will then be developed. This is a written document that lists the goals (outcomes) your child is working on in each developmental area, and the services your child and family require to reach those goals. An example of a goal might be for your child to learn to feed himself independently with a spoon. Services provided to help your child reach that goal might include physical therapy to help your child learn to sit in a highchair without leaning on his hands for support, and possibly also occupational therapy if your child has feeding difficulties or fine motor problems.

IFSPs are "family driven"—that is, they must take *your* concerns and *your* priorities into account. For example, your family's priorities might include making sure that mobility is as easy as possible for your child and that car travel with him is safe. Since you will be part of the meetings to develop an IFSP, you will be able to make sure your concerns are addressed.

As your child nears the age of three, early intervention specialists can help you plan for your child's transition into early childhood special education services, which are provided through the public school system.

▪▪ Preschool

When your child is between three and five years old, he may be eligible to receive preschool education services based on the diagnosis of spina bifida. Depending on your child's needs, he may qualify for a variety of services. These may include occupational therapy, perhaps to assist with hand writing; physical therapy to address mobility issues; speech and language therapy; appropriate school health services; and transportation to and from school.

These services are provided within your community. It is important to remember that while your child may need special assistance in one area, he will also benefit from being with other children within the *least restrictive environment*. The least restrictive environment means the setting that is as close as possible to the general education environment of your child's peers but which still enables your child to learn. (See Chapter 15 for more information about the least restrictive environment.)

Before your child can begin receiving preschool special education, he must be assessed to help you and the professionals better understand where he is experiencing difficulties. An education plan can be developed for your child using information from the evaluation, previous plans, your observations, and other sources. This time, however, the plan will be known as an Individualized Education Program (IEP), rather than an IFSP. (See the section on IEPs later in this chapter.)

▪▪ One Size Does Not Fit All: Evaluation and Eligibility

When you pick out a hat for your child, you do not shape your child to fit the hat. You choose the hat that fits your child. Likewise, when you design a plan to assist your child with educational goals, you must start with the child and the goals and then determine what activities will help your child meet those goals.

A starting point for children who are believed to need special education is with a *multidisciplinary evaluation*—that is, a series of tests conducted by a team of professionals with many different areas of expertise. For children aged five and up, this type of evaluation must be performed to determine whether a child is eligible for special education. For children aged three and up, the multidisciplinary evaluation is also used to determine appropriate goals and services for children who qualify for special education. If your child is making the transition from an early intervention program, the early intervention staff will likely assist you in arranging for the evaluation for your child. If your child is older, you can contact the principal at the school your child attends, or will attend, and ask him or her how to get the evaluation process started.

Your school district is required by law to provide your child with an evaluation in a timely fashion and at no cost to you. Assessments might include standardized testing of cognitive abilities, speech and language skills, academic skills, gross motor and fine motor skills, and physical abilities. Information about your child's abilities might also be collected from people who know your child. Sources might include a classroom teacher, a special education teacher, a speech therapist, a principal, a nurse, an occupational therapist, a psychologist, experts, friends, and your own good observations of your child's strengths and weaknesses. Just as you might measure to determine a hat size, you need to measure and evaluate to determine the current abilities and needs of your child. When your child's team has gathered information from many sources, you are ready to develop a plan.

When the evaluation is complete, your child's multidisciplinary team will be able to determine whether your child qualifies for special education services. To do so, he must be found to have one of the qualifying disabilities listed under federal and state law. Spina bifida is not specifically listed as a qualifying disability in the Individuals with Disabilities Education Act. There are a number of qualifying disabilities that children with spina bifida may be found to have, however. These include: "orthopedic impairment" (gross motor and/or fine motor problems), "specific learning disability," "speech or language impairment," and "other health impairment" (a catchall category for conditions that result in "limited strength, vitality, or alertness" that are due to a chronic or acute health problem and adversely affect a child's educational performance).

If your child is *not* found to be eligible for special education services, you may request that an independent evaluation be done through private sources in the community. If your child does not qualify for special education services in the early years of school, he may qualify later. If at any time during your child's education you feel that he is having a difficult time, let the principal of your school know and request that your child be evaluated. Schools can assist all children with individualized learning activities.

If your child *is* found to need special education, the next step is to draw up an Individualized Education Program (IEP).

:: Individualized Education Program (IEP)

The IEP is a plan for the student's education that begins with the family's vision for the child. Where do you see your child by the time he is wearing a graduation cap? With careful planning, short-term goals can be set to help the child make gradual progress toward meeting his family's long-range goals. Your child, your family, the school, and other people can all contribute information, knowledge, or ideas to formulate the plan. Everything is eventually written down on a piece of paper that gets signed by the student (when appropriate), the parents, and the school. It then becomes a legal document that specifies what the school system will do to help your child reach his educational goals.

An IEP covers many facets of your child's education. Chapter 15 provides a complete list of everything it encompasses. The information below is designed to get you thinking about what you think should be included in your child's IEP. Remember, you should be prepared to contribute your thoughts to the plan.

Goals are an important part of an IEP. What are your long-range goals for your child? To be a productive citizen? To live independently? What are the intermediate goals your child needs to meet to reach the long-range goals? For example, a short-term goal for independent living might include the ability to budget a monthly income. However, before your child can learn to budget a monthly income, he might need a goal to learn to calculate using decimals.

What services does your child need to help him reach his goals? Just as when he was in early intervention, your child may need therapy or certain kinds of educational assistance to assist him in making progress. For instance, he might need speech-language therapy to help him meet his goals for reading comprehension. On the IEP, these types of services are referred to as *related services*. (See below.)

Another important component of an IEP is a description of where these services take place. As explained in the next section, the "least restrictive environment," or the one closest to the general education environment, falls within a variety of possible settings. It might be in the general classroom with other children of the same age, or in a separate classroom with a special purpose. It is important to remember that the decision about where to provide the services can be discussed only after the goals, objectives, and needs of the individual student are known.

Your child's IEP must also state how his progress will be measured. Will he participate in standardized tests? Will the teacher measure his progress with teacher-made evaluations? How often will measurements of progress be made?

The IEP is meant to be a flexible document that can be reopened at the request of any member of the team to reassess how progress is being made. To change an IEP, someone must call the team together. A teacher in a class cannot simply decide to change a goal and not provide something for the student that was agreed upon by the team. Everyone needs to know what is going on. The law requires that the team meet to review a student's IEP at least once a year, and that parents be invited to participate in the meeting. Individual school districts may have policies that include more frequent meetings. Parents can request meetings on a schedule they prefer and have them written into the IEP.

No child's IEP will look just like another child's IEP. Remember, it is an *individualized* educational plan.

■■ Don't Wear a Top Hat When a Baseball Cap Is Right: Your Child's Placement

As discussed above, one of the key decisions made during the IEP meeting is where your child will receive his educational services. Obviously, it is important to choose the environment for learning that will best help your child reach his goals. Not so obviously, the right environment for one child is not necessarily the right environment for another child. And sometimes even the right environment for achieving one goal for one child is not the same as it is for another goal.

When choosing a hat that can go from environment to environment, we would look for one that can be adapted. For example, if we have a hat with earflaps, we can tie them up on top if it is warm outside or pull them down over our ears and tie them under our chin if it gets cold.

In special education, that same kind of versatility is available through what is termed a *continuum of services*. Education settings can vary from activity to activity depending on the student's needs. For example, during any given classroom activity, a student may be:

- included in regular classroom instruction;
- included in regular instruction with supports, such as additional time to complete written work or a tape recorder for taking notes;
- included in regular instruction with additional staff or faculty attending; for example, with an aide assigned to the student or to the classroom as a whole;
- given individual instruction within the framework of class interactions on a theme, such as completing a project on the topic of study rather than writing an essay, or individualizing vocabulary;
- attending a one-on-one tutorial inside or outside of the regular classroom;
- participating in a small group, perhaps for discussions;
- given extra help in a resource room.

In addition, if your child is hospitalized or homebound for medical reasons, the school district is responsible for educating your child in those settings, if necessary.

Sometimes a student may need a great deal of extra help. Sometimes a student may need less help. Just like we use ear flaps on some days and not on others.

The Least Restrictive Environment

Under federal law, the educational settings for a child are to be in the *least restrictive environment* in which that child can accomplish his goals. This means the educational setting that will best prepare that student to be a full participant within the broader community as an adult—to contribute to his community, as well as to access assistance from it. Since the broader community is made up primarily of people who do not have disabilities, the least restrictive environment for a student is the one that allows him to have the most contact with typically developing peers while meeting his goals.

When considering what learning environment might be best for your child, it is a good idea to visit the different settings available—specific schools, as well as specific classrooms within those schools. See for yourself which setting looks like an appropriate place for your child.

Remember, don't wear a top hat when a baseball cap is right. Choose the environment for learning that is right for the goal you want to reach.

▪▪ The Essential Features of a Well-Fitting Hat: Related Services

A straw hat might not be any good without a chin strap to hold it on in the wind. A baseball cap without a bill would not allow you to look into the sun. Without related services at school, some children might not be able to learn.

As defined by federal law, a related service is one that is necessary for a child to benefit from special education. For example, your child might need assistance with medical needs (such as catheterization) to attend a class. Or he might need speech and language therapy to develop the skills needed to talk with the other students and the teacher in the classroom. Other examples of related services include:

- Occupational therapy and physical therapy (discussed under "Early Intervention")
- Transition services to assist in making a smooth transition from one setting to the next, such as from early interven-

tion to the public school system or from high school to the work force. Sometimes other agencies can be involved. For example, professionals from the Bureau of Vocational Rehabilitation.

- Adaptive physical education to meet your child's goals for physical well-being and fitness.
- Assistive technology services, such as a word processor or tape recorder for completing written assignments.
- Transportation to and from school, using an adapted bus or van, if necessary.

Related services must be provided based on a student's need for those services. If your child needs a particular service to benefit from programming or to meet an IEP goal, then he must have the service. It is important to remember that we fit the hat to the child, not the child to the hat. If your child needs a size medium, then a size large or a size small will not do. This means that if your school district does not currently provide that service, they still must provide it for your child if that is what he needs. This may mean that the school will purchase the services from an outside agency (for example, contract with an OT to come to your child's school).

Remember, just like any student, your child has a right to an education that will allow him to be a full participant in the broad community. If he needs related services to make educational progress to reach that goal, then he must receive them.

◾ Making Sure the Hat is Right for the Occasion: An Appropriate Education

Under federal law, schools are required to provide all students with disabilities with a "free and appropriate public education." This means that every aspect of a child's education plan detailed in his IEP must be provided at no cost to the family within the public school system. This much is usually easy for parents to understand. However, parents, educators, and others sometimes have a difficult time understanding what an "appropriate" education means.

When we think about choosing an appropriate hat for a specific occasion, we think about finding one that fits our needs. What kind of weather does the hat need to protect us from? How dressy do we need to look? How long will we need to keep the hat on?

Likewise, an appropriate education needs to fit a child's needs to meet specific goals. Generally, an appropriate education is interpreted to mean one in which the student can make reasonable progress in several different areas. These include academic preparation, personal growth, independence in the community, and wise use of leisure time. An appropriate education does *not* necessarily mean the best possible education for a child, just as an appropriate hat is not necessarily the top-of-the-line model.

As a parent, it is important for you to understand this concept of "appropriate education." This is because nothing is going to be added to (or subtracted from) your child's IEP without considering its "appropriateness" for your child. For example, you might think that your child would benefit enormously if the school provided occupational therapy. The school, however, might not agree to provide OT unless you can convince them that your child's education would not be appropriate without it. To do so, you might have to show that your child is failing to make good progress in several academic areas because he can't keep up with the written work in the classroom.

In looking at your child's IEP, you need to ask yourself whether it is a good fit for your child and his goals. Do the activities and goals specified on it tie in with what you want for your child in the distant future? In other words, do you feel the hat looks good?

❚❚ Making Sure the Hat Still Fits: Accountable Progress

As explained above, an appropriate education is one in which a student makes progress. To know if a student is making progress, we must measure his successes. Just as we must check to see if last winter's stocking cap is too small, we must check to see if a child has outgrown a goal on his IEP.

By law, a student's progress must be monitored in several ways. The IEP must specify how progress will be measured and the IEP must be reviewed at specified times to check the student's progress. Parents can request an administrative review at any time if they are concerned about the progress of their child. School districts have written information regarding the appeals procedure that must be given to the parents.

If a student is not making the expected progress, parents and educators will ideally agree on what to do. In the event of a disagreement, parents have several options. These options include mediation and due process procedures, which will be written as part of the school's special education policy and will be made available to parents by the school. See Chapter 15 for more information about grievance procedures.

▮▮ Different-Colored Bonnets: Common Challenges to Learning

All children are born with an innate potential to learn, and the variety of learning potentials among children with spina bifida is as wide as it is among any group of children. Having spina bifida, however, does make it more likely that a child will experience at least some difficulties in the classroom. This section describes the most common challenges to learning, as well as strategies to help overcome them.

Gross Motor Problems

Spina bifida may delay the acquisition of skills that require movements of the large muscles. Generally, however, these delays do not affect a child's abilities to learn alongside other children in the classroom. If motor delays affect the ability to learn specific material, then *accommodations* must be made. (An accommodation is any change made to the regular environment that will help a child succeed.) Accommodations for gross motor delays could include assistance from a physical therapist, changing the location of a class, or providing special equipment such as a ramp.

If motor delays do not affect your child's classroom learning, they must still be taken into account when planning his IEP. One reason is that accommodations may need to be made to help him manage his physical needs. For instance, if he requires assistance or extra time in the bathroom, strategies need to be developed so that he won't miss out on important classroom activities or feel stigmatized.

Accessibility of classrooms and activities also needs to be carefully considered. Your child needs equal access not just to his classroom, but also to the playground, the lunchroom, field trips, assemblies, and extracurricular activities. Otherwise, he will have difficulty practicing the social skills that he will eventually need to be a full participant in the

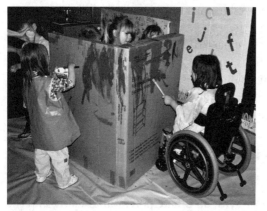

economic and social structure of adult society. Federal law requires that your child be allowed to participate in the full range of school activities.

It is important for your child's classmates to be educated about physical disabilities. They need to understand, for example, that poor motor skills do not equal poor cognitive or thinking abilities. Programs to assist peers with adjustment and attitudes are available. Parents may wish to speak with the school psychologist to assess which programs might be beneficial for their child's school. Personnel from hospitals or spina bifida clinics may also be helpful in educating your child's classmates about disabilities.

Fine Motor Problems

Fine motor problems are common in children with spina bifida. They are not as immediately obvious as gross motor problems, however. Typically, the fine motor skill that children with spina bifida have the most trouble with at school is handwriting. This is because their hands tire easily and they may have less strength in their fingers. It may be helpful to limit the amount of paper work a child must complete or to teach him keyboarding skills. Another common problem is poor spatial orientation, which results in messy looking papers. Encouraging your child to dictate reports may be helpful if this is a problem for him. Other options are to allow your child to dictate his answers to a scribe or to try voice recognition software.

If your child has extreme difficulties, he may need to be assessed by an occupational therapist, who works with fine motor skills necessary for daily activities.

Communication Difficulties

Some children with spina bifida have language difficulties such as poor comprehension, difficulty sequencing ideas, or misunderstanding directions. With guidance from the speech-language pathologist, the teacher may be able to handle these problems with special techniques within the classroom. For example, the teacher could provide outlines of lecture materials or give clues as to the sequence or order of a task. Young children may benefit from picture clues. Older children may require written graphic organizers or diagrams to assist in understanding.

If your child has speech or language difficulties that affect his ability to learn in the classroom, he can receive therapy from a speech-language pathologist. This therapy may be individual therapy, small group instruction, or collaboration with the classroom teacher by the speech and language professional. An IEP can be developed with information from the speech-language pathologist to assist in individualizing your child's goals.

Spatial Orientation

Some children with spina bifida have trouble with spatial orientation tasks. Spatial orientation tasks include knowing where your body is in relationship to other objects, as well as being able to judge space requirements and distances and understand abstract mathematical concepts. A student with spina bifida may therefore have difficulty with tasks that require him to make judgments about what he sees. For example, it may take him longer to put together a puzzle or to figure out how to do geometry problems or solve a word problem in math.

Strategies or adaptations that can help a child with spatial orientation problems in school might include the use of graph paper or clearly drawn margins and lines on writing paper.

Attention and Memory

For children with spina bifida, concentrating can be very difficult due to the differences in their central nervous system. Memory skills, which can be related to concentration skills, might also be somewhat weak. If you suspect that these are problem areas for your child, you might start by helping him find ways to compensate. You might remind him to:

- Write down things to do such as his homework;
- Establish a routine such as leaving homework by the door for morning;
- Keep a calendar for school activities and home responsibilities;
- Tape record messages to himself.

Some children with spina bifida have attention deficit disorders (AD/HD), with or without hyperactivity. That is, if a specialist compares their behavior with the list of behaviors generally believed to be indicative of an attention deficit disorder, they exhibit enough of the behaviors to be diagnosed with the inattentive or hyperactive form of the disorder. Characteristics of attention deficit disorders may include difficulties with the following:

- finishing work;
- finishing games;
- concentrating;
- planning;
- turn-taking;
- sitting still;
- relaxing.

If you or your child's teachers are concerned that he may have AD/HD, you can make an appointment to have him evaluated. Start by consulting your physician or your spina bifida team.

If you are told that your child meets the criteria for a diagnosis of attention deficit disorder, you would likely be referred to a psychologist who specializes in behavior management. He or she can recommend changes to your child's home and classroom environment that may reduce the likelihood that your child will have behavior problems. At school, the school psychologist could provide classroom consultation or develop a plan with your child to address specific behaviors. For example, suggestions might include ways: to increase the time that your child remains in his seat, to encourage him to raise his hand before answering in class, to assist him to refocus on an activity, and to provide clear external structure to his environment.

Stimulant medication such as Ritalin™ or Dexedrine™ or the nonstimulant medication Strattera™ is also an avenue that can be explored. In many children, these medications can reduce at least some of the behaviors associated with AD/HD. Be sure to ask your physician about side effects. How will follow-up be done to determine whether the appropriate dose is being given? Your physician would likely want behavior questionnaires completed by you and the teacher to assess whether medication is working. These would be completed on a regular basis, likely in cooperation with a psychologist.

Learning Difficulties

Students with spina bifida often have difficulties with mathematics, reading comprehension, or writing. They may also have problems with organization and study skills.

If these difficulties need to be addressed on your child's IEP, he may be diagnosed with a specific learning disability. As mentioned above, this is one of the diagnoses that can qualify a child for special education services. Under federal law, a learning disability is defined as a "disorder in one of more of the basic psychological processes involved in understanding or in using spoken or written language, which may manifest itself in an imperfect ability to listen, think, speak, read, write, spell or to do mathematical calculations." According to the federal definition, these learning difficulties are not the result of visual, hearing, or motor disabilities, mental retardation, emotional disturbances, or environmental, cultural, or economic disadvantage.

Individual states have their own criteria for determining whether a student has a learning disability. Until the most recent amendments to IDEA in 2004, schools generally looked for evidence of a significant discrepancy between a child's ability and his achievement in the classroom. For example, was the child having much more difficulty reading, doing math, or mastering some other skill than would be expected based on his scores on standardized IQ tests? IDEA 2004 now specifies that states do *not* need to look for a severe discrepancy between achievement and overall intelligence. Instead, states can develop other policies for identifying learning disabilities, including by trying interventions that usually help students with learning disabilities and observing to see whether these interventions help a particular struggling student.

When learning difficulties are seen, they should be addressed on the IEP. The goal should be to find ways to help the child succeed despite these problems. Some examples of accommodation are: pulling the child out of the classroom to work on problem subjects in a resource room with a specially trained teacher; providing assignments that are shortened, simplified, or otherwise adapted; using special teaching techniques, such as Touch Math (in which a child learns to add or subtract by counting dots placed at certain positions on numerals); and allowing the child to use technology or equipment in the classroom, such as a word processor with a spell check program or a tape recorder for note taking.

Health Care Issues

Obtaining routine medical care such as immunizations, physicals, and prescription medications is your family's responsibility. School health services, however, must be provided as a related service if your child needs them to benefit from his education. Under federal law, these services must be provided by a school nurse or other qualified professional. Health services that students with spina bifida commonly receive in school include help with catheterization, changing of undergarments, putting on and taking off braces, and receiving medications while at school. Your child is entitled to these services whether or not he qualifies for special education services under IDEA (see the section below).

■■ What If Your Child Is Not Covered by IDEA?

Not all children with spina bifida qualify for special education services under IDEA. This is because IDEA covers only those children whose disabilities are found to have an educational impact on them. A child who uses a wheelchair but is able to do the same schoolwork expected of his peers would usually not be considered to have a qualifying disability under IDEA. Even if your child does not qualify under IDEA, however, he will probably still be eligible for accommodations at school under Section 504 of the Rehabilitation Act of 1973.

As Chapter 15 explains, Section 504 is an antidiscrimination law. It prohibits any program or activity that receives money from the federal government from discriminating against people with disabilities. Subpart D—Preschool, Elementary, and Secondary Education—guarantees a "free appropriate public education to each qualified person with a disability . . . regardless of the nature or severity of the person's disability."

Almost every child with spina bifida would be found to have a disability under Section 504, as discussed in Chapter 15. If your child qualifies under Section 504, but not IDEA, he will be eligible for aids, equipment, and accommodations that will allow him to receive an education comparable to that of the students without disabilities at his school. In contrast to IDEA, however, these accommodations can only be provided if they do not impose an "undue financial and administrative burden" on the school system. Examples of accommodations that might be provided under Section 504 include:

- moving the location of a class to make it accessible (for example, if the chemistry lab is on the third floor, where it is inaccessible to students in wheelchairs);
- allowing a student additional time to change out of gym clothes or to travel from class to class so he does not miss out on valuable instructional time;
- providing a bus that is equipped to carry children with disabilities for transportation to school and on field trips;
- allowing extra time for writing assignments or shortening writing assignments;
- providing seats, desks, and tables appropriate for wheelchair users;
- providing assistance in the cafeteria line if the student cannot carry a tray and propel his wheelchair at the same time.

In addition, any educational program that receives federal funding must be available to students with disabilities. This includes preschools or vocational teaching programs. Likewise, students with disabilities must be given an equal opportunity to participate in their school's extracurricular programs. For example, they cannot be excluded from the drama club because the school stage is not wheelchair accessible. (These provisions apply to *all* children with disabilities, not just those seeking accommodations under Section 504.)

By law, every school system must have written procedures for carrying out the requirements of Section 504. Among other things, these should describe: 1) the school system's procedures for determining who is eligible for accommodations under Section 504; and 2) the elements of the individualized plan for a qualified student, which may be called the 504 Plan or Individualized Determination Plan. Each school system is required to have at least one 504 coordinator on staff. The 504 coordinator can answer your family's questions and concerns about how Section 504 might apply to your child.

■■ Hats to Wear after High School: The Transition to Vocational Programs, Colleges, and Jobs

When your child is in the public education system, the ultimate goal is for him to learn skills that will enable him to be fully included

within society. This goal can be met through academic preparation, vocational experiences, or both.

IDEA requires that a plan be developed to help each student in special education make the transition from school to adult life. This transition plan must be incorporated into the IEP by the time a student is 14 years old.

Transition plan goals might include academic preparation, career exploration, vocational training, or supervised work experience within the broader community. To help a student reach his long-range goals, the plan will list the skills the student needs to learn.

Transition topics for college-bound students might include:

- time management skills,
- self-advocacy,
- time spent on a college campus,
- assistance learning how to apply for financial aid, or
- how to interview.

Transition topics for students interested in vocational opportunities might include:

- job preparation,
- personal finance,
- independent living skills,
- and how to interview.

Transition plans typically include lots of activities designed to assist your student with making a gradual change from school life to adult life. A transition plan might include opportunities for job shadowing (following an employed person throughout the work day). It might also include activities designed to help the student decide whether he would like to make a particular field of interest his life's work—perhaps through an unpaid or paid supervised experience, an internship, or a course offered through an agency other than the school.

Transition planning can also include working with other agencies such as the Bureau of Vocational Rehabilitation (B.V.R.), which can assist with training for specific jobs, or with college planning. See Chapter 16 for more information about services of the Bureau of Vocational Rehabilitation.

Your Child's Role in Transition Planning

By his teenage years, your child will have come a long way from the days when he wore a sunbonnet and depended on others to make all his decisions. Here are some questions that might help your child focus on his transition needs as he looks toward wearing the hat of personal responsibility:

Thinking about the Future in General
- What do I enjoy doing the most?
- How can I fit that into my transition plan for after high school? Is it a career?
- What skills do I have now?
- What skills do I need?
- How can I obtain those skills?

Choosing a Job Hat
These are questions to ask your young adult to help narrow down job possibilities:
- Do I like to be indoors or outdoors?
- Do I like to work with people or with objects?
- Who are some interesting people I know and what do they do for a living?
- What types of support services will I need to succeed in the work environment?
- What is the future of the job?
- Can I change positions or jobs and use the skills I have learned?

Wearing the College Beanie

If your young adult is thinking about college, urge him to think through these questions:

- Do I know what I want to be when I graduate from college, and if so, which schools teach those skills?
- Do I like big schools or small schools?
- What kind of support services should I ask about when I go to visit the campus?
- Do I like the students that I meet on a campus visit?
- Can I succeed academically at this school?
- Do I know how to obtain financial assistance if I need it?
- Are extracurricular activities available to me?
- Have I researched a variety of college options by talking with my high school guidance counselor and by going to the library to find books that tell about various colleges?

Whether your child chooses work, further vocational training, or college, the Bureau of Vocational Rehabilitation may be able to assist him with training skills, funding, or necessary support services. Call them. They are in your local phone book, most likely listed in the state government pages.

❚❚ Pulling Together Our Wardrobe of Hats

When it comes to education, one size definitely does not fit all. Fortunately, there are laws and rules to help you obtain a free appropriate education that meets your child's needs. If you put on your various hats and work with your child's teachers and therapists, you have a good chance of developing the right educational plan for your child. Just be sure to keep a wide range of options open for making choices, so when the hat no longer fits, you can change it.

❚❚ Parent Comments

Patrick got a late start with early intervention services because he was hospitalized a lot that first year. I wish we could have started sooner. Once we did start, an early intervention specialist visited our home once a week. She did a little bit of everything with Patrick—OT, PT, and Speech. She showed

*me a lot of things I could do at home with him. She provided me with dif-
ferent kinds of equipment to use with Patrick. A speech therapist also came
to our home and we came to the hospital for extra physical therapy.*

❧

*Early intervention is a lot like playtime to my daughter. Some of the
things the therapists ask her to do are hard for her, but they are good at
motivating her with cool toys and praise.*

❧

*We have been fighting our school system for a room for preschoolers who
cannot walk up steps. We have been denied because the superintendent
claims there is no room available in the four buildings in our district.*

❧

*When Angela was starting kindergarten I called the district we were in,
and they were not helpful. We moved to a district that provided an RN
or LPN in every building and that had inclusive classrooms. Angela has
blossomed with the innovative teaching styles and made a great many
"normal" friends.*

❧

*I sometimes get discouraged when my son needs orthopedic surgery and
he misses valuable school time. It's very frustrating not to be able to get
everything working consistently together for very long.*

❧

*The school district should pay for therapy if your child is three years or
older and needs it to be able to function better in the classroom. Kids
may need OT if they have trouble with using scissors or using their hands;
speech, if they have trouble with language; and PT, if they have difficulty
with motor activities such as getting around the classroom and school.
Our school district only wanted to pay for a half hour of PT, OT, and
speech therapy for our son, but I insisted on a full hour of each and got
it. All the therapists were surprised. All you need to do is ask, and if they
say "no," ask someone higher up!*

❧

My child received OT/PT, speech, and group counseling in school. I was glad to receive the services. Their help in her therapy needs gave me time for other interests.

❧❀❧

My daughter got a variety of therapies through the early intervention program, but we also paid for private physical therapy. The private PT seemed so much more responsive to our needs and concerns and was much better at making sure we knew what activities we should be doing with Sarah at home to keep her motor skills moving forward.

❧❀❧

My daughter is in a special education classroom for part of the day and the regular classroom the other part, so I think we have the best of both worlds. She also has PT and speech therapy integrated into her program. Time will tell how successful this will be.

❧❀❧

The school offered OT and PT every other week for my daughter. I said she needed these weekly because of a fractured femur and surgery in the past. The school declined because of their budget. Our IEP representative called for a meeting. We also got a doctor's opinion and an outside OT/PT opinion. At that meeting and every year since, there has never been any argument. Brenda gets OT and PT weekly.

14

NURTURING AN EMOTIONALLY HEALTHY CHILD

Mary Ann Mulcahey, Ph.D.

As the parent of a child with spina bifida, you may sometimes be overwhelmed by your daily care-giving routine. In addition, you probably have concerns about the future. Will your child have friends? Will she go to college? Will she have a job that she enjoys?

No parent wants to inadvertently limit their child's opportunities. Childhood behaviors, however, can sometimes become obstacles to achievement if not handled effectively. The purpose of this chapter is, therefore, to describe the environment that your child needs in order to become an emotionally healthy adult, ready to take advantage of her abilities.

■■ A Systematic Approach

In the popular book, *The Seven Habits of Highly Effective People,* Steven Covey discusses the idea of beginning a project with the result in mind. Most of our undertakings begin with a goal. Weight loss programs, for example, begin with the establishment of a weight that we want to reach. Parenthood is a long-term project. Like any big project, parenthood consists of small steps in a positive direction, toward a goal. Just like the answer to the famous question, "How do you eat an elephant?" parenting happens one "bite" at a time. Most parents are just trying to get through today. It is wise, however, to occasionally stop and consider whether you are taking the right steps; steps that will result in an emotionally healthy adult. If your child is not turning out as you would wish, remember, it is never too late to get a problem under control. No child's behavior is impossible or hopeless. Let's eat a few bites of our elephant!

■■ Project Parenthood

The First Step: What Are the Qualities of a Well-Adjusted Adult?

You want your child to grow up to be a well-adjusted adult. But first, what qualities does someone *need* in order to be considered well-adjusted? Remember, you need to know your destination in order to plan the trip. The five qualities discussed below are certainly not the only ones that could be singled out. There will be others that are unique to your family and your child.

The Ability to Interact Comfortably with Others

Social skills are critical in the workplace. Indeed, a major reason that adults with disabilities fail on the job, regardless of profession, is lack of appropriate social skills, not lack of ability. The types of skills needed range from the ability to make social chitchat at the coffee machine to the ability to demonstrate self-control in withholding inappropriate remarks. Other desirable skills include conversing with others about their interests and not asking embarrassing personal questions.

Even young children can demonstrate social ease by shaking hands when introduced or making eye contact when speaking with others. Likewise, addressing adults as "Mr., Mrs., Ma'am, or Sir" is something that all children can be trained to do. Polite behavior does not require a high level of intelligence to learn—just some simple instruction and a little practice.

All children need opportunities to develop their ability to interact with peers. Participating in Scouting, having friends over, and being involved in activities at a place of worship are all good ways to develop social skills. Through structured, supervised, and organized activities, your child can become accustomed to not always being the center

of attention. She can learn to interact with others appropriately in different situations—an important skill for the future.

Respect for Authority

Having respect for authority is part of being a responsible adult. A child's first experience with authority is with parental authority. As parents, we must be careful to enforce the rules we have set. If the rule is no TV before homework, and our child has failed to complete her homework, she doesn't watch TV. Simple, right? But, children cry, plead, throw a tantrum, or try to make deals to get around rules. That is the toughest part of parenting; being firm with the youngster whom we love with all our heart. How can you say "no" to that charming smile?

Letting rules slip communicates that adults, especially you, really don't mean what they say. Your child may learn to expect to get away with noncompliance at school, home, and the workplace using moderate complaining or a sweet smile. Or, she may learn that testing an adult when the adult is tired increases the chance of getting away with something. Before you know it, your little sweetheart is a con artist.

Another common problem is that rules may be unequally enforced for some members of the family. Who among us has not heard the oldest child complain of higher standards being applied to him or her? Siblings complain that the brother or sister with spina bifida gets away with murder. Sometimes the other children are correct. If your child has a history of medical problems or seems fragile, you may feel that reprimanding her or putting her in "time out" could upset her and cause something terrible to happen to her. Then you would really feel guilty! Besides, what is the harm in letting your child call you "stupid," for example? She is just reacting in frustration. True, but being an understanding parent and being a doormat are two different things.

The understanding parent can acknowledge that an inappropriate remark or behavior is the result of frustration. But, you further explain that there are consequences. Of course, your child will be upset. She may get upset for the next five times that you turn off the TV for ten minutes after she calls you "stupid." Loss of TV privileges will not cause her health to decline. It will let her know that Mom and Dad mean business. The doormat parent, on the other hand, gets a child who follows rules at her own convenience and eventually misbehaves in all settings.

Applying consequences is hard for most parents, but essential for a happy home and happy child. If you find it hard to set and enforce limits, there are books on parenting available in most libraries. Several examples include: *The Good Kid Book,* by Howard Sloan and *SOS Help for Parents,* by Lynn Clark. In addition, community education programs frequently have classes or workshops on parenting.

Respect for Oneself

In popular literature, the term "self-esteem" is often used to refer to respect for oneself. Sometimes the term is used so often that people become tired of hearing it. The truth is, people who believe that they have value will not tolerate abuse or exploitation by others. They stand

up for themselves. They are cooperative but assertive when others cross inappropriate boundaries. When friends invite them to do something they know is wrong, they find within themselves the courage to say "no." They know that they have worth and treat others as valuable people (respecting authority, interacting in a respectful fashion). People who feel valued respect the opinions of others. They do not feel a need to ridicule, or require that others agree with them.

How do we help our children develop a sense of their value as human beings?

The sense of one's value as a person develops over time. When your child is an infant, it is important to respond to her cries and other attempts at communicating. This helps your infant learn that she can influence what happens to herself. She smiles at you and you smile back, for example. When your child is a toddler, your behavior will communicate your child's importance to the family. Clap when your child picks up toys or puts dirty clothes in the hamper. Listen to her attempts at speaking and play and laugh with her. It is crucial to allow your child the freedom to make choices; for example, to choose which shirt to wear or what she wants to eat for lunch. By simply allowing your child to make choices, you show respect for her choices. This will help her develop confidence in her decisions. For example, allowing your child to wear what she chooses demonstrates your respect for her decision.

The child who constantly seeks help with small decisions is one who has been second-guessed by an adult. Her simple selections in clothing or toys have undoubtedly been met with disapproval. She lacks confidence in expressing her wants, and is fearful of disapproval from authority figures.

Sometimes, as the parent of a child with spina bifida, you have to be more aware of opportunities for your child to assert herself. If your toddler does not crawl, have her indicate where she wants to be placed in the room. Does she want to sit by the toy box, or by the DVD to watch a movie? Your child's choices may be inconvenient for you. For instance, she may want to wear overalls today, not the stretch pants. The overalls are the style, but harder to manipulate for toileting. Point that out to her, but let the choice be hers. You could also strike a bargain: wear the overalls to school but change to stretch pants after school, when you can help with toileting.

All this discussion of choice sounds great, you may be saying to yourself, but sometimes you feel used or manipulated by your child. She thinks she is royalty, and you are the faithful servant. Remember, your child can make choices for herself, but within limits. You could agree that once an outfit has been chosen and is on, she has to wear it! Or, when she indicates that she wants to play with blocks, and you have given her blocks, she needs to play with them for ten minutes (set a kitchen timer with a loud bell). When the bell goes off, you will return to offer another choice.

Confidence in Solving Problems

When you look around at acquaintances and friends who are successful as people, one quality you may note is their ability to deal with setbacks or disappointments. This will be an important trait for your child to develop.

Some children with spina bifida are skilled at finding alternative routes to solving a problem. This ability develops over time. If your child becomes easily frustrated and continues to approach a problem the same unsuccessful way, she needs some extra guidance from you. Teaching her some basic relaxation techniques, such as taking deep breaths when she feels herself becoming upset, can help her stay calm. Closing her eyes for a few seconds and visualizing what her best friend might do in this situation could also be helpful.

Another technique called "anticipatory coping" can help children to be calm when confronting a problem. You may already have shown your child how to use this technique by role playing what to do when a stranger is at the door, how to answer the phone, or by walking the family through a home fire drill. In using this technique, you try to anticipate challenges that may occur in a new situation, generate possible solutions, and identify who may be of help.

Whenever your child is about to enter a new situation, walking her through the steps of anticipatory coping can increase her feeling of confidence. One example would be an invitation to a birthday party in an unfamiliar recreation center. You and your child would go to the location in advance and check that the bathroom is accessible, that there is a ramp into the building, that the incline is not too steep for a walker, or that there are activities in which she will be able to participate. Likewise, when your child enters a new grade in school, you would both "scout" the new location for possible problems. On the first day of school, then, she can be comfortable maneuvering among her peers. Brainstorming with your child will help demonstrate to her that there is frequently more than one way to solve a problem.

The Ability to Accept or Ask for Help When Needed

No adult is completely independent—rather, we are interdependent. We depend on the auto mechanics to diagnose the problem with our car. We might pay someone to cut the grass, paint, fix a leaky roof, hang wallpaper, or perform other tasks for us because we have limited skill in that area. We recognize that, although we have many skills, we can't do everything. We pay people to do some things for us, because they are better at that job than we are. It just makes sense.

Your child with spina bifida may also need to learn to cope with the necessity of receiving assistance from nonfamily members. Assistance can run the gamut from needing someone to open a door when there is not a power door, to needing help with very private activities such as using the toilet. Your child might feel demeaned when she needs help, or she can react in a way that maintains her own dignity. Role playing with your child at home can help her learn to distinguish between appropriate and unwanted assistance and how to deal with potential helpers accordingly. For example, a simple "Thank you" to someone who holds a door for you is usually appropriate.

On the other hand, if someone is trying to dominate your child by helping her, a different response is in order. Humor, rather than anger, is a good skill to employ in this case. Role-play a few lines your child could use to turn aside the unwanted assistance. Saying, "Thanks, but I'm tougher than I look. I'll take it from here," with confidence and a smile, should discourage the helper without leaving them feeling angry at your child.

The degree of physical disability that your child has will determine the amount of personal assistance she requires. Many children will need instruction in directing personal care assistants, whether health aides at school, or paid assistants who come to their home as an adult. Teach your child to instruct others how to perform the tasks in a way that is most comfortable for her. She can participate in her care, rather than being a passive recipient. For example, if your child needs help in transferring to the toilet at school, role-play with her how to instruct her "helper" in assisting her.

You might feel that the people hired to assist your child are professionals, so it is inappropriate to give them directions. But your child, as the consumer, does have the right to give an opinion on how she wants the service provided. If there is a medical reason why the service cannot be performed in a particular way, expect the service provider to explain those reasons to you and your child.

Your child will feel less vulnerable if she feels confident in directing her own care. That confidence develops from starting small, building on her successes, and practicing various ways of handling problem situations.

❚❚ The Meaning of Disability— To You and Your Child

All children with spina bifida eventually notice that they differ from their peers. They may remark on physical differences—that a sibling walks unaided, while they do not. Or they may remark that they use the bathroom differently than others do. Frequently they voice observations or questions that we, as parents, have been pondering in our own hearts. It will be painful for you to see your child struggle with ideas of fairness, because you struggle with those ideas too. When you see a "bad child" who does not have any of the struggles that your delightful youngster does, you may question the idea of fairness or your own values and religious beliefs. It can be a frightening experience.

To hear your child's questions about her differences might seem like more than you can bear. How can you try to answer your child's questions about why something happened, or when some skill will develop? You want to know these answers, too. Your child's concerns, as reflected in her questions, will not go away if you ignore them. Furthermore, your child will sense that some things are not to be discussed with you. A wedge will develop in your relationship, a lost opportunity for closeness.

In thinking about how you will respond, think about the people with whom you feel comfortable discussing your child's disability. Think about the people who provided you with emotional support when you were young, or who do so now. They do not tell you that everything will be OK. They don't try to talk you out of being worried or sad. You know they accept your feelings, whatever your feelings may be, at that moment. These favorite people are not afraid to be with you when you feel down. They may not have any experience with disability. They listen, maybe squeeze your hand. Most often, they have no answers for you. So, what makes them special? Somehow they communicate a willingness to walk the road with you, wherever it takes you. Many of these special people have a personal knowledge of suffering. They have struggled with issues of fairness or lived with uncertainty, too. Your concerns do not threaten their beliefs, or make them fearful of the future. Let's consider how you can be one of these support people for your child.

The questions are coming, so what do you do? First, you need to take your child's perspective. What is motivating her question at this time? Is this an observation? For example, perhaps she has remarked that a friend draws neatly. A door-opening response would be to agree with the specific observation: "Yes, that *was* a nice ship that Joe made." You have left the door open to further discussion of the varying amounts of drawing ability or other talents that people have. If you don't know what to say, silence frequently is sufficient to elicit further observations from your child. A simple "Hmmm" may be enough to encourage your child to share her thoughts with you. Just as your special person does not try to soothe or disagree with your observations, avoid doing so with your child.

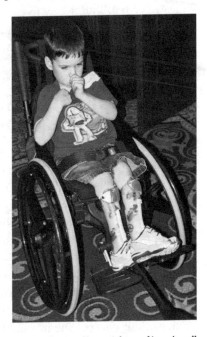

There are times when there is nothing you can say to make it better. "It's so unfair," your child may say, or, "I am smarter than Cindy, but she walks without limping." Statements to that effect may tempt you to try to talk your child out of her feelings: "Oh, dear, you know that's not true." Or, "But Cindy has other things that she struggles with." These types of responses are roadblocks to your child's sharing her feelings with you. In fact, disagreeing with your child or trying to point out your child's many talents to her may only lead her to make additional negative observations in an attempt to prove you wrong. A much better response to your child would be something like, "I guess sometimes it seems that way." This type of statement communicates your willingness to share and accept negative feelings too. Remember, there are times when your child may be feeling sorry for herself and does not want to be talked out of her mood. Everyone feels like that sometimes. Neither agree nor disagree, just walk along the path with her.

At times your child's questions may spark your own anger at how life has turned out. If you feel that you cannot cope with your own feelings, share them with a spiritual advisor, therapist, or members of your parent group. If your own anger or sense of disappointment is frightening to you, you may try to avoid touchy or painful subjects with your child. That avoidance will be communicated to your child. Then she may hesitate to share her angry or negative feelings with you. Anger will find a way to express itself, frequently in ways that are not healthy. Anger can also be a mask for depression. Lashing out at others, impatience, or quick shifts in mood may signal a need for professional help.

▪▪ When Being a Supportive Parent Is Not Enough

There may be times when your support and encouragement will not be enough to help your child with her concerns. For example, your child may feel as if her physical health is deteriorating, and develop an attitude that "it's hopeless." She may reach a point where she feels tired of working hard at activities that are easy for others. There are any number of occasions when your child may be more than just discouraged; she may be depressed.

Depression can be expressed in many ways. For instance, your child may seem very angry. Or she may seem lazy—neglect her grooming, lack energy, spend too much time in her room alone, or stop doing homework or chores. She just may not seem to care about things the way she used to. She might look unhappy. She might have no appetite, or not want to do anything except eat. Some youngsters suddenly sleep excessively; you can't get them up in the morning. Other youngsters have trouble going to sleep at night, or wake in the middle of the night and can't go back to sleep. If your child exhibits this type of behavior for more than four weeks, it may be time to seek professional help.

Getting Professional Services

A variety of professionals, including social workers, psychologists, or psychiatrists, can help a child who is feeling depressed. Ask your acquaintances, your physician, or the school counselor for names of mental health professionals with whom your child might talk. You might also want to investigate group settings where your child could share her concerns with other youngsters who are experiencing similar issues.

Be sure to obtain services from a licensed professional. A license is an indication that some minimum education or training standard has been met in an area of expertise. Your insurance company will likely have a list of approved professionals. In any case, do not be afraid to call the professional's office and ask about his or her credentials. Try to speak directly with the professional, rather than with the office staff. Does the professional have experience in treating children with special needs? Is the office accessible? If you are not comfortable, try another person. If you are not comfortable after the first office visit, make an appointment with someone else. If you are not successful with the list from your insurance company, call the insurance company and let them know that none of the people on the list were appropriate and give specific reasons why. It could be that no one has experience with children.

Counseling takes time to be successful. Problems that have taken years to develop will not be cured in two sessions. Parents and other family members will likely be asked to participate in counseling. When a child has a problem, the family's participation can speed the solution.

∷ Attention Deficit Disorders

It is not unusual for children with spina bifida to also have a diagnosis of attention-deficit/hyperactivity disorder (AD/HD). As discussed in Chapter 13, there are specific strategies for managing AD/HD in the classroom. There are also strategies that can make it easier to manage in the home. You will need to have a direct parenting style, a consistent household routine, and be ready to give swift feedback. It can help to pair verbal directions with visual cues, such as pictures of the steps to complete assigned chores. Checklists help with organization and keeping track of rewards for task completion.

Your child may talk excessively and interrupt other family members when they are talking. Giving her visual and verbal cues can help place limits on interrupting and excessive talking. For example, if your child asks you the same question repeatedly, set the kitchen timer for five minutes and tell her you'll answer the question when the bell rings. This technique helps your child learn self-control and gives her a signal when you're ready to be approached. There are many useful books and videotapes on AD/HD that can help you learn to manage your child's behavior at home. See the Reading List for some suggested titles.

❚❚ Some Closing Thoughts

What if you are not the perfect parent? What if you sometimes yell at your child when you are stressed? What if you don't listen to 100 percent of the things that your child tells you? It is likely that your child will still turn out OK. If we miss something important, our children have a talent for reintroducing the topic again. Children have tremendous resiliency. They face challenges, they conquer fears, they grow up—sometimes in spite of nature's obstacles. A child with a disability is not disabled or "unable." Your family is not disabled. You, your child, and your family will develop a unique way of being. Learn what your child has to teach you, and let your child's behavior provide clues to the type of guidance she needs. Be open to sharing with other parents and seek help when you need it. The best parents are not perfect; the best parents make mistakes and learn from them.

❚❚ Parent Statements

I was afraid that other kids would make fun of Thomas and tease him when he started school. I told my nieces and nephews to protect Thomas if anyone gave him a hard time.

❦

Once I was playing a game with Tina where she had to make a wish. She didn't say, "I wish I could walk." I asked her why and she said, "But Mom, I wouldn't be me then."

❦

I have observed that our daughter inspires and brings a smile to everyone she meets. A few people may pity her, but by far most are impressed and encouraged by her attitude and happiness. When I see the effect she has on people and her happy approach to life, it lifts me up.

❦

LEGAL RIGHTS
AND HURDLES

James E. Kaplan
Ralph J. Moore, Jr.

■■ Introduction

As the parent of a child with spina bifida, it is important to understand the laws that apply to your child and your family. There are laws that guarantee your child's rights to attend school and to live and work in the community; laws that can provide your child financial and medical assistance; and laws that govern your long-term planning for your child's future.

If you know what your child is entitled to, this knowledge can help to ensure that your child receives the education, training, and special services he needs to reach his potential. You and your child will also be able to recognize illegal discrimination and assert his legal rights if necessary. Finally, if you understand how laws sometimes create problems for families of children with disabilities, you can avoid unwitting mistakes in planning for your child's future.

With one exception—the Agent Orange Benefits Act that specifically mentions spina bifida and is described later—the rights of children with spina bifida are found in the federal laws and regulations for children and adults with disabilities in general. In other words, the same laws that protect all persons with disabilities in the United States also protect your child. This chapter will familiarize you with these federal laws so that your child's rights can be protected and enforced when necessary.

That being said, it is impossible to discuss here the law of every state or locality. For information about the particular laws in your area, contact the national or local office of the Spina Bifida Association of America or your state Parent Training and Information Center (PTIC). (In Canada, contact the Association for Community Living or ACL for information about national or local laws.) You should also consult with a lawyer familiar with disability law when you need specific advice.

▪▪ Your Child's Right to an Education

Until the middle of the twentieth century, children with disabilities were usually excluded from public schools. They were sent away to residential "schools," "homes," and institutions, or their parents banded together to provide private part-time programs. In the 1960s, federal,

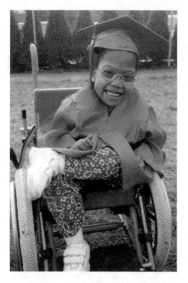

state, and local governments began to provide educational opportunities to children with disabilities; these opportunities have expanded and improved to this day.

Perhaps no law has done more to improve educational opportunities for children with spina bifida than the Individuals with Disabilities Education Act ("IDEA"). This law, originally enacted in 1975 and amended extensively in 1997 and 2004, used to be called "The Education for All Handicapped Children Act of 1975" and was better known as Public Law 94-142. IDEA vastly improved educational opportunities for almost all children with disabilities, including children with spina bifida. Administered by the U.S. Department of Education (DOE) and by each state, the law works on a carrot-and-stick basis.

Under IDEA, the federal government provides funds for the education of children with disabilities to each state with a special education program that meets certain standards set forth in IDEA and regulations issued by DOE. To qualify, a state must demonstrate that it provides all children with disabilities a "free appropriate public education" in the "least restrictive environment" that meets IDEA's standards. These terms are defined in detail below. At a minimum, however, states must provide approved special educational services, opportunities for participation in the regular curriculum (inclusion), and a variety of procedural rights to children with disabilities and their parents. The lure of federal funds has been attractive enough to induce all states to provide special education for children with disabilities, including children with spina bifida.

IDEA has its limits. The law only establishes the *minimum* requirements in special education programs for states desiring to receive federal funds. The law *does not* require states to adopt an ideal educational program for children with disabilities or a program that you might feel is "best" for your child. Because states have leeway under IDEA, there are differences from state to state in the programs or services available. For example, the student-teacher ratios and the quality and quantity of teaching materials can vary widely from state to state.

States are certainly allowed to create special education programs that are better than the minimum required by IDEA, and some have. Check with the placement or intake officer of the special education department of your local school district to determine exactly what classes, programs, and services are available to your child. Parents, organizations, and advocacy groups continually push states and local school districts to exceed the federal requirements and provide the highest quality special education as early as possible. These groups need your support, and you need theirs.

What IDEA Provides

As you can imagine, IDEA is a large and complex set of laws and regulations. The Resource Guide at the end of this book tells you how to obtain copies of these laws and regulations from the U.S. Senate or national organizations. The following summary highlights the provisions most important for you and your child.

Coverage

IDEA is intended to make special education available to all children with all kinds of disabilities, such as learning, behavioral and emotional, developmental, and physical disabilities (regardless of origin), including spina bifida.

Identification and Evaluation

Because IDEA applies only to children with disabilities, your child with spina bifida must be evaluated to determine whether he is eligible for special education. The law requires states to develop testing and evaluation procedures designed to identify and evaluate the needs and abilities of each child before he is placed in a special education program. All evaluation and reevaluation procedures are required to take the parents' input into account.

In most cases, a diagnosis of spina bifida is adequate to establish that IDEA applies to your child. Regardless of how your child's intellectual or physical abilities are evaluated, he qualifies for services if the condition hinders learning or otherwise interrupts the normal educational processes.

"Free Appropriate Public Education."

At the heart of IDEA is the requirement that children with disabilities receive a "free appropriate public education" in the "least restrictive environment." Children with spina bifida are entitled to receive an education at public expense that takes into account their special learning needs and abilities and their right to go to school with their peers without disabilities. This section examines more precisely what each of the elements of "free appropriate public education" means. The following section explains the term "least restrictive environment."

Free and Public. The words "free" and "public" mean that every part of your child's special education program must be provided at public expense, regardless of your ability to pay. This requirement is often satisfied by placement of your child in a public school, but the school district must pay the cost of all services and reasonable accommodations necessary for your child. If no suitable public program is available, the school district must place your child in a private program and pay the full cost. IDEA does not pay tuition for educational services for your child *not* agreed to by the school district or other governing agency (unless, as explained later in this chapter, the school district's decision is overturned). As a result, if you place your child in a program that is not approved for your child by the school district, you risk having to pay the full cost of tuition.

Appropriate Education. As already mentioned, the law's requirement for an "appropriate education" does not guarantee the best possible education; IDEA simply requires states to achieve some reasonable measure of educational success. A state must establish measurable performance goals for children with disabilities designed to lead toward independence, community living, and employment as adults, all consistent with a child's particular disability. The nature and extent of services provided typically depend on the need.

Special Education. The term "appropriate education" also encompasses "special education and related services." In turn, "special education" means instruction designed to meet the unique needs of the child with disabilities, which may be provided in a full range of settings, including general education classrooms, separate classrooms, separate schools, home instruction, or instruction in private schools, hospitals, or institutions. General education teachers, special education teachers, therapists, and other professionals—all provided by the school district at public expense—are responsible for delivering these educational services.

Related Services. "Related services" are defined as transportation and other developmental, corrective, and supportive services necessary to enable the child to benefit from special education. Services provided by an occupational therapist, physical therapist, psychologist, social worker, school nurse, aide, or other qualified person may be required under IDEA as related services. For instance, given the motor problems that often result from spina bifida, physical and occupational therapy for your child can be essential.

Some services, however, are specifically excluded from the requirement to provide "related services." Most important, medical services ordinarily provided by a physician or hospital are not considered to be related services, although the U.S. Supreme Court decided in 1984 that a school nurse must provide catheterization as may reasonably be necessary for a child with spina bifida to attend school. You should demand that your child receive the related services he needs, as they are your child's right under the law and are often critical to the child's ability to be part of the educational community, whatever the setting.

Not surprisingly, the law in this area is constantly evolving. We suggest that you check with your local Arc, ACL, or state PTIC for the current state of the law. Of course, you can also seek advice from a lawyer who specializes in the field.

"Least Restrictive Environment"

IDEA requires that children with disabilities must "to the maximum extent appropriate" be educated in the "least restrictive environment." This requirement has become a major emphasis of the law, largely due to the successful efforts of parents who have advocated for their children to be educated in public school with their peers.

The "least restrictive environment" means the educational setting that permits your child to have the most contact appropriate at school with children without disabilities and to be involved in the general education curriculum. For example, your child should have the

opportunity to learn the same subjects in the same classrooms as other children his age, provided he can learn successfully there. IDEA contains a strong preference for children with disabilities, including children with spina bifida, to be educated in the schools and classes they would attend if they did not have a disability. IDEA is specifically intended, at least in part, to end the historical practice of isolating children with disabilities either in separate schools or out-of-the-way classrooms and to open the doors of your neighborhood school to your child with spina bifida.

Most children with spina bifida can receive their instruction with peers without disabilities for all or part of the school day, so long as proper supports and therapy are in place. Neither your child's spina bifida itself nor any developmental delay is a sufficient reason for a school district to refuse to provide opportunities for your child to learn with his typically developing peers.

IDEA supports many different types of educational placements. Many children spend all their time in general education classrooms with teachers or aides who can help them with the general education curriculum. (You may hear this referred to as "full inclusion.") Others spend most of their time in general education classrooms, but go to a resource room to receive special education services in certain subjects.

Still others spend most of their time in separate special education classrooms, but have opportunities for inclusion in school activities such as assemblies, physical education, sports teams, music, and lunch and recess. The extent of your child's inclusion depends on a variety of factors that will be set forth in your child's individualized education program (IEP), as explained below.

IDEA also recognizes that public schools may not be suitable to provide all educational and related services required for some children. In these cases, federal regulations allow for placement in private schools or residential settings if your child's IEP team determines that such a placement is required to meet the child's individual educational needs. When placement in a public school is determined to be inappropriate, the law still requires that the child be placed in the least restrictive educational environment suitable to his individual needs, which can include some participation in regular school classroom programs and activities. Even a student whose parents enroll him in a private school without school district approval or funding may still be eligible for some school-provided services.

When Coverage Begins under IDEA

IDEA requires all states to provide special education services to eligible children with disabilities aged three and older. In addition, IDEA also provides funding to states that create an approved program for early intervention services to infants with disabilities from birth until age three.

Some form of early intervention services under IDEA is available in each state. But there is wide variation in what services are provided, how and where those services are provided, and which agency provides them. You should check with your local school district, the state education agency, your local Arc, or your state PTIC about the availability of early intervention services. (See Chapter 13 for information about the therapies and other types of early intervention services your child may receive.) You may be charged for early intervention services—perhaps on a sliding scale. Your health insurance or Medicaid may cover these costs.

IDEA requires special education services to continue until children reach at least age 18. If your state offers education to all students until age 21, however, it must also provide special education services for eligible students until age 21.

Length of School Year

Under IDEA, states must provide more than the traditional 180-day school year when the needs of a child with a disability indicate that year-round instruction is a necessary part of a "free appropriate public education." In most states, the decision to offer summer instruction depends on whether your child will "regress," or lose a substantial amount of the progress made during the school year without summer services; this is called "anticipated regression." States may also use other criteria in determining which students need extended school year (ESY) special education services. ESY must be provided at no cost to families. If you think your child needs year-round services, you should not hesitate to request an ESY program, but you should be prepared to document your child's need for this program.

"Individualized Education Program"

IDEA recognizes that each child with a disability is unique, and the law requires that your child's special education program be tailored to his individual needs. Based on your child's evaluation, a program specifically designed to address his developmental problems must be devised. This is called an "individualized education program" or, more commonly, an "IEP."

The IEP is a written report that describes:
1. your child's present level of development in all areas;
2. your child's developmental strengths and needs;
3. the annual goals for your child;
4. the specific educational services that your child will receive;
5. the date services will start and their expected duration;
6. standards for determining whether the goals of your child's educational program are being met;
7. the extent to which your child will participate in regular educational programs;
8. the behavior intervention programs, if necessary, that will be used to enable your child to participate in regular education classrooms without impeding his or other students' learning; and
9. parent concerns.

Under federal regulations, educational placements must be based on the IEP, not vice versa. That is, the services your child receives and the setting in which he receives them should be determined by your child's needs, not by the availability of existing programs. "One size fits all" is not permitted by IDEA.

A child's IEP is usually developed during a series of meetings among parents, teachers, and other school district representatives. Your child may be present at these meetings. The group who develops your child's IEP may be referred to as the IEP Team, Child Study Team, Pupil Evaluation Team (PET), or Administrative Placement Committee.

Designing an IEP is ideally a cooperative effort, with parents, teachers, therapists, and school officials conferring on what goals are appropriate for the child and how best to achieve them. Because of IDEA's emphasis on inclusion, general education teachers are required to be on the IEP team. Preliminary drafts of the IEP are reviewed and revised in an attempt to develop a mutually acceptable educational program.

The importance of your role in this process cannot be overemphasized. IDEA requires the IEP team to consider "the concerns of the parents for enhancing the education of their child." This means that your goals for your child's education must be taken into account in drafting the IEP. You cannot always depend on teachers or school officials to recognize your child's unique needs. You should make sure school officials recognize these needs—the needs that make him different from children with other disabilities and even from other children with spina bifida. To obtain the full range of services, you may need to demonstrate that withholding certain services would result in an education that would *not* be "appropriate" or that would be inadequate to satisfy the "least restrictive environment" requirement.

IEPs should be very detailed, and crafted with care. You and your child's teachers should set specific goals for every area of development in which he needs special education services, and specify how and when those goals will be reached. Although the thought of specific planning may seem intimidating at first, a detailed IEP enables you to closely monitor the education your child receives and to make sure he actually receives the services prescribed. In addition, the law requires that IEPs be reviewed and revised at least once a year, and more often if necessary, to ensure that your child's educational program continues to meet his changing needs. Parents can also request a meeting with school officials at any time.

How can you prepare for the IEP process? First, explore available educational programs, including public, private, federal, state, county, and municipal programs. Observe classes at the neighborhood school, as well as schools with specialized programs for students with your child's disabilities, to see what different programs and placements have to offer. Local school districts and organizations such as the Arc or chapters of the Spina Bifida Association of America (SBAA) can provide you with information about programs in your community.

Second, collect a complete set of developmental and medical evaluations to share with school officials—obtain your own if you doubt the accuracy of the school district's evaluation. Third, think about appropriate goals for your child, based on your knowledge of his strengths and needs. Finally, decide for yourself what placement, program, and services are necessary for your child, and request them. If you want your child educated in his neighborhood school, request the services (such as catheterization assistance or physical therapy) necessary to support him in that setting. If no program offers enough of what your child needs, request that an existing program be modified to better meet your child's needs.

To advocate for your child's placement in a particular type of program, you should collect evidence about your child's special needs. Then gather letters from physicians, psychologists, therapists, teachers, developmental experts, or other professionals supporting your position. This evidence may help persuade a school district that the requested placement or services are the appropriate choices for your child.

A few other suggestions are:

1. Do not attend IEP meetings alone—bring a spouse, nurse, lawyer, advocate, physician, nurse, teacher, or whomever you would like for support, including, of course, your child;
2. Keep close track of what everyone involved in your child's case—school district officials, psychologists, therapists, teachers, and doctors—says and does;
3. *Get everything in writing*; and
4. Be assertive and speak your mind. Children with unique developmental challenges need parents to be assertive and persuasive advocates during the IEP process. This does not mean that you should expect school officials to be your adversaries, but you are your child's most important advocate. You know him best.

"Individualized Family Service Plan"

Parents of children from birth to age three use a plan that is different from the IEP used in schools for older children. States receiving grants to provide early intervention services must draft an "individual-ized family service plan" (IFSP). This plan is similar to the IEP, but with an early intervention focus. Unlike an IEP, which focuses primarily on the needs of the child, an IFSP emphasizes services for the family. In other words, the law recognizes that families with young children with special needs often have special needs themselves. Consequently, IF-SPs do not simply specify what services are provided for the child with spina bifida. They also describe services that will be provided to: 1) help parents learn how to use daily activities to teach their child with spina bifida, and 2) help siblings learn to cope with having a brother or sister with spina bifida. The procedures and strategies for developing a useful IFSP are the same as described above for the IEP. IFSPs are reviewed at least every six months.

An important IDEA requirement is that early intervention services be provided to children and families to the "maximum extent appropriate" in the child's "natural environment." This means that services should be provided at the child's home or a place familiar to the child. This requirement reflects IDEA's strong preference for inclusion.

As your child approaches age three, IDEA requires a written plan for your child's transition into preschool services. This transition process can begin six months before your child turns three. Parents, teachers, and a representative of your local school district are required to partici-pate. The plan must contain the "steps to be taken to support the transi-tion of the toddler with a disability to preschool or other appropriate services" to ensure "a smooth transition" into preschool services.

Disciplinary Procedures

IDEA includes provisions governing how children with disabilities are to be disciplined in public schools. These provisions apply to situ-ations in which a child would be suspended from school, and restrict school district actions, depending on the length of a suspension.

In general, schools must continue to provide a free appropri-ate education in the least restrictive environment even if a child is suspended. Schools that have previously failed to address behavior problems with appropriate functional behavior intervention cannot suspend a child for that behavior. If the school already has a behavior intervention plan, school personnel must meet to review and, if neces-sary, revise the plan. If a suspension of ten days or more is considered (or if a series of shorter suspensions amounts to more than ten days), the school must present its plan and its proposed interim placement to a neutral hearing officer for approval. The school must also demonstrate that the behavior was not a manifestation of the child's disability and that the IEP was appropriate for the child at the time. If the behavior is determined not to be a manifestation of the disability, the school can move him to a different placement, but still must provide special education. Parents have the right to appeal all disciplinary actions under procedures described below.

Resolution of Disputes under IDEA

IDEA establishes a variety of effective safeguards to protect your rights and the rights of your child. For instance, written notice is always required before any change can be made in your child's identification, evaluation, or educational placement; the school district is required to inform you of your rights under IDEA at each step of the process; and you are entitled to review all of your child's educational records at any time.

Despite these safeguards, conflicts between parents and school officials can arise. When they do, it is usually best to resolve disputes over your child's educational or early intervention program *during* the IEP or IFSP process, before firm and inflexible positions have been formed. Although IDEA establishes dispute resolution procedures that are designed to be fair to parents, it is easier and far less costly to avoid disputes by reaching agreement during the IEP or IFSP process. As a result, we believe that you should first try to accomplish your objectives by open and clear communication and by persuasion. If a dispute arises that simply cannot be resolved through discussion, you can and should take further steps under IDEA and other laws to resolve that dispute.

First, IDEA allows you to file a formal complaint with your school district about *any matter* "relating to the identification, evaluation, or educational placement of the child, or the provision of free appropriate public education to such child." This means that you can make a written complaint about virtually any problem with any part of your child's educational or early intervention program. This is a very broad right of appeal, one that parents have successfully used in the past to correct problems in their children's education programs.

The process of challenging a school district's decisions about your child's education can be started simply by writing a letter of complaint, explaining the nature of the dispute and your desired outcome. This letter ordinarily is sent to the special education office. You have an absolute right to file a complaint—you need not ask the school district for permission. For information about starting complaints, you can contact your school district, your local Arc or SBAA, your state PTIC, local advocacy groups, or other parents.

Mediation. After the school district has received your complaint, they may request that you consider mediation of the dispute. Mediation is a process of negotiation, discussion, and compromise in which parents and school officials meet with a neutral third party and try to reach a mutually acceptable solution. IDEA requires that education agencies establish a means to mediate disputes, but you are not required to pursue mediation, nor may mediation be used to delay or postpone a resolution of your complaint. Mediation is just another voluntary approach aimed at reducing the costs of resolving disputes and avoiding costly lawsuits.

Due Process Hearings. If you decline mediation or mediation fails, you can request an "impartial due process hearing" before a hearing examiner. This hearing, usually held locally, is your opportunity to explain your complaint to an impartial person, who is required to listen to both sides and then render a decision. At the hearing, you are entitled to be represented by a lawyer or lay advocate; present evidence; and examine, cross-examine, and compel witnesses to attend. Your child has a right to be present at the hearing as well. After the hearing, you have a right to receive a written record of the hearing and the hearing examiner's findings and conclusions.

To prevail, you must present facts at the hearing that show that the disputed placement or program does not provide your child with the "free appropriate public education" in "the least restrictive environment" required by IDEA. Evidence in the form of letters, testimony, and expert evaluations is usually essential to a successful challenge.

Parents or school districts may appeal the decision of a hearing examiner. The appeal usually goes to the state's education agency or to a neutral panel. The state agency is required to make an independent decision upon a review of the record of the due process hearing and of any additional evidence presented. The state agency then issues a decision.

The right to appeal does not stop there. Parents or school officials can appeal beyond the state level by bringing a lawsuit under IDEA and other laws in a state or federal court. In this legal action, the court must determine whether there is a preponderance of the evidence (that is, whether it is more likely than not) that the school district's placement is proper for your child. The court must give weight to the expertise of the school officials responsible for providing your child's education, although you can and should also present your own expert evidence.

During all administrative and judicial proceedings, IDEA requires that your child remain in his current educational placement, unless you and your school district or the state education agency agree to a move or a hearing officer agrees to an interim change of placement for disciplinary reasons. Again, if you place your child in a different program without agreement, you may have to pay the full cost of that program. If the school district eventually is found to have erred, it may be required to reimburse you for the expenses of the changed placement. Accordingly, you should never change your child's educational program without carefully considering the potential cost of that decision.

Attorneys' fees are another expense to consider. Parents who ultimately win their dispute with a school district may recover attorneys' fees at the court's discretion. Even if you prevail at the local or state level (without bringing a lawsuit), you likely are entitled to recover attorneys' fees. You may not recover attorneys' fees for a mediated settlement, and attorneys' fees will be reduced if you fail to properly notify the school district or state education agency of your complaint. And, a court can limit or refuse attorneys' fees if you reject an offer of settlement from the school district, and then do not obtain a better outcome. Finally, and perhaps most onerous, parents can be required to reimburse the school's legal fees if the complaint is found to be "frivolous, unreasonable, or without foundation," or if the parents acted with an "improper purpose" in filing their complaint.

As with any legal dispute, each phase—complaint, mediation, hearings, appeals, and court cases—can be expensive, time-consuming, and emotionally draining. As mentioned earlier, it is wise to try to resolve problems without filing a formal complaint or bringing suit. When informal means fail to resolve a problem, formal channels should be pursued. Your child's best interests must come first. IDEA grants important rights that you should not be bashful about asserting vigorously.

IDEA is a powerful tool. The law can be used to provide unparalleled educational opportunities to your child. The Reading List at the end of this book includes several good guidebooks about IDEA and the special education system. The more you know about this vital law, the more you will be able to help your child realize his fullest potential.

∷ Programs and Services When Your Child Is an Adult

Many adults with disabilities who meet eligibility requirements receive Supplemental Security Income (SSI), Social Security Disability Insurance (SSDI), Medicaid, Medicare, housing assistance benefits, and food stamps. These benefit programs are discussed later in this chapter. Most children with spina bifida grow up to live independently or semi-independently as adults, however, and may not meet eligibility requirements for these benefits. Whether eligible for these benefits of not,  many adults with spina bifida may need special services and supports to enable them to engage in productive employment or to live in the community. Regrettably, employment, job training, and community residential services are in short supply because federal laws do not in general require states to offer such services for adults with disabilities and few states offer adequate services on their own. The programs that exist usually are underfunded and have long waiting lists. As a result, many parents must provide the necessary support and supervision on their own for as long as possible.

Now is the time to work to change this sad reality. The unemployment rate for people with disabilities is appallingly high, especially for young adults. Waiting lists for training programs continue to grow, and programs sponsored by nonprofit organizations and private foundations are limited. Most families do not have the resources to pay the full cost of providing employment and residential opportunities.

The only other remedy is public funding. Just as parents banded together in the 1970s to demand enactment of IDEA, parents must band together now to persuade local, state, and federal officials to take the steps necessary to allow adults with disabilities to live in dignity. Parents of *children* with disabilities should not leave this job to parents of *adults* with disabilities; children become adults all too soon. One great way to become involved is to begin to work with local or national advocacy organizations.

Vocational Training Programs

Vocational Rehabilitation educational programs, overseen by the federal Rehabilitation Services Administration, make funds available to states to support vocational training and rehabilitation programs for qualified people with disabilities, including people with spina bifida. As with IDEA, states that desire federal funds for this program must meet certain standards established in the funding laws.

Adults must fulfill two requirements to qualify for job-training services: 1) they must have a physical or mental disability that constitutes a "substantial handicap to employment"; and 2) they must be expected to benefit from vocational services. Under the law, services and training must be provided to people even if they are not expected to be competitively employed, but to achieve "supported employment"—employment in a setting with services such as a job coach or special training that allows an individual to work productively.

The state Departments of Vocational Rehabilitation, sometimes called "DVR" or "Voc Rehab," are charged with administering these laws. Adults who apply for Voc Rehab services are evaluated, and an "Individualized Plan for Employment " (IPE), similar to an IEP, is developed. The IPE sets forth the services needed to enable a person with a disability to work productively. The law requires that IPEs be developed in partnership between the individual and his vocational rehabilitation counselor so that the individual can make informed choices about his vocational training.

You should contact your state vocational rehabilitation department for specific information on services available to your child when he is an adult. Despite limited federal and state budgets, some states, communities, and organizations offer their own programs, such as group homes, supported employment programs, social activity groups, continuing education, and life-skills classes. Other parents and community organizations likely will have information about these local programs.

∷ Developmentally Disabled Assistance and Bill of Rights Act

Under a federal law called the Developmentally Disabled Assistance and Bill of Rights Act, states can receive grants for a variety of programs.

Important among them is a protection and advocacy (P&A) system. A P&A system advocates for the civil and legal rights of people with developmental disabilities. P&A offices have been leaders in representing people living in institutions seeking to improve their conditions or to be placed in the community. In addition, P&A offices may be able to represent your family if you cannot afford a lawyer for an IDEA due process hearing or a discrimination suit. Because some people with spina bifida may not be able to protect or enforce their own rights, state P&A systems offer necessary protection. You can locate your state P&A office by calling or visiting the website of the National Dissemination Center for Children with Disabilities; look under State Resources. (See Resource Guide.)

■■ Anti-Discrimination Laws

In a perfect world, no one would be denied opportunities or otherwise discriminated against solely on the basis of disability, race, sex, or any other factor beyond his control. Unfortunately, our world remains imperfect, and the federal government has enacted several laws to ensure that children, adolescents, and adults with disabilities are given the right to live and work in the community to the fullest extent possible. This section reviews the highlights of the Americans with Disabilities Act and the Rehabilitation Act of 1973, both of which prohibit discrimination against all people with disabilities, including your child with spina bifida.

The Americans with Disabilities Act

The Americans with Disabilities Act (ADA), enacted in 1990, prohibits discrimination against people based on their disabilities. The law is based on and operates in the same way as other well-known federal laws that outlaw racial, religious, age, and sex discrimination. The ADA applies to most private employers, public and private services, public accommodations, businesses, and telecommunications.

Employment

The ADA states that no employer may discriminate against a qualified individual with a disability "in regard to job application procedures, the hiring or discharge of employees, employee compensation, advancement, job training, and other terms, conditions, and privileges of employment." In other words, private employers cannot discriminate against employees or prospective employees who have a disability. The law defines "qualified individual with a disability" as a person with a disability who, with or without reasonable accommodation, can perform the essential functions of a job. "Reasonable accommodation" means that employers must make an effort to remove obstacles from the job, the terms and conditions of employment, or the workplace that would prevent an otherwise qualified person from working because he has a disability. Accommodations can include job restructuring, schedule shuffling, modified training and personnel policies, and modifications to the workplace to improve accessibility. Failing to make reasonable accommodations in these respects is a violation of this law.

The law does not *require* employers to hire people with disabilities or to make accommodations if an "undue hardship" will result for the employer. Rather, employers may not refuse to employ qualified people with disabilities solely because of the existence of the disability. For example, if a person with spina bifida applies for a job as a computer programmer or travel agent, the employer may not refuse to hire him if he is as qualified as or *more* qualified than other applicants to perform the job's duties and the employer's refusal was based on the applicant's spina bifida. The employer is not required to hire qualified people with spina bifida, but cannot refuse to hire a person, who otherwise can perform the job, because of his disability. The employer may also not inquire whether the applicant has a disability or fail to make some reasonable accommodation to enable a person with spina bifida to work productively. The employment section of the ADA applies only to companies that employ fifteen or more persons.

Perhaps even more important for parents of children with spina bifida is that the ADA also prohibits employers from discrimination against an employee or prospective employee because that person has a child with a disability, based on concerns that the parent will not be reliable or will have an absenteeism problem because of the needs of his child.

The ADA sets forth procedures for individuals with a disability who believe they have been victims of employment discrimination. A person must file a complaint with the federal Equal Employment Opportunity Commission (EEOC), the agency responsible for resolving employment discrimination complaints. If the agency does not satisfactorily resolve the dispute, a lawsuit may be brought to prohibit further discrimination and to require affirmative action. The ADA allows an award of attorneys' fees to a person with a disability who wins a lawsuit. Your local Arc or SBAA may be able to provide basic information about how to challenge discriminatory employment practices, but a lawyer likely will be required.

Public Accommodations.

One of the most potentially far-reaching provisions of the ADA is its prohibition of discrimination in public accommodations. Mirroring the approach of the civil rights laws of the 1960s, the ADA bans discrimination against people with disabilities virtually everywhere, including in hotels, inns, and motels; restaurants and bars; theaters, stadiums, concert halls, auditoriums, convention centers, and lecture halls; bakeries, grocery stores, gas stations, clothing stores, pharmacies, and other retail businesses; doctor or lawyer offices; airports and bus terminals; museums, libraries, galleries, parks, and zoos; nursery, elementary, secondary, undergraduate,  and postgraduate schools; day care centers; homeless shelters; senior citizen centers; gymnasiums; spas; and bowling alleys. Virtually any place open to the public must also be open to people with disabilities, unless access is not physically or financially feasible.

Businesses cannot exclude people with disabilities just because they are different. The excuse that people with disabilities are "not good for business" is now unlawful thanks to the ADA. For example, a theater, restaurant, or museum cannot exclude people with spina bifida from their facilities, cannot restrict their use to certain times or places, and cannot offer them only separate programs, unless to do otherwise would impose unreasonable cost on these facilities. The end result is that the new law does not merely prohibit active discrimination, but rather imposes a duty to open our society to all people with disabilities.

Like other civil rights laws, the ADA also requires integration. The law bans the insidious practice of "separate but equal" programs or facilities that offer separate services to people with disabilities, rather than access to programs offered to everyone else. The law prohibits the exclusion of people with disabilities on the grounds that there is a "special" program available just for them. For example, a recreation league (public or private) cannot uniformly exclude people with disabilities on the ground that a comparable separate league is offered.

People who are the victims of discrimination can file a lawsuit to prohibit further discrimination. And if the U.S. Department of Justice brings a lawsuit to halt a pattern and practice of discrimination, monetary damages and civil penalties may be imposed. Again, your local office of The Arc, as well as your state P&A office, will be able to provide information and assist in a discrimination complaint.

Public Services

This part of the ADA prohibits discrimination against people with disabilities by state and local public agencies that provide such services as transportation. It is a violation of the ADA for agencies to purchase buses, rail cars, or other transportation equipment that are not accessible to people with disabilities. The ADA also requires that private companies providing transportation services make their buses, trains, or rail cars accessible.

Accessibility

For many people with spina bifida, the most significant provisions of the ADA require buildings and facilities to be physically accessible. All federal, state, and local government buildings and facilities, such as town halls, airports, and schools, and all commercial buildings covered by the ADA's public accommodations provisions (discussed above) must be "readily accessible to and usable by individuals with disabilities." This requirement applies to both new construction and modifications to existing buildings, unless it would be "structurally impractical" to meet the requirements. This section of the ADA is intended to enable persons with physical disabilities, including people with spina bifida, to have the same access to public and commercial buildings as everyone else.

The ADA protects rights and opportunities for people with disabilities. By prohibiting discrimination and requiring reasonable accommodation and accessibility, the ADA stands as a true Bill of Rights for people with all disabilities, including spina bifida.

The Rehabilitation Act of 1973

Before the ADA was enacted, discrimination on the basis of disability was prohibited only in certain areas. Section 504 of the Rehabilitation Act of 1973 continues to prohibit discrimination against qualified people with disabilities in federally funded programs. The law provides that "No otherwise qualified individual with handicaps in the United States . . . shall, solely by reason of his handicap, be excluded from the participation in, be denied the benefits of, or be subjected to discrimination under any program or activity receiving federal financial assistance. . . ."

An "individual with handicaps" is any person who has a physical or mental impairment that substantially limits one or more of that person's "major life activities," which consist of "caring for one's self, performing manual tasks, walking, seeing, hearing, speaking, breathing, learning, and working." The U. S. Supreme Court has determined that an "otherwise qualified" individual with disabilities is one who is "able to meet all of a program's requirements in spite of his handicap." Programs or activities that receive federal funds are required to make reasonable accommodation to permit the participation of qualified people with disabilities. The law covers programs such as day care centers, schools, and jobs in programs receiving federal funds.

Section 504 has been used to enforce the right of children with disabilities to be integrated in their school district, to challenge placement decisions, and to assert the right to special education services for children who do not qualify for services under IDEA, which likely will be the federal funding "hook" required for the school to be subject to Section 504. Even if a child functions at a level that disqualifies him from services under IDEA, his right to services may be enforceable under Section 504. Similarly, if the child goes on to college—where IDEA does not apply—Section 504 will require the college to make reasonable accommodations to enable him to succeed at school, again so long as the college receives some federal funding in some area.

As with other legal issues, you should consult a qualified lawyer to explore claims under Section 504. Section 504 permits the recovery of reasonable attorney's fees if you prevail in your challenge.

Fair Housing Laws

Under federal fair housing laws, it is illegal to discriminate against a person with a "handicap" in the sale or rental of housing. "Handicap" as defined by federal law and regulations includes spina bifida. Under these laws, landlords cannot refuse to rent to a person with spina bifida or a family with a member with spina bifida because of his disability. In addition, landlords may not isolate people with disabilities in one part of a building or deny them access to any common facilities available to other tenants. They must also make "reasonable" accommodations for all people with disabilities, including modifications that make buildings "readily accessible to and usable by individuals with disabilities." This law is enforced by the federal Department of Housing and Urban Development (HUD) where discrimination complaints can be sent or filed by telephone or even over the Internet. Some states also have their own fair housing laws, which are sometimes helpful in situations not covered by the federal laws.

▪▪ Private Health Insurance

Finding and maintaining health insurance that covers a child with spina bifida can be extremely difficult. Unfortunately, in many states, insurance companies do not offer health or life insurance at a fair price, or sometimes at any price, to children or adults with spina bifida. This practice results from the belief that these children and adults are likely to submit more insurance claims than others. Until they become adults, children who are covered from birth by their parents' insurance face fewer problems, but coverage depends on the particular terms of the insurance.

Federal and many state laws prohibit insurance companies from denying coverage based on a disability like spina bifida, although certain preexisting conditions attributable to spina bifida (just like all preexisting health conditions) can be excluded for one year from the date of coverage. The drawback to all of these laws, however, is that insurance companies generally are allowed to deny coverage based on "sound actuarial principles" or "reasonable anticipated experience." Insurers rely on these large loopholes to deny coverage. In short, the laws often are ineffective. Even the ADA does not prohibit these same "sound actuarial" practices that frequently result in denied coverage.

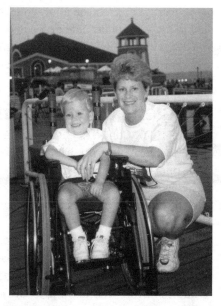

A few states have begun to lessen the health insurance burdens on families with children with disabilities. These states have passed insurance reform laws that prohibit exclusion of children with disabilities from coverage or prohibit exclusion of preexisting conditions. Other states offer "shared risk" insurance plans, under which insurance coverage is offered to people who could not obtain coverage otherwise. The added cost is shared among all insurance companies (including HMOs) in the state. To be eligible, a person must show that he has been recently rejected for coverage or offered a policy with limited coverage. The cost of this shared risk insurance is usually higher and the benefits may be limited, but even limited coverage is usually better than no health insurance at all.

Some state laws also cover people who have received premium increases of 50 percent or more. In addition, Medicare, Medicaid, and other federally funded programs aimed at improving health care for children might well be available to help with medical costs (see below). Check with your state insurance commission or your local office of the SBAA for information about health insurance programs in your area.

As your child approaches his eighteenth birthday, it is important to be aware of any changes in coverage that may occur due to his aging out of insurance coverage. Employer-provided private insurance plans usually discontinue coverage for dependents when they reach the age of eighteen, or twenty-two, if the child continues in school. However, many plans will continue coverage for dependent children with disabilities after they become adults. Coverage under a federal employee plan can be continued for the lifetime of the child with disabilities, but under most private employer plans, coverage for the child ends when the parent's own coverage ends. If you allow your adult child's coverage as a dependent to lapse, you may not be able to obtain any substitute coverage for him. Even if he is eligible for Medicaid or Medicare, you may not be able to obtain some benefits available under your workplace plan.

■ Agent Orange Benefits Act

In 1996, Congress passed the Agent Orange Benefits Act. This legislation provides both healthcare and financial benefits to children with spina bifida whose parent or parents served in Vietnam. This law was enacted in response to the concerns of many Vietnam veterans over the effects of the use of Agent Orange, a chemical sprayed widely during the war.

Under this law, children with spina bifida who have a parent or parents who are Vietnam War veterans are entitled to a monthly allowance to pay for medical care and vocational training and rehabilitation. In addition, these children are entitled to free health care services (including medications, nursing care, and assistive technology) for the symptoms and effects of their spina bifida. Medical services are provided through various federal health care providers, such as the Veterans Administration. If one or more of the parents of your child with spina bifida served in the Vietnam War, contact the Veterans Administration at 800-827-1000 or the Spina Bifida Association of America (see Resource Guide) for information about how to obtain benefits under this law.

■ Federally Funded Government Benefits

A number of programs funded in whole or in part by the federal government provide benefits for children and adults with disabilities, including those who have disabilities associated with spina bifida. The most important of these programs provide income (Supplemental Security Income and Social Security Disability), supplement income (housing assistance and food stamps), and pay for medical care (Medicaid and Medicare).

Some of these programs are "means tested" and some are not. "Means-tested" programs are available only for people with limited means—that is, people whose assets ("resources") and income are below certain maximum amounts. SSI, Medicaid, housing assistance, and food stamps are means-tested programs. Social Security Disability and Medicare are not means tested, so eligibility is not affected by an applicant's or recipient's resources or income. (The exception is for earned income, which at certain levels is deemed to establish that the applicant/recipient is not disabled.)

SSI and SSD

There are two basic federally funded programs that can provide additional income to people with disabilities, including people with spina bifida whose disabilities preclude substantial earnings. The two programs are "Supplemental Security Income" (SSI) and "Social Security Disability" (SSD), both of which are administered by the Social Security Administration (SSA). SSI pays a monthly cash benefit for children and adults with disabilities who are too disabled to work and who lack other income and resources. SSD pays a monthly cash benefit to adults with disabilities based on their own past earnings record or to children or adults who have a disability that began before age 18 and who are the children of deceased or retired persons who earned Social Security coverage. SSI is means tested. SSD is not.

SSI

As of 2007, SSI paid eligible individuals a maximum federal benefit of $603 per month and eligible couples $934 per month. Many, but not all, states supplement the basic federal SSI benefit. These amounts, which are adjusted each year to reflect changes in the cost of living, are reduced by other income of the recipient. If the recipient lives at home or is otherwise provided with food or shelter by others, the benefit is reduced by not more than about one-third of the basic federal benefit. SSI recipients in states other than California may also be eligible for food stamps. (California's state supplement is in lieu of food stamps.)

To establish eligibility for SSI, an individual must meet both a disability test and means tests (tests of financial need). To qualify as "disabled," an adult applicant's condition must be so disabling that he cannot engage in "substantial gainful activity." This means that he cannot perform any paid job, whether or not he can actually find such a job. The test of disability for minor children is different: whether the child's condition "results in marked and severe functional limitations." The disabling condition must be one that is expected to last not less than twelve months or to result in death.

SSA uses a complex, five-step process in making disability determinations. (See SSA Publication No. 05-16029, "Disability Benefits," for more information.) The criteria include your child's:

1. physical disabilities resulting from spina bifida;
2. ongoing health problems; and
3. cognitive ability, as measured by standardized IQ tests.

In making an eligibility determination, SSA is required to consider all the factors that can affect the recipient's ability to work (or the equivalent criteria for children under age 18). Both the symptom and its intensity are considered as part of a functional analysis.

SSI's eligibility requirements do not end with the disability test. Eligibility is also based on financial need. To establish need, one must satisfy both a "resource" test and income tests. Assets ("resources") cannot exceed $2,000 for an individual or $3,000 for a couple. The income of an SSI applicant or recipient also affects eligibility. The SSI rules allow a $20 "disregard" for monthly income of all kinds and an additional $65 "disregard" per month for earned income. Unearned income in excess of the $20 disregard reduces SSI benefits dollar for dollar. Earned income in excess of the disregard reduces SSI benefits $1 for every $2 earned, under a statutory work incentive program. In calculating an applicant's income, SSA also disregards certain impairment-related work expenses. In addition, under the PASS program (Plans for Achieving Self-Support), an SSI recipient can receive additional income or assets if they will be used to make it possible for the recipient to work in the future or to establish a business or occupation that will enable him to become gainfully employed.

In these determinations, SSA "deems" the resources and income of the parents of a child under age 18 who lives at home to be resources and income of the child. Thus, children with disabilities under age 18 who live with their parents are eligible only if their parents are very poor. When a child is 18, however, the attribution ("deeming") of parental resources and income to the child stops, and eligibility is determined on the basis of the child's own resources and income. Thus, many people with disabilities first become eligible for SSI on their eighteenth birthday. To be eligible, however, they cannot have excess resources or income. If a child reaches his eighteenth birthday with more than $2,000 in assets in his own name, he will not be eligible for SSI as long as he continues to own the excess assets.

Many people with spina bifida work. Finding a job for a son or daughter with spina bifida is a goal most parents strive hard to achieve.

Yet earning a salary can lead to a reduction or elimination of SSI benefits, because SSI is intended to provide income to people whose disabilities prevent them from working. Furthermore, in many states, the loss of SSI may lead to a loss of Medicaid, discussed below. Congress has enacted various work incentive programs that may postpone loss of benefits and Medicaid while individuals are seeking to join the productive workforce. See the SSA publications listed in the Reading List.

SSD

People with disabilities may also qualify for Social Security Disability—disability benefits provided under the Social Security program. The test for disability is the same as it is for SSI, discussed above. People do not have to be poor to qualify for SSD, however. There are no financial eligibility requirements based on resources or unearned income, although an applicant must not have earned income exceeding $900 per month to be eligible for SSD (as of 2007).To be eligible, an applicant must qualify on the basis of his own work record for Social Security purposes, or he must be unmarried, have a disability that began before age 18, and be the child of a retired or deceased parent who was covered by Social Security.

As with SSI, your child's employment can cause serious problems with respect to SSD eligibility. Earnings affect SSD differently than they affect SSI. Under SSD, a person who earns more than $900 per month (as of 2007) is deemed not to be disabled and thus is ineligible. That is not true of SSI, under which someone who is eligible for the full individual federal benefit with no other income can earn up to $1291 per month (as of 2007) before his federal SSI benefit stops. SSD work incentives may postpone ineligibility for benefits, as explained further in the SSA publications in the Reading List.

Although most people with disabilities that are severe enough to meet the SSA tests become eligible for SSI at age 18, they may become eligible for SSD on their parents' work record when their parents retire or die, thus subjecting them to the SSD rules described above. However, if SSD rules reduce benefits below SSI levels, SSI generally will make up the difference.

Medicare

Medicare is a federal health insurance program that helps pay the medical expenses of people who qualify. Medicare is not means tested.

People who are eligible for SSD benefits, either on their own earnings record or on a parent's account, will also be eligible for Medicare, starting at any age, after a 24-month waiting period. These individuals will automatically receive Part A (hospital) coverage, and they can elect Part B (medical) and D (prescription drug) coverages, for which they must pay a premium. If a person can also qualify for Medicaid, discussed below, Medicaid may pay the Medicare premium. Some children or adults with disabilities who would not otherwise be eligible for Medicare may qualify if someone pays the Medicare premiums. Called "third party buy-in," this works very much like purchasing private health insurance and may be useful when private health insurance is not available. Check with your local SSA office for details.

Medicaid

Medicaid is also important to many people with spina bifida. It pays for medical care for people who do not have private health insurance or Medicare and lack sufficient income to pay for medical care. It also provides certain benefits that are not covered by Medicare, such as financial aid for the purchase of wheelchairs. In many states, under so-called "Medicaid waivers," it pays for residential services for many people with disabilities.

Because Medicaid is funded by both federal and state governments, there are differences among states in the range of benefits offered. For example, some states provide "optional" services such as dental care, speech-language therapy, and occupational therapy. Consequently, parents must check with their state or local SSA office to make sure they are receiving the maximum range of Medicaid benefits available in their state.

In many states, if your child meets the eligibility criteria for SSI, he will automatically qualify for Medicaid. In these states, SSI eligibility is the key to Medicaid for most individuals with disabilities. In many of these states, disabled individuals whose income and resources are limited but who do not meet the financial eligibility requirements for SSI may still qualify for Medicaid as "medically needy" by "spending down" excess income and resources. Other states, in which SSI eligibility does not automatically establish Medicaid eligibility, have their own Medicaid financial eligibility requirements.

There are certain other services that may be available under Medicaid for people with spina bifida:

1. Under current law, Medicaid pays for residential services for people with disabilities in large Medicaid-certified residential institutions, called intermediate care facilities (ICFs). Most people with disabilities such as spina bifida are best served in the community, not in institutions, however. The Secretary of Health and Human Services has the authority to "waive" the ICF requirement. As a result, most states have received waivers allowing Medicaid funding of services provided in community-based facilities. The services that can be provided under these waivers include respite care, adaptive technologies, nutritional counseling, social services, homemaker services, and case management.

2. Another Medicaid service that may be important for some people with spina bifida involves personal assistance services. Personal assistance services are essential to enable some people with spina bifida to achieve an independent community life. Federal Medicaid rules allow (but do not require) states to provide certain "personal care" services under their Medicaid programs, but many states do not provide them. These services can include help with bathing, cooking, and grooming. It is up to people with disabilities and their families to advocate for these services to be more widely available under Medicaid.

3. Medicaid also provides an Early and Periodic Screening, Diagnosis, and Treatment Program (EPSDT). Under this program, states provide periodic medical and developmental assessments of children under the age of 21 whose parents qualify for Medicaid, and provide medical and other services needed to treat any diagnosis. These services can include physical, occupational, and speech therapies; immunizations; assistive devices; and vision, dental, and medical treatment. Your state or county department of health services should have an EPSDT contact who can help you determine if your child is eligible for services under this program. Your county or state P&A office may also be able to help you obtain EPSDT services.

It is important for parents to become generally familiar with the complex rules governing SSI, SSD, Medicare, and Medicaid. You can contact your local SSA office, call their national toll-free number (800-772-1213), or visit their website at www.ssa.gov.

Children with Special Health Care Needs Program

Under a program of grants administered by the Maternal and Child Health Bureau of the U.S. Department of Health and Human Services, states receive funds to pay for a wide variety of health-related services to children of low- and middle-income families. Services can include evaluations, clinic visits, hospitalization, surgery, medications, physical, occupational, and speech therapy, dental care, and genetic testing. Each state sets its own financial eligibility requirements based on a family's annual income. States can select the conditions that will be covered. This list is generally broad; children with spina bifida qualify for services if their parents are eligible financially. Individual states set the age at which these services cease to be available, but children are usually covered until age 18 or 21. Each state has a coordinator for this program, typically at the state departments of health or human services.

State Children's Health Insurance Program (SCHIP)

In 1997, Congress enacted the State Children's Health Insurance Program (SCHIP) to provide free or low-cost health insurance to children whose parents' income is too high to qualify for Medicaid and too low to be able to afford private family insurance. In most states, uninsured children age 18 and under qualify for coverage under SCHIP if their families have an income of less than $36,200 (family of four). Most states currently participate in this program and offer a range of medical services for covered children, including checkups, immunizations, doctor visits, prescription drugs, and hospital care. Applications for coverage under the CHIP program can be obtained from state or local health and human services departments, by calling 1-877-KIDS-NOW, or by going to www.insurekidsnow.gov.

Congress recently voted to reauthorize the program and to cover additional children whose parents have limited incomes, but President George W. Bush vetoed the bill. Therefore, at this writing, the future of the program is uncertain.

Housing Assistance

Federally funded housing assistance programs are available for people of limited means, including individuals with disabilities associated with spina bifida. These programs are operated by local housing authorities. The U.S. Department of Housing and Urban Development prescribes means-tests for these programs. These programs make affordable housing available for people with disabilities in many communities.

‖ Planning for Your Child's Future: Estate Planning

Although most children with spina bifida grow into independent adults, some may not be able to manage completely on their own. This section is written for parents whose children may need publicly funded services or help in managing their funds when they are adults.

The possibility that your child may always be dependent can be overwhelming. To properly plan for your child's future, you need information in areas you may never have considered before. Questions that deeply trouble parents include: "What will happen to my child when I die? Where and with whom will he live? How will his financial needs be met? How can I be sure he receives services he needs to assure his safety, health, and quality of life?

Some parents of children with spina bifida delay dealing with these issues, coping instead with the immediate demands of the present. Others begin to address the future when their child is young, adding to their insurance, beginning to set aside funds for their child, and sharing with family and friends their concerns about their child's future needs. Whatever the course, parents of children with spina bifida need to understand certain serious planning issues that arise from their child's disabilities. Failure to take these issues into account when planning for the future can have dire consequences both for the child and for other family members.

The central issues that any family needs to consider in planning for their children's future concern: 1) adequacy and allocation of assets; and 2) assignment of responsibilities. This chapter discusses aspects of these two issues that may affect families of children with spina bifida somewhat differently than they affect families whose children don't have potential impairments.

With respect to allocation of resources, families of children who may need publicly funded services or benefits in the future need to consider establishing a special needs trust for the child rather than leaving the child's inheritance to him outright when the parents die. These trusts are usually established after the parent dies, under the parent's will or revocable living trust. Less frequently, they are established while the parents are alive. Either way, parents need to plan, draft, and sign appropriate wills and trusts while they are alive—which means now, since no one knows when he will die. Failure to deal with the issue while parents are living may result in the child's disqualification for needed benefits and services, or may result in funds unnecessarily being claimed by public authorities. In addition, parents need to consider the adequacy of their resources to meet their children's needs—including the special needs of a child that may last for the child's lifetime instead of ending when the child completes his education. This leads to consideration of life insurance.

With respect to assignment of responsibilities, parents need to consider whether a child has impairments that will interfere with his ability to manage his own affairs as an adult. All parents with minor children need to consider who will look after their children if they die before their children are adults. But parents of children with spina bifida may need to make arrangements extending over their child's lifetime. These arrangements involve designating trustees and guardians and giving family members, trustees, and guardians guidance in addressing the special needs of their child. This is frequently done with what is sometimes called a "letter of intent"—a notebook of useful information. Again, the time for this planning is now, since no one knows when he will die or become incapacitated.

The sections below cover basic estate planning documents; special needs trusts; life insurance; choice of trustees; need for and choice of guardians; and letters of intent.

Basic Estate Planning Documents

The fundamental estate planning document is the will. Wills can: 1) name trustees, guardians, and executors; and 2) dispose of property at the owner's death. Property that passes to others under a will goes through a court-administered process called probate.

The will usually contains the basic estate plan for disposition of a person's property at death, unless the person making the will also establishes a revocable living trust. These trusts are usually used to avoid probate of assets that have been transferred to the trust during the lifetime of the person establishing the trust. When these trusts are used, they usually contain the basic estate plan for disposition of property, and in any event, must be coordinated with the provisions of the will.

Some kinds of property do not pass under a person's will or living trust at death and are not subject to probate. These include property held in joint tenancy with right of survivorship ("JTWROS") and tenancy by the entireties, a form of joint ownership with right of survivorship by a husband and wife. Property held in this form passes to the surviving joint owner at the death of one of the owners by right of survivorship rather than under a will or through probate. However, when the surviving joint owner dies, the property will pass under his or her will and be subject to probate. If you use these arrangements, you must coordinate them with your will and any revocable living trust.

Other property that does not pass under a person's will or living trust includes property with a designated beneficiary. Property of this kind includes life insurance, retirement plans and accounts, and "transfer on death" (TOD) and "payable on death" (POD) accounts. These arrangements also need to be coordinated with your will and your revocable living trusts, if any.

Wills, revocable living trusts, beneficiary designations, and other trust documents (such as the special needs trust, below) are referred to in this chapter as "estate planning documents."

Special Needs Trusts

If your child with spina bifida may need to qualify for government benefits and services other than educational services, you need to consider the effect of giving your child any assets, both during your lifetime and at death. Likewise, if you fail to execute estate planning documents, you need to consider what may happen if you allow your child with spina bifida to inherit by intestacy (dying without a will). If your child receives gifts and inheritances in excess of $2000, it will disqualify him for SSI and may also disqualify him for other "means-tested" benefits. Also, such gifts and inheritances may be subject to claims by the state for reimbursement ("cost-of-care liability") for services provided by the state. (See "Common Estate Planning Mistakes," below.)

Therefore, if your child may need to qualify for government benefits and services as an adult, you should be very cautious about making gifts to him or allowing him to inherit assets. There are two basic strategies you can use to deal with the benefit eligibility and cost-of-care liability issues: 1) disinheritance; and 2) use of special needs trusts.

Sometimes parents disinherit a child with special needs, relying on siblings to look after that child's needs after their deaths. Except where very small sums of money are involved, this strategy is usually not a desirable solution. If you leave funds intended for your child with spina bifida to a sibling, they may not be used as you intended. Even if the "favored" sons or daughters are sympathetic to the needs of their disabled brother or sister, the needs of their spouses, their own children, and their creditors may take precedence.

The alternative commonly recommended is for parents to establish a "special needs trust" for their child with disabilities. When properly drafted, these trusts do not constitute "resources" and trust income is not attributed to the beneficiary for purposes of determining his eligibility for benefits. Further, these trusts are not generally subject to cost-of-care liability. Special needs trusts do not require that assets be distributed for the support and maintenance of the beneficiary; instead the trustee pays out the funds at his or her sole and absolute discretion to benefit the beneficiary. Since trust distributions may constitute "income" for purposes of determining benefits eligibility, it is up to the trustee to use the trust funds in ways that minimize or eliminate any effect on eligibility.

Special needs trusts can be established during the lifetime of the parent or other donor, or at the death of the parent or other donor. Most frequently they are established at the donor's death.

Sometimes people with disabilities acquire assets that disqualify them from means-tested government benefits—for example, from an inheritance or a personal injury settlement. If it is not feasible to spend these assets to reestablish eligibility for benefits, it is frequently desirable to transfer them to a special needs trust. However, when assets of a disabled trust beneficiary (as distinguished from assets from his parent or someone other than the disabled beneficiary) are transferred to a special needs trust, the special needs trust must contain certain provisions prescribed by federal law. Otherwise, the trust will not accomplish its intended purpose, to allow the beneficiary to qualify for means-tested benefits. These special provisions require what is left in the trust at the beneficiary's death to be used to repay the state for Medicaid benefits received by the beneficiary during his lifetime ("payback provision") or to be retained in a "pooled trust" for other disabled individuals instead of going to heirs of the disabled beneficiary. Theses special provisions are not required and are not desirable in special needs trusts that are funded with the assets of a parent or other third party instead of the beneficiary's own assets.

Life Insurance

Parents of children with spina bifida should review their life insurance coverage. The most important use of life insurance is to meet financial needs that arise if the insured person dies. Many people who support dependents with their wages or salaries are underinsured. This problem is aggravated if hard-earned dollars are wasted on insurance that does not provide the amount or kind of protection that could and should be purchased. It is therefore essential for any person with dependents to understand basic facts about insurance.

The first question to consider is: Who should be insured? Life insurance deals with the financial risks of death. The principal financial risk of death in most families is that the death of the wage earner or earners will deprive dependents of support. Consequently, life insurance coverage should be considered primarily for the parent or parents on whose earning power the children depend, rather than on the lives of children or dependents.

The second question is whether your insurance is adequate to meet the financial needs that will arise if you die. A reputable insurance agent can help you determine whether your coverage is adequate. Consumer guides to insurance can also help you calculate the amount of insurance you need.

The next question is: What kind of insurance policy should you buy? Insurance policies are of two basic types: term insurance, which provides "pure" insurance without any build-up of cash value or reserves, and other types (called "whole life," "universal life," and "variable life"), which, in addition to providing insurance, include a savings or investment factor. The latter kinds of insurance, sometimes called "permanent" insurance, are really a combined package of insurance and investment.

People with children who do not have disabilities try to assure that their children's education will be paid for if they die before their children finish school. Many people use life insurance to deal with this risk. When their children are grown and educated, this insurance need disappears. Term insurance is a relatively inexpensive way to deal with risks of this kind.

On the other hand, people with spina bifida may need supplemental assistance throughout their lives. That need may not disappear completely during their parents' lifetimes. If the parents plan on using life insurance to help meet this need when they die, they must recognize, in deciding what kind of insurance to buy, that term insurance premiums rise sharply as they get older. Consequently, they should either adopt and stick to a savings and investment program to eventually replace the insurance, or consider purchasing whole life or universal life.

Whether you buy term insurance and maintain a separate savings and investment program, or instead buy one of the other kinds of policies that combine them, you should make sure that the insurance part of your program is adequate to meet your family's financial needs if you die. A sound financial plan will meet these needs and will satisfy savings and retirement objectives in a way that does not sacrifice adequate insurance coverage.

Finally, it is essential to coordinate your life insurance with the rest of your estate plan. This is done by designating the beneficiary—choosing who is to receive any insurance proceeds when you die. If you name your child with spina bifida as a beneficiary, your child's share of the proceeds may interfere with eligibility for government benefits or be subject to cost-of-care claims, as described earlier. Therefore, if you wish any or all of your life insurance proceeds to be used for the benefit of your child with spina bifida, you may wish to designate a trustee of a special needs trust, either under your will or revocable living trust or under a separate life insurance trust, as the beneficiary of your child's share of the life insurance proceeds. Upon your death, the trustee will receive the insurance proceeds and use them for the benefit of your child in accordance with the trust.

Choice of Trustees

If your child with spina bifida will not be able to manage his own affairs or may need to qualify for means-tested benefits as an adult, you will need to choose trustees or provide methods for designating trustees who will be able to manage the funds in any trust you establish over the course of your child's lifetime. Choices included professional trustees—banks and trust companies, lawyers, and accountants—and family members and friends. No one size fits all, so you need to thoughtfully discuss the selection of trustees with your attorney. Here are some considerations:

1. Commercial trustees charge fees. Other trustees may or may not. Think carefully about whether it is desirable to compensate a family member or friend for serving as a trustee. Sometimes it is; sometimes it isn't.

2. Banks and trust companies do not die or become incapacitated. People do. Therefore, you must plan for succession in the event of the disability or death of a trustee or co-trustee, and consider naming co-trustees.

3. Not everyone is suited to the trustee's role. Trustees have three basic jobs: a) investing trust assets; b) using trust assets for the beneficiary's benefit; and c) keeping records and paying taxes. Professional trustees are sometimes the only reasonable candidates for one or all of these duties. Sometimes individuals are desirable, particularly for the second role. Again, co-trustee arrangements may be used to fill these different roles.

4. Give consideration to providing a mechanism to remove and replace a trustee who is not doing the job well or whose fees are too high.

5. The trustee needs to be willing and able to take into account the rules governing benefits when making distributions.

6. Special needs trusts are discretionary trusts. The trustee only makes the distributions of assets that he deems appropriate and no one can review his decisions except in case of "abuse of discretion" (extreme misconduct). In the absence of co-trustees, there will be nobody to look over his shoulder.

7. Siblings are frequently appointed as trustees and they or their children are often named to receive the remainder of the trust after the beneficiary dies. Pay careful attention to the tax and other implications of this potential conflict of interest.

As indicated above, no one choice of trustee arrangements is best for all cases. Furthermore, no one is likely to be as well informed about your child's needs as you, his parents, so no choice will be entirely satisfactory from your standpoint. Parents often put off their estate planning for this reason. Nevertheless, some choices are better and some are worse, and the proper choice can make a great deal of difference to your child. Therefore, it is important not to postpone estate planning until too late because of the difficulty of choosing guardians and trustees. Your lawyer should be able to help you sort out the issues in order to make the best choices available.

Guardians

A guardian is a person appointed by a court or by law to manage the legal and financial affairs of someone else. Although few adults with spina bifida require guardians, parents frequently ask whether they should nominate themselves or others as guardians once their child with spina bifida becomes an adult. The appointment of a guardian costs money and may result in the curtailment of your child's rights—the right to have a checking account, to vote, and so on. Therefore, a guardian should be appointed only if and when needed. If one is not needed during your lifetime, it usually is sufficient to nominate guardians in your will.

Spina bifida is not by itself a sufficient reason to establish a guardianship for your child when he becomes an adult. A guardian may be needed in certain situations, however. For example, guardianship may be necessary if your child inherits or acquires property that he lacks the capacity to manage. Also, a guardian may be required if a medical provider refuses to serve your child without authorization by a guardian. Occasionally it is necessary to appoint a guardian to gain access to important legal, medical, or educational records. Unless there is a specific need that can be solved by the appointment of a guardian, however, there is no reason to consider guardianship for adults with disabilities.

Letter of Intent

You know a great deal more about your son or daughter and his strengths and needs than anyone else does. You have a vision for his future that is based on your knowledge of your child. No one stepping into your shoes—no sibling of your child, no trustee, no guardian—is in a position to fill your shoes unless you help. You can do this by making sure you share your knowledge and vision with those who succeed you.

Much literature on estate planning for families of children with special needs suggests writing a "letter of intent" that tells those who succeed you everything you would want to know if you were starting from scratch. Your successor needs to know:

- what you want your child's future to be like;
- what your vocational, social, residential, and recreational vision is;
- what your son's or daughter's strengths and abilities are;
- what he or she needs help with;
- who your child's friends are;
- who your child's care providers are;
- your child's medical record and educational history;
- what financial resources your child has;
- what benefits your child is receiving and what he may be eligible for in the future;
- what you know, and where your successors can obtain, advice about rules governing benefits.

This "letter of intent"—which is actually more like a notebook than a mere letter—is a living document that needs to be reviewed frequently and updated continually. That way, your family and trustees and guardians will have a readily available source of all the information you have about your child to which they can turn immediately, without undue difficulty, when they must step into your shoes.

Common Estate Planning Mistakes

Here are some common mistakes to avoid:

No Will

In most states, the children (including a child with a disability) of a married person who dies without a will are entitled to equal shares in a portion of the assets the parent owns at death. The result is that your child with spina bifida will inherit property in his own name. His inheritance could jeopardize eligibility for government benefits or be subject to cost-of-care claims. These and other problems can be avoided with properly drafted estate planning documents. Do not allow your state's laws to determine how your property will be divided upon your death. No parent of a child with spina bifida should die without a will and other estate planning documents.

A Will Leaving Property Outright to Your Child with Spina Bifida

A will that leaves property to a child with spina bifida in his own name is often just as bad as no will at all, because it may disqualify him for government benefits or subject the inheritance to cost-of-care liability. Parents of children with spina bifida do not need just any will; they need appropriate estate planning documents that meet their child's special needs.

A Will Creating a Support Trust for Your Child with Spina Bifida

A will that creates a support trust for your child, instead of a discretionary special needs trust, presents much the same problem as a will that leaves property outright to a child with spina bifida. A support trust is a trust that directs the trustee to make distributions for the person's "health, support, and maintenance," instead of directing the trustee to make such distributions for the benefit of the beneficiary as the trustee deems appropriate, at the trustee's sole and absolute discretion. A support trust may jeopardize government benefits or be subject to cost-of-care claims. A discretionary special needs trust avoids those problems.

Insurance or Retirement Plans Naming Your Child as a Beneficiary

Many parents own life insurance policies that name a child with spina bifida as a beneficiary or contingent beneficiary, either alone or in common with siblings ("share and share alike"). The result is that insurance proceeds may go outright to your child with spina bifida, creating problems with eligibility for government benefits and cost-of-care liability. The same is true of many retirement plan benefits. Often the solution is a properly drawn special needs trust, as discussed above.

Use of Joint Tenancy in Lieu of Wills

Spouses sometimes avoid making wills by placing all their property in joint tenancies with right of survivorship. When one of the spouses dies, the survivor automatically becomes the sole owner. Parents try to use joint tenancies instead of wills, relying on the surviving spouse to properly take care of all estate planning matters. This plan, however, fails completely if both parents die in the same disaster, if the surviving spouse becomes incapacitated, or if the surviving spouse neglects to make a proper will. The result is the same as if neither spouse made any will at all—the child with spina bifida shares in the parents' estates. Therefore, even when all property is held by spouses in joint tenancy, it is necessary that both spouses have appropriate estate planning documents.

Establishing UTMA Accounts for Your Child with Spina Bifida

Well-meaning parents and grandparents sometimes open bank accounts for children with disabilities under the Uniform Transfers to Minors Act (UTMA). When the child reaches age 21, the account becomes the property of the child, and may interfere with eligibility for SSI and Medicaid. Parents and relatives of children with spina bifida who are likely to need government-funded services or benefits should never set up UTMA accounts for their child with spina bifida, nor should they open other bank accounts in the child's name.

Failing to Advise Grandparents and Relatives of the Need for Special Arrangements

Just as the parents of a child with spina bifida need properly drafted wills or trusts, so do grandparents and other relatives who may leave (or give) property to the child. If these people are not aware of the special concerns—government benefits, cost-of-care liability, and competency—their plans may go awry and their generosity may be wasted. Make sure anyone planning gifts to your child with spina bifida understands what is at stake.

Children and adults with spina bifida are entitled to lead full and rewarding lives. But many of them cannot do so without continuing financial support from their families. The only way to make sure your child has that support whenever he needs it is to plan for tomorrow today. Doing otherwise can rob him of the future he deserves.

∷ Conclusion

Parenthood always brings responsibilities. These responsibilities are greater when you have a child with spina bifida. Understanding the pitfalls for the future and planning to avoid them will help you to meet these special responsibilities. In addition, knowing and asserting your child's rights can help guarantee that he will receive the education and government benefits to which he is entitled. Being a good advocate for your child requires more than knowledge. You must also be determined to use that knowledge effectively, and, when necessary, forcefully.

∷ Parent Statements

We were very active in the IEP process. We knew that we wanted our child to be given a chance to try everything and to be included in regular gym. We have had our battles, but for the most part, were able to work well with the various schools in the three states we've lived in.

❧

They wanted to bus our son to a school in another district that is 25 minutes away. I refused. To accommodate us they have agreed to pay for his day care that he has attended since he was a year old. There are laws that the school districts must abide by. (They know these laws, but they hope you don't.)

❧

I have had to write a lot of letters, make a lot of phone calls, and do a lot of research, but Heather has always received everything I felt she needed. I utilized the Department of Education, Parent Training Centers, and Protection and Advocacy Services.

❧

My daughter had been in the public school system for five years. It always seemed like she was struggling to catch up or keep up with the rest of the students her age. Her grades were always poor. Despite all the evaluations the school did, as well as the independent evaluations we obtained, the school would never write up an IEP that included anything other than her needs for catheterization. Whenever I asked for academic assistance of any kind, I would be told such things as "that belongs in a different kind of IEP" or "she doesn't qualify." I think I pretty much heard every excuse there was, but I never was able to get an appropriate IEP that addressed her needs.

When I had had enough, I filed a formal complaint with the State Board of Education. They found all my complaints valid and ordered the school to correct their violations. I then filed due process against the school system (upon the State's recommendation), pulled her from the public school, and placed her in a private school that could and would give her the help she needed.

❧⚜❧

Our due process case took two and a half years and was very hard on the entire family. I couldn't afford a lawyer who was trained in the education laws, but did end up with one who was willing to try to help me. In the end, they helped the other side. I did, however, find some advocates who knew the law and helped me more than any lawyer could have.

❧⚜❧

I get upset when Jeanie and I go out to a public restaurant and her wheelchair can't fit under the table or booth due to posts, etc. Finding a wheelchair entrance in the back of a building is frustrating.

❧⚜❧

Waiting for a handicapped bathroom in a public facility is particularly difficult to take when an able bodied person comes out of it.

❧⚜❧

It is extremely frustrating to be told that a facility is accessible only to find out, after you arrive with your child, that the information you were given was not exactly accurate. You almost have to personally check out the facility ahead of time to be sure. Some people's definition of accessible is different than mine.

❧⚜❧

My husband is a Vietnam veteran, so when I heard about Agent Orange Benefits, I applied. Will now gets health benefits through them, as well as monthly stipends.

❧⚜❧

Insurance and paperwork are unending chores. Sometimes it takes two years to get a test covered. My insurance company is usually pretty good, but it definitely helps if you go to a "participating provider."

❧

The keys to managing paperwork and insurance issues are:
1. *Stay on top of them.*
2. *Learn to play the game.*
3. *Be persistent.*
4. *Stick up for your child's rights and make sure he or she gets the services needed.*

❧

My main concern is what is going to happen to Carl when we die. Will he be able to go into a group home? Will any of our children be able to help care for him? Will there be any outside services to help support them if they do decide to help him out? What will be best for Carl? What will be best for my other children?

❧

Our society is trying to accommodate people with disabilities. A lot of stores now have riding carts and wheelchairs to make shopping easier. With a little help, I think Brian should be able to do about anything.

16

THE ADULT WITH SPINA BIFIDA

Timothy J. Brei, M.D.

No matter how young your child with spina bifida is, you probably have spent at least some time wondering about her future. This chapter will focus on some issues relating to adulthood and independence, as well as on ways to overcome barriers to independence.

The ultimate goals for an adult with spina bifida are the same as for any other adult: to live as independently as possible; to work; to have deep, meaningful relationships; and to be a contributing member of society. Families committed to promoting independence in their young children will help make these goals realistic and achievable, There are, however, many possible obstacles and/or challenges that the individual with spina bifida may face.

1. **Societal Barriers.** These can range from something as simple as inaccessibility of buildings and transportation to something as complex as attitudes and prejudices.
2. **Health Care Issues.** Some of the medical concerns that come up in individuals with spina bifida may make achieving independence more difficult.

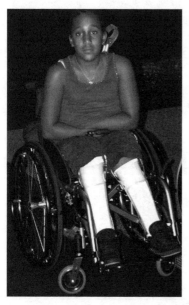

3. **Family Attitudes.** If children with spina bifida are viewed as less capable or are overprotected, they may not learn the skills necessary for independent living.
4. **Emotional Concerns.** Poor self-esteem and depression make it harder to learn the tasks necessary to be independent.
5. **Learning Difficulties.** The learning difficulties that are often seen in individuals with spina bifida can make learning or organizing everyday activities at home and at school more challenging. Identifying the appropriate ways of dealing with learning disabilities and then finding jobs that match an individual's unique learning style is difficult and time consuming.

This chapter highlights some of the most important of these issues. It is not possible to cover all of the issues thoroughly in one chapter; but this will at least give you an idea of what may lie ahead for your child as she grows older.

▟▙ Health Issues

Until the development of the shunt in the early 1960s, very few individuals with spina bifida survived into adulthood. Even today, medical professionals do not yet have a complete picture of the medical issues in adults with spina bifida. We do know, however, that adults with spina bifida have both the medical issues related to spina bifida to deal with, as well as the medical concerns common in all adults as they age.

In adults, we think of *primary conditions* as those that are specifically related to spina bifida, while *secondary conditions* are those other medical factors of aging or complications that may arise that interact with spina bifida to cause problems. Indeed, the secondary issues may have a greater effect on how healthy adults with spina bifida are than the spina bifida itself. Much of this discussion will therefore deal with secondary conditions seen in adults with spina bifida. The Spina Bifida Association recently published the *Health Guide for Adults Living with Spina Bifida* (available at www.sbaa.org). This guide is helpful for adults to manage their health or to families of adolescents to begin to teach their children health management skills. The topics below, and many other topics, are covered in greater detail in this Guide.

Obesity

Adults with spina bifida are more likely to be overweight. This relates in general to being less active and relying more on the use of wheelchairs to move around, as well as to the fact that most adults have a tendency to put on weight as they get older. Obesity in all people increases the risks of heart disease, high blood pressure, and diabetes. In individuals with spina bifida, being overweight can make getting around more difficult, contribute to pressure sores, affect circulation, and make activities of daily living particularly challenging.

Weight loss in people with or without spina bifida is difficult to achieve, so the best strategy is prevention. The first step is to eat wisely. Everyone should strive to eat a well-balanced diet that is low in fat, high in fiber, and includes many servings of fruits and vegetables. Most spina bifida clinics have dietitians who are available to consult with you should you have specific questions or want more information.

A second important step is aerobic exercise and strength training. In addition to helping in weight loss, this is beneficial for overall health, particularly cardiovascular fitness. An added benefit is that it improves mood. It is important to make exercise a part of your child's lifestyle so that she will be more likely to incorporate exercise into her life as she ages.

Unfortunately, many individuals with spina bifida are limited in the types of exercises that they can do, and there are few individuals or fitness centers that understand the special issues of exercise in individuals with disabilities. This makes it important to make exercise a part of your child's lifestyle in childhood. Members of spina bifida clinics, particularly the orthopedists, psychiatrists, or physical therapists, can serve as a resource. Additionally, many universities have departments of physical education that offer classes and instruction in adaptive physical education. Assistance might also be obtained through adult rehabilitation centers, particularly those with experience in spinal cord injuries. Finally, many larger cities have adult wheelchair sports leagues. While some opportunities may be less available in rural areas, it should be possible to find a way to provide both aerobic and strength training to almost all individuals with spina bifida,

For individuals with spina bifida, good types of exercise include swimming, upper extremity exercise, or power wheeling in their wheelchairs. Traditionally, much of the equipment in gyms has not been accessible to people with spina bifida. Recently, however, more and more companies have begun making equipment that can be used by people with various disabilities. Additionally, many gyms hire certified fitness instructors who may be able to recommend ways of utilizing available equipment. Numerous exercise videos designed for individuals with disabilities have also been produced. A useful website is that of the National Center on Physical Activity and Disability (wwww.ncpad.org). NCPAD serves as a national clearinghouse and information center about exercise and recreation related resources available to individuals with disabilities, including spina bifida.

Osteoporosis

Osteoporosis refers to the loss of bone density that occurs naturally with aging. Women are more prone to this condition as they age and their estrogen levels decrease. People with spina bifida who are nonambulatory are at an even higher risk for developing osteoporosis. This can even occur in early childhood. Spontaneous fractures may occur as a result.

Preventative strategies include: eating dairy products and dark green leafy vegetables such as collard greens and broccoli; taking daily calcium and vitamin D supplements, if recommended; and engaging in regular physical exercise. It also helps for a person with spina bifida to remain on a therapeutic standing program for as long as possible. Regular weight bearing on the lower extremities will help offset the physiologic bone changes that occur with osteoporosis.

Joint Pain/Arthritis

Pain appears to be a common problem for many adults with spina bifida and can affect their quality of life. Everyone knows that as you get older, more aches and pains occur. Muscles and joints get tired. Because of their altered gait patterns, adults with spina bifida put extra strain on joints in an effort to continue walking. If they are also overweight, their joints have to work still harder. All of this extra wear and tear on the joints can lead to pain or arthritis—a connective tissue disorder that results in inflamed joints.

The best preventative strategy is to exercise daily to maintain muscle strength and joint range of motion. Walking, weight lifting, and sitting aerobics are all good forms of exercise. A physical therapist can evaluate a person's walking and make appropriate suggestions to minimize wear and tear on the joints. Losing weight also helps by decreasing the amount of pressure on the weight-bearing joints in the lower extremities. An adult who is experiencing pain should consult his or her physician, as there may be many causes of pain and many options for pain management that can be helpful.

Complications

An adult with spina bifida needs to keep in mind that complications related to her disability can occur at any time. Periodically, neurosurgical evalua-tions are necessary to assess shunt functioning and the presence of tethered cord, syringomyelia, or Chiari complications. (See Chapter 5.) Tests such as renal ultrasound and renal profiles, as well as blood pressure monitoring, are also necessary. Otherwise, urinary problems such as chronic infections and stones can go undetected and permanent damage can occur. (See Chapter 7.) In addition, braces and wheelchair need to be checked for proper fit and maintained so that they function properly. And any skin without feeling should be inspected daily for signs of redness or breakdown.

Access to Health Care

Clearly, adults with spina bifida need good, comprehensive medical care—specialty care plus routine medical care. However, locating providers of that care and sources of payment for it is not always easy.

Locating Appropriate Health Care Providers

There are still very few adult spina bifida clinics in the country, so the coordinated, multidisciplinary approach to care that many children receive is often not available. Instead, adults with spina bifida often need to seek out routine medical care, as well as care related to spina bifida issues, themselves. In some instances, pediatric orthopedists, urologists, and neurosurgeons will continue to follow adults with spina bifida, or they may refer them to adult specialists. Of equal, if not more importance, is the need to identify primary care physicians who are knowledgeable about spina bifida and/or willing to consult specialists when necessary, to provide the overall health care for adults with spina bifida. As mentioned above, having a good primary care provider is essential because the overall healthcare issues of adults may begin to eclipse the medical concerns related to spina bifida in importance. The specialists who deal with spina bifida are not equipped to provide total health care, but only to assist in medical issues related to spina bifida.

A primary care physician is needed to supervise general healthcare concerns and to do routine medical care and physical exams. For adults, this care may be provided by a family practice physician or an internist. A relatively new type of primary care physician is a "med peds" physician, whose training enables him to become board certified in both pediatrics and internal medicine. This type of primary physician is well versed in dealing with childhood birth defects such as spina bifida, and also understands the importance of routine medical care in adulthood.

Even when high quality primary care is available for adults with spina bifida, difficulties can still arise if someone lacks the motivation to go to a physician for routine care. This makes it crucial for the adult with spina bifida to know her body and know when to seek medical care.

Paying for Health Care Services

For an adult to have full access to care, she also must have the ability to pay for care. This is difficult for many young adults, not just for young adults with spina bifida. Often young adults are too old to be covered by their parents' insurance, but not yet covered by an employer. Insurance coverage is usually available for individuals employed by large companies that have group insurance policies already in place. This is not necessarily the case in small companies. These individuals may be able to participate in a state-run "shared risk" insurance plan that provides coverage to people who otherwise could not get coverage.

Contact your state insurance commission to find out whether your state has such a plan and what kind of coverage is available.

For people who are unable to work, healthcare costs may be covered by government programs. Medical coverage may be available through Medicaid or Medicare programs. As Chapter 15 explains, both of these programs provide medical assistance for people with disabilities who meet eligibility requirements. Through the "Medical Waiver" program, Medicaid and Medicare may also help meet these needs on a community basis and potentially pay for some personal assistance. These requirements vary from state to state, so you and your adult child need to become familiar with the rules in your particular state.

▪▪ Psychosocial Concerns

"Psychosocial" concerns arise when there are difficulties with behavior, mood, or interactions with significant others. These concerns are just as important as other adult health issues because they have a big impact on the happiness and well being of your adult child. A variety of psychosocial issues are crucial in working toward independent living in adults with spina bifida. Some of the most important issues are discussed below.

Self-Esteem

How we feel about ourselves and our capabilities—our self-esteem—plays a big role in our success as adults. Poor self-esteem interferes with attempts to be independent. For example, if someone doesn't feel good about herself, she may not be motivated to manage her healthcare needs or spend time grooming, which will affect her ability to get and keep a job.

Creating a sense of self-confidence and self-esteem is a lifelong process that begins in

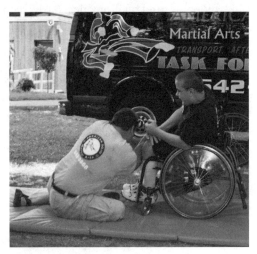

childhood. Do not wait until adolescence to help your child begin this process in preparation for adulthood. Indeed, adolescence is a time when self-esteem can really be put to the test. After all, this is when young people tend to become acutely aware of differences. Encouraging social interactions, providing exposure to a variety of activities, finding out what your child is good at, and allowing her to make her own decisions as appropriate are all examples of ways you can help your child achieve the self-esteem necessary to achieve independence as an adult. See Chapter 14 for more guidance.

Education

Education is an important building block in independence. Most individuals with spina bifida have "normal" intelligence, but many have learning problems that can interfere with education. These learning difficulties may include problems with attention, visual-motor skills (hand-eye coordination), organizational skills, complex planning and problem solving, and developing strategies. Frequently, these areas of difficulty may not become apparent or be recognized until late childhood and early adolescence, when the demands of school and life increase.

The presence of learning disabilities can affect your child's independence in adulthood in several ways. First, they can affect the selection of career choices that will be appropriate for your child. Second, difficulties in these areas can make it harder to manage various aspects of adult life, such as jobs, medical concerns, transportation, paying bills, shopping, and relationships. Early identification of these kinds of difficulties will allow individuals with spina bifida to develop strategies in order to better manage them.

An appropriate educational program will help to identify not only weaknesses or areas of difficulty for your child, but also areas of strengths. The educational plan developed should work to identify ways of working with the weaknesses, as well as ways of building on the strengths. See Chapter 13 for more information.

Mental Health

Depression is a mental illness that is fairly common among the general population, as well as among people with physical disabilities. Adolescents and adults with spina bifida may feel depressed or alone and isolated. Depression can occur as a reaction to a particular situation such as unemployment or limited social opportunities, or it may be a general feeling of hopelessness and sadness.

Depression limits a person's ability to plan and finish tasks. This can make it difficult, if not impossible, to live alone without proper supports. Treatment with psychotherapy and/or medication is vital if your child is going to be successful at living independently as an adult.

Social Skills

Difficulties with social skills can affect all areas of independent functioning, including jobs, friendships, dating, and intimate relationships. Poor social skills also contribute to the sense of social isolation that many adults with spina bifida may feel. Some problems with social skills may be related to  certain aspects of learning disorders. However, many difficulties with social skills result from lack of practice at these skills due to having overprotective parents or limited time interacting with peers or adults. Although new social skills can be learned in adulthood, they are best learned over a lifetime. If you want your child to learn the skills necessary for work and for maintaining friendships, make sure she has ample opportunities to be around others, learn from others, and take risks.

Sexuality

Many parents have trouble thinking of their children as sexual beings. But having spina bifida does not change the need to be loved or to express love. Indeed, this is the most important task and desire of all adults. An important component of being a loving adult is sexuality, but sexuality is only a part of intimacy. Other important prerequisites for adult intimacy include: a sense of self-worth, knowledge that what is important is what's inside rather than what's outside, and good communication skills so that you can develop friendships and intimate relationships. Because of spina bifida, the mechanics of sexual intimacy and intercourse may be different, but the ability to express intimacy in a sexual way is possible.

It is important that parents understand and talk with their children about issues of sexuality because children with spina bifida, both male and female, may start going through puberty earlier than children without spina bifida. (See Chapter 10.) Women with spina bifida can have intercourse, although lubrication is often a problem. They are just as fertile as any other woman, and are quite capable of getting pregnant. Women who become pregnant should be followed by an obstetrician who specializes in high-risk pregnancies and is knowledgeable about possible difficulties, which may include not being able to feel when labor is occurring. Close medical follow-up by other physicians, particularly experts in treating issues related to spina bifida, is also important. They can help monitor potential problem areas such as bladder function, which may change during pregnancy.

Sexual function in men with spina bifida is more variable. Men who have very low lumbar or sacral level lesions are often able to have erections and may achieve normal ejaculation. The ability to have erections decreases with higher level lesions. Males with thoracic level lesions are often not able to achieve erection or to have ejaculation. For males unable to achieve erection, there are a variety of erection aids that may assist them in being able to have sexual intercourse. Options can be discussed with a urologist. Males who are unable to ejaculate are infertile. Men who can ejaculate may have decreased fertility, but this is not easily predicted. Since some men can father children and there is no easy way to predict fertility, the safest course is to teach males appropriate birth control methods.

For additional information about this subject, consult the booklet entitled *Sexuality in the Person with Spina Bifida*, published by the Spina Bifida Association of America.

▪▪ Independent Living

As discussed above, to live independently requires a variety of skills, including independence in medical care, competence in social interactions, knowledge of academics and other "school" skills, and an ability to handle emotional concerns. These skills are best acquired beginning in childhood.

Learning daily household chores may be more difficult or take more time due to the unique learning styles in individuals with spina bifida or due to home accessibility or mobility issues. There are also several issues related to independence that people with spina bifida typically do not begin focusing on until adolescence or later. These include job skills, transportation, and housing, which are discussed below. A particularly useful website for disability-related information, including employment, education, housing, transportation, health, benefits, and community services, is www.disabilityinfo.gov. Additional topic-related resources are included below.

Job Skills

An important part of independent living is to identify a job that will provide an adequate income. Despite their limited mobility, individuals with spina bifida can succeed in many occupations. It may, however, take some investigation to find out your child's interests and abilities. If your child is receiving special educational services through the school system, her IEP in high school should include a transition-to-work plan to help her narrow down possible career options and learn needed job skills. Many states call this an individual transition plan (ITP). Included on her transition-to-work plan might be such services as: vocational assessment and testing, job training, and instructional support.

Adults with disabilities have much greater career opportunities now than ever before, in large part due to the Americans with Disabilities Act (ADA). As Chapter 15 explains, this act protects a person's right to equal opportunities in jobs and other services. Title I of ADA deals with employment issues and prohibits discrimination against "qualified individuals with disabilities." An individual with a disability must meet legitimate skill experience, education, and other requirements for a position and be able to perform the "essential functions of the position with or without reasonable accommodation." However, the employer is required to make reasonable accommodations for a disability if those accommodations will allow a person to perform the job adequately. Examples of reasonable accommodations include acquiring or modifying equipment so a wheelchair user can perform the job or making facilities more accessible to, and useable by, an individual with a disability.

An employer may not ask about a disability during an interview or make a job candidate take a medical exam, but may ask whether the person can perform specific job functions or activities. Individuals with disabilities, however, should share specific needs with potential employers so that reasonable accommodations can be made. Anyone who feels they have been discriminated against can turn to services such as the Legal Aid Society or lawyer referral and information services listed in the phone book. A complaint may be filed with the nearest office of the U.S. Equal Employment Opportunity Commission (EEOC), usually listed in the phone book under U.S. Government. For further information, contact the EEOC at 1-800-669-EEOC, or the ADA information hotline, 1-800-514-0301.

Adults with spina bifida who are seeking jobs may qualify for assistance from State Bureau of Vocational Rehabilitation programs. These agencies provide services such as evaluation of vocational needs, counseling and guidance, work-related placement services, and other training services. Check under the state government offices in your phone book for the nearest vocational rehabilitation department.

Transportation

Most people with spina bifida are able to drive a car or a van, but may need special adaptations to the vehicle. A first step is often an evaluation to determine what equipment, if any, is needed to assist in driving.

The Bureau of Vocational Rehabilitation may be able to help young adults access and pay for this service. Evaluations will determine whether there are vision problems or difficulties with motor skills that would make driving more difficult.

The next step involves learning how to drive in order to pass licensing tests. Special driver's education courses may be funded by the Bureau of Vocational Rehabilitation. Classroom training, as well as on-the-road training, may be required.

Once your child has obtained a license, the Bureau of Vocational Rehabilitation may help pay for needed modifications to your own car or van. Payment for these modifications is always a difficult issue. In some instances, the Bureau of Vocational Rehabilitation may pay part of the costs. In other instances, you may be able to get insurance companies to agree to pay, although this happens only rarely. Some families contact other family members, churches, or charitable organizations to help with payment. Families should also check with their accountant or with the Internal Revenue Service (IRS) as to whether these modifications may be tax deductible.

Some people with spina bifida may not be able to drive, or may choose to use public transportation. Title II of the Americans with Disabilities Act (ADA) prohibits discrimination against individuals with disabilities in all programs, activities, and services of public entities. This includes public transportation systems. If you live in a city with public transportation, the ADA requires that they have buses available that are accessible to individuals with disabilities. Smaller cities that do not have bus transportation may have other transportation services for individuals with disabilities, including special vans that go door to door. Check with your city government about accessible transportation available in your area.

Housing

One of the things most people want to do as they get older is to move out of their parents' home and into their own housing. Sometimes, however, it is difficult for adults with spina bifida to find housing that is accessible. One option is to look for an apartment building that was built fairly recently. Because of the Fair Housing Amendment Act, many apartment buildings built since 1992 have individual apartments that have been designed to be accessible to people with physical disabilities. Check with the individual complexes you are interested in to see whether they have accessible units. Accessible apartments may also be available through subsidized housing. These apartments are likely to have built-in conveniences such as lower light switches and handle bars in the showers.

Sometimes the best option is to modify an existing home to make it more accessible. There are currently architectural guidelines available which discuss handicapped accessibility (also known as Universal Design) and private housing. If you or your adult child are attempting to modify a home, these guidelines will be useful. You may also be able to consider these residential improvements as medical deductions for income tax purposes. For more information, contact the local IRS office under the U.S. Government listing.

If an adult with spina bifida needs more assistance with living, she might consider an assisted living situation. "Assisted living" usually refers to places that provide some supervision or direct services to their occupants. For example, they might offer help with cooking meals or with bathing. This type of housing is more scarce, but resources are available. For more information, you might get in touch with the National Council on Independent Living, a community resource that helps individuals with disabilities locate affordable and accessible housing. See the Resource Guide for contact information.

‖ Conclusion

Some of this discussion about adults with spina bifida may be new to you. There are, however, many people thinking about these issues, including doctors and individuals and families affected by spina bifida. I hope that this chapter provides some useful information.

My own situation is a little unique. I am a doctor who works with children with spina bifida, but I also have spina bifida. For those of us with this condition, spina bifida is a part of who we are, but it is only a part. I think that other parts of our lives become more important as we get older. To be sure, individuals with spina bifida face challenges throughout life; but spina bifida does not define who we are.

I can tell you that adults with spina bifida can lead successful lives filled with happiness and meaning. In the ways that are most important, we do not have to be limited by having spina bifida. We can live independently; we can work successfully in jobs we enjoy (yes, even as doctors); we can be married; we can have good friendships; we have ideas and abilities to share with the world around us.

The role for parents of children with spina bifida is to foster skills that encourage and equip them for independence and adulthood. Our task as adults with spina bifida is to use those skills to the best of our ability. The time to get started is now.

‖ Parent Statements

I want my daughter to be independent someday. It is so easy to do things for her, but I know her adult future depends on how much she can do by herself. If she is to be a productive, successful adult, she will need to learn to take charge of her life.

❧

My goals for my child with spina bifida are the same as those for my other children. I want all of them to obtain an education, live on their own, and hold down a job. I want them to be happy and lead fulfilling lives.

❧

My son is four and a half and I know a lot about what his childhood is like, but I wonder about his adult life. What happens when he is ready to date, marry, and have children?

❧

I worry about dating, dancing, driving, and going out with friends. These are the same issues I worried about with my other children, but in Kate's situation, I worry a little more.

❧

I didn't think about adult life too much when my daughter was small, but now that she is in middle school, I find myself thinking more and more about what jobs she might enjoy and be successful at. The choice of careers will be up to her, of course, but I've been keeping a mental list of jobs that might be possibilities for her so I can provide guidance when she's receptive to it.

❧

Right now I'm not putting any limits on what my child will be able to do as an adult. I encourage all her interests wholeheartedly and encourage her to dream about her future.

❧

I think it is good to have high expectations, because children pick up on that. Brian has surprised me at times with things he does that I might not have expected him to do. Sometimes my expectations have been too low. Brian is learning to drive now and his driving instructor says he is doing well. His car has hand controls.

Brian is receiving help through the Bureau of Vocational Rehabilitation to go to school and eventually gain employment. They are paying his tuition, transportation costs, and for driver's education.

Someday, I hope Brian gets married. I think he would be a good husband because he is caring and easy to get along with.

17

Growing Up
with Spina Bifida

Jessica Newbauer

I was born on September 7, 1978 in Cincinnati, Ohio. I was born with spina bifida, and as a result, I have very little feeling and no movement below my knees. I also have a shunt in the ventricles of my brain that reroutes the excess fluid. I am the youngest of four children and the only girl. My brothers would probably all tell you that I got lots of attention since I was the baby of the family, the only girl, and had special needs.

▪▪ Childhood

When I was growing up, my parents tried to give me a normal childhood, but at times that was difficult, since I was in and out of the hospital a lot. When I wasn't in the hospital, I spent a lot of time watching my brothers' sporting events or going to our local YMCA for swimming lessons. My best friend was Josie. She and I have been friends for almost twenty years now, and we have shared a lot of secrets and good times together. I don't know what I would have done without her listening ear when life sometimes seemed unfair and I just had to express my frustrations. It can be kind of difficult to fit in when you have to catheterize yourself several times a day and follow a bowel management program to achieve continence, but my differences never bothered Josie.

School and homework and good grades did not come easy for me. It always seemed like the other kids caught on to everything more quickly. I had tutors on and off throughout school, but I managed to graduate from high school on time, with my peers.

Although school was hard for me, there were high points in my life even at a young age. In fact, one of the best experiences of my life occurred while I was in grade school. Right after I started kindergarten, my mom registered me in a contest to be the poster child for the March of Dimes for Hamilton/Clermont counties in Ohio. I was chosen from the many children who entered the contest, which made it possible for me to participate in a lot of fun things. I was on TV commercials, I got to meet a lot of different local celebrities, and I attended all kinds of fundraising events. I held the honor of being the March of Dimes poster child for three years. Along with the March of Dimes activities, I was also in Girl Scouts. I was a Girl Scout from elementary school through my senior year of high school.

After graduating from high school, I attended Cincinnati State Technical and Community College. I graduated with an Associate degree in Liberal Arts after five years of classes. My parents and I were so proud that I had persevered and achieved a worthwhile goal—obtaining a college degree!

‼ Surgeries

Even though I had a lot of great experiences during my childhood, I also had a lot of difficult times as well, mostly because of the number of surgeries I needed and the amount of time I spent recovering in the hospital and at home. Although most of my surgeries were simple, such as the operations to straighten my legs to help me walk better, some were more serious, such as the shunt revision I needed in 1998. When the doctor started to remove the shunt, I started bleeding in my brain. I ended up staying in the hospital for three weeks and had to go through three emergency surgeries. This was by far the worst period in my life. During that complicated recovery, I lost a lot of strength and was no longer able to use my crutches and spend time walking. I had to switch to using use my wheelchair exclusively for mobility. Although using a wheelchair made it possible for me to get around quicker, it was still a loss and I missed walking.

▪▪ Dating/Marriage

The dating scene was completely different for me than for most people I know. I didn't meet the love of my life, Shaun, until I was eighteen years old. We met on the Internet through AOL's pen-pal ads. We were friends for a year before we started dating, and we dated for four years before we were engaged. Our wedding on June 18, 2005 was exciting, to say the least, and the most memorable day of my life.

One of the most amazing things was that, after seven years of not walking, I walked down the aisle to meet my groom! I had made up my mind that I wanted to walk, not use my wheelchair, and nothing was going to stop me. Shortly after Shaun proposed to me, I started physical therapy and for six months I worked very hard. Only a few people knew of my plans. I wanted to surprise everyone, including my father. Boy, was he amazed when I took his arm, at the rehearsal, and walked down the aisle. It had been so long since my parents had seen me walk, they both broke down and cried. The next day at the wedding ceremony, most of the guests also shed a few tears as they witnessed the proud father escorting his "little girl" down the aisle. I am not sure who was holding up whom at this point, but we made it to the altar. It was a perfect day and one I will, of course, remember for a lifetime.

Shaun and I lived with my mother both while we were dating and also for a little while after we got married. After we had been married a year, we started looking at houses. It took us quite a while to find a house that would be accessible for me, but eventually we did find one. In October of 2006 we moved into our own house. I had never been on my own before, so this was a new and exciting experience for me.

▪▪ Conclusion

All in all, I'm very happy with how my life has gone. At present, I am twenty-eight years old, and have a great job as a customer service representative. When I was young, I never dreamed that I would get married and be living on my own before I was thirty. I feel fortunate to have had all the great experiences I have had throughout my life.

GLOSSARY

Abduction—movement away from the body.

Accommodations—Changes made to the regular environment that will help someone with disabilities succeed. Accommodations made at school change the way information is presented or the way the student responds without changing the content the student is expected to learn.

Acetabulum—the cavity on the hip bone into which the head of the femur fits.

ADA (Americans with Disabilities Act)—a federal law that prohibits discrimination against people with disabilities by employers, by public accommodations, by public and private services, and in the area of telecommunications.

Adaptive Behavior—the ability to adjust to new environments, tasks, objects, and people and to apply previously learned skills to those situations.

Adduction—movement toward the body.

Advocacy—the act of speaking out in behalf of a cause or someone else's interests.

Agent Orange—a chemical used during the Vietnam War. Agent Orange Benefits Act is a federal law that mandates monetary compensation to families of Vietnam veterans who subsequently had a child with spina bifida.

Ambulatory—having the ability to walk, with or without braces.

Amniotic fluid—fluid that surrounds the fetus.

Anomaly—a change or deviation from what is considered normal, such as a malformation of a body part.

Anticonvulsant—a drug used to control seizures.

Anus—the body opening through which feces are expelled.

Apnea—an abnormally long pause in breathing, which can be caused by blockage in the throat or upper airway or by problems in the part of the brain that controls breathing. In children with spina bifida, apnea may signal problems with the Arnold Chiari formation.

Arnold Chiari Malformation—an abnormality in the formation of the brainstem which may result in breathing and eating problems.

Assessment—the process of testing and observation used to determine a child's needs for special education.

Atonic—lacking normal muscle tone.

Attention-Deficit/Hyperactivity Disorder—A condition that results in excessive activity (hyperactivity), impulsivity, and difficulties focusing attention.

Beneficiary—the person named in a trust or insurance policy to receive any payments that become due.

Bladder Augmentation—a surgery that involves making the bladder larger so it can hold more urine at low pressures. This can preserve kidneys and decrease urine leakage between catheterizations.

Brace—*See* Orthosis/Orthotic.

Brainstem—the base of the brain that connects the upper part of the spinal cord with the cerebral hemispheres and regulates breathing, heart rate, and temperature.

CAT Scan or CT Scan—Computerized Axial Tomography, a diagnostic test that produces pictures of cross sections of the body. May be used to view the ventricles in the brain.

Catheter—a thin tube used to drain fluid.

Cecostomy—a surgically created opening in the right lower abdomen that is used to introduce enemas directly into the colon to flush out feces.

Cecum—the beginning of the large intestine.

Cerebellum—the part of the brain that makes it possible to perform complex motor activities.

Cerebrospinal Fluid—fluid that is produced in the ventricles and surrounds the brain and spinal cord.

Cervical—pertaining to the cervical region of the spinal column (the neck region).

Child Life Specialist—a professional who is part of the health care team and specializes in therapeutic play and providing activities for hospitalized children.

Chromosomes—strands in the cell nucleus that contain the genes that determine or influence the traits a child inherits. Normally, there are 46 chromosomes in each cell.

Clubfoot—a condition that occurs when the muscles on one side of the foot are stronger than the muscles on the other side, so the foot is pulled out of alignment.

Cocktail Party Language—chatty, fluent speech that may mask a child's difficulties in understanding language.

Congenital—existing at birth.

Continence—the ability to control urine and/or bowel movements.

Contract—to tighten.

Contracture—a shortening of a muscle, resulting in reduced joint movement.

Convulsion—involuntary contractions of the muscles accompanying a seizure. The word is sometimes used interchangeably with seizure.

Cost-of-Care Liability—the right of a state to charge for the care of someone with disabilities and collect from that person's assets.

Cranial Nerves—The twelve nerves that originate from the brain.

CSF—*See* Cerebrospinal fluid.

Cystic Fibrosis—a genetic disease that causes the production of thick mucus to develop in the lungs and pancreas.

Decubitus—skin ulcer.

Defecate—to have a bowel movement.

Developmental Delay—a label that may be used under IDEA to qualify children aged 3-9 for special education services. The label may be used for children who are experiencing delays in physical, cognitive, communication, social, or adaptive development.

Developmental Disability—a disability or impairment beginning before the age of eighteen that is expected to continue indefinitely and that causes a substantial disability.

Dietitian/Dietician—a professional who assesses nutritional status, recommends specific foods and quantities to eat, and assesses growth status.

Diphtheria—an acute infectious disease that is caused by bacteria and particularly affects the throat.

DNA—molecules that store information and tell cells how to make the proteins that are responsible for the metabolic activity that occurs in cells.

Down Syndrome—a genetic disorder caused by an extra copy of chromosome 21 in some or all of the cells. It results in developmental delays, low muscle tone, characteristic facial features, and other effects.

Due Process Hearing—under IDEA, a method of resolving disputes about a child's special education program in which a hearing is held before an impartial person.

Early Intervention—instruction and therapy provided to children ages birth to three that is intended to minimize the effects of conditions that can delay early development.

EEG—Electroencephalogram: a test often used to diagnose seizure activity which produces a graphic picture of the electrical impulses of the brain.

Efferent—originating from the central nervous system, a nerve impulse that travels to a nerve or muscle.

Encephalocele—a birth defect in which the brain, meninges, or both protrude through an opening in the skull. Brain damage usually results due to the brain tissue exposure.

Enema—instilling fluid into the rectum to facilitate a bowel movement.

Epilepsy—a condition characterized by recurrent seizures.

Equilibrium—balance.

Estate Planning—formal, written arrangements for handling the possessions and assets of people after their death.

Expressive Language—the use of gestures, words, and/or written symbols to communicate.

Fine Motor—relating to the use of the small muscles of the body, such as those in the face, hands, and fingers.

Folic Acid—a B vitamin that the human body needs in order to make DNA. Folic acid is normally found in green, leafy vegetables, liver, and beans and is also in fortified baked goods; taking a folic acid supplement before conception and during the first three months of pregnancy can reduce the chances of having a baby with spina bifida.

Fontanel—soft spot on a baby's skull where bones have not grown firmly together, usually closed by age two.

Gait—the way a person walks.

Genes—bits of DNA and protein located along the chromosome that determine what characteristics (such as eye or hair color) are inherited by an individual.

Genetic—related to a condition that is inherited or caused by an alteration in genetic material (chromosomes or genes).

Genetics—the study of how genes are passed from one generation to the next and of genetic conditions.

Gestation—length of pregnancy.

Gross motor—relating to the use of the large muscles of the body, such as those in the legs, arms, and abdomen.

Guardian—a person appointed or designated legally to manage the property or financial affairs and to exercise the rights of another person.

Hemophilus Influenza—a bacteria that can cause severe respiratory symptoms that can develop into meningitis.

High tone—a tightness or spasticity in the muscles, also called hypertonia.

Hives—an allergic response resulting in a skin rash.

Hydrocephalus—an accumulation of excess amounts of cerebrospinal fluid in the ventricles of the brain, resulting in increased pressure.

Hydromyelia—an increase of fluid in the central canal of the spinal cord.

Hypertonia—*See* High Tone.

Hypotonia—*See* Low Tone.

IDEA—Individuals with Disabilities Education Act. The federal law that guarantees children with disabilities the right to a free, appropriate education.

IDEIA—Individuals with Disabilities Education Improvement Act. The official name of the 2004 revisions to IDEA.

IEP—Individualized Education Program. The written plan that describes a child's special education goals, as well as the instructional and related services he will receive, in what setting.

IFSP—Individualized Family Service Plan. The written document that describes an infant's or toddler's early intervention goals, as well as the services he and the family will receive, in what setting.

Immobilized—restricted in movement.

Inclusion—the practice of including a child with disabilities in a classroom alongside typically developing students. In full inclusion, the child remains in the general education classroom for the entire school day.

Incontinence—inability to control urine and/or bowel movements.

Individuals with Disabilities Education Act—*See* IDEA.

Influenza—flu.

Intermittent Catheterization—using a catheter to remove urine from an individual's bladder at periodic intervals.

I.Q.—abbreviation for Intelligence Quotient: a measure of cognitive ability based on standardized tests in which a score of 100 is considered exactly average.

IV—an intravenous tube or needle placed into a vein for injecting medication or fluid into the bloodstream.

Joint—the point where two bones connect.

Kidneys—the two organs located on each side of the spine that filter waste products from the blood (in the form of urine) so it can be eliminated from the body.

Kyphosis—an exaggerated forward curving of the spine.

Learning Disability—a condition that causes someone to have more difficulty learning in one or more specific areas (such as reading or math) than would be expected considering the person's overall cognitive abilities.

Least Restrictive Environment (LRE)—under IDEA, the educational setting that allows a child to participate in the general educational environment to the maximum extent appropriate while still achieving the goals on his IEP.

Lesion—in spina bifida, lesion refers to the area on the spinal column where the opening occurs.

Low Tone—decreased muscle tone (less tension when muscles are at rest), resulting in muscles that seem floppier than usual.

Lower Extremities—the legs and feet.

Lumbar—pertaining to the lower back area or lumbar region of the spine.

Malformation—a variation in structure from what is considered normal.

Measles—*See* Rubeola.

Medicaid—a joint state and federal program that offers medical assistance to people who are entitled to receive Supplementary Security Income.

Medicare—a federal program that provides payments for medical care to people who are receiving Social Security payments.

Meninges—the membranes surrounding the brain and spinal cord.

Meningomyelocele—another word for myelomeningocele.

Mental Retardation—below average intellectual functioning (I.Q. lower than 70) combined with below average adaptive skills, beginning before the age of eighteen.

Motor Patterns—the ways in which the body and limbs work to make sequenced movements.

Motor Planning—the ability to think through and carry out the steps involved in carrying out a physical task such as getting into a chair.

MRI—Magnetic Resonance Imaging. A test that uses electromagnets to give a detailed image of the interior of the body, and is particularly useful in looking at the brainstem.

Multidisciplinary—refers to professionals from many disciplines working together; for example, Nursing, Pediatrics, Physical Therapy, Neurosurgery, Psychology, etc.

Mumps—a disease that typically causes fever, headache, and inflammation of the salivary glands.

Muscle Tone—the amount of tension or resistance to movement in a muscle.

Muscular Dystrophy—a disease that causes progressive muscle deterioration.

Myelodysplasia—abnormal development of the spinal cord. This term is sometimes used to mean spina bifida or myelomeningocele.

Myelomeningocele—a birth defect in which part of the spinal cord and its membranes (meninges) protrude through an opening in the vertebrae. A type of spina bifida.

Neural Tube Defect—a group of congenital defects that involve the spine or brain. Spina bifida is one of the most common neural tube defects.

Neurodevelopmental Treatment (NDT)—a specialized therapy approach that concentrates on encouraging normal movement patterns and discouraging abnormal reflexes, postures, and movements. Used by some physical, occupational, and speech therapists.

Neurogenic Bladder—a bladder that fails to function adequately due to damage to the spinal cord and or nerves that supply the bladder.

Neuromotor—involving the brain, nerves, and muscles.

Neutral Position—the position in which the foot and leg are in proper alignment for weight bearing.

Occupational Therapist—a professional who specializes in helping people regain or develop fine motor skills and/or self-care skills.

Orthopedic—having to do with bones and joints.

Orthopedic Disability (Impairment)—an impairment that affects the bones, joints, or muscles and also has some educational impact on a child. This label may be used under IDEA to qualify children with spina bifida for special education.

Orthosis/Orthotic—a device that provides stability to a body part or stretches the muscles to help with movement. A brace.

Osteoporosis—a condition in which bone mass decreases, making fractures more likely.

Paralysis—complete or partial loss of muscle movement.

Paraplegic—an individual with paralysis of the lower extremities.

Parapodium—a body brace mounted on a platform base that allows a child to stand upright and walk with the aid of a walker or crutches.

Pavlov Harness—a brace to correct dislocated or subluxed hips in infants.

Peritoneal Cavity—the abdominal cavity.

Pertussis—whooping cough, a disease that causes severe spells of coughing.

Phlebitis—inflammation of a vein.

Physical Therapist—a professional who helps people regain or develop gross motor skills.

Placenta—the structure through which the fetus receives oxygen and nourishment from the mother.

Polio—an acute viral disease that can lead to paralysis and death.

Posture—the way the body is positioned or aligned.

Prenatal—before birth.

Pressure Sore—a sore that develops from too much pressure on the skin, usually over a bony prominence. Also called a decubitus.

Puberty—the stage in which reproductive organs develop and sex characteristics appear.

Range of Motion (ROM)—the degree of movement that a joint has.

Reasonable Accommodation—efforts made to make a building, job, classroom, etc. more accessible to someone with a disability but do not result in an unreasonable financial burden.

Receptive Language—the ability to understand language (spoken, written, or gestures).

Rectum—the lower portion of the large intestine.

Reflex—an involuntary movement in response to stimulation such as touch, pressure, or joint movement.

Rehabilitation—the process of learning how to function to one's fullest potential despite a chronic or disabling condition.

Rehabilitation Act of 1973—*See* Section 504.

Related Services—services such as physical or occupational therapy and transportation that enable a child to benefit from special education.

Rh Disease—a condition that occurs when a woman produces antibodies against Rh factor in the blood of her fetus. This is a very serious condition for the baby but not for the mother. It may occur if the mother has Rh negative blood and the baby's father has Rh positive blood. Rh disease can be prevented if RhIg is medically administered to the woman at the appropriate times.

Rubella—a contagious viral infection that produces a rash and sometimes joint pain (also known as German measles or three-day measles). Usually a mild disease in children, but can cause birth defects in unborn children if the mother is infected during pregnancy.

Rubeola—a very contagious viral infection also known as measles. Usually causes a rash, fever, cough, and runny nose lasting for 7 to 14 days. Serious complications can occur.

Sacral—pertaining to the sacral (lowest) region of the spinal column.

Scoliosis—a lateral (side-to-side) curvature of the spine.

Section 504—a part of the Rehabilitation Act of 1973 that prohibits any program or activity (including schools) that receives federal funds from discriminating against people with disabilities.

Seizure—involuntary movement or changes in consciousness or behavior brought on by abnormal electrical activity in the brain.

Self-help—skills such as eating, dressing, and bathing that enable a person to care for himself.

Serum—blood.

Service Coordinator—the person responsible for coordinating services and information from a child's multidisciplinary team (either medical or educational). Formerly known as the case manager.

Sickle Cell Anemia—a hereditary disease that results in clumping of red blood cells and reduced oxygen to tissues.

Special Education—specialized education aimed at meeting the unique learning strengths and needs of a student with disabilities from age three through high school.

Speech-Language Pathologist—a therapist who evaluates difficulties with speech and language skills, as well as feeding skills, and works to improve them.

Sphincter—muscles that contract or relax to control the passage of urine or stool.

Spina Bifida—a congenital condition in which part of the spinal column fails to close completely during fetal development, leaving the meninges or the meninges and spinal cord exposed.

Spinal Column—the spine or backbone. *See also* Vertebrae.

Spinal Cord—the portion of the central nervous system (nerve tissue) contained within the spinal column that relays information about sensation and movement between the brain and the rest of the body.

Standing Frame—an orthosis that helps support a child in a standing position without the need to depend on his own balance.

Stool—waste matter released from the bowels; feces.

Subluxation—partial dislocation.

Supplemental Security Income (SSI)—financial assistance for people with low incomes who have a disability or are elderly.

Suture—a surgical stitch.

Tendons—the connective tissue that attaches bone to muscle.

Thoracic—relating to the chest area, or to the vertebrae in the chest area (below the cervical vertebrae and above the lumbar vertebrae).

Transfer—to move from one position to another, such as from a wheelchair to a chair.

Trisomy—a congenital condition in which there is an extra copy of a particular chromosome (bringing the total to three, rather than two) in the cells of the body.

Trisomy 13—a congenital condition in which there is an extra (third) chromosome number 13 in the cells of the body. Characteristics include mental retardation, deafness, heart defect, cleft lip and palate, and a (usually) short lifespan.

Trisomy 18—a congenital condition in which there is an extra (third) chromosome number 18 in the cells of the body. Characteristics include mental retardation, low muscle tone, failure to thrive, heart defects, facial, hand, and foot anomalies, and a (usually) short lifespan.

Trisomy 21—another name for Down syndrome, a condition caused by an extra (third) copy of chromosome number 21 in the cells of the body.

Ureter—the tube from each kidney that drains into the bladder.

Urethra—the tube from the bladder that carries urine to the outside of the body.

Urinary reflux—a condition in which urine backs up into the ureters and kidney.

Ventricles—cavities within the brain through which cerebrospinal fluid flows.

Vertebra—one vertebrae.

Vertebrae—any of the 33 bones that form the spine (spinal column). The first seven vertebrae form the cervical spine (in the neck area). The next 12 vertebrae form the thoracic spine (in the chest area). The next five vertebrae form the lumbar spine (in the lower back area). The next five vertebrae are joined together and form the sacrum. The last four vertebrae are joined together and form the coccyx (the tailbone). The vertebrae are separated by spongy disks called intervertebral disks.

Vesicostomy—an opening made surgically from the abdomen into the bladder to allow urine to flow continuously out of the bladder into a diaper.

■■ READING LIST

■■ Chapter 1

Batshaw, Mark L. **Children with Disabilities.** 5th ed. Baltimore: Brookes Publishing Co., 2002.

This parent-friendly reference book contains information on a variety of childhood disabilities. It includes a chapter on neural tube defects, as well as information on many conditions commonly associated with spina bifida, including hydrocephalus, learning disabilities, and seizures.

PM Medical Health News. **21st Century Complete Medical Guide to Spina Bifida and Related Neural Tube Defects: Authoritative Government Documents, Clinical References, and Practical Information for Patients and Physicians.** Progressive Management Publishing, 2004.

This book on CD-ROM provides a collection of information and documents on the subject of spina bifida from authoritative sources such as National Institute of Health (NIH), Centers for Disease Control (CDC), and Combined Health Information Database (CHID).

Sandler, Adrian. **Living with Spina Bifida: A Guide for Families and Professionals.** Rev. ed. Chapel Hill, NC: The University of North Carolina Press, 2003.

Information on the medical, developmental, and psychological aspects of spina bifida.

■■ Chapter 2

Adams, Amy. "What Is Genetic Counseling?" www.genetichealth.com/resources_What_Is_Genetic_Counseling.shtml.

Genetics Center at Children's Hospital Medical Center of Akron, Ohio. "What You Should Know about Folic Acid: A Booklet for Parents Who Have Lost a Pregnancy or Had a Child with Spina Bifida, Anencephaly of Encephalocele" (1997).

This booklet is available at no charge from the National Maternal and Child Health Clearinghouse, 2070 Chain Bridge Rd., Ste. 450, Vienna, VA 22182; 703-356-1964 or NMCH@circsol.com.

∷ Chapter 3

"Your Baby Has Spina Bifida." Booklet available from NSGC Publications, 4061 Paysphere Circle, Chicago, IL 60674. Or order online: www.nsgc.org.

Booklet includes a description of spina bifida, management, cause, recurrence, risks, and supportive resources.

Wexler, Keith & Wexler, Laurie. **The ABC's of Prenatal Diagnosis: A Guide to Pregnancy Testing and Issues.** 2nd ed. Denver, CO: Genassist, 2002.

This book covers every important question regarding diagnostic techniques and results, and pays special attention to the latest technology and parental issues.

∷ Chapter 4

Disability-Related Resources on the Internet. Seattle: DO-IT, University of Washington.

A directory of disability-related discussion lists, electronic newsletters, and World Wide Web (WWW) sites. Print copies can be ordered from DO-IT, University of Washington, Box 355670, Seattle WA 98195-5670 or down-loaded at www.washington.edu/doit/Brochures/DDR.

Exceptional Parent. P.O. Box 3000, Dept. EP, Denville, NJ 07834. PH: 800-562-1973. www.familyeducation.com.

A monthly magazine for families of children with disabilities, which includes articles on family life, daily care concerns, medical concerns, educational issues, laws and benefits, etc.

Hower, Wayne. **Does a Disabled Child = A Disabled Family?** Bloomington, IN: AuthorHouse, 2006.

The writer provides anecdotes, personal examples, and professional information to help parents and siblings achieve balance while living with a disabled child.

Klein, Stanley & Schive, Kim. **You Will Dream New Dreams: Inspiring Personal Stories by Parents of Children with Disabilities.** New York: Kensington, 2006.

A collection of stories by parents of children with a variety of special needs. Shared narratives come from those with newly diagnosed children, adult children, and everything in between.

Kushner, Harold S. **When Bad Things Happen to Good People.** Reprint ed. New York: Anchor, 2004.

Written by a rabbi whose son died of a rare disorder (progeria) in his early teens, this book can be helpful in working through all the "why's" that parents feel when facing unexpected news.

Meyer, Donald J. **Uncommon Fathers: Reflections on Raising a Child with a Disability.** Bethesda, MD: Woodbine House, 1995.

A collection of essays by fathers of children of all ages who have various disabilities, including hydrocephalus and physical disabilities. The writers interweave thoughts on practical, emotional, and philosophical issues with their personal experiences.

Miller, Nancy B. **Nobody's Perfect: Living & Growing with Children Who Have Special Needs.** Baltimore: Brookes Publishing Co., 1997.

The author's advice about coping with the challenges of raising a child with special needs is interwoven with thoughts and experiences of four mothers, including the mother of a child with spina bifida.

∷ Chapter 5

Bellush, Terri Rice. **All About Me (and My Shunt).** Victoria, BC, Canada: Trafford Publishing, 2004.

Introduces hydrocephalus to a child with the condition or to other children to help them understand.

Icon Health Publications. **The Official Parent's Sourcebook on Hydrocephalus: A Revised and Updated Directory for the Internet Age.** San Diego, CA: Icon Health Publications, 2002.

This sourcebook has been created for parents who have decided to make education and Internet-based research an integral part of the treatment process.

Lutkenhoff, Marlene. **Detour Ahead.** Washington, DC: Spina Bifida Association of America, 2007.

An illustrated children's book about hydrocephalus and how it is treated with a shunt. Order from the SBA website (www.sbaa.org) or call 800-621-3141.

Sandler, Adrian. **Living with Spina Bifida: A Guide for Families and Professionals.** Rev. ed. Chapel Hill, NC: The University of North Carolina Press, 2003.

This parents' guide to spina bifida includes information on closure of myelomenigoceles and treatment of hydrocephalus.

Toporek, Chuck & Robinson, Kellie. **Hydrocephalus: A Guide for Patients, Families, and Friends.** Sebastopol, CA: O'Reilly & Assoc, 1999.

Topics covered in this practical guide include selecting a neurosurgeon, understanding treatment options, keeping records to aid in home monitoring, and living with hydrocephalus.

:: Chapter 6

Joseph, David B. **Urologic Care of the Child with Spina Bifida.** Washington, DC: Spina Bifida Association of America.
> Order from the SBA website (www.sbaa.org) or call 800-621-3141.

Lutkenhoff, Marlene. **Another Way to Go.** Washington, DC: Spina Bifida Association of America, 2005.
> An illustrated book designed to reassure children aged 5-8 that cathing is OK, at home or at school. Two versions of this book are available: one for boys and one for girls. Order from the SBA website (www.sbaa.org) or call 800-621-3141.

Urinary Tract Infections - A Medical Dictionary, Bibliography, and Annotated Research Guide to Internet References. San Diego, CA: ICON Health Publications, 2004.
> This reference book includes a medical dictionary covering hundreds of terms and expressions relating to urinary tract infections, lists of bibliographic citations, and information on using various Internet resources.

:: Chapter 7

Gilpin, Michelle & Harris, Dorothy. **Toilet Teaching with Your Special Child.** 2nd ed. London, Ontario: Thames Valley Children's Centre, 1996.
> Covers general concerns related to toilet training a child with physical disabilities including managing constipation, choosing a potty seat, and motivating the child.

Liebold, Susan. **Bowel Continence and Spina Bifida.** Washington, DC: Spina Bifida Association of America, 2006.
> An excellent book aimed at anyone trying to attain bowel continence with sample menus, bowel tracking charts, and glossary of terms.

Schuster, Marvin M. & Wehmueller, Jacqueline. **Keeping Control: Understanding, and Overcoming Fecal Incontinence.** Baltimore: Johns Hopkins University Press, 1994.
> A compassionate, medically reliable, and thoroughly informative resource for anyone who wants to understand the possible causes of fecal incontinence and learn about important advances in management and treatment.

:: Chapter 8

Hooper, Nancy J. **Stopping Scoliosis: The Complete Guide to Diagnosis and Treatment.** New York: Avery, 2002.
> Although not specific to spina bifida, this book offers useful information about the causes and treatments of scoliosis, including braces and surgery.

Jacobs, Lee & Zucker, Gale. **The Orthopedist.** Woodbridge, CT: Blackbirch, 1998.
> Written for children in upper elementary or middle school, this book shows what an orthopedist does in his office and at the hospital.

▪▪ Chapter 9

Dobbs, Jean, editor. **Kids on Wheels: Vol. 1: A Young Person's Guide to Wheelchair Lifestyle; Vol. 2: A Guide to Wheelchair Lifestyle for Parents, Teachers, and Professionals.** Horham, PA: No Limits Communications, 2004.

A guide to helping young wheelchair users lead an active independent life, with information on sports and recreation, fun activities, making friends, school issues, and more. Available from www.kidsonwheels.com.

Goldberg, Barry, editor. **Sports and Exercise for Children with Chronic Health Conditions.** Champaign, IL: Human Kinetics, 1995.

Spina bifida is one of the 20 conditions covered in this book. Includes information on appropriate activities, exercise tolerance, and potential problems that may develop.

New Mobility. **Consumer Guide.** Malibu, CA: Miramar Communications (P.O. Box 8987, Malibu, CA 90265), annual.

This annual guide is full of information about finding and funding adaptive equipment for health and hygiene, fitness and sports, seating, technology, and more.

Paciorek, Michael J. & Jones, Jeffrey A. **Disability Sport and Recreation Resources.** Traverse City, MI: Cooper Publishing Group, 2001.

Information on 47 sports and recreational activities that are accessible to individuals with disabilities.

Pain, Helen. **Choosing Assistive Devices: A Guide for Users and Professionals.** London: Jessica Kingsley Publishers, 2002.

Brings together the research on people with disabilities with the equipment available for them and shows how choices can be matched to an assessment of need.

Steadward, Robert & Wheeler, Garry D. **Adapted Physical Activity.** Alberta, Canada. The University of Alberta Press, 2003.

Based on a core theme of "inclusion," this text examines the spectrum of adapted physical activity from school, community, and international disability sports perspectives.

▪▪ Chapter 10

Barber, Marianne, Scott, Maryanne, & Greenberg, Elinor. **The Parent's Guide to Food Allergies: Advice from the Experts on Raising Your Food Allergic Child.** New York: Henry Holt, 2001.

Practical advice and reassurance for parents on dealing with a child's food allergies at home, at school, and in the community.

Blackburn, Lynn Bennett. **Growing Up with Epilepsy.** New York NY: Demos, 2003.

A short parents' guide that explains the types of seizures and why they happen, then examines typical "challenges" that children with epilepsy face from birth through young adulthood.

Freeman, John M., Vining, Eileen P.G., & Pillas, Diana J. **Seizures and Epilepsy in Childhood: A Guide.** Baltimore: The Johns Hopkins University Press, 2002.

An optimistic guide to raising a child with epilepsy, this book covers causes, diagnosis, treatment, and coping strategies.

Keene, Nancy & Prentice, Rachel. **Your Child in the Hospital: A Practical Guide for Parents.** Sebastopol, CA: O'Reilly & Associates, 1999.

Includes tips on preparing your child for a hospital stay, minimizing discomfort, handling insurance claims, keeping your family life on an even keel, and school concerns.

Pacific Northwest Foundation. **The Complete Guide to Latex Allergy.** Portland, OR: PNF, 2005.

This brief guide covers information on diagnosis and treatment of latex allergy, related food allergies, survival strategies, and a list of latex-free products.

SBA Editorial Board. **Health Guide for Parents of Children Living with Spina Bifida.** Washington, DC: Spina Bifida Association of America, 2006.

Order from the website (www.sbaa.org) or call 800-621-3141.

■■ Chapter 11

Greenspan, Stanley I. & Weider, Serena. **The Child with Special Needs: Encouraging Intellectual and Emotional Growth.** New York, NY: Perseus, 1998.

The authors explain their methods for parents to use in increasing communication and social skills of children with disabilities at home.

Hamaguchi, Patricia M. **Childhood Speech, Language & Listening Problems: What Every Parent Should Know.** New York: John Wiley & Sons, 2001.

A thorough overview of many types of speech, language, and listening problems is provided, with information on diagnosis and treatment.

Healy, Jane. **Your Child's Growing Mind: Brain Development and Learning from Birth to Adolescence.** 3rd ed. New York: Broadway, 2004.

A reader-friendly look at the development of cognitive skills in children; also provides an overview of learning styles and abilities to learn in school.

Lollar, Donald J. "Social Development and the Person with Spina Bifida." Washington, DC: Spina Bifida Association of America, 2006.

See Resource Guide for address.

Schwartz, Sue. **The New Language of Toys: Teaching Communication Skills to Children with Special Needs.** 3rd ed. Bethesda, MD: Woodbine House, 2004.

Describes how parents can use toys and games (commercially available and homemade) to help their children develop speech and language skills.

▪▪ Chapter 12

Baker, Bruce L. **Steps to Independence: Teaching Everyday Skills to Children with Special Needs.** 4th ed. Baltimore: Brookes, 2003.

Each chapter breaks down into specific steps on how to teach everyday skills like toilet training, homecare skills (dressing, feeding) as well as behavior management - it contains advice and charts on how to monitor and assess improvement in a systematic way. Also explains the use of rewards for motivation, etc.

Baskin, Amy & Fawcett, Heather. **More Than a Mom: Living a Full and Balanced Life When Your Child Has Special Needs.** Bethesda, MD: Woodbine House, 2006.

Strategies and advice for mothers who are trying to be good parents of children with disabilities while continuing to have a career and pursue their own interests.

Marshak, Laura & Prezant, Fran. **Married with Special-Needs Children: A Couples' Guide to Keeping Connected.** Bethesda, MD: Woodbine House, 2007.

This book explores common stresses and pitfalls in marriages where one or more children have a disability and suggests strategies for preventing and handling marital problems.

Meyer, Donald. **The Sibling Slam Book: What It's Really Like to Have a Brother or Sister with Special Needs.** Bethesda, MD: Woodbine House, 2005.

In this book, over 80 teens candidly answer questions about living with a sibling with a disability; a valuable resource for parents and professionals as well as teens and older children.

Phelan, Thomas. **1-2-3 Magic: Effective Discipline for Children 2-12.** 3rd ed. Glen Ellyn, IL: Parentmagic, Inc., 2003.

Describes a method of discipline that has proven to be especially useful in managing the behavior of children with attention deficit disorders.

SpeciaLiving Magazine (P.O. Box 1000, Bloomington, IL 61702-1000; www.specialiving.com)

A quarterly magazine designed for "mobility-impaired consumers" that covers such topics as home modifications, travel and leisure, and health issues.

▪▪ Chapter 13

Barkley, Russell A. **Taking Charge of ADHD: The Complete, Authoritative Guide for Parents.** Rev. ed. New York: Guilford Press, 2000.

A guide to the nature and treatment of ADHD, with useful strategies for managing behavior at home and at school.

Coleman, Jeanine G. **Early Intervention Dictionary: A Multidisciplinary Guide to Terminology.** 3rd ed. Bethesda, MD: Woodbine House, 2006.

Includes parent-friendly definitions of terms that parents are likely to encounter in dealing with medical professionals, therapists, educators, psychologists, and other early intervention professionals, as well as when reading research in print or online.

Fisher, Gary L. & Cummings, Rhoda. **The Survival Guide for Kids with LD: Learning Differences.** Minneapolis, MN: Free Spirit, 2002.
A reader-friendly introduction to the topic of learning disabilities.

Hayden, Deirdre & Takimoto, Cheryl. **Negotiating the Special Education Maze: A Guide for Parents and Teachers.** 4th ed. Bethesda, MD: Woodbine House, 2008.
The classic guide to the federal special education laws and to advocating for the educational program and services your child with disabilities needs. Includes extensive information on preparing for and surviving the IEP process.

Levine, Mel. **A Mind at a Time.** New York: Simon and Schuster, 2002.
The author, an expert on learning disabilities, explains why a "one size fits all" philosophy of education is not helpful for children and explores how problems and strengths with attention, memory, spatial or sequential skills, and other areas can lead to success or failure at school.

Lollar, Donald. "An Overview of Educational Issues among Children with Spina Bifida" and "Learning Among Children with Spina Bifida" [brochures]. Washington, DC: Spina Bifida Association of America, 2001.
See Resource Guide for address.

Pierangelo, Roger & Giuliani, George A. **Assessment in Special Education.** 2nd ed. Boston, MA: Allyn & Bacon, 2005.
This book provides future special educators comprehensive coverage of the latest tests and evaluation procedures for all areas of exceptionality—for every age group—for students with mild, moderate, and severe disabilities.

Rief, Sandra. **How to Reach and Teach Children with ADD/ADHD: Practical Techniques, Strategies, and Interventions.** 2nd ed. San Francisco: Jossey-Bass, 2005.
A reader-friendly guide to helping children with attention deficit disorders succeed at school, with separate chapters describing strategies for preschoolers, elementary aged students, and older students.

Voss, Kimberly S. **Teaching by Design: Using Your Computer to Create Materials for Students with Learning Differences.** Bethesda, MD: Woodbine House, 2007.
Step-by-step instructions for creating customized learning materials such as lotto boards, flashcards, and games for children with disabilities.

Wright, Peter W. D. & Wright, Pamela. **Wrightslaw: Special Education Law.** 2nd ed. Hartfield, VA: Harbor House Law Press, 2007.
This manual includes the full text of IDEA 2004 and Section 504, together with helpful commentary about how to use various sections of the laws to assert your child's rights to an education, argue for inclusion, etc.

▪▪ Chapter 14

Clark, Lynn & Robb, John. **SOS: Help for Parents.** 3ʳᵈ ed. Seattle: Parents Press, 2005.
Practical suggestions from a clinical psychologist to help parents deal with behavior problems.

Covey, Stephen R. **The 7 Habits of Highly Effective People.** Parsippany, NJ: Free Press, 2004.
A manual designed to help readers achieve success by learning to balancing both personal and professional effectiveness.

Davis, Martha, et al. **The Relaxation and Stress Reduction Workbook.** 5ᵗʰ ed. Oakland, CA: New Harbinger, 2000.
This book outlines a variety of relaxation methods, explaining what type of attitude works best in its use, variations on the method, and the time that is necessary to see the effects.

Kurcinka, Mary Sheedy. **Raising Your Spirited Child: A Guide for Parents Whose Child is More Intense, Sensitive, Perceptive, Persistent, and Energetic.** New York, NY: Harper, 2006.
A guide to help parents understand their child's temperament, as well as their own, with an eye towards understanding differences and developing a more harmonious family life.

Lutkenhoff, Marlene & Oppenheimer, Sonya. **SPINAbilities: A Young Person's Guide to Spina Bifida.** Bethesda, MD: Woodbine House, 1997.
Intended to help young people with spina bifida become as independent as possible, this guide covers medical issues and personal care; relationships; school and career issues; and staying healthy. The book is out of print, but still available on the SBA website: www.sbaa.org.

Ratto, Linda Lee. **(dis)Ability.** Malibu, CA: Power Press, 2004.
A two-book volume that includes collections of young people's stories about successfully coping with a disability as well as strategies to help children and teens cope with their own disability.

Turecki, Stanley & Tonner, Leslie. **The Difficult Child: Expanded and Revised Edition.** New York: Bantam, 2000.
Tips for dealing with "normal" misbehavior.

▪▪ Chapter 15

Elias, Stephen. **Special Needs Trusts: Protect Your Child's Financial Future.** 2ⁿᵈ ed. Berkeley, CA: Nolo, 2007.
Explains how to leave money to a family member with disabilities, without jeopardizing government benefits. It provides plain-English information and forms that let you create a special needs trust by modifying your will or living trust document.

IRS. **Disabled Persons with Disabilities.** Order by calling 1-800-876-1715, or on the Forms and Publications page of the IRS web site: http://www.irs.ustreas.gov.

Describes forms that can be used for tax assistance and tax deductions by individuals with disabilities or their parents.

Jones, Nancy Lee. **The Americans with Disabilities Act (ADA): Overview, Regulations and Interpretations.** Hauppauge, NY: Novinka Books, 2003.

Provides explanations of how the ADA applies to employment, public services, public accommodations, and telecommunications.

Schlachter, Gail Ann. **Financial Aid for the Disabled & Their Families, 2006-2008.** San Carlos, CA: Reference Service Press, 2006.

Information about federal aid for families of children with a disability, as well as sources of scholarships, fellowships, and grants in aid.

Simons, Jo Ann. **Footprints for the Future.** East Middlesex, MA: The Arc, 2005.

This online booklet will guide you step-by-step through the process of writing a "letter of intent" for a child with disabilities. It can be downloaded at www.theemarc.org, under "Resources."

Social Security Administration. **Social Security Benefit Publications:** *Disability Benefits (No. 05-10029); Supplemental Security Income (No. 05-11000); Benefits for Children with Disabilities (No. 05-10026); Working while Disabled—How We Can Help (No. 05-10095); Your Ticket to Work (05-10100).*

These free publications can be ordered by calling 800-772-1213 or can be downloaded online at: www.ssa.gov/pubs/englist.html (in English) or www.ssa.gov/espanol/publist2.html (in Spanish).

"VA Department of Veteran Affairs Health Administration Center Overview: Spina Bifida Program." Washington, DC: U.S. Department of Veterans Affairs, 2007. Available at: www.va.gov/hac/aboutus/programs/spina.asp.

Washington Watch. United Cerebral Palsy, 1660 L St., NW, Ste. 700, Washington, DC 20036. 800-872-5827; www.ucpa.org

A bimonthly newsletter that reports news on legislation and court rulings that will affect people with disabilities.

Zevnik, Richard. **The Complete Book of Insurance: Understand the Coverage You Really Need.** Napierville, IL: Sphinx Publishing, 2004.

This book is designed to help consumers make intelligent insurance-buying decisions.

▪▪ Chapter 16

Kaufman, Miriam. **Easy for You to Say: Q & As for Teens Living with Chronic Illness or Disability.** Buffalo, NY: Firefly, 2005.

The author answers real teenagers' questions about growing up with a disability or chronic illness, including questions about sexuality, medical issues, and drugs.

SBA Editorial Board. **Health Guide for Adults Living with Spina Bifida.** Washington, DC: Spina Bifida Association of America, 2005.
Order from the website (www.sbaa.org) or call 800-621-3141.

Sloan, Stephen. **Sexuality and the Person with Spina Bifida.** Washington, DC: Spina Bifida Association of America, 1995.
Order from the website (www.sbaa.org) or call 800-621-3141.

Wehman, Paul, ed. **Life Beyond the Classroom: Transition Strategies for Young People with Disabilities.** Baltimore: Paul Brookes, 2006.
Written for professionals, this book may be useful for parents of teens who are preparing to transition out of high school; includes chapters on the transition process, vocational selection and training, and independent living.

▪▪ Books for Childen

Beatty, Monica Driscoll. **Blueberry Eyes.** Santa Fe, NM: Health Press, 1996.
An illustrated story for children aged 3-8 about a little girl who has strabismus and wears a patch and has eye muscle surgery to correct it.

Bemelmans, Ludwig. **Madeline.** New York, NY: Viking, 1967.
In this illustrated, rhyming children's classic, Madeline is stricken with appendicitis and whisked to the hospital, where she awakens to find she now has a scar (and many presents). May be helpful in talking to young children about the hospital.

Bourgeois, Paulette & Clark, Brenda. **Franklin Goes to the Hospital.** New York, NY: Scholastic, 2000.
Franklin the turtle gets a crack in his shell and needs to go to the hospital for an operation to fix it. The story walks children through many common hospital procedures such as getting a wristband and an IV.

Dobbs, Jean, editor. **Kids on Wheels: Vol. 1: A Young Person's Guide to Wheelchair Lifestyle.** Horsham, PA: No Limits Communications, 2004.
A guide to helping young wheelchair users lead an active independent life, with information on sports and recreation, fun activities, making friends, school issues, and more. Available from www.kidsonwheels.com.

Dwight, Laura. **We Can Do It!** Starbright Books, 1998.
Candid color photographs show five young children with different disabilities, including spina bifida, going about their daily lives.

Headley, Justina Chen. **The Patch.** Watertown, MA: Charlsebridge, 2006.
An illustrated story about a five-year-old girl who needs to wear a patch to correct amblyopia and initially resists it because it does not fit in with her image of herself.

Lears, Laurie. **Becky the Brave: A Story about Epilepsy.** Morton Grove, IL: Albert Whitman, 2002.

Told through the eyes of Becky's big sister, this story weaves in basic information about epilepsy while recounting how Becky surmounted her fear of having seizures at school.

Lutkenhoff, Marlene. **Another Way to Go.** Washington, DC: Spina Bifida Association of America, 2005.

An illustrated book designed to reassure children aged 5-8 that cathing is OK, at home or at school. Two versions of this book are available: one for boys and one for girls. Order from the SBA website (www.sbaa.org) or call 800-621-3141.

Lutkenhoff, Marlene. **Detour Ahead.** Washington, DC: Spina Bifida Association of America, 2007.

An illustrated children's book about hydrocephalus and how it is treated with a shunt. Order from the SBA website (www.sbaa.org) or call 800-621-3141.

Meyer, Donald. **Views from Our Shoes.** Bethesda, MD: Woodbine House, 1997.

A collection of essays by four dozen children who have a brother or sister with a disability, suitable for readers in grades 2-7.

Meyers, Cindy. **Rolling Along with Goldilocks and the Three Bears.** Bethesda, MD: Woodbine House, 1999.

A picture book for children aged 3-8 in which Baby Bear uses a wheelchair and receives physical therapy, and, in a departure from the original story, befriends Goldilocks.

Moss, Deborah. **Shelley, the Hyperactive Turtle.** 2nd ed. Bethesda, MD: Woodbine House, 2006.

In this brightly illustrated picture book for ages 3-8, Shelley the Turtle is always getting in trouble at home and school until he is diagnosed with AD/HD and begins to receive proper support and treatment.

Rey, H.A. & Rey, Margaret. **Curious George Goes to the Hospital.** New York, NY: Houghton Mifflin, 1973.

The mischievous monkey spends some time in the hospital after swallowing a puzzle piece. Although parts of the book are dated (e.g., how X-ray machine looks), the book may help to quell some children's worries about hospitalization.

Senisi, Ellen. **All Kinds of Friends, Even Green!** Bethesda, MD: Woodbine House, 2002.

This book stars Moses, a seven-year-old boy with spina bifida who is included in regular classes at his elementary school. In glossy color photographs, the book shows Moses interacting with friends and grappling with a writing assignment at school, and playing with a neighbor's iguanas after school.

RESOURCE
GUIDE

The organizations, companies, and other resources listed below offer a variety of services that can be helpful to families of children with spina bifida living in North America. For further information about any of these organizations, call, write, or visit their webpage and request a copy of their newsletter or other publications.

There are now thousands of resources online. Since it can be difficult to determine which ones are reputable, however, you may want to start with some long-established, authoritative websites:

- **PubMed** (a service of the U.S. National Library of Medicine) at www.pubmed.gov—This website enables you to search medical journals and read the "abstracts" of most articles. These are short summaries of the articles. Sometimes you receive the full article. You can go to the website and search for—spina bifida, hydrocephalus, Attention Deficit Disorder, Sensory integration—whatever specific topic you are looking for.

- **Google Scholar** at www.scholar.google.com—This is another good online search engine that searches through scholarly papers on many different topics.

- **Education Resources Information Center (ERIC)** at www.eric.ed.gov—This website, associated with the U.S. Department of Education, enables you to search over a million articles on education topics, and, in many cases, retrieve the full text of the original article.

▪▪ Organizations

Abiding Hearts

abidinghearts@yahoo.com

Abiding Hearts is a not-for-profit organization dedicated to providing support and information to parents continuing their pregnancies after prenatal testing has revealed the presence of birth defects, some of which may be life-threatening. Provides a network of contact parents in a growing number of areas across the United States; promotes patient advocacy; provides referrals to support groups and other services; and offers educational and support materials.

All Kinds of Minds

1450 Raleigh Road, Suite 200
Chapel Hill, NC 27517
888-956-4637
www.allkindsofminds.org

A nonprofit institute that helps students who struggle improve their success in school and life. Their website provides resources to help parents, educators, and clinicians understand why a child is struggling in school and how to help each child become a more successful learner. The website includes a free monthly newsletter, articles, discussion groups, and a LearningBase and Parent Toolkit with practical strategies for supporting learning differences.

Alliance of Genetic Support Groups

4301 Connecticut Ave., NW
Suite 404
Washington, DC 20008-2369
202-966-5557; 202-966-8553 (fax)
www.geneticalliance.org

Distributes publications and newsletter; provides technical assistance to new and existing genetic support groups; links families to the appropriate group or needed service.

American Latex Allergy Association

3791 Sherman Road
Slinger, WI 53086
888-972-5378; 262-677-0324 (fax)
www.latexallergyresources.org

A national nonprofit, tax exempt organization that provides information about latex allergy and supports latex-allergic individuals.

American Physical Therapy Association

1111 North Fairfax Street
Alexandria, VA 22314
703-684-APTA (2782) or 800-999-APTA (2782); 703-684-7343 (fax)
www.apta.org

This professional organization for physical therapists offers publications of interest to parents and educators and has an online searchable database of physical therapists to help you find a PT in your area.

American Speech-Language-Hearing Association

10801 Rockville Pike

Rockville, MD 20852

800-638-8255

www.asha.org

ASHA can provide information on speech and language therapy and audiologists in your area. It also distributes brochures on speech and hearing disorders.

Asthma and Allergy Foundation of America

1233 20th Street, NW

Suite 402

Washington, DC 20036

800-7-ASTHMA (1-800-727-8462)

www.aafa.org

AAFA provides practical information, community-based services, and support through a national network of chapters and support groups.

Canadian Association for Community Living

Kinsmen Building, York University

4700 Keele Street

Toronto, Ontario M3J 1P3

Canada

416-661-9611; 416-661-5701 (fax)

www.cacl.ca

An association of family members and others working for the benefit of individuals with intellectual disabilities. Offers a newsletter and other publications.

CHADD

8181 Professional Place

Suite 150

Landover, MD 20785

800-233-4050; 301-306-7070; 301-306-7090 (fax)

www.chadd.org

Children and Adults with Attention-Deficit/Hyperactivity Disorder (CHADD), is a national organization providing education, advocacy and support for individuals with AD/HD. CHADD also publishes a variety of printed materials to keep members and professionals current on research advances, medications, and treatments.

Children and Adults with Spina Bifida and Hydrocephalus Web Page

www.waisman.wisc.edu/~rowley/sb-kids/index.html

An excellent starting point for families of children with spina bifida who are looking for information and support on the Internet. Users can join a list serve (on-line newsgroup) for parents; find a variety of links to other Internet resources; view web pages created by parents of children with spina bifida; read essays and articles written by parents and professionals; and more.

Children's Defense Fund
25 E Street N.W.
Washington, DC 20001
202-628-8787; 800-CDF-1200 (800-233-1200)
www.childrensdefense.org
A legal organization that works to expand the rights of children, including children with disabilities. It can provide information on topics such as insurance and childcare.

The Council for Exceptional Children (CEC)
1110 North Glebe Road, Suite 300
Arlington, VA 22201
703-620-3660; 703-264-9494 (fax)
www.cec.sped.org
This is a membership organization for educators in the U.S. and Canada who are interested in the needs of children who have disabilities or are gifted. Their publication catalog offers a number of books and other materials on education-related topics.

Disabled Sports USA
451 Hungerford Drive
Suite 100
Rockville, MD 20850
301-217-0960; 301-217-0968 (fax)
www.dsusa.org
DS/USA offers nationwide sports rehabilitation programs to anyone with a permanent disability. Activities include winter skiing, water sports, summer and winter competitions, and fitness and special sports events.

Epilepsy Canada
2255B Queen Street
Suite 336
Toronto, Ontario M4E 1G3
877-734-0873; 905-764-1231 (fax)
Dedicated to improving the quality of life for people with epilepsy and their families, Epilepsy Canada offers a variety of facts sheets and brochures in English and French; website includes a list of treatment centers in Canada.

Epilepsy Foundation of America
4351 Garden City Drive
Landover, MD 20785-7223
800-332-1000; 301-577-2684 (fax)
www.efa.org
A national organization that works for the prevention and cure of seizure disorders and promotes independence and optimal quality of life for people with epilepsy. Services commonly provided in local communities are information and referral, counseling, patient and family advocacy, school alert, community education, support groups and camps for children.

Families USA – The Voice for Health Care Consumers
1201 New York Ave NW, Ste 1100
Washington, DC 20005
202-628-3030; 202-347-2417 (fax)
www.familiesusa.org/index.html
This national nonprofit, nonpartisan organization provides information and resources related to healthcare public policy and tracks the progress of legislation affecting managed care and Medicaid. Lists links to pertinent web sites and has publications, which can be mailed or downloaded on computer, regarding health insurance, especially Medicaid, and prescription medications. Lists relevant information state by state.

Family Village
www.familyvillage.wisc.edu
This website describes itself as "a global village of disability-related resources." It includes full text articles on specific disabilities, education issues, legal issues, recreation, and more, as well as opportunities to connect with others and extensive links to information, products, and resources.

Hydrocephalus Association
870 Market Street, Suite 705
San Francisco, CA 94102
415-732-7040; 888-598-3789; 415-732-7044 (fax)
www.hydroassoc.org
Provides support, education, and advocacy for individuals, families, and professionals. Has free information packets, a newsletter, and information in Spanish.

International Dyslexia Association
Chester Building
Suite 382
8600 LaSalle Road
Baltimore, MD 21286
410-296-0232; 410-321-5069 (fax)
Voice Message Requests for Information: 800-ABCD123
www.interdys.org
A nonprofit organization dedicated to helping individuals with dyslexia, their families, and the communities that support them. Provides a forum for parents, educators, and researchers to share their experiences, methods, and knowledge through periodicals and books; offers information and referral services.

LD Online website
www.ldonline.com
Online articles, resources, and forums to help parents, teachers, and people with LD understand many different types of learning disabilities and learn strategies and information to help individuals with LD be more successful at home, school, and on the job.

Learning Disabilities Association of America
4156 Library Road
Pittsburgh, PA 15234
412-341-1515; 412-344-0224 (fax)
www.ldaamerica.us
LDA is the largest non-profit volunteer organization advocating for individuals with learning disabilities and has over 200 state and local affiliates in 42 states and Puerto Rico. The national office can provide publications and information on education, laws, and advocacy.

The Learning Disabilities Association of Canada
323 Chapel St.
Ottawa, Ontario K1N 7Z2
613-238-5721; 613-235-5391 (fax)
www.ldac-taac.ca
The LDA of Canada works to support people with learning disabilities, their parents, teachers, and other professionals. Works with a network of provincial/territorial and local partners, to provide cutting edge information on learning disabilities, practical solutions, and tools for use.

March of Dimes
1275 Mamaroneck Avenue
White Plains, NY 10605
800-663-4637
www.modimes.org
The March of Dimes works to prevent birth defects through research and education. The organization offers publications for parents of children with disabilities, and answers specific questions about disabilities through their toll-free number.

MOMS (Management of Myelomeningocele Study)
c/o Catherine Shaer, M.D.
GWU Biostatistics Center
6110 Executive Blvd., Ste. 750
Rockville, MD 20852
www.spinabifidamoms.com
The MOMS study is conducting research to determine whether it is to the advantage of a baby with spina bifida to have the opening in his spine repaired prenatally or after birth. See the website for information on participating in the study (as well as results, once published).

MOVE International
1300 17th Street
City Centre
Bakersfield, CA 93301
800-397-MOVE (6683); 661-636-4045 (fax)
www.move-international.org

MOVE (Mobility Opportunities Via Education) helps children and adults with disabilities acquire increased independence in sitting, standing, and walking. MOVE publishes a newsletter and curriculum.

National Center for Learning Disabilities

381 Park Ave So, Ste 1401
New York, NY 10016
212-545-7510; 212-545-9665
888-575-7373
www.ncld.org

This parent-professional organization dedicated to working for the success of individuals with learning disabilities of all ages has a great website on learning disabilities organized by age group with resources, publications, advocacy, and online experts.

National Council on Independent Living

1710 Rhode Island Avenue, NW, 5th Floor
Washington, DC 20036
202-207-0334; 877-525-3400; 202-207-0341 (fax)
www.ncil.org

Advances independent living and the rights of people with disabilities through consumer-driven advocacy. Provides information on affordable and accessible housing.

National Dissemination Center for Children with Disabilities (NICHCY)

P.O. Box 1492
Washington, DC 20013-1492
800-695-0285
www.nichcy.org

This clearinghouse specializes in providing information on educational programs and laws and other issues of importance to families of children with disabilities. Publications can be downloaded from the website or ordered in hard copy (usually for no charge). Especially useful are NICHCY's "State Sheets," which list a variety of support and other organizations in each state.

National Easter Seal Society

230 W. Monroe
Suite 1800
Chicago, IL 60606
800-221-6827; 312-726-1494 (fax)
www.easterseals.com

Supports families of children with disabilities by offering direct services such as screening and therapy through local affiliates; through public education; and through advocacy. Some local affiliates provide childcare and sponsor summer camps.

National Health Information Center
P.O. Box 1133
Washington, DC 20013-1133
800-336-4797; 301-565-4167; 301-984-4256 (fax)
www.health.gov/nhic
    The National Health Information Center (NHIC) is a health information referral service. NHIC links consumers and health professionals who have health questions to organizations best able to provide answers.

National Organization on Disability
910 Sixteenth St., NW, Suite 600
Washington, DC 2006
202-293-5960; 202-293-7999 (fax)
www.nod.org
    The National Organization on Disability (NOD) provides a wide range of resources and information on increasing the participation of people with disabilities in all aspects of life. Whether you are searching for contact information, facts and figures, or a specific program, their website is a great place to begin your search.

National Rehabilitation Information Center (NARIC)
4200 Forbes Blvd., Suite 202
Lanham, MD 20706
800-346-2742; 301-459-5900;
www.naric.com
    An online source of disability and rehabilitation-oriented information on education, advocacy, financial assistance and benefits, resources, etc. for people with disabilities, their families, and researchers.

Office of the Americans with Disabilities Act
U.S. Department of Justice
950 Pennsylvania Avenue, NW
Disability Rights Section - NYAV
Washington, D.C. 20530
800-514-0301; 202-307-1198 (fax)
www.ada.gov
    The U.S. Department of Justice provides free ADA materials. Printed materials may be ordered by calling the ADA Information Line at 800-514-0301 (Voice) or 800-514-0383 (TDD). Automated service is available 24 hours a day for recorded information and to order publications.

Senate Printing and Document Services
B-04, Hart Senate Office Building
Washington, DC 20510-7106
9:00 a.m. - 5:30 p.m., Monday - Friday
202-224-7701 (availability inquiries only); 202-228-2815 (fax)
E-mail: orders@sec.senate.gov

The Senate document room provides copies of publications generated by the Senate, including bills and resolutions; legislative and executive reports, including conference reports; documents; and committee assignment lists (pdf). The document room also supplies copies of public laws and treaties. Bills, resolutions, and committee rosters are available for the current Congress only. All other items are held 10 years or more. You can request documents in person, in writing, via e-mail, or via fax.

Sibling Support Project
www.siblingsupport.org

This website has a variety of useful links for families, including information on finding events for siblings of children with disabilities of all ages, separate listservs for adult and child siblings, and thoughts from siblings about what it is like to have a brother or sister with special needs.

Social Security Administration
Office of Public Inquiries
6401 Security Boulevard
Room 4-C-5 Annex
Baltimore, MD 21235-6401
800-777-1213
www.ssa.gov

A government program offering economic protection to retirees and people with disabilities, as well as their survivors. Website offers online application for SSI and Medicare, downloadable forms and many pertinent publications, and an explanation of Social Security statements.

Spina Bifida Association of America
4590 MacArthur Blvd., NW, Suite 250
Washington, DC 20007
800-621-3141; 202-944-3285; 202-944-3295 (fax)
www.sbaa.org

SBAA is the only national voluntary health agency solely dedicated to enhancing the lives of those with spina bifida and those whose lives are touched by spina bifida. Members include people with spina bifida, family members, and professionals. Services include: toll-free information and referral service; a newsletter, legislative updates, pamphlets and other publications; information on clinics that specialize in spina bifida treatment and care; Agent Orange Class Assistance Program; conferences; research; and advocacy.

Spina Bifida and Hydrocephalus Association of Canada
#977-167 Lombard Avenue
Winnipeg, Manitoba R3B 0V3
204-925-3650; 204-925-3654 (fax)
800-565-9488
www.sbhac.ca

The Spina Bifida and Hydrocephalus Association of Canada focuses on education, public awareness, and research of spina bifida and hydrocephalus. Has fact sheets and other publications, sponsors conferences, has bursary (scholarship) programs for college students with spina bifida.

Spina Bifida Webring

http://v.webring.com/hub?ring=sb

A collection of websites by and for anyone with an interest in spina bifida and related conditions such as hydrocephalus.

State Children's Health Insurance Program (SCHIP)

Centers for Medicare & Medicaid Services

7500 Security Blvd.

Baltimore, MD 21244

877-543-7669

www.cms.hhs.gov/home/schip.asp

Information on the SCHIP program, including links to state programs and benefits for qualifying children.

TASH

29 W. Susquehanna Avenue, Suite 210

Baltimore, MD 21204

410-828-8274; 410-828-6706 (fax)

www.tash.org

TASH is an international association of people with disabilities, their family members, other advocates, and professionals fighting for a society in which inclusion of all people in all aspects of society is the norm. Publishes a newsletter and sponsors conferences.

United Ostomy Associations of America, Inc.

UOAA

P.O. Box 66

Fairview, TN 37062-0066

800-826-0826

www.uoaa.org

UOAA is a national network for bowel and urinary diversion support groups in the United States. Provides online fact sheets and guidebooks about different types of ostomies, publishes a magazine, hosts online discussion groups.

Wheelchair Sports USA

1236 Jungermann Road

Suite A

St. Peters, MO 63376

636-614-6784; 636-329-1090 (fax)

www.wsusa.org

This organization sponsors recreational and competitive sporting events for wheelchair athletes.

:: Sources of Equipment and Supplies

This section provides only a representative sample of the many companies in the United States and Canada that offer adaptive equipment, toys, and clothing suitable for children with spina bifida. To locate additional sources, check *The Exceptional Parent* magazine, which includes advertisements for all kinds of special toys, equipment, and educational products.

Abilitations
3155 Northwoods Pkwy
Norcross, GA 30071
800-850-8602; 800-845-1535 (fax)
www.abilitations.com

Products for professionals and parents working with and raising children with special needs. Offers equipment for balance, movement, positioning, exercise, etc.

ABLEDATA
8630 Fenton Street, Suite 930
Silver Spring, MD 20910
800-227-0216; 301-608-8958 (fax)
www.abledata.com

ABLEDATA provides objective information about assistive technology products and rehabilitation equipment available from domestic and international sources. Although ABLEDATA does not sell any products, they can help locate the companies that do.

Achievement Products for Children
P.O. Box 9033
Canton, OH 44711
800-373-4699
www.specialkidzone.com

Mobility and positioning products, products for improving gross motor and oral motor skills, and sensory stimulation products for children with disabilities.

ARC Home Health Products
174 Roundhouse Road
Oneonta, NY 13820
800-278-8595; 607-433-6745 (fax)
Incontinence products.

Beyond Play
1442A Walnut St., #53
Berkeley, CA 94709
877-428-1244
www.beyondplay.com

A wide variety of toys and learning materials for young children with disabilities.

Dragonfly Toy Company
291 Yale Ave.
Winnipeg, MB, Canada
R3M 0L4
   and
5725 South 5th Street
Pembina, ND 58271
800-308-2208; 204-453-2320 (fax)
www.dragonflytoys.com
   Dragonfly specializes in products, from toys to technology, for children who have special needs. Products include: aids for daily living, assistive technology, software, furniture, and toys suited for children with a variety of disabilities.

Easy Access Clothing
P.O. Box 6521
San Rafael, CA 94903
800-775-5536
www.easyaccessclothing.com
   Clothing that is easy to put on and take off, in sizes for children and adults.

Enabling Devices
385 Warburton Ave.
Hastings-on-Hudson, NY 10706
914-478-0960; 800-832-8697; 914-479-1369 (fax)
www.enablingdevices.com
   Toys and switches for people with physical disabilities.

Equipment Shop
P.O. Box 33
Bedford, MA 01730
800-525-7681
www.equipmentshop.com
   Seating and positioning aids, therapy balls, adaptive tricycles, eating aids, balance products, and more.

Fat Wheels
Mechanical Innovations
P.O. Box 220649
Charlotte, NC 28222-0649
888-241-3486
www.fatwheels.com
   Extra large, stable training wheels for bicycles.

Flaghouse
601 FlagHouse Dr.
Hasbrouck Heights, NJ 07604
800-793-7900; 800-793-7922 (fax)
www.flaghouse.com
     Flaghouse's catalog includes gross motor equipment, assistive technology, toys to assist with motor development, and other products for people with physical disabilities.

HDIS, Inc. (Home Delivery Incontinent Supplies Co.)
9385 Dielman Industrial Dr.
Olivette, MO 63132
800-269-4663
www.hdis.com
     HDIS provides incontinence products (catheters, underwear, wipes).

KAPLAN Early Learning Company
1310 Lewisville-Clemmons Road
Lewisville, North Carolina 27023
800-334-2014; 800-452-7526 (fax)
www.kaplanco.com
     Kaplan sells toys, curricula, books, and other materials for educating children of all ages.

Kaye Products
535 Dimmocks Mill Rd.
Hillsborough, NC 27278
800-685-5293; 800-685-5293 (fax)
www.kayeproducts.com
     Mobility aids, adaptive positioning equipment, and therapy products for infants, children, and young adults with special needs.

North Coast Medical
18305 Sutter Blvd.
Morgan Hill, CA 95037
800-821-9319; 877-213-9300 (fax)
www.ncmedical.com
     Products that increase independence by making everyday activities easier and safer: adaptive utensils, transfer devices, dressing aids, etc.

Pocket Full of Therapy
P.O. Box 174
Morganville, NJ 07751
732-441-0404; 800-pfot-124; 732-441-1422 (fax)
www.pfot.com
     Specializes in resources for developing fine motor skills, including scissors, pencil grips, and toys.

Rifton Equipment
P.O. Box 260
Rifton, NY 12471-0260
800-571-8198; 800-865-4674 (fax)
www.rifton.com
　　Rifton manufactures gait trainers, equipment for dynamic and static standing, adaptive tricycles, seating systems, and bathing and toileting aids.

Sammons Preston Rolyan
270 Remington Blvd., Suite C
Bolingbrook, IL 60440
800-323-5547; 630-226-1300; 630-226-1389 (fax)
www.sammonspreston.com
www.sammonspreston.com/ca (in Canada)
　　Positioning, seating, and mobility equipment (including walkers); adaptive bikes.

Special Clothes for Special Children
P.O. Box 333
East Harwich, MA, 02645
508-430-5172
www.special-clothes.com
　　A catalog of adaptive clothing for toddlers through young adults with disabilities, featuring inconspicuous snaps, Velcro, etc. to make dressing easier.

SpecialNeedsToys.com
4537 Gibsonia Rd.
Gibsonia, PA 15044
800-467-6222
www.specialneedstoys.com
　　A wide variety of toys that can help children improve gross or fine motor skills, communication skills, sensory processing, or just have fun.

TherAdapt
11431 N. Port Washington Rd.
Suite 103-B
Mequon, WI 53092
800-261-4919; 800-892-2478
www.theradapt.com
　　Adaptive chairs, standing aids, mobility aids, desks, therapy toys, and other products for children with disabilities.

CONTRIBUTORS

Drake Ash is a mother of three. Her youngest daughter, Emily, has spina bifida. Drake is also an accomplished violinist and plays with the Cincinnati Symphony Orchestra.

Roberta E. Bauer, M.D., is a developmental pediatrician at Cleveland Clinic Children's Hospital for Rehabilitation.

Timothy J. Brei, M.D., is a developmental pediatrician. He is director of the Spina Bifida Program at Riley Hospital for Children in Indianapolis, Indiana. He is an Associate Professor of Clinical Pediatrics at Indiana University School of Medicine. He is past president of the Professional Advisory Council (PAC) for the Spina Bifida Association (SBA) and is currently on the Board of Directors for SBA, serving as liaison to the PAC.

Katherine Lyon Daniel, Ph.D., is a behavioral scientist and epidemiologist specializing in health risk communication and health promotion at the Prevention and Health Communication Branch of the Birth Defects and Pediatric Genetics Division, Centers for Disease Control and Prevention.

Luciano S. Dias, M.D., is Professor of Orthopaedic Surgery at the Feinberg School of Medicine/Northwestern University, Chicago, Illinois. He also serves as the Medical Director for the Motion Analysis Center at the Children's Memorial Hospital and is Director of Orthopaedic Services for the Spina Bifida Clinic. Dr. Dias has coauthored numerous articles in professional refereed journals, written chapters for several books on pediatric orthopaedics, and cowritten a book on the orthopaedic management of spina bifida.

Alina L. Flores, M.P.H., C.H.E.S., is a Health Education Specialist with the Prevention Research team of the National Center on Birth Defects and Developmental Disabilities, Centers for Disease Control and Prevention. Previously, Mrs. Flores served as the Education Director for the Spina Bifida Association of Georgia. During her time at the Centers for Disease Control and Prevention, Mrs. Flores has assisted in the development, implementation, and evaluation of a national Spanish-language folic acid campaign, as well as assisting with other domestic and international neural tube defects prevention programs and development of educational materials and school curriculums. She has presented folic acid promotion strategies to international, national, state, and community-based agencies.

Melody Campbell Goettemoeller is also known as Melody Campbell, R.N., M.S.N., C.E.N, C.C.R.N., C.C.N.S. She is a practicing critical care clinical nurse specialist at Good Samaritan Hospital in Dayton, Ohio. She has published other works related to critical care and emergency nursing. She is married to Duane Goettemoeller, an attorney, and is the mother of three children: Drew, Megan, and Anne Marie.

Jill Harris, M.A., P.T., has been a physical therapist for more than 30 years, working at Children's Hospital Medical Center of Akron, Ohio, and for the past two years at Children's Home Care Group and PRN Therapy Services, Inc. She has worked with children with spina bifida through Children's Hospital's Spina Bifida Clinic, inpatient and outpatient services, Camp Ability, and in their homes through Children's Home Care Group. Jill has worked in the school system for 10 years as a contracted physical therapist, and served as a member of the Myelodysplasia Advisory Board to the Bureau for Children with Medical Handicaps for 14 years. She has published an article in the physical therapy journal *Clinical Management* based on bracing used with children with spina bifida and other paralytic conditions. She authored the chapter on physical therapy in the first edition of this book.

Joy Ito, R.N., B.A., is a Research Nurse for the Division of Neurosurgery at Children's Memorial Hospital in Chicago. She was previously the Spina Bifida Coordinator for the Spina Bifida Clinic at Children's Memorial Hospital. She also served as the coordinator for the adult spina bifida clinic at the Chicago Institute of NeuroResearch and NeuroScience from 1990-1997. She remains active in the field of spina bifida and has presented at various local, national and international meetings on various topics related to spina bifida.

Vickie Jahns, M.Ed., has worked in the field of education for 40 years. She has served as a Clinical Special Educator with the Cincinnati Center for Developmental Disorders and as the Special Education Liaison for the Division of Adolescent Medicine at the Children's Hospital Medical Center since 1987. Mrs. Jahns, working with the Division of Adolescent Medicine and Cincinnati Children's Hospital Medical Center, the Cincinnati Center for Developmental Disorders, and the Center for Continuing Education for Adolescent Health, wrote and narrated an award-winning video, *In Their Own Words,* which explores family feelings related to disabilities and educational goals.

James E. Kaplan is Executive Director of the Jeremiah Cromwell Disabilities Center in Portland, Maine.

Dr. Ajay Kaul, M.D., is an Associate Professor of Pediatrics in the Gastroenterology, Hepatology and Nutrition Department at Cincinnati Children's Hospital Medical Center. He is also the Director of the Motility Disorders Program.

Marlene Lutkenhoff, R.N., M.S.N., is the clinical nursing manager in the Division of Developmental and Behavioral Pediatrics at Cincinnati Children's Hospital Medical Center. She is the coeditor of *Spinabilities* and editor of the first edition of *Children with Spina Bifida: A Parent's Guide.* She served on the National SBA Board for four years and during that time participated in the following publications by SBA: *Health Guide for Adults Living with Spina Bifida* (Lead Editor); *Health Guide for Parents of Children Living with Spina Bifida* (Lead Editor); *Another Way to Go* (Author); *Detour Ahead* (Author).

Patricia Manning-Courtney, M.D., is a developmental pediatrician in the Division of Developmental and Behavioral Pediatrics at Cincinnati Children's Hospital Medical Center.

Debbie Mason, R.N., M.S.N., C.P.N.P., was the inpatient pediatric nurse practitioner for the division of Gastroenterology, Hepatology and Nutrition at Cincinnati Children's Hospital Medical Center for many years. More currently she is the acting project coordinator for Pediatric Ethic Center and supports education of Advance Practice Nurses at Cincinnati Children's Hospital Medical Center.

Ralph Moore is a lawyer in Isleton, CA, practicing in Maryland, the District of Columbia, and California. He has lectured frequently on the rights of persons with disabilities and is coauthor of *Planning for Disability* (Tax Management Institute) and *Estate Planning for Families of Developmentally Disabled Persons in Maryland, the District of Columbia, and Virginia* (Maryland DD Council).

Mary Ann Mulcahey, Ph.D., is a psychologist in private practice in Cincinnati, and the Program Coordinator for Springer School and Center. Dr. Mulcahey was at Cincinnati Center for Developmental Disorders and the University of Cincinnati from 1996 to 2006.

Joseph Mulinare, M.D., M.S.P.H., is a pediatrician and Chief of the Prevention Research team of the National Center on Birth Defects and Developmental Disabilities, Centers for Disease Control and Prevention.

Jessica Newbauer is a young woman with spina bifida. She has an Associate's degree in Liberal Arts and currently works as a Customer Service Representative for Federated Department Stores in Mason, Ohio.

Sonya Oppenheimer, M.D., is a developmental pediatrician in the Division of Developmental and Behavioral Pediatrics at Cincinnati Children's Hospital Medical Center.

Geri S. Pallija, R.N., M.S.N., C.S., is a pediatric nurse practitioner in Akron, Ohio.

Paula Peterson, R.N., M.S., P.N.P, is the coordinator of the spina bifida program at Primary Children's Hospital Medical Center in Salt Lake City, Utah. She is active in the local and National Spina Bifida Association (SBA). She has served on the Professional Advisory Council of SBA and has served as the nurse liaison on the Board of Directors of SBA.

Renee S. Rodrigues, M.D., is a fellow in the Developmental and Behavioral Pediatrics program at the Cincinnati Children's Hospital Medical Center, Division of Developmental and Behavioral Pediatrics.

Kathy B. Santoro, M.Ed., R.D., L.D., C.S.P., is a pediatric dietitian working with the Interdisciplinary Feeding Team at Cincinnati Children's Hospital Medical Center in Cincinnati, Ohio. She treats children with feeding and swallowing disorders, as well as children with intractable seizures on the Ketogenic Diet.

Alysoun Taylor is the mother of a teen with spina bifida. She is a technical editor and program coordinator at Wright State University and lives in Centerville, Ohio.

Nan Tobias, R.N., M.S.N., C.S., P.N.P., is a urology nurse practitioner at Cincinnati Children's Hospital Medical Center. For the past eighteen years she has worked with a variety of children's problems ranging from enuresis to neurogenic bladder.

Harriet Hadley Valentin, M.D., is a staff pediatrician in the Cincinnati Children's Hospital Medical Center Division of Developmental and Behavioral Pediatrics.

Marion L. Walker, M.D., is Professor of Neurological Surgery at the University of Utah and the Primary Children's Medical Center in Salt Lake City, Utah. He attends the Spina Bifida Clinic and is actively involved in the management of children with hydrocephalus and spina bifida. He is on the Medical Advisory Board of the Hydrocephalus Association.

Martha E. Walker, M.S., C.G.C., has practiced as a genetic counselor in pediatric and prenatal genetic counseling at Cincinnati Children's Hospital Medical Center in Cincinnati, Ohio, since 1989.

INDEX

ABOUT THE EDITOR

Marlene Lutkenhoff, RN, MSN, is a Clinical Manager in the Outpatient Department of Cincinnati Children's Hospital Medical Center. She is the nursing manager for the Division of Developmental and Behavioral Pediatrics and Ophthalmology. She served on the National SBA Board for four years and during that time served as Conference chair for the National Conference in 2006 and 2007. She has also advocated on Capitol Hill three times for individuals with spina bifida.